ISLAM: TO REFORM OR TO SUBVERT?

Other Works by Mohammed Arkoun

In English

'Algeria', in *The Politics of Islamic Revivalism*, Shireen T. Hunter (ed.), Indiana UP, 1988.

Arab Thought, S. Chand, New-Delhi, 1988.

Rethinking Islam Today, Center for Contemporary Arab Studies, Georgetown, Washington, 1987.

The Concept of Revelation: From Ahl al-Kitāb to the Societies of the Book-book, Claremont Graduate School, California, 1988.

'Islam, Europe, the West: Meaning-at-stake and the Will-to power', in *Islam and Modernity: Muslim Intellectuals Respond*, J. Cooper, R. Nettler and M. Mahmoud (eds), I.B. Tauris, 1998.

Rethinking Islam: Common Questions, Uncommon Answers, Westview Press, Boulder, 1994.

'Present-day Islam between its Tradition and Globalisation', in *Intellectual Traditions in Islam*, F. Daftary (ed.), I.B. Tauris, 2000.

In French

Deux épîtres de Miskawayh, édition critique, BEO, Damascus, 1961.

Aspects de la pensée islamique classique, IPN, Paris, 1963.

Traité d'éthique: Traduction, introduction, notes du Tahdhīb al-akhlāq de Miskawayh, 1st edn, 1969; 2nd edn, Institut d'Etudes Arabes, Damascus, 1988.

L'humanisme arabe au IVe/Xe siècle, 1st edn, J. Vrin, Paris, 1970; 2nd edn, 1982.

Essais sur la pensée islamique, 1st edn, Maisonneuve et Larose, Paris, 1973; 2e éd. 1984.

La pensée arabe, 1st edn, PUF, Paris, 1975; 5th edn, 1995. (Translations in Arabic, English, Spanish, Swedish and Italian.)

L'islam, hier, demain, 1st edn, Buchet-Chastel, Paris, 1978; 2nd edn, 1982.

L'islam, religion et société, Cerf, Paris, 1982. (Italian translation, RAI, 1980.)

Lectures du Coran, 1st edn, Paris, 1982; 2nd edn, Aleef, Tunis, 1991.

Pour une critique de la raison islamique, Maisonneuve et Larose, Paris, 1984.

L'islam, morale et politique, UNESCO-Desclée, 1986.

Ouvertures sur l'islam, 1st edn, J. Grancher, 1989; 3rd edn, *L'islam: Approche critique*, 1998.

Religion et laïcité: Une approche laïque de l'islam, L'Arbrelle, Centre Thomas More, 1989.

Combats pour l'humanisme en contextes islamiques, Paris, 2002.

With Joseph Maila: *De Manhattan à Bagdad: au-delà du bien et du mal*, Desclée de Brouwer, Paris 2003.

Mohammed Arkoun

ISLAM:

To Reform or to Subvert?

Saqi Essentials

ISBN 0-86356-765-7
EAN 9-780863-567650

A previous edition was published in hardback in 2002 as
The Unthought in Contemporary Islamic Thought
by Saqi Books in association with The Institute of Ismaili Studies

This updated edition published 2006 by Saqi Books

A full CIP record for this book is available from the British Library
A full CIP record for this book is available from the Library of Congress
Library of Congress catalog card: available

Saqi Books
26 Westbourne Grove
London W2 5RH

www.saqibooks.com

To my wife,
who helped with the elaboration of this book
with conviction and deep affection

Contents

Preface to the Second Edition

The publication of the second edition of the present work provides me with a fitting occasion for re-stating the theoretical perspective which inspired its writing and indicating its relevance to the copious output of opinion and debate that has followed in the wake of the tragic events of 11th September, 2001.

The relevance of the book's overarching theme to these events, though by no means premeditated (for the work was issued only six months after the events, and thus was written much earlier) remains, to my mind, as fresh as ever. Indeed, it seems to me that the never-ending stream of publications, whether popular or scholarly, whether written for the benefit of journalists, politicians, government officials or the public at large, or by academics or religious believers – publications which seem ceaselessly to diagnose, elucidate or otherwise explain these events and the conditions that allegedly gave rise to them – serve only, primarily by default, to underline the importance of the themes broached in my work. It was my intention, in writing this book, to draw attention to what remains systematically unthought, not merely out of neglect but out of the active resistance of what one might call the **mytho-historical mind**, such as it is, in what passes for Islamic thought. The present occasion is an opportune moment for suggesting that this mentality remains as stubbornly in place as ever. It is to be encountered, moreover, not only in Muslim conceptions of their own history and culture but, as is only too apparent in the very stream of publications just mentioned, in accounts of Islam, including those by scholars with impeccable academic credentials, published in the West.

The book by Bernard Lewis, entitled *What Went Wrong?*, whose phenomenal sales attest to its mass appeal, is an excellent case in point. This is not the place for a detailed critique of this work. It will suffice to point out that both its title and its contents betray the intellectual impasse born of a frame of mind intent on thinking in terms of the polarity of an imaginary 'Islam' and its equally imaginary counterpart of the 'West'. So long as this fictional dualism remains in place, the intellectual impasse which is thereby engendered is destined to remain irresolvable.

From my earliest to most recent publications on Islam,[1] I have consistently sought to raise the question of the **cognitive status** of what Muslim theologians, exegetes, historians and jurists have long thought of as **revelation**, a concept which they have taken, without further question, as a gi -ven. In thus resting their elaborate formulations on a notion which itself remains immune to the operations of critical reason, Muslim authors were responsible for creating a tradition which, though rich and intricate on its own terms, depended for its very potency on a vast terrain of the **unthought** and the **unthinkable**. Contemporary Islam, heir to this tradition, further reinforced by the ideological strains resulting from their experience of modern history, resorted to the strategy of sanctifying classical, textual definitions of Islam, turning these effectively into the ultimate bedrock of legitimacy and authority for its own axioms and proclamations. It was this whole enterprise that I have consistently attempted to deconstruct, so as to push back the boundaries of what is intellectually possible to envisage in this area, and thereby to open new avenues of thought and investigation, not only for the Islamic tradition of thought, but most significantly for all other religious legacies and for the Western modern secularised Enlightenment. This means that my ambition is to embrace in the same intellectual gesture a radical critique of reason in all its productions, methodologies and epistemological postures.

The title of what I consider to be an important embodiment of my work along these lines, *Towards a Critique of Islamic Reason*, was self-evidently devoted to this aim. Far from suggesting that there is such a thing as a generically 'Islamic' reason, let alone advocating its claims, the treatise was intended to show how such a mythical construct could arise, and to demonstrate the advantages of probing it by means of the critical tools of modern linguistic, anthropological and historical scholarship. It was dismaying to find, therefore, scholars such as Leonard Binder or (to a lesser degree) Robert Lee or Olivier Carré[2] and others who have commented on my work, evidently

1. M. Arkoun et Joseph Maila: *De Manhattan à Bagdad: au-delà du bien et du mal*, Desclée de Brouwer, Paris 2003.
2. In his recent essay on *Mystique et Politique. Le Coran des islamistes: Lecture du Coran par Sayyid Qutb, frère musulman radical*, Cerf, Paris 2004.

failing to grasp the radicalism of my intent, took my work as a species of modern, reformist (*islahi*) Islam; whereas, in my whole approach, Islamic 'reform' of the familiar type, represents precisely the kind of mythologising and ideologising that I am concerned to lay bare and to help overcome.

In short, my aim in this regard is to advance an epistemological critique at the level pioneered by Kant and developed further, with due additions or modifications, by a small number of authors whom I prefer to place in the category of *les chercheurs-penseurs* ('researchers-scholars' being the literal though admittedly inelegant equivalent in English).[1] Unlike the strictly philosophical scope of Kant's work, however, I take as the object of my critical endeavour the phenomenon which may be best described as **'historical epistemology'**, which happens, in part, to be that of Islam, in both its classical and contemporary manifestations.

I say, 'in part' because the same approach is applicable, indeed cries out to be applied, to the West's understanding of itself. This understanding is the other, if hidden, side of the West's current discourse on Islam. It should be evident now why I find in the recent flood of publications on Islam, as mentioned above, a reminder not only of the continuing timeliness of my strictures on Islamic mytho-history, presented in this work, but of the need to expose to view what remains unthought in the West's self-understanding. This feature would seem to have been thrown into clearer relief in the wake of recent events, for the type of publications to which I allude above, and the commonality of the discourse which underlies their superficial diversity, are symptomatic, precisely, of this very problem.

It is instructive to remark, in this regard, that the numerous commentaries we have seen on the events of 11th September, their character as the sort of human disorder which was the central subject of Greek tragedy, has been totally missed. In other words, the question before us is as to what genre of interpretation and analysis might help identify the disastrous responses to what should ideally have been recognised as the product of a collective *psyche* which has not yet been emancipated from a mytho-historical mode. This mentality is further encumbered by mytho-ideological procedures of thought and perception designed to exploit this way of thinking so as to produce spurious impressions of legitimacy. The period since the first

1. See my recent essay Rethinking Mediterranean Space, in *DIOGENE*, UNESCO, 2004, vol. 206.

appearance of this book has given me ample opportunity to observe the persistence of this mentality, and the utter failure of Western scholars and commentators to recognise its existence and its effects.

I have thereby been led to the conclusion that what requires urgently to be identified and studied are the reasons for what could be termed the sociology of success and failure in the sphere of intellectual, scientific and artistic production, in both the Western and Muslim contexts. These factors are to be observed equally in both developed and undeveloped societies, in democratic countries as well as those marked by despotic or authoritarian orders and in societies with an abundance of resources as much as those which are impoverished and deprived.

Meanwhile, after long thought and consultation, I have decided, as the reader will have noticed, to issue this second edition under a new title. The idea behind the earlier title, far from redundant, is in fact subsumed into its successor. For to identify the *unthought* and the *unthinkable*, it is necessarily to *subvert*. This effect is secured by employing new methodologies, by problematising unquestioned ideas and by achieving a shift of paradigms. The operation, moreover, has a dual target, as noted above. It is directed at Islamic thought, which has been distorted from within, in recent history in particular, through physical and structural violence, resulting in irreparable disintegration, oblivion (in the sense of an extension of the *unthought*), and a perversion of the mind itself. Not least, this element of **structural violence** is utterly destructive to the ethical and spiritual sentiments of the human subject – a regression notwithstanding Nietzsche's cry, '*God is dead, and it was we who killed him*', which was a subversive theme intended to herald a second phase of the Enlightenment.

In the same breath, it is directed at the ironic perversion of reason in the modern West – ironic, because it was here that in the eighteenth century a celebrated advance was made on the part of critical reason and its power to emancipate the human mind, over what Voltaire called *la bête féroce*, 'the savage beast'. Far from being carried further, this legacy has been betrayed today by cynical or self-serving ideologues, including many academics who, ignoring the universalist ideals of reason, promote such dubious notions (in the contemporary context) as the '*just war*'. In castigating these interpretations, I have in mind the positive goal of advancing the resources of the human intellect. Human beings have a *right* to this good which supervenes what we are currently accustomed to call human rights, much of which is only a legitimising masquerade for *Machtpolitik* and *Realpolitik*. The goal, then, is a **subversion** of reason for the sake of reason – a critical, sober, honest, fruitful, consequential reason, worthy of universal respect.

There is a great need today to study as a single entity what I call the historical **Mediterranean space** as it has existed already under the sovereignty of *Pax romana* extended to *Mare Nostrum*. In his famous *Mahomet et Charlemagne*, first published in 1938, the Belgian historian Henri Pirenne defends the thesis that Islam as the new emerging historical force in the seventh century imposed an end to the *Pax romana* opposing irreversibly the South-East to the North-West of Mediterranean area. This thesis received a so strong 'confirmation' in the Western imaginary since 9/11/01 that the book has been recently re-edited as if nothing contrary to the thesis has been published since 1938. It remains evident that with a handful of exceptions like the vast contribution of David Goitein, the concept of historical Mediterranean space has not yet found its way in scholarly output in the field of Islamic Studies. In the meantime, we witness a ceaseless production of works, ostensibly drawing on the social or political sciences but subscribing alike to the same fundamental polarity of a substantialised Islam on one hand, and on the other (depending on the side of the divide) an 'enlightened' or Satanised West. The result, in my view, is not only a failure to address the root complex of the unthought and the unthinkable on both sides, but a perilous extension of it, with untold harm, in consequence, to the prospects of a proper understanding.

Because I have been unsparingly critical of this mentality in the Muslim context, I consider myself entitled to draw attention to its counterpart in the West. However, most scholars in the West assume their domain to be somehow immune to this intellectual distortion. Regrettably, I have observed that the present work has not so far managed to dent this outlook. It may be that its style, vocabulary and mode of analysis are in part responsible for this fact. If this is the case, it itself constitutes a subject for critical analysis. A sociology of contemporary reading, designed to demonstrate the prevalence in these times of what I call **disposable thought**, *la pensée jetable* (and disposable elements of culture, more generally) is all too necessary. It goes hand in hand with the supremacy today of what I call **'tele-techno-scientific'** reason. The laws of the free market, operating with a brute force of their own, have the effect of trivialising the world of ideas by reducing them to the status, the rampant consumption and the ready disposability of gadgets of everyday life. Whether, in these circumstances, the endeavour of painstaking, fundamental intellectual ana -lysis has a place, and what chances it has for success, remains an open, disturbing question. Nevertheless, trust in the fruitfulness of such endeavour must guide and inspire continued efforts in this mode. It is in this spirit that I offer the second edition of this work to the discerning public at large.

I cannot end this preface without expressing my deep gratitude to my friend Aziz Esmail, who has supported, shared and enriched my intellectual struggle through numerous conversations and exchanges in London. He shares the spirit of **intellectual responsibility** for the role of what I call **'scholar-teacher-thinker'**. It is the spirit in which we have each taught successive classes of graduate students in London. Aziz was generous enough to devote precious time to correcting the 'French-English' style of this preface, and converting it into the lucid prose which is characteristic of him thanks to his love of English language and literature. The reader will have no difficulty in distinguishing his elegant, nuanced, expressive sentences from my purely intellectual English.

Paris, 15 September 2004

INTRODUCTION

Thinking the Unthinkable and the Unthought in Contemporary Islamic Thought

Nous vivons une époque étrange, dominée par une idéologie douce et une pensée molle: aux uns le savoir dur et la science, aux autres les apparentes évidences du social et du culturel; à chacun, enfin, les mystères du 'vécu' et les interrogations sans réponse. Il faudra bien jeter un pont entre ces trois continents à la dérive, sous peine de les voir livrés à leurs formes respectives et peut être complices de totalitarisme.

Marc Augé, *Le Monde*, 3/9/1999.

All human knowledge, insofar as a man is a 'member' of a society in general, is not empirical, but 'a priori' *knowledge. The genesis of such knowledge shows that it* precedes *levels of self-consciousness and consciousness of one's self value. There is no 'I' without a 'we'. The 'we' is filled with contents prior to the 'I'.*

Max Scheler, *Problems of a Sociology of Knowledge*, 1980, p. 67.

What this book proposes is a way of thinking, rather than essays in traditional scholarship based on primary sources. Not that I do not use such sources extensively, but my interpretation of them is informed by a strategy which differs from that usually employed for the purpose of providing a descriptive, narrative, factual and cumulative presentation of what they contain. My intention is to combine a critical review of modern studies devoted to early and contemporary periods of what is generally called 'Islam', with the systematic deconstruction of the original texts used in these studies as sources of genuine information. Primary and secondary texts are not read in order to discuss the facts themselves, but to **problematize**[1] the epistemic and epistemological framework underlying the articulation of each discourse. This cognitive strategy has never been used before in interpreting the types of discourse produced by Muslims to express their Islam, or in approaching them as a subject of study, alongside the Western literature on Islam and Muslim societies. From this perspective, **historical epistemology** has a priority over the purely descriptive, narrative presentation of what 'Islam' teaches, or what Muslims say, do or achieve as social and historical protagonists. To what extent are these protagonists aware of the ideological dimensions of their discourse and historical actions? Which cognitive structures do they use for the purpose of interpreting their religion, applying it to their actual life or reshaping it on the basis of historical pressures? To what extent do they develop a critical relationship with their past and their present in order to have better control over their future, and how relevant, effective and creative would such a relationship be? These questions constitute the itinerary of this self-interrogation. Such an itinerary can be proposed and achieved only by those who accept the need to combine respect for the rules of scientific research with the capacity to submit to philosophical criticism every stance of reason, every intellectual initiative and every question arising therefrom.

For a time, during the late 1970s, I called this approach **'applied Islamology'**[2] following the example set by a group of

1. All the words and expressions in bold type are concepts which I have elaborated for the specific purpose of thinking the yet unthought in Islamic thought; beyond the example of Islam, I hope to extend the relevance of these concepts to the social sciences applied to the study of the religious phenomenon.
2. I have re-written as an introduction to my coming book *Penser l'Islam aujourd'hui*, under the title *Les réponses de l'Islamologie appliquée*, the

anthropologists who started the practice of '*applied anthropology*'. During the 1980s and 1990s, political scientists focused on political Islam, and in particular, fundamentalist movements, to such an extent that they succeeded in marginalizing classical Islamology, ignoring the methodological breakthrough offered by **Applied Islamology**. This situation applies both to classical Islamicists, long confined to the philological, historicist application of the most 'representative' classical texts, and to the new wave of Islamicists who have had no philological training in the main Islamic languages (Arabic, Persian, Turkish and Urdu) and who have confined their research to socio-political issues considered from a short-term perspective. **Applied Islamology** insists on the need to practise a **progressive-regressive** method, combining the long-term historical perspective with the short-term perspective, because all of the contemporary discourse emerging in Islamic contexts, inevitably refers to the emerging period of Islam, and the 'Golden Age' of its civilization used as mythological references to reactivate 'values' – ethical and legal paradigms – which need to be reassessed according to what I call a '*Critique of Islamic Reason*'. Not only do political scientists occupy key positions in academic institutions, they also have a strong relationship with the political decision-makers as well as a tacit solidarity with the most powerful media. As far as Islamic studies are concerned, the move from classical Islamology, dominated by the classical Orientalist *épistémè* and epistemology, to the pragmatic, factual, too often ideological practice of the social sciences by the political scientist, has had little material effect in improving the intellectual shortcomings of scholarship applied in the Islamic sphere of influence in research and teaching. It is my contention that Islam as a religion, a world vision perpetuated by a still living tradition, with a great variety of cultural, social and political expressions, remains, like all religions other than Christianity, a challenge to the social sciences. In the same way, social sciences, if applied properly, are a challenge to Islam, especially as a living tradition. For many reasons, the most

presentation of this notion which I hope to promote to the dignity of a discipline.

decisive one being geopolitical, it can clearly be seen that the challenge has not yet been fully taken up by the opposing side. The intellectual and scientific reasons for what has been a recurrent failure since the nineteenth century will, I hope, be clarified, in this book.[1]

Although I often refer to the dialectic, creative tension between the **thought** and the **unthought**, the **thinkable** and the **unthinkable**, I feel there is still a need to explain this terminology which has always been unusual and remains so in current parlance and even in philosophical discourse. The question arises as to why there is such a focus on the achievements of reason, on the critical control of the rationalities it elaborates within the spatial limits assigned to the thinkable. What does a tradition of thought allow us to think in a particular period of its evolution, concerning a particular subject, within a particular domain of human existence? When we speak today about the modes of communication required by political correctness, we are clearly referring to limits imposed by political and social pressures on the innovative and critical faculties of reason. A number of ideas, values, explanations, horizons of meaning, artistic creations, initiatives, institutions and ways of life are thereby discarded, rejected, ignored or doomed to failure by the long-term historical evolution called tradition or 'living tradition' according to dogmatic theological definitions. Voices are silenced, creative talents are neglected, marginalized or obliged to reproduce orthodox frameworks of expression, established forms of aesthetics, currently received rules of judgement, evaluation, communication, transmission, teaching, relating to others ... When social, economic,

1. My critical remarks are not addressed to the informative side, the quality of erudition displayed in the academic production during the two periods of classical Islamology and contemporary political sciences; this aspect remains valuable and has contributed to the enrichment of the understanding of historical evolution; my restrictions concern the lack of theoretical discussion of epistemological issues among scholars and the cognitive status of reason in the texts used as historical sources as well as in texts written by scholars of all disciplines, as applied to a 'foreign' object. See my remarks on the work of Cl. Cahen in *Arabica*, 1996/1, reworked in my forthcoming book *Penser l'Islam aujourd'hui*.

and political conditions change and new possibilities for creative thought and action open up, a struggle begins between the defenders of the living sacred and sacralizing tradition and the supporters of reformist or revolutionary change. This dialectic tension is at work, with differing intensity, in all societies, from the most conservative and traditional to our democratic, dynamic, 'free' societies. We know how horizons and themes of discourse change depending on whether a leftist or rightist majority accedes to power; not only are some laws changed, but the philosophical rationale underlying the creation of law shifts to a different thinkable.

When the field of the unthinkable is expanded and maintained for centuries in a particular tradition of thought, the intellectual horizons of reason are diminished and its critical functions narrowed and weakened because the sphere of the unthought becomes more determinate and there is little space left for the thinkable. The unthought is made up of the accumulated issues declared unthinkable in a given **logosphere**. A logosphere is the linguistic mental space shared by all those who use the same language with which to articulate their thoughts, their representations, their collective memory, and their knowledge according to the fundamental principles and values claimed as a unifying *weltanschaung*. I use this concept to introduce the important dimension of the linguistic constraints of each language on the activities of thought. When a language such as Arabic or English is currently used by different peoples, with different cultural backgrounds, it becomes a common **logosphere** which will affect the configuration of the faculties of the human mind and, consequently, will contribute to the creation of frontiers between the **thinkable** and the **unthinkable**, the **thought** and the **unthought**. This is evident in the case of the Arab philosophers who introduced the Greek philosophical **thinkable** into the Arabic language, thereby creating friction with the religious **thinkable** defended by the traditionalist builders of Islamic orthodoxies. Similarly, the concept of the logosphere assists in the understanding of how Islamic values taught in Arabic to Indonesian, Bangladeshi or Tajik peoples, for example, share the same **unthinkable** about religion with the rest of the world's Muslims. The impact of the **unthinkable** and the **unthought** is immediately identifiable in the discourse articulated in a given language; language is the authentic memory of what thought has achieved, or failed to achieve, in each **logosphere**. From this perspective, an hypothesis could be attempted to explain why the terminology that I am trying to produce on the subject of **thinkable/unthinkable, thought/unthought**, has so far been neglected by the historians of thought. Historiography has always been linked to a political focus, such as a king, a prince or other leader; it reports what is relevant in order to illustrate the glory of the ruler, the authority of a spiritual leader; only positive achievements and the related outstanding cultural, and intellectual works achieved by thinkers, artists, jurists and orthodox religious authorities are quoted, celebrated and regularly taught as classical references for the living collective memory. The modern nation-state has been built and is supported by the selective creation and reproduction of the glorified national **identity**. A highly convincing illustration of this ideological practice, in contradistinction with the free, open, creative quest for meaning, is provided in *Les lieux de mémoire*, edited by Pierre Nora, which discusses the strategies used by the French Third Republic to unify the nation in accordance with the principles of the Republic. All the post-colonial states that emerged in the late 1950s, used the same strategy, with a much more authoritarian, obscurantist, intolerant will-to-power. In Muslim countries, this policy helped to expand the space of the **unthinkable** and the **unthought** because a dual censorship has been and still is imposed on intellectual and cultural activities, censorship from above exercised by the state and censorship from below imposed by public opinion, especially on matters related to religion. Many intellectuals came to interiorize this dual control in the name of the Nation, or the religion, adding self-censorship to that already imposed from outside.

An important remark is in order here. I have explained in my various writings how my Algerian origins, and my involvement in Algerian contemporary history since the late 1950s (especially in the War of Liberation) imposed on me, as a scholar and professor of the History of Islamic Thought, the obligation to rethink and rewrite this entire history within the dialectic framework of the **thinkable/unthinkable, thought/unthought**. As an historian, I have been struck by two major historical facts, namely the spectacular success of Greek philosophy and sciences in the Arabic logosphere under the political control of an Islamic regime from the eighth to the thirteenth century, and in the same period, the expanding of the horizons of religious reason through dynamic schools of theology and law. The Mu'tazilite school contributed to having **thinkable** issues – such as the issue of God's created speech – declared **unthinkable** afterwards by the Caliph al-Qādir. Many schools of thought started to be weakened and disappear after the thirteenth century. Philosophy, as inherited from Classical Greece, disappeared after the death of Ibn Rushd (1198), though it survived in Iran in the form of theodicy and theosophy; the Mu'tazilī school was banned by the well-known decrees of al-Qādir in 1017–18 and 1029 and to this day, the *'ulamā'* officially devoted to the defence of orthodoxy, refuses to reactivate the **thinkable** introduced and developed by original, innovative thinkers in the classical period.

Historians report these facts without opening up new fields of historical research devoted to the interaction between the changing sociological frameworks of knowledge and the emergence, or disappearance, of fields of intellectual and scientific endeavour. The same sociological, political, linguistic, economic and demographic factors that eliminated Ibn Rushd in his own **logosphere** helped to tremendous and enduring success of the same Ibn Rushd in Latin Catholic Europe until as late as the sixteenth century. Historical research reveals the consequences generated in Islamic thought by the elimination of the philosophical standpoint of reason, while we know the decisive role played by this standpoint in the development of scientific reason as well as the democratic regimes in modern Europe.

It is not sufficient to describe the increasing gap that has emerged between modern Europe and the so-called Muslim societies since the sixteenth century; we need to determine whether this evolution is related to internal forces and mechanisms operating independently in each historical sphere, or whether it is also subject to correlative factors. The development of 'material civilization' in Europe since the eighteenth century, accelerated the collapse and the conquest of all the non-European societies in the world. In other words, material modernity has been used to enhance the political and economic expansion of the European capitalist bourgeoisie; it prevented, deviated or perverted the simultaneous transmission of intellectual modernity in non-European cultures and traditions of thought. This ambiguous process, often described as the clash between tradition and modernity, conservatism and progress, religious fundamentalism and historical change, led to the ideology of liberation with its radical political and social opposition to colonial domination from 1945 until today. During the Cold War, the struggle against 'Western imperialism' was inspired by the dialectical materialist option of the Socialist-Communist vision of human liberation. The philosophical dimension of political liberalism had been rejected as the weapon of the imperialist bourgeoisie. The dogmatic totalitarianism of the nation-state controlled by a single political party has dominated the intellectual and cultural life of all the countries emancipated from colonial domination. After the collapse of the Soviet Union and its ideological support of third-world countries, an 'Islamic' vision of the historical process of emancipation replaced the previous secularized socialist model in the so-called Muslim societies. Both visions share the will to eliminate the struggle of reason to autonomously perform the specific function of enabling unrestricted criticism of the initiatives of social protagonists through historical development (discourse, behaviour, political and economic options, cultural and intellectual achievements). From this perspective, more attention should be paid by historians to making explicit the historical correlation between the expanding European hegemony and the reactions, the ideological responses and the regressive changes seen more in the unthought, than in the thought in contemporary Islamic thought.

As a member of a society which went to war to liberate itself from colonial domination and had to 'welcome' a 'democratic popular republic' based on the model of the Soviet Socialist Republics, I felt more keenly than scholars without this revolutionary background, the intellectual responsibility to rethink in terms of social sciences and **historical epistemology**, the whole legacy of Arabic culture in what I came to call the 'Maghrebian space'.[1] The Algerian one-party state tried to legitimize its 'socialist' collectivist option in a strong, formal political will to protect and recover the 'Arab-Islamic personality' of the Algerian nation. Morocco followed suit, defended by the *Istiqlāl* party, but under the supreme authority of a king opposed to any kind of socialist revolution as defined and imposed by the leadership of Nasser, Tito, Nehru and other 'historical' leaders who met at the famous Bandung Conference of 1955. The spirit of Bandung was an significant reference point for all those who embraced the socialist model of economic and political action as a way of quick deliverance from historical backwardness. The great majority of leading intellectuals, scholars and artists supported the socialist revolution with their works, teaching, militant rhetoric and their strong desire to reach high positions as political decision-makers. Historians, sociologists and political scientists have not yet assessed the negative intellectual and cultural consequences of this massive adhesion to a dogmatic, totalitarian ideology imposed on societies in which peasant cultures, traditional modes of thinking and oral communication were still the norm. That is why I have chosen to concentrate on this neglected aspect of the history of thought in contemporary Islamic contexts. To do this, I had to create methodological and epistemological options in order to conquer new territory not only to explore new fields of meaning, but primarily to initiate new levels and types of understanding of many inherited issues which remain unexamined. Religion, and all matters related to religious life and

1. I have devoted several essays to problematize the history of Maghrebian space beyond the ideological definitions of national identities imposed by the one-party-states and also the representations developed by Arab-Islamic historiography since the political triumph of a 'Muslim' state. These essays will be collected into a forthcoming anthology entitled *Lecture de l'espace maghrébin*.

expression, is one of the most important fields where political and social forces generate a confusing and obscurantist thought which requires the problematisation suggested in my title *The Unthought in Contemporary Islamic Thought*. Islam everywhere has been put under the control of the state (*étatisé*); but the religious discourse developed by the opposing social forces shifted to a **populist** ideology which increased the extent of the **unthought**, especially in the religious, political and legal fields.

1. Identifying the Unthinkable and the Unthought

It seems necessary to be more precise and explicit – more didactic – on the subject of the identification and practical evaluation of what I call 'the unthinkable' and the 'unthought'. English-speaking readers may be less familiar with these concepts than French speakers, owing to the fact that French school pupils all experience some philosophy teaching in their final year at the *lycée*. It will become apparent, however, that I have given these concepts historical, sociological, psychological and political ramifications which go beyond abstract philosophical speculation.

Let me start with a paragraph from Jean De Munck's recent book *L'institution sociale de l'esprit* (PUF, 1999). I have italicized those terms and expressions that need critical or additional commentary in relation to my own concerns as a critical historian of Islamic thought.

> While liberalism only promises a long process of planetary alignment of institutions with the *rational references* of human rights and the rights of the market, the very idea of *homogenizing historical evolution* is contested, criticized, dismantled by a *post-modernism* that sees only contexts and their '[*small*] *narratives*', unalignable with the '[*wider*] *history*' of emancipation. At a moment when the *formalism* of an *economic* and *political Reason* is being redeployed on a large scale, *post-modernism* is unmasking its persistent *irrationality*,

> the *injustice* that it generates, the untruth it transmits and the *violence* that upholds it. The fission of the Cold War has been replaced by the great new distribution: no longer *human rights* against *collective rights*, but *human rights* against the right to *difference*; no longer the *market* against the *state*, but the market against *cultures*; no longer the *Individual*, universal and abstract, against the material worker, but the *Individual*, still universal, still abstract, against the *diversity of faces*, the *plurality of tribes*, the diversification of *values*, styles and convictions (p. 3).

Clearly, this is a condensation of the history of thought in its European trajectory with its irresistible expansion into all contemporary societies to the point that the very destiny of the human species, even of planet Earth, is now at stake. What is inexorably decided or imposed upon all living beings is presented as the result of a play of forces, mechanisms and interactions that, in the final analysis, harks back to the workings of the human mind in historical contexts exclusive to that geopolitical space called 'Europe' or 'the West'. Outside this European/Western context, the intellectual, spiritual, cultural and especially the scientific and technological performance of the human mind is not radically different, but is considerably out-of-step when considered from the point of view of the effects of meaning and the practical consequences for the emancipation of the human condition and the price to be paid for what is considered progress, but which, in reality, is both alluring and dangerous.

Seen from the historical trajectory of Islam, Europe/the West is a hostile, hegemonic geopolitical sphere, unavoidable since the eighteenth and nineteenth centuries, and broadly responsible for a historic decline which began in the thirteenth and fourteenth centuries. As a geocultural, intellectual and spiritual sphere, Europe, before the emergence of the economic, technological and monetary powerful sphere called the West, is in many ways an extension and expansion of the thought and the scientific knowledge accumulated in the Islamicized area of the Mediterranean during the classical age of Arab-Islamic civilization (750–1300). The change of direction in intellectual, scientific and cultural exchanges between the Muslim Mediterranean and Europe can be dated from the year 1492 AD. Two major events signalled the inversion: Catholic Spain drove the Muslims and Jews out of Andalusia, and Europe discovered the American continent and opened up the Atlantic route, which resulted in supplanting the Mediterranean route with the growth of United States power, especially after 1945. This is not the place for a detailed account of all the stages and conditions of these developments, which include notably the dismantling of the Ottoman Empire, the colonization of all the Muslim countries, the liberation wars of the 1950s and the ideological peregrinations of the so-called national states since the achievement of political 'liberation'. What interests us here is the accumulation of **unthinkables** and **unthoughts** during the four centuries from the sixteenth century to the present, during which Europe/the West was constructing intellectual, political, legislative and cultural modernity in Western Europe. Not only did Islamic thought play no part at all in this development; it cut itself off from its own classical heritage by eliminating the practice of philosophy and even theology, which so enriched religious thought in the past and has yet to be reinstated.

That is why the historical summary I have just provided is strictly unthinkable in the historical and cognitive contexts in which Islamic thought has been imprisoned since the political triumph of nationalist ideologies in the struggle for liberation, and the ensuing construction of single-party states either on the apparently claimed liberal European model or, until 1989, that of the 'people's democratic republics' of Communist Europe. From 1950 to 2000, two determining factors substituted a sociologically dominant **populist ideology** for a liberal culture, restricted to circumscribed and fragile urban élites: education systems, manipulated by one-party states universally promoted a nationalistic, militantly ethnic vision, sometimes openly xenophobic, in the guise of vigilance – not entirely unjustified – against imperialist exploitation by the 'West'; and the social settings of knowledge were thrown into confusion by a demographic growth rate unprecedented in the history of human society. In all Islamic contexts, the situations created in this way will never be superseded as long as the military and police-state regimes endure, with their total hostility to the most unarguable values of democratic development in modern societies.

It is in terms of these weighty and complex factors that we should interpret the militant 'argument' proclaiming the radical and definitive incompatibility of 'Western' science and thought with that of 'Islam'; in which 'Islam' has its own conceptual apparatus and horizons of meaning which admit absolutely no theoretical or pragmatic validity in the intellectual and spiritual 'wanderings' of Western positivist science. This position is defended in the education systems and the religious rhetoric of Islamicist militants issuing from the sacred enclave of the mosques, and also by the official media compelled to take part in a mimetic escalation concerning the unsurpassable 'validity' of 'Islam' as the source and foundation (*aṣl*) of all religious, ethical, political, social and economic legitimacy. All discursive utterances in contemporary Islamic contexts are inspired to a greater or lesser degree by this ideological perception of the 'Western' protagonist of contemporary history, just as in that 'West' constructed by the politico-religious imaginary, the world of 'Islam' is generally perceived as radically incompatible with, and therefore threatening to, the superior 'values' of the West. This is the highly successful 'clash of civilizations' theory that has haunted the Western political imagination since the end of the Cold War. There certainly is a clash, but it is between collective **imaginaries** constructed and maintained on both sides through **unthinkables** and **unthoughts** cultivated by the education systems, the discourse of political and academic establishments, and the media that feed on this rhetoric and seek to increase their following by outdoing each other with anticipations of interpretations from the leading minds.[1]

1. The gaffe by the then French prime minister Lionel Jospin on the subject of Ḥizbullāh terrorism is a perfect example of the connivance of official discourse with what I have called anticipations of 'meaning' from the dominant **imaginaries**, something that occurs on the Islamic

Let us return to J. De Munck's historical summary. His critique of the dominant forms of rationality seeks to lay the groundwork for substituting what he calls *procedural* or pragmatic reason for the *substantive* reason of classical theology and metaphysics as well as the positivist *instrumental* reason of today, which others have called *tele-techno-scientific* reason. J. De Munck is a researcher at the Centre for the Philosophy of Law headed by Jacques Lenoble at the Catholic University of Louvain La Neuve. He follows a line of critical thought that seeks to supersede the contradictions of the forms of jurisprudence linked to the dominant cognitive postures of classical modernity as well as post-modernity. This orientation illustrates the most enduring feature of modern thought which never stops questioning its own structures and exploring its limitations; but it is noticeable that, like all the great critical interventionists (Nietzsche, Heidegger, J. Rawls, Ch. Taylor, H. Gadamer, J. Habermas, L. Wittgenstein, Gödel, etc.) who have tried to regain control of this reasoning, it leaves one essential question unexplored, since it has never, in practice, managed to master its own de facto solidarity with all the forms of government in place, including liberal democracies. The question consistently locked away in the **unthought** is that of a strategy for integrating into the same critical and cognitive movement, the trajectories of reason historically linked to non-'Western' contexts for the production of meaning. By 'strategy of critical and cognitive integration' I mean that which inspired and made into essential reading the works of J. P. Vernant and M. Détienne on thought and politics in classical Greece. 'Orientalist' explorations of the so-called 'Oriental' civilizations have never reached that threshold of intelligibility beyond which any cognitive and critical exercise of 'Western' reason should include the relevant data on all the epistemic and epistemological routes travelled within civilizations that until now have been explored as exotic places – 'primitive', 'archaic', 'traditional' or 'conservative' in their learning and culture. The

side as well as on the Western one. There are numerous examples of this sort in both camps, going back to the theological and military confrontations of the Middle Ages (see Chapter 6).

undeniable advances in cultural anthropology have not succeeded here even in casting doubt on the universality of the struggles waged by 'Western' reason, let alone in introducing a more humanist rationality into the perception of non-Western cultures by the dominant ideological **imaginaries** (*imaginaires*). Philosophically, J. De Munck's critique of postmodernism is pertinent, but insufficient, implying as it does no effort to get out of the Western European trajectory of reason, which continues to construct its pertinencies and legitimacies in the linear, chronological deployment of successive or concomitant forms of substantive, instrumental, post-modern reason which may be overtaken, still in the same line of development, by '*procedural reason*'. The author does not even draw all the conclusions from the relevant and productive critique he makes on the basis of the philosophically new approach of '*the social institution of the mind*'; just as the great theoreticians in political science failed to draw conclusions from what C. Castoriadis called '*the imaginary institution of society*'. There is no sign of the emergence of the idea of using any means other than *procedural* modifications within the Western enclosure, to progress beyond the functional solidarity of Enlightenment reason, in its deployments as economic and political reason, with the so-called democratic institutions for the exercise of power and the social settings of knowledge established and instrumentalized by and for these institutions to ensure their survival. Irrationality, injustice, social exclusion, structural and physical violence, are not just persistent, as is recognized; they are being spread on a global scale in all types of societies across the frontiers drawn and maintained by the geopolitical and geo-economic strategies of the 'élites' of specialists, experts, engineers and technocrats who everywhere have a monopoly on practical decisions. Holders of political power are themselves mere 'executive officers' who carry out major decisions prepared, justified, 'founded' by these experts on the basis of national criteria and internal strategies for taking and holding power, or for increasing the profits of huge multinational firms.

A transition is now taking place from the ideological polarities of the time of the '*great narratives*' of emancipation of the human condition led by the abstract humanism of Enlightenment reason to the no-less ideological opposition of '**human-rightsism**' and humanitarian action to the identity-related demands of the many groups, peoples, communities, languages and cultures that passed from colonial domination to the oppressive political voluntarism of single-party nation-states in the second half of the twentieth century – states wanted, supported, 'enlightened' by the geopolitical strategists of the great powers, themselves divided by nationalist rivalries that have still not been overcome. Since the 1960s, people have been calling in vain for a new economic and monetary order, and for the creation of an international law which would not only abolish the baleful inheritance of the dispossession of the world by a conquering Europe, but set up a juridical authority on an adequate scale for the violence unleashed by so many wills-to-power across the world. To prepare institutions to accept the diversity of faces, values, styles and cultures? Yes of course; but only on condition that the problems posed by the 'plurality of the new tribes' (political parties) are radically rethought, to undermine demands for 'difference' or 'identity' which are just dialectical responses (themselves bringing violence and antihumanism) to the devastating effects of the structural violence introduced everywhere by tele-technoscientific reason.

A purely philosophical critique of the cognitive standpoints of reason in the West cannot – we can see – go as deep as the more radical, fundamental and liberating critique of all the uses of reason, the irrational and the imaginary in all socio-political contexts in the contemporary world. I believe that I have already established that there is a need, both epistemological and political (in the sense of a political philosophy covering all the situations generated by the geopolitical manipulation of powers on a world scale), for this expansion of the horizons of criticism in the *Critique of Islamic Reason*. This work in effect comes up against the limits and arbitrary aspects of hegemonic reason and is involved in the most useful debates on the passage from the *Phenomenology of the*

Mind, trapped in the 'mytho-historico-transcendental thematic',[1] to '*the social institution of the mind*'. Like all high-profile thinkers in the contemporary West, the young researcher J. De Munck never mentions hegemonic reason, or the **unthinkable**; when he refers to the **unthought**, it is only to announce the schedule for procedural reason; but the **unthinkable** and the **unthought** are inherent in the linear structure of any discursive statement; and also in the fact that any proposition is an act of power whether followed by a result or not; for a proposition implies selection from the range of significations in any tradition, thus an orientation of meaning in a particular direction from all the possible horizons of expectation of any given speaker of a particular language. To that may be added the selective pressures brought to bear by all protagonists in positions of power in every political and linguistic context. From clan leader, tribal chief or village mayor to king, caliph, sulṭān, emperor or president, from the smallest republic or kingdom to today's United States; from bishop, rabbi, village imām to pope, chief mufti or chief rabbi: all of these exercise control over the **thinkable** and the **unthinkable**, over the selection of what is thought in the orthodox line, and over what has to be eliminated and remain **unthought** if intellectually subversive. Among agents of the transmission of learning, even among the producers of knowledge which is presented as new, none escapes this dialectic of the powers and the residues.[2]

The residues, brought about by the centralising powers, liberal as well as communist, since the nineteenth century, have been trying to find ways and means of expression under today's democratic regimes; but in the new nation-states under construction

1. See Michel Foucault, *Order of Things: An Archeology of the Human Sciences*, London, Routledge, 1970. It is essential to be acquainted with this basic notion, to grasp the difference between history of ideas and history of systems of thought.
2. See 'Modes de présence de la pensée arabe en Occident musulman', in *Critique de la raison islamique*, Paris, 1984; and 'Transgresser, déplacer, dépasser', in *Arabica*, 1996/1, op. cit. The concept of the dialectic of powers/residues (*les puissances et les résidus*) is a key to interpret the current evolution of the ex-Third World societies.

within borders arbitrarily drawn by the colonizers, centralising voluntarism tends rather to erase the traces of languages, ethnic groups or cultures declared to be unassimilable by nationalism, communalism or fundamentalism, themselves products of the dialectic of the powers and the remainders. It is a sure fact, though one which would induce despair in the oppressed, excluded and eliminated millions, that the political rationale currently engaged in the construction of the European Union, and to an even greater extent, the one running the strategies of the US presence in the world, devote a lot more effort to manipulating this dialectic of the powers and the remainders than to recognising this dimension of the general history of human societies as one of the weightiest **unthoughts**, one that limits and continues to invalidate all the theologies and political philosophies past and present.

We need to dig a little deeper to identify the structural conditions for the exercise of a type or level of reason that intends to go beyond all these **unthoughts** and **unthinkables**. Religious reason in its Hindu, Buddhist, Confucian, Jewish, Christian, Islamic and animist traditions; secular reason in its African, Chinese, Indian, Indonesian, Arab, Persian, Turkish, etc., expressions; in short, all forms of thought emerging from non-Western contexts, must face the same philosophic refutations, the same denials by critical history, the same challenges and tests from anthropology, the neurosciences and biology, that theologies, philosophies and moral values had to face in the birthplaces and nurseries of modernity. It is from this *fait accompli* in the evolution of modern thought that the hegemonic reason on power in the West, draws its certainty that apart from the undeniable hegemonic situation existing since at least the eighteenth century, it also represents the paradigmatic forms, the cognitive stages and the extreme limits of the social and historical institution of the human mind, and not just the mind in its Western historical trajectory. We lack the data and the cognitive resources necessary to discuss this aporia; all we can do is furnish some elements of analysis and advise the principle of caution: we cannot prejudge the adequacy, the relevance and achievements, or on the other hand the digressions, the illusions and failures, of reason and imagination at work in all the contexts listed above; it is necessary to register all that occurs in these contexts and incorporate it into the critical work of what I prefer to call **emergent reason**, or reason in crisis : meanings, effects of meaning and horizons of meaning do not emerge only where hegemonic reason is active, along with its unequalled means of action, creation and invention; we have to be able to hear voices reduced to silence, heterodox voices, minority voices, the voices of the vanquished and the marginalized, if we are to develop a reason capable of encompassing the human condition.

This utopia is blocked for the present by the current conditions of the expansion of hegemonic reason. In all the satellite countries, we are witnessing the formation of political, economic and financial 'élites', very restricted in size and found in social settings where the middle classes are desperate either to join these 'élites' or at least to avoid sinking down into the masses and being doomed to live precarious lives. The élites for their part focus more on their own standard of living compared with that of their opposite numbers in the wealthy countries, than on tackling the fundamental problems of their own societies. They feel overwhelmed by the scale of these problems when they confront the national and international roots of these problems and their remorseless complication. The result is a tendency towards resigned and self-protective behaviour and an expectation of uncertain solutions. Those who succeed in amassing scandalous fortunes add the arrogance of wealth to that of power and in the meantime, make use of nationalist rhetoric. In Islamic contexts, they defend the superior values of Islam, thus absolving themselves from taking part in the courageous struggles for emancipation being waged by women and the very few male intellectuals who dare to attack the taboos of religious beliefs.

Women represent a particularly disadvantaged social body; it is they who have to suffer the oppression of regimes that instrumentalize religion to compensate for their own lack of political legitimacy; the resistance of the popular mentality to any questioning of the status of women as fixed by God Himself in the Qur'ān; and the weight of beliefs and customs they have themselves internalized through the rearing process handed down by their mothers and grandmothers in the lineage of an ancient feminine memory. I was able to verify all these mechanisms recently in a broad debate taking place in Morocco around the '*Plan for the integration of women in the development process*' launched by the present government (April 2000). The fault line dividing society on the plan is not easy to trace; the simplistic terminology of opposition between progressives and conservatives, left and right, modernists and traditionalists, secular and religious, etc., is unsatisfactory. The use of these trivial, obsolete categorisations in political sociology is both an unavoidable ideological necessity and a backward conceptualisation damaging to proper critical thought: in politics, one has to be effective at manipulating the social imagination with words and slogans that elicit immediate adhesion or rejection, while this manipulation avoids the intellectual need to introduce a more relevant emancipating critical discourse. This, of course, would require more enlightened political élites able to share intellectual concerns, accurate scientific references, and with the educational skills to use social debate as an opportunity to enhance the democratic culture and political consciousness of all citizens. There are many factors still delaying any significant move to this unavoidable trend towards modern political thought and practice. One of the most determining in this regard is the total irrelevance of the educational system as it is imposed everywhere at all levels, especially as concerns the teaching of social sciences.

Another determining, and totally **unthought** factor is sexuality. At the deepest level of the individual and collective psyche lies this unexplored, taboo continent of sexuality, apparently 'regulated' by religious codes, which really stem from anthropological structures in place long before the appearance of these religions in time. All religions have simply covered with a so-called sacred law, the archaic codes and structures prevailing in all societies. In the case of Islam, we know how the Qur'ānic categorisations of the licit and illicit (*ḥalāl/ḥarām*) are still enforced as divine and intangible, rejecting any kind of secularized definitions. On top of this hard layer, invisible but determining, are deposited the customs, beliefs, representations and legislations appropriate to each socio-cultural environment, as shown by dialectology and ethnolinguistics. So long as this field of reality remains veiled, and under-analysed, it will be difficult to make progress in women's emancipation, unless legislators speed up the evolution of mentalities by introducing not only audacious reforms that will have educational effects on all social categories and all levels of culture, but also a subversive philosophy of Law (see my Concept of Islamic reason in *Penser l'Islam aujourd'hui*).

2. The Cognitive Status of Emerging Reason

I had to clarify my position on the attempt to assess the epistemological relevance of procedural reason so that I could propose my own elaboration of the concept of Emerging Reason (E. R.). I have alluded to it just to express my reluctance to follow the line of procedural reason which might be relevant to the critique of juridical discourse, but cannot fulfil all the tasks and the explorations I described above. Emerging Reason goes beyond the punctual, particular methodological improvements actualized in some fields of research, or in some disciplines applied to the study of different aspects of Islam and other non-Western cultures. It is concerned with the philosophical subversion of the use of reason itself and all forms of rationality produced so far and those which will be produced in the future so as not to repeat the ideological compromises and derivations of the precedent postures and performances of reason. In that sense, E. R. will be continuously emerging to reassess its critical function.

Paying prior attention to the epistemological postures of reason is an essential requirement of philosophical activity. Social and political scientists are supposed to share this fundamental concern not only in their contributions to theoretical confrontations, but even more in the process of working out their concepts and articulating their discourse. It is easy to show that many western philosophers, not to mention the great majority of scholars, limit their epistemological control to what I would call the western historical logosphere. The common *weltanshaung* can be criticized, revised, opened or closed inside ideological frontiers fixed by binding historical, existential solidarities linking the members of a group, a minority, a majority, a large community or a powerful nation. There are hegemonic logospheres like the Arabic Muslim, the Greek, Latin Christian logospheres in the Medieval Ages and the English and French ones today; there are smaller, satellite logospheres where dialects, not written languages survive under the threat of expanding languages with their related civilizations. From that perspective, S. Huntington is right in trying to identify competing logospheres which might develop violent clashes if they remain indifferent, if not openly hostile, to any intellectual or cultural attempt to cross the ideological frontiers and create historical opportunities for sharing transnational, multicultural solidarities as the European Union is doing under the pressure of the internal European wars that have prevailed since the sixteenth and seventeenth centuries.

The European Union's experience is rejected, as we know, by defenders of the well-established national sovereignties; in France they are known as *les nationaux-républicains.* Within the political frontiers of each national sovereignty, there is another ongoing conflict between the foreign migrants of different nationalities who disturb the 'peaceful', fruitful functions of each national logosphere. Such debates have a paramount influence not only on political life, but also on the cognitive options of political and social scientists and even on leading philosophers in Canada and the United States. This is clearly reflected in titles like Richard Bernstein's *Dictatorship of Virtue: How the Battle Over Multiculturalism is Reshaping Our Schools, Our Country, Our Lives*; John J. Miller's *The Unmaking of America: How Multiculturalism Has Undermined the Assimilation Ethic* and Yehudi O. Webster's *Against the Multicultural Agenda.* For supporters of multiculturalism, I mention Will Kymlicka, *Multicultural Citizenship: A Liberal Theory of Minority Rights*, and Charles Taylor 'The politics of recognition' in *Multiculturalism: Examining the Politics of Recognition.* The most significant contribution to the discussion in French has just been made by Sylvie Mesure and Alain Renaut in *Alter ego: Les paradoxes de l'identité démocratique*.

But beyond the debates limited to national logospheres, we must also consider the prolific literature related to the process of globalization for further indications of the way the frontiers of the human mind are moving at the turn of the century. Those who are in control of economic, financial, technological and telecommunications, globalization tend to be satisfied with the triumph throughout the world of a **tele-techno-scientific reason** with its purely pragmatic, empiricist expertise. Social and political sciences will continue to serve this new, expanding stage in material civilization, just as they did in the nineteenth century for the industrialized and industrializing societies. The rest of the world will be obliged either to travel in the same boat if it can afford such an uncertain and expensive journey, or to live in the margins until it is eliminated. In the nineteenth and twentieth centuries, industrialized capitalist Europe used colonial strategies to 'civilize' backward, traditional societies, just as Communist Europe announced the end of the history of the bourgeoisie with the triumph of the final proletarian revolution. After 1989, Francis Fukuyama declared from the United States that it was the end of history and the inauguration of the era of mastered, liberal, humanist history. All these debates emerge and develop in one hegemonic logosphere called the West; the hegemonic visions and concrete, constraining practices are discussed, refuted and rejected with the very tools of the abstract, helpless, polemical, ideological, religious discourse of the victims, or the new slaves. To the discourse of political, economic, financial and intellectual domination, the only response has been the discourse of victimization tempered occasionally by the discourse of 'co-operation'.

In these world-wide battles, we have to note the phenomenon that Julien Benda has called '*la trahison des clercs*' on both sides. Benda fulminated against writers who betrayed the specific function of literature by their political options in the late twenties. Today, the phenomenon is often pointed to as the '*silence of the intellectuals*' and the treason of political and social scientists who continue to serve the national interests of their nations or their communities while they ascribe their scholarship to a scientific, objective, humanist, intellectually-driven endeavour. It is true that scholars and intellectuals have much less easy access to the fields of research controlled by the nation-states that emerged after colonial liberation. Economists or experts in technology are admitted with official and limited contracts, restricting their freedom and presence to their specific field of expertise. Even the most innovative books and articles devoted by Western scholarship to Islamic studies, for example, long remain unknown in Muslim countries for several reasons. Either they are too expensive, or they are written in foreign languages, or they are censored by political or religious authorities. As long as the critical function of the social sciences is restricted for all the reasons mentioned, the intellectual, cultural, and scientific gap between the West and the former Third World societies will increase and have a negative effect on all the current debates between cultures and civilizations. It should be added that inside Western and Eastern Europe itself, there are gaps and discrepancies between the cognitive standpoints, the conceptual tools, and the collective representations that actually dominate each society. Nevertheless, the ongoing conflicts in Ireland, Yugoslavia, Russia and even Israel/Palestine are perceived, 'explained' and interpreted using criteria, vocabulary and perspectives that are very different from those used in connection with similar conflicts in Africa, the Muslim world and Asia.

These remarks help to identify the cognitive status and the new functions of Emerging Reason. We need to elaborate the concept, to establish its philosophical relevance and its specific role among the still-conflicting cognitive postures of reason in the geopolitical contexts designed by recent historical developments and the rivalry between ancient and new aspirations for power.

I have explained why the concept of post-modernity cannot be used here, as a result of all the criticism it has attracted from various disciplines and schools of thought in the West itself. It had some relevance for a while in the 1970s and 1980s in the elimination of the limited, abstract postulates used by the rationale of the Enlightenment – the formalistic, vacuous humanism, especially during the period of the conquering liberal bourgeoisie on one side, and the Socialist-Communist proletarian revolution on the other. The definition and the tasks assigned to post-modern reason have remained limited to the European/Western historical perspective. During the 1970s, the political, cultural and economic failure of the revolutionary claims which had spread throughout the colonized countries during the wars of liberation (1945–1967) started to become evident with the decline of Soviet support. Some anthropologists, such as Margaret Mead, Malinovski, Cl. Geertz, J. Goody, Cl. Lévi-Strauss, L. Dumont and G. Dumézil, preferred to open the cognitive horizons of the Western mentality to other cultures and mentalities. But anthropology as a pluralist cognitive framework for interpretation still remains limited to specialists. Even in United States where this discipline is actively practised in several universities, it has little impact on the current way of thinking and of interpreting foreign cultures. The gulf between *us* and *them*, *I* and *he*, *we* and *others* is still determined by traditional religious systems of belief and non-belief, used and corroborated by political nationalist constructions of the self. In the most democratic regimes, the struggle between the so-called 'identities', claims for individual and communitarian 'difference' are encouraged and multiplied by an abstract discourse on human rights which is not enlightened by what James Clifford has called *anthropology as cultural criticism*, or what P. Bourdieu defends as *the theory of the social world* (see Louis Pinto: *P. Bourdieu et la théorie du monde social.*).

I am not suggesting that this option is purely materialistic and should be limited, or rejected in the name of so-called spiritual and ethical values. I published a book in Arabic with the ambitious and unusual title, *al-Fikr al-uṣūlī wa-istiḥālat al-ta'ṣīl.* The title is more challenging and more evocative in Arabic than in any European language, because it refers to a long tradition of the search for foundations. In English it means: *The foundational thought and the impossibility of providing foundations. Uṣūl* is the plural of *aṣl*, meaning roots, basic foundations, primary sources, origins. The teachings of the Qur'ān and the Prophet (*ḥadīth*) are received as divine, revealed by God; thus, they all have the power, the value of sanctifying, transcending and ontologizing all spiritual principles, and the ethical, legalistic norms derived from the teachings articulated by God in the Arabic language. Two 'scientific' disciplines have been developed and taught in Islamic thought under the name of *uṣūl al-dīn* and *uṣūl al-fiqh* which mean the roots/divine origins/foundations of religion and Law. The equivalent of the same disciplines commanding the same rationalizing procedures is to be found in Jewish and Christian traditions of thought. That is why one can speak of a religious reason with its Islamic, Jewish Christian instruments, references and procedures. This religious reason has been challenged, shaken, politically marginalized and intellectually disqualified by the reasoning of the Enlightenment and especially since the French Revolution which was more radical in this regard than the English and American Revolutions. It is a historical fact that Christian theological, legalistic reasoning has been more exposed than any other to the intellectual, scientific challenges and political marginalization generated by the reasoning of the Enlightenment. We know how the Muslim orthodox community reacted against Ibn Rushd and the Jewish community against Spinoza. We know also how Judaism has been involved in a nationalist struggle since the creation of the State of Israel, just as Islam had to support nationalist movements of liberation from colonial domination. Religious reason itself is differentiated by these different historical evolutions and contexts. These differences have been explicitly recognized in the inter-religious confrontations and dialogue since Vatican II. But neither the reasoning of the Enlightenment, nor so-called post-modern reason have been able so far to propose new possibilities to go beyond the principles, categories, definitions and forms of reasoning inherited from theological reason on one side, and enlightened, scientific reason on the other. The inherited frontiers of the mind are displaced by the *culture of disbelief* (see Stephen Carter, *Culture of disbelief: How American Law and Politics trivialize Religious devotion*) and sustained by scientific discoveries; but, as Marc Augé puts it in the quotation at the start of this introduction, new frontiers have been drawn between the conqueror mentality, shaped by 'hard' sciences and computer sciences, and the fragile disputed evidence proposed by human and social sciences and the unreachable mysteries of the lived experiences of the individual; these mysteries are left without any relevant answer because they remain beyond the scope and the speculation of **tele-techno-scientific reason**.

The philosopher Paul Ricœur who made so many important contributions to identifying the need to rethink all the problems related to the articulation of the religious field and the intellectual field with all its epistemological concerns, recently completed an illuminating new book, entitled *La mémoire, l'histoire, l'oubli* (*Memory, history, oblivion*). This deeply perceptive and innovative work reflects the growing dimension of intelligibility offered by Emerging Reason. The three concepts are applied to history as a scientific discipline which has the responsibility of shaping again and again the inaccessible 'objective' past, using an ocean of archives that are never explicit and exhaustive enough to correct the discrepancies between collective oral memories, the necessary work of *anamnesis* and the selective pressures of social groups to adapt the representation of the past to their present convictions, values and options. He introduces the correct distinction between history written just as the time over, *le révolu* (facts, events, personalities and historical monuments belonging to a past chronology) or as what has been, *l'avoir été* which requires the historian to go beyond the written record in order to revive by memory, imagination and historical sensibility the dead protagonists as those who have been living, acting, continuously placed as we ourselves are, in conditions of negotiation and decision-making. '*I challenge*', says Ricœur, '*the being for death*'; like Michel de Certeau, Michel Foucault, Emmanuel Lévinas, Bernard Lepetit and J. Revel, he denies the principle of fatalism in history. If the dead are considered as living persons in time, then the changing scales of such a person's actions must be considered within the contexts of micro-history and macro-history. Using this line of reasoning, Ricœur ends the book with an epilogue on the pardon as a dimension of the obligation to retain the memory and the need to go beyond justice which has to judge the criminal and say to the condemned person: '*your value as a human being goes far beyond your deeds as a criminal*'. Pope John Paul II visited his would-be assassin in prison, but he let the trial end with the verdict.

Now we are in a better position to grasp the meaning and to perceive the tasks of Emerging Reason. First of all, it does not necessarily emerge as an expanding evolutionary linear process of modern reasoning; certainly, it cannot ignore the abundant achievements of modernity; but neither can it disqualify *a priori* all the legacies of the living cultural traditions still linked to religious inspiration. Emerging Reason operates, creates, and innovates in the new contexts of **intercultural dialectic** which open up more possibilities for **intercreativity** at all levels, in all fields, all expectations, all possible politics of hope, all debates on human existence. It assumes the intellectual responsibility of helping so many people uprooted from their active cultural codes, systems of beliefs and values to be left aside from the main historical stream, the new political institutions of social integration. This is true for all Muslim communities. The majority of Muslim migrants to Europe are manual workers or youngsters looking for low-paidjobs rejected by jobless citizens. These exiled populations do not so far have any adapted spaces for learning, any opportunity to replace their disqualified cultural, religious references with 'modern', European standards of thought and life. Yet at the same time, sociologists describe them as 'fundamentalists', dangerous social categories, elements that threaten 'Western values'.

Here, E. R. faces two tasks. It points out the ideological solidarity of social and political sciences with hegemonic reason and it undertakes the neglected duties of the state in the fields of education, cultural activities, relevant criticism of the 'return of religion', the resurgence of the sacred, all of which mean, in fact, a dialectic response to an arbitrary policy or a total lack of effective policy. These tasks are not only required for the migrants in European/Western contexts; they are all the more urgent in

Islamic contexts where many 'national' states are even more cynical and obscurantist in their religious, cultural and social policy. In other words, E. R. carries on several battles simultaneously in all contemporary contexts, namely the epistemological battles in the West, the didactic and educational battles in the traditional, marginalized societies and the political battles with all categories of establishments that monopolize the decision-making process in academic, bureaucratic, governmental and economic institutions. It is interested in all types of silenced voices throughout history, like all those voices silenced today in Islamic contexts, either by official censorship or by the pressures of public opinion manipulated by political activists; it reactivates the persecuted, innovative mind, it refuses to write a history of thought, literature and the arts based exclusively on the so-called representative authors and works selected, in fact, by the dominant tradition in each period and each milieu, neglecting to use the methodology of what, in relation to Ibn Rushd, the Mu'tazilites, and philosophy in general, I called the sociology of failure combined with the sociology of success.[1]

3. Proposed Illustrations

Each of the essays presented in this book deals with a complex topic referring to a number of problems which remain **unthought** in contemporary Islamic thought. I do not mean that these topics are all unknown and have never been tackled in classical or contemporary Islamic thought. As I have mentioned in several contexts, some problems have been intensively discussed at some time or another and have been rejected and relegated to the domain of the **unthinkable**. One example is the famous theory of God's created speech defended by Ḥanafī, Djahmī, and

1. I did this already in my thesis about the generation of Miskawayh and al-Tawḥīdī, in *L'humanisme arabe au 4e/10e siècle*; see also 'La place d'Averroès dans l'histoire de la pensée', (Averroes' Place in the History of Thought) in *Rencontres d'Averroès. La Méditerranée, frontières et passages*, Thierry Fabre (ed.), Actes Sud, 1999.

Mu'tazilī thinkers especially between 800–848; others, like religious freedom, human rights, the individual and the citizen, toleration, logocentrism, historical epistemology, symbolic function, metaphoric organization of religious discourse, and so on, refer to the yet **unthought** as far as these themes are currently known and debated in Western thought, while contemporary Islamic thought remains suspicious, more polemical and apologetic than critically concerned and challenged by them and by intellectual modernity in general.

The first chapter deals with the frontiers of mind, a concept proposed by the Library of Congress as the subject of an international conference held in Washington in June, 1999. I took this unexpected opportunity to clarify my attempts to differentiate the cognitive status, the functions and the horizons of meaning and action of three competing cognitive types of reasoning – religious reason, philosophical reason and scientific reason. Since I began my research for a *Critique of Islamic reason*, I have had to determine how this reason integrates, ignores, or rejects the concerns, attitudes and goals of the three interacting attitudes or paradigms. I hope that the concepts developed through this enquiry will facilitate and contribute to the understanding of the analysis devoted throughout the book to the many delicate issues related to Islamic thought.

I have insisted on what I call the foundational posture of religious reasoning in general. By this, I mean the search for ontological, spiritual and intellectual foundations upon which to base systems of belief, knowledge and interpretation, the normative law supposedly derived and currently taught as the genuine expression of the 'true religion'. In Islamic thought, this fundamental exercise (*ta'ṣīl*) has persisted thanks to the two central disciplines of *uṣūl al-dīn* and *uṣūl al-fiqh*; both disciplines have developed a systematic methodology to establish the divine origins, the textual sources and meaningful roots (*uṣūl*) on which theological propositions and legalistic norms have to be based. The discursive procedures used for this purpose are called *ta'ṣīl.* The scholarly impact of these disciplines on religious perception of what is called the Divine Law (*sharī'a*), has been confused with the regulations collected in the form of bodies of law (*majmū'āt fiqhiyya*), resulting in the present fundamentalist discourse coupled with the political activism of the so-called fundamentalist movements, not only in Islam, but in several political movements, religious and secular.[1] That is why I have introduced a firm distinction between fundamentalist vision and discursive practice and the foundationalist standpoint of reason looking for ontological origins, theoretical principles and coherent reasoning on which to base beliefs, ethical values, the law and 'scientific' knowledge. All these problems will be examined in several contexts, especially in Chapters 2, 3 and 4.

The concept of logocentrism merits special consideration. I wrote this essay in 1970. Since the publication of J. Derrida, *De la grammatologie*, an interesting discussion has ensued concerning the deconstruction of classical metaphysics. It was more than a new field of research in the history of ideas as still practised, especially in the history of Islamic thought. Derrida was aiming to introduce new cognitive strategies in the interpretation of the long philosophical tradition of thought in the ontological framework of classical metaphysics which has influenced theological thinking in the three 'revealed' religions. As usual, not one historian of Islamic philosophy and theology paid any attention to the ensuing debate which, while far-reaching, was limited to the linear history of Western thought from classical Greece to the present day, bypassing the Middle Ages from Plato and Aristotle to Descartes, Leibniz and Spinoza. It is true that the concept of deconstruction as Derrida used it, raised objections and rejection even among Western historians of philosophy. At the present stage of the history of Islamic thought, I do not need to enter into a theoretical debate about the philosophical legitimacy and the methodological relevance of deconstructivism and logocentrism. I do not support any specific position, but I think that it is important to show that the impact of logocentrism on Islamic thought is as strong,

1. A good example of this foundational activity was provided recently by Cardinal Joseph Ratzinger in his presentation of the Declaration 'Dominus Jesus'. See *L'Osservatore romano* 17/10/2000, the answers of Cardinal Ratzinger to the critiques raised by his positions.

although less durable, as it was on European mediaeval thought. For further developments on the issue, I refer to John M. Ellisin *Against Deconstruction*; Christopher Norris: *Deconstruction. Theory and Practice*, where some interesting points are made.

I wanted to react against the prevailing scholastic division of Islamic thought into specialized disciplines (theology, philosophy, historiography, law, literature) without pointing out a more significant unifying differentiation, using the criteria of *epistémè* and discourse analysis. Abū-l-Ḥasan al-'Āmirī's *al-I'lām* was published as long ago as 1967; it set an inspiring example to test in a so-called 'oriental' culture, the relevance of the deconstructivist analysis of classical metaphysics and theology expressed in the Arabic language and in an Islamic context. Since the publication in 1972 of my essay in *Studia Islamica*, no scholar writing on al-'Āmirī or any other subject related to the history of thought, had referred to my text until Ian Richard Netton published his *al-Fārābī and his School* (1992) in which he writes 'in a stimulating, erudite and wide-ranging article, Professor M. Arkoun stresses that the *On Making known the virtues of Islam* operates within, or employs, a lexicon and cultural paradigm which is already well established. It is clearly a lexicon which gives a certain primacy to the noetic in its technical aspects ...' (p. 75).

I am not complaining about the lack of interest in my contributions to scholarship. I know that my way of sharing the concerns of scholarship is different from the merely descriptive, narrative, informative style of scholarship; it is the style specific to what I call the scholar-thinker (*chercheur-penseur*) who pays as much attention to finding the epistemological options underlying each type of discourse used in the past and the present, as to the development of facts, events, ideas, beliefs, performances, institutions, works of art and individual biographies, based on reliable archives (see above, Paul Ricœur). Writing history without making an issue of each word, each concept, each attitude used by the social protagonists, is misleading and even dangerous for people who assimilate the representations of the past as proposed by historians as the undisputable truth about this past. That is why each social group has itself built an image of its past without having the means of differentiating this mythical, or ideological image from the critical problematization provided by modern historians.

My point is about the epistemic and epistemological barrier that has always separated 'Orientalist' scholarship from the innovative, creative standpoints of reason emerging in the scholarship applied to European cultures and societies since the late sixties. In my attempt to identify a logocentrist attitude in classical Arab thought, I wanted to demonstrate that the axiomatic propositions, the postulates, the categories, the forms of demonstration used in Medieval thought expressed in the Syriac, Hebrew, Arabic, Persian, Greek, and Latin languages, were in fact shared and common to the Medieval mental space. And this strongly logocentrist frame of thinking imposed an epistemic **regime of truth** different from the other discursive frame represented by what I call the **prophetic discourse**. The mental dividing-line between the technical logocentrist corpus and the wider and more diversified corpus of prophetic discourse (the Bible, Gospels, Qur'ān considered apart from inherited theological definitions) runs at that 'deep' encompassing level, not on the 'surface' level particular to Jewish, Christian, Islamic logospheres on one side, to Western secularized, scientific sphere more and more separated from the monotheist religious sphere on the other side. I use the concepts deep and surface in the sense used by N. Chomsky in linguistics to discuss 'deep' and 'surface' structure. With this approach, the dividing-line does not stop with the advent of the modern age; the logocentrist frame was strengthened with the rationale of the Enlightenment, and to a greater extent today with tele-techno-scientific reason, while the religious frame is driven away from the prophetic discourse by the secularising forces operating in all religious traditions to shift the discourse from the religious to the ideological and militant.

We can then reinterpret the linguistic, semiotic and historical genesis, the semantic content and the functions of the three competing interacting logospheres: the religious, the scientific, and the philosophical in their changing sociological, historical contexts. I know that this terminology is too technical to be easily grasped and applied. To reach its full cognitive dimensions and its critical import, one needs to become familiar with several disciplines which are not currently properly taught with their interrelated conceptualisations and with the common concern for the epistemological shift of the frontiers of mind. All cultures and the languages used as vehicles, map the human mind with frontiers drawn and reproduced by systems of beliefs, non beliefs, representations and empirical knowledge. The problem for social sciences is to re-map the mind with a constant effort to retrace the frontiers according to the requirements of successive scientific revolutions and with radical criticism of the stance of reason. But we know that social sciences prefer to stick to the empirical, functionalist description of the 'facts', the 'objective realities' which are ultimately the result merely of social, psychological, conceptual constructions. If these remarks are in order on the cognitive status of the social sciences defined, taught and applied in Western societies, what would be the relevance of their practice and their products in the fields of foreign, sometimes hostile societies? We know how the exclusion of what is currently called 'Islam' from the Western intellectual and spiritual legacy, is more militant and more explicit than ever;[1] as I point out repeatedly, some Muslims themselves contribute to the extension and radicalisation of this exclusion with their apologetic endeavour to 'Islamise' modernity, to reject the Western 'materialism', 'immorality', 'atheism' labelled 'Westoxication'!

Seven other themes related to large and complex domains of Modern debates are introduced in the following chapters: problems of the state, civil society, individual and human rights; the concept of the person, the individual and the citizen; belief, non-belief and the construction of the human subject in Islamic contexts; authority and power, religious imaginary. I have dealt with many other themes in articles published in journals or collective books like the inter-religious dialogue and the recognition of the religious

1. On this important aspect, see *Islam and the West in the Mass Media: Fragmented Images in a Globalizing World*, edited by Kai Hafez, Hampton Press, Creskill, 1999.

phenomenon; toleration, intolerance, intolerable; anthropology as a key discipline for rethinking the religious phenomenon and for deciphering many till now ignored aspects of traditional, pre-modern societies; the functions of religion in the quest for peace and legitimizing wars (see the Bibliography).

We cannot say that these themes are totally absent in the ongoing confrontations, the recurrent programs proposed in many conferences, seminars, colloquia organized throughout the world by different institutions and organisations. It is true that Western institutions, private associations are eager to enhance a dialogue with Muslims on these burning issues with the hope of reaching a better mutual understanding, to build a culture of peace through repeated exchanges, meetings, international conferences. Particular efforts are displayed in that perspective by Christian institutions; since talks for peace have been initiated between Israel and Palestine, Jewish personalities are taking part more than before in this international endeavour. Finally, UNESCO has recently shown interest in supporting and enlarging the activities aimed at the construction and the teaching of a culture for universal peace with the decisive participation of all the existing religions. Such an ambitious program cannot be fulfilled if religious reason continues to stick to the inherited tools and systems of thought. It is clear that the participants in these activities do not share the same values, the same social and historical solidarities; more than that, they come from very different epistemological backgrounds; most of them cannot stick to a rigorous historical reasoning, or conceive of the existence of several rationalities supporting different types and levels of what all of them call currently 'reason', truth, reality, history, culture, religion, society and so on. For example, when I try to explain the methodological necessity to suspend – not to ignore totally – all theological interference with a linguistic analysis of the Qur'ānic discourse, Muslims – ordinary believers as well as cultivated 'intellectuals' – would ask immediately 'how can you carry on a linguistic discourse analysis on a *divine* word expressed in Arabic which is itself elected as a *divine* language'? Or 'what you consider as a text is actually an indivisible part of the *uncreated Qur'ān* collected in the *Muṣḥaf*. Not only do these questions reveal the intellectual impossibility of grasping a very simple methodological rule, but they stop the proposed exercise with naïve so-called theological objections betraying a total ignorance of the rich theoretical debates generated in classical theology on the issue of God's created speech. This is clearly what I call the unthinkable and the unthought in contemporary Islamic thought. The usefulness of such meetings and dialogues lies in the opportunities given to each participant to increase awareness of the urgent necessity to create an adequate cultural and intellectual frame of communication, analysis and interpretation, whenever or wherever traditions of thought, belief systems, emotional claims of identity and 'values' are used to face challenges of modernity and globalisation.

Because I often had to introduce my own cognitive strategy and option for a general criticism of all forms of rationality, all procedures and postures of reason in various historical and cultural contexts, I felt obliged to repeat elementary explanations as a pedagogical device to enhance the intellectual communication with my changing audiences. Traces of this oral delivery will be noticed in the written version of the essays collected in this volume. My readers too belong to different cultural and epistemological, ideological backgrounds; they complained to me about the difficulty of going through several fields and levels of conceptualisation. Although Western scholars remain reluctant to share the task of rethinking the whole Islamic tradition, some of them dare to combine several methodologies, to rely on multiple disciplines and confer a more critical purport to their new scientific practice.[1] I mention many titles in the general bibliography to illustrate this new initiative of what I prefer to call Western scholarship on 'Islam' and 'Muslim' societies to avoid the heavily and polemically loaded word Orientalism. In a recently published book by Ḥamīd Dabashi, *Truth and Narrative: The Untimely Thoughts of 'Ayn al-Quḍāt al-Hamadhānī*, we read a vehement reactivation of the controversy about

1. Many titles can be mentioned here like Uri Rubin, *The Eye of the Beholder*, or J.Van Ess, *Theologie und Gesellschaft* (see the bibliography).

> *the unbelievable power of Orientalism as a colonialist ideology that even now, a good two decades into Said's destruction of the whole Orientalist discourse, people continue to exercise it in university halls and dissertations, conferences and journals* [p. 39].

I mention this author here just to avoid an intolerable amalgam between an illusionary deconstructivist discourse, a so-called critique limited to a polemical rhetoric and a legitimate epistemological reassessment of the systems of thought, the levels and types of knowledge transmitted, reproduced uncritically by all religious as well as modern, secularised traditions of thought and knowledge. Dabasbi calls for a subversive epistemology and instrumentalises in 1999 – just as I have done since the seventies – the same vocabulary, the same option for deconstructing all the 'masternarratives, the nomocentricity of Islamic Law, the logocentricity of philosophy, the intoxicated theo-erotic counter narrative of the *taṣawwuf* … the power-based language of all discourses of Islamic thought', as well as for pursuing the 'de-essentialisation of what Muslims and Orientalists have hegemonically called "Islamic" history.' Not only he does this as if no one author has used this cognitive strategy for more than three decades, but he fails to recognize the still-needed rigorous philological methodology and even historicist writing in Islamic studies. He is also unfair to the significant moves made by Western Islamicists since the last twenty years towards new epistemological postures and cognitive explorations (see the bibliography). The book of Dabashi is in my view an eloquent counter-example to the intellectual and scholarly profile I try to illustrate under the concept of the **scholar-thinker.** I totally share the critical remarks made by Julie Scott Meisami in her review of the book (*Journal of Islamic Studies, vol. 11, 3, September 2000*); she rightly stresses the discrepancy between 'the theoretical pretensions of the author and the weakness, the inconsistencies of his scholarship and style. This should not authorize on the other side, the dismissal, with the same unfair irony used by Dabashi against the "the neo-Orientalist enterprise", the ritualistic invocation of Weber, Durkheim, Derrida, Foucault and a whole panoply of others in … jargon-ridden statements.' It remains true that the most admirable scholars who limit their search and their 'writing' to the erudite accumulation of factual knowledge, neglect to read and enhance their critical thinking with the conceptualisations and the epistemological shifts imposed by those scholars-thinkers who contributed so efficiently to the successive 'scientific revolutions' of intellectual modernity. The unique valid point in discussion here is how to bring Islamic thought and studies to the level of fertile criticism we witness since the seventeenth-eighteenth century in European scholarship and historical development.

I cannot end this introduction without mentioning other essays prepared in French for a book to be published soon under the title *Penser l'Islam aujourd'hui.* All these essays illustrate the large fields and important themes belonging to the *Unthought in Contemporary Islamic Thought.* Two chapters in particular should be added to the present work: *Inaugurating a Critique of Islamic Reason* and *Introduction to a Critique of Juridical Reason in Islamic Contexts.* For various reasons I have preferred to delay this publication until reactions to the French edition are collected and evaluated. I hope the readers of the present book will also take into consideration the whole project and the common vision which inspired the English and the French versions of the same lifetime work.

ONE

A Critical Introduction to Qur'ānic Studies

*Therefore, take heed (*fa'tabirū*), you who have eyes.*

Qur'ān, 59, 2.

Surely, We have sent down to you the Book with the Truth, so that you may judge between the people by that which God has shown you.

Qur'ān, 4, 105.

Scientific reason is not questioned according to the criterion of the true or false on the (paradigmatic) axis of the message/referent, but according to the performative level of the pragmatic axis of the addresser/addressee.

F. Lyotard, in *L'état des sciences sociales en France*, p. 15.

A critical introduction to Qur'ānic Studies should not only evaluate the content of the most significant contributions published in the last 20 years, it should also discuss the theoretical aspects of the approaches required by religious discourse as it is employed in Islamic contexts as well as in other religious traditions. Muslims avoid or reject radically such a comparative inquiry; they focus on the Qur'ān as the Word of God providing all the believers with clear, eternal, indisputable norms, teachings and ideal commandments to enlighten this life and lead to Salvation in the next. An increasing number of books and commentaries in all languages are invoked in order to support and spread this purely religious acceptance of the heavenly Book. What place is left in this practice to the scholarly works devoted to the interpretation of the Qur'ān? And how can scholarship, with its specific tools and methodologies, incorporate or discard the pious literature produced by the believers? Should scholars accept the wide gap generated by the contrast between 'scientific' and 'traditional' attitudes to the religious phenomenon, or should they include in their inquiry all the facts relating to the Qur'ān as a source of life, an ultimately constraining point of reference, a global, complex, recurrent, commanding historical force? The cognitive status of modern scholarship is challenged by the phenomenon of what I called the religions of the **Book-book**; critical scholarship has certainly shed light on several aspects of this phenomenon, but the recent emergence of religion as a refuge, a springboard for historical action in many societies, has convincingly unmasked the failure of 'scientific' interpretations of religion to enhance the rational, cultural dimensions of religious belief and emancipate popular/populist religion from its mythological, ideological and fantastical expressions. This failure should itself be the subject of scientific inquiry in order to enrich the cognitive ambitions of modern scholarship.

To illustrate these observations, I shall consider the following aspects:

- From *'ilm al-yaqīn* to the end of certainty.
- Reading the Qur'ān today. Faithful readings and 'scientific' readings
- Methodological priority and the limits of historical-anthropological reading.
- An analysis of religious discourse.
- From traditional exegesis to the hermeneutical circle.
- New horizons of meaning and action.

Under these six headings, I shall focus on the contemporary methodology operative in the critical study of the Qur'ān, especially in the West, as well as the historical, anthropological, linguistic, literary, philosophical and epistemological questions, problems and queries relating to the study of the Qur'ān as the focal point of Islam, Islamic tradition, Islamic Law, and Islamic thought, which are themselves confronted by the challenges of classical and meta-modernity.

1. From 'Ilm al-Yaqīn to the End of Certainties

Qur'ānic discourse has given ontological, psychological, thematic and rhetorical support to the concept of *'ilm al-yaqīn*, certainty-based science. Not only does the revealed Word of God provide full intangible certainty and defines the limits thereof, but it functions as the source and the fundamental root of every type of knowledge derived therefrom, taking due account of the rules, procedures and methods. Islamic law, *sharī'a*, is called 'Divine Law' because it is presented as fully, correctly derived from the teachings of holy texts (the Qur'ān and the *ḥadīth*). The quest for certainty in Law, for the purpose of undermining the role of doubt, is richly expressed in the following statement by Bihbahānī, a Shī'ī, a scholar who died in 1792:

> *You know that the cause of the difference between the akhbārī and the mujtahid is ijtihād itself, that is acting on the basis of opinion (ẓann). Whoever acts on its basis is a mujtahid, and whoever claims not to, but rather claims to be acting on the basis of religious science ('ilm) and certainty (yaqīn), is an akhbārī.*[1]

Theology (*'ilm al-kalām*) is more controversial; some schools prefer to avoid it, or at least to prevent the unprepared masses from having any exposure to it. Ṣūfī search and spiritual exercise

1. See the comments on this statement in R. Gleave, *Inevitable Doubt: Two theories of Shī'ī Jurisprudence*, Brill, 2000, p. 252.

are another field in which a more emotional, subjective, less logocentrist certainty is conquered, possessed and used as a path by which to reach the level of unification with God (*ittiḥād, ittiṣāl*).

In classical modernity (1680–1945, according to Paul Hazard in *La crise de la conscience européenne*), positivist reason has fostered the imaginary of scientific progress with a sense of mathematical, experimentally based certainty that has become the solid foundation of a culture of disbelief replacing the traditional culture of religious belief and eschatological hope in eternal Salvation. Historians of science, such as Ilya Prigogine, have dated the '*end of certainties*' based on scientific reasoning and experimentation from 1945 onwards. Social sciences are contributing to the dissolution of the inherited systems of knowledge and the subversion of the cultural and legal regimes of truth both in their religious and modern versions. Qur'ānic studies. as the majority of Muslims continue to pursue them, distance themselves from these intellectual shifts and scientific revolutions, maintaining the 'orthodox' theological and legal frameworks of belief and interpretation in order to legitimize the 'universal' perspective of the Islamic regime of truth, sustaining the Islamic model of human history as an alternative to the Western secularized model. The emergence of a meta-modern horizon of meaning, knowledge and action is simply ignored or misunderstood in the current ideological debate opposing 'Islam' and the 'West'.

There is a need for a new ranking of rational processes; we cannot stick to the ranking established and imposed for centuries by the two foundational disciplines developed by Muslim theologians and jurists under the name of *uṣūl al-dīn* and *uṣūl al-fiqh*. Contemporary reason no longer offers the certainty and the uniqueness of a Truth that is still defended by all those who think, interpret, decide and act in the dogmatic, conservative belief patterns and knowledge. Even in the Middle Ages, these frameworks were pluralistic and conflicting, much less monolithic than what the fundamentalist discourse has been imposing for several decades. Ranking rational processes means maintaining constantly open the theoretical debate on the epistemological axioms and postulates commanding each implicitly or explicitly assumed hierarchy of approaches (*l'ordre des raisons*) in every cognitive construction. From that point of view, the social sciences are not always helpful, especially for those who aim to displace the *ordre des raisons* elaborated by *uṣūlī* thinking in the mediaeval context to the meta-modern criticism of any foundationalist attempt. I have shown this intellectual and methodological discrepancy in my 'Critique of legalistic reasoning in Islamic contexts' (to be published in *Penser l'Islam aujourd'hui*). So-called 'tele-techno-scientific reasoning' is spreading a new pragmatic instrumental form of reasoning lead by the principle of '*just do it*', as long as so doing ensures concrete, significant technological and economic success. Facing the hegemonic achievements of tele-techno-scientific reasoning, academic scholastic reasoning, such as P. Bourdieu has presented its cognitive status in his *Méditations pascaliennes*,[1] is unlikely to elicit any fruitful response to the type of issues we are introducing about the radical critique of the cognitive status of the Qur'ānic discourse, itself, that are considered here as a mere example among others of an attempt to reach all types and levels of 'holy Scriptures', or sacred foundational texts.

European modernity, at least since the eighteenth century, has left us with the impression that reason would finally be liberated from the constraints of dogmatism in order to be placed in the service of objective knowledge alone, once a radical separation between every institutionalized religious law and the 'neutral' state has been accomplished. When this latter body is free to exercise its undisputed sovereignty, it does not, however, struggle with the same determination for such a radical separation between cognitive reasoning and the reasoning of the state (*raison d'état*). This is not the place to explore this subject further; it is enough to recall now that in the various Islamic contexts, reason multiplies the constraints

1. The author is not indicating the reason submitted to the orthodox teachings of the theological magisterium of the Middle Ages, but to modern academic practices, imposing the scholarly reproduction of a methodological and epistemological framework of analysis and interpretation in strict conformity to that favoured by the supervisor of a thesis, or a leading figure of a given school of thought.

which it had itself created for the sake of its independence in the face of the strict control of the state which unilaterally proclaims itself the exclusive administrator of orthodox religious truth and law.

Such are the two contexts in which the Qur'ān has been read, consulted and interpreted for fourteen centuries by the Muslims and for some two centuries by the modern scholarship. This introduction of a hierarchy of approaches (*ordre des raisons*) makes the debate on Orientalism irrelevant at least in the manner it has hitherto been conducted, i.e., devoid of any preliminary critique, devoid of scholastic reasoning (as defined above) and devoid of recognition of the fact that cognitive reasoning has willingly accepted the actual hegemony of the utilitarian, pragmatic, experimental, instrumental reasoning which is becoming all-powerful under the name of tele-techno-scientific reason. One must, however, remember two troublesome issues for the western scholar of the Qur'ān who is using the tools and assumptions of the social sciences of religions (see the French journal *Archives des Sciences Sociales des Religions*), after the long domination of a positivist, historicist, philological methodology and epistemology:

1. During the long academic supremacy of *Formgeschichte* and philology, Qur'ānic scholars had little regard for questions of an epistemological nature, if they were even aware of them at all. Methodological discussions were restricted to the ways in which philological rules were applied to reach 'facts' and solve problems in relation to both authentic and apocryphal documents. The philosophical implications of the cognitive framework chosen in which to conduct this criticism have not yet been adequately considered even in the new framework introduced by social sciences.

2. Apart from specialists who are themselves believers and bring their Jewish or Christian theological culture to bear on the question at hand, all who declare themselves agnostic, atheist or simply secular dodge the question of meaning – its genesis and

metamorphoses – in religious discourse and thus refuse to enter into a discussion of the content of faith, not as a set of life rules to be internalized by every believer, but as a psycho-linguistic, social and historical construct. The concept of religious discourse differentiated from theological, philosophical, historiographical and legalistic discourses, has not yet been shown to become operative and meaningful when it is applied to the sacred, religious, basic texts currently called the Holy Scriptures. Hence the essential question about truth, for religious reasoning as well as that of the most critical philosophical kind, is totally absent in the so-called scientific study of a corpus of texts of which the *raison d'être* – the ultimate goal to which all rhetorical and linguistic utterances bear witness – consists in providing for its immediate audience, who have multiplied and succeeded one another throughout the centuries, the unique, absolute and intangible criterion of Truth as a True Being, a True Reality and a True Sense of Righteousness (*al-ḥaqq*). Doubtlessly, from the time when was first announced orally between 610 and 632 C. E., the *ḥaqq* has developed in a way that must be taken into account by history of thought and cultural sociology.

It is not a matter of establishing the true meaning of texts as lived and received by the faithful, i.e., as sacred and revealed, or of articulating that which is taken as a certainty insofar as recorded in a process of sacralization, transcendantalization, ontologization, spiritualization, etc., in the manner of the great systems of theological, philosophical, legal or historiographical thought inherited from the Middle Ages; the task of the researcher is to problematize all the systems that claim to produce meaning, all the forms, whether or not they are still extant, which offer meaning and assumptions of meaning (*effets de sens*). This is a necessary distinction that refers to many problems yet to be raised or, if they have been raised, they have been raised inadequately or without full recognition. In the case of the Qur'ān and similar corpuses in other cultures (a comparative approach is always in order), the activity of the human mind can be found nearest to its own utopian vision, its hopes, both those which are unfulfilled and those which recur, its struggle to attain the full exercise of its 'will to know,' combined with its critical and creative freedom. The purpose in the case of the Qur'ānic corpus and its vast historical development, is to test the capacity of reason to decipher the mysteries which it has itself produced in a previous age.

With this idea of utopia, it is important not to lose sight of the fact that Qur'ānic studies lag considerably behind biblical studies to which they must always be compared (see scripture and Qur'ānic study). This could be said to reflect the different concerns in the historical development of societies in which the Qur'ān continues to play the role of ultimate and absolute reference point and has never been replaced as the sole criterion for the definition and function of all true, legitimate and legal values. The stakes in the violent and passionate rejection of what political Islam calls 'the West' lie less in the grasping of an ephemeral power than in the progress of the secular model of the production of history, and could ultimately render the 'divine' model obsolete, as it is in the West. This point is noteworthy in order to release the Qur'ānic studies from its isolation *vis-à-vis* the historical perspective of modernity as well as that of the religious problem, which has been at one and the same time, appropriated by and disqualified along with its former force. This premise is essential for clarifying the strategy of mediating a solution and thus guiding the pedagogy of the **scholar-thinker** (*chercheur-penseur*).[1]

During the years of struggle for political independence (1945–1970), one could have hoped that an opening toward modern historical criticism, as shown in the Middle East and North Africa

1. This combination is unusual in the current discourse of scholarship, and might lead to misunderstandings. I do not mean a mixture of scholarship and critical thinking on problems raised by scholarly presentations of the matters under inquiry; I mean even less any theological or philosophical speculation on problems related to practices of scholarship. I have only in mind that scholars dealing with disputed, delicate issues like Qur'ānic studies, should insert in their writing explicit definitions of their methodological and epistemological options.

during the so-called Renaissance (*nahḍa*, 1830–1940), would have expanded to include such taboo subjects as Qur'ānic studies, including the sanctified areas of law appropriated by the *sharīʿa* and its legal statutes and rulings (see law and the Qur'ān), the corpus of *ḥadīth* which enjoys the status of foundational sources (*uṣūl*) as defined by al-Shāfiʿī (d. 204/820). However, certain historical events have altered this potential course, beginning with the 1979 Islamic Revolution in Iran, which was in turn, extended globally by so-called fundamentalist movements. This revived, in the already very complex and inadequately explored area of Qur'ānic studies, the rather archaic combination of violence and the sacred, which was still able, with some effect, to bring its weight to bear upon the global civilization of disenchantment, desacralization and the supremacy of science over all dimensions of human existence.

Like Christians during the modernist crisis of the nineteenth century, Muslims have reacted – and still react – against former works marked by historicist-philologist positivism as well as against more recent research that is relatively free of the assumption of a triumphalist, even intolerant 'scientific' attitude. Under the pretext of not wanting to confuse different kinds of science, so-called pure researchers refuse to address the conflict between full-blown scientific reasoning and religious reasoning that is apparently vanquished intellectually or forced on to the defensive, despite its historical persistence and its revolutionary potential. We know how political scientists portray fundamentalist movements according to their own political options, either legitimizing their political action against totalitarian, oppressive regimes, or condemning them as violent, fanatical, irrational and opposed to the Western rational, democratic values. The theological and spiritual background of religiously inspired movements is rarely mentioned, at least as a psychological cultural reference to ancient collective memories that are still very much alive.

This means that historical epistemology is not integrated into social and political science as an important dimension of any historical and sociological research or writing. Whenever non-Western traditions of thought and cultural systems are involved, social and political scientists refer implicitly to the epistemological framework tacitly received as reliable by the scientific community; their interpretations, their writing would then reflect the impact of that framework more than the historical, sociological, psychological framework that is proper to contingent time and social milieu taken as the object of study. Philologists would insist on chronological formal authenticity, but not on the epistemological postulates commanding the articulation of the discourses studied.

It is thus a matter of moving towards the use of historical psychology, historical sociology and historical anthropology for vast areas of the past, long ignored by the historian interested in narration, description and taxonomy. The recently published survey by J. van Ess, entitled *Theologie und Gesellschaft* (Theology and Society) demonstrates all the richness of which we have been deprived and that which will potentially escape us for even longer, if not forever.

As a rather marginal discipline, history of religions is looked upon askance both by theological authorities, as the guardians of orthodoxy, and by secular states which advocate a political 'neutrality' that has still to be thought through philosophically and anthropologically. Furthermore, this field remains uncertain of its precise scope since it spills over into many other disciplines. The same uncertainty applies to its aims which largely involve the invisible, the untouchable, the unnamable, the supernatural, the miraculous, the mysterious, the sacred, the holy, hope, love, violence and so on; as well as its instruments, analytical framework and inevitable relationship to other disciplines, themselves groping their way forward in the dark. There is another rarely mentioned fact about the history of religions: specialists writing for their colleagues are fully aware of the academic constraints by which they will be judged and admitted to the profession or excluded therefrom, no less differently than theologians who must practice self-censorship in order to obtain the *imprimatur* of doctrinal authorities. In any case, the populace at large, long confined to the discourse of oral culture, does not appear in scholarly writing, although they are the most directly concerned audience for this research and form by far the largest and most convinced corpus of consumers of systems of belief and non-belief which science has submitted to their examination. Mediaeval élites (*khawāṣṣ*) already taught openly that the masses (*'awāmm*) should be kept away from scholarly debates. Today, it is left to the scorned popularizers of knowledge to transmit to a large audience bits and pieces of a highly specialized science. The distinctive feature of religion, however, is that it is a source of inspiration, hope and legitimatization for all and primarily for those who have not received instruction in critical thought. In the case of the contemporary Muslim world, this observation bears considerably on Qur'ānic studies.

2. Reading the Qur'ān Today

'Today' means that we need to articulate the cognitive, critical strategies used by social sciences since its epistemological shifts from classical modernity framework to meta-modern perspectives:

- Structure and form of the Qur'ān – form and meaning.
- Early Meccan revelation and Medinan revelation as differentiated corpora.
- Rational, imaginative, marvellous – the psychology of knowledge (angels, djinns, salvation). (A new area of work that has not been touched so far.)
- Emergence of a responsible person (sin, virtue, vice, law, interpersonal relations); the construction of an individual as a creator, a believer, a social agent, a moral, legal and spiritual subject.
- Society, law, culture, governance (authority, continuity; non-violence and truth as opposed to violence, the sacrosanct and the true; male, female, children, slaves, warfare, commerce).

Each chapter will refer extensively to the work done so far so as to evaluate it and show our commitment to exploring new areas of work that have not been undertaken, or even thought of as relevant subjects for scholarship. A select bibliography will follow at the end of the book.

These are categories that would apply to all religious texts (Islamic and others) and would, therefore, also be a useful categorization for a full long-term programme of Qur'ānic studies.

As far as what is commonly called the Qur'ān is concerned, it must be said that this term has become so heavily loaded by theological inquiry, legalistic instrumentalization and the ideological manipulations of contemporary political movements that it must be subjected to a preliminary deconstruction in order to make manifest levels of function and significance that have been side-stepped, suppressed or forgotten by pious tradition as well as by text-oriented philology, to say nothing of the savage exegesis of the so-called fundamentalist Muslims. This situation has a long history. It is known that from the moment the Qur'ān was written down throughout its propagation in manuscript form until it was finally printed, there was an inexorable rise of the clerics to political and intellectual power. This process is at odds with the social and cultural conditions prevailing at the time of the emergence and growth of that which the initial Qur'ānic discourse calls *Qur'ān*, the celestial text (*al-Kitāb*, the Book), recited as a confession of faith, aloud and in public. This annunciation can be called **prophetic discourse** and establishes an arena of communication between three grammatical persons, a *speaker* who articulates the discourse contained in the Heavenly Book;[1] a first *addressee*, who transmits the message of the enunciation[2] as an event of faith; and a second *addressee*, *al-nās* (the people), who constitute the group, large or small depending upon circumstances, whose members are nevertheless all equal and free, given their status as *addressees*. They are equal because they share the same discourse situation, i.e.,

1. On this concept, see G. Widengreen, *The Ascensionof the Apostle and the Heavenly Book*, Upsula, 1954.
2. There is a difference between *enunciation*, a linguistic concept, and *annunciation*, loaded with theological context.

access to the same oral language used in the enunciation of the Message. They are free because they respond immediately by assent, understanding, rejection, refutation or the demand for further explanation. More will be said about the crucial importance of the psycho-socio-linguistic analysis of what will henceforth be called **prophetic discourse**. (Justification will be given for the use of this description of the term 'prophetic,' which, historically, is strongly contested by the second *addressee*, after the adage that 'a prophet is without honour in his own country'). It must be remembered that all Orientalist scholarship, in limiting itself to the curiosities of the task of a philological restoration of the text (grammar, morphology, lexicography, syntax) along with an historical reconstruction of the simple facts, has ignored the concepts of the structure of interpersonal relationships (E. Benvéniste), of the discourse situation as conditioned by its context (as described by P. Zumptor for mediaeval literature by use of the term *orature* after French *écriture*, 'writing'), and of the dialectic between the powers and the residue (*dialectique des puissances et des résidus*) which encompasses the interaction between *orature* and *écriture*, knowledge of the structure of myth and critical historical knowledge, in other words the functional solidarity between 1) the centralizing state, 2) writing *écriture*, 3) the learned élites, and 4) orthodoxy. Thus, four dynamic socio-historical forces can be seen to be dialectically related to four other forces in the social arena which appear universally (as in Mecca and Medina at the time of the emergence of the Qur'ānic event (*fait coranique*) no less than in the social milieu of the contemporary nation-state): 1) segmentary societies, 2) *orature*, 3) culture which is called **popular** and disintegrates into **populist** culture in the contemporary megalopolis and 4) heterodoxies. This conceptual framework enables an integration of all levels at which Qur'ānic discourse functions – linguistic, social, anthropological, along with all historical periods – when we displace the analysis from the theological perspective to the procedures and rules of **discourse analysis**.

One can still be grateful, in fairness to orientalist scholarship, for the efforts and achievements of such pioneers as J. Wellhausen,

H. Grimme, T. Nöldeke, F. Schwally, G. Bergsträsser, O. Pretzl, I. Goldziher, T. Andrae, A. Guillaume, A. Jeffery, M. Bravmann, whose work has been continued by R. Paret, R. Blachère, H. Birkeland, R. Bell, W. M. Watt, J. Burton, J. Wansbrough, A.T. Welch, U. Rubin and so on. It should also be noted that for an area of studies which is so rich and vital, the names of those who really matter in this past century are quite few, as can be seen from the bibliography; the current generation seems promising, but the number and isolation of the researchers remain the same, along with the meagre scope of the projects and the less-than-considerable importance of the publications. Two remarks can be made:

1. The question of knowledge – reductionist, scientific, positivist – that goes so far as to support, openly and aggressively, an atheism that does not acknowledge itself to be merely one simple doctrinal option, must be examined, especially where it concerns comparative history and the anthropological analysis of religion. This problem must be re-addressed and re-discussed in relation to every scholarly work concerning the religious phenomenon.

2. J. Van Ess, whose contribution to Islamic studies is exceptionally rich, is another kind of scholar, belonging to that school which undertakes to censor itself, constantly and strictly, when it comes to the arena of faith, going so far as to respect the expression of this faith which proclaims itself to be orthodox by virtue of the sole fact of its sociological influence and political dominance. Here, it must be emphasized that the deconstruction of every form of orthodoxy falsely rendered sacred by historical figures who happened to succeed politically or psycho-sociologiaclly (saints), is one of the most essential critical tasks for the social sciences. Here is a surprising quote from this great scholar:

   I could have brought examples from the Mu'tazila (q.v.) but since they were considered to be heretics by the majority of Sunnī Muslims, I would have had to reckon afterwards with the objection that they

> *were ultimately unrepresentative of Islam ... He [Bishr al-Marīsī] is an interesting man, but, as in the case of the Mu'tazila, I do not want to put the Islamic view of history upside down. This would be something for the Muslims themselves to do ... As an historian and non-Muslim, I should not ask who was right, and who was wrong ... Indeed, whoever believed the recitation to be uncreated committed a sacrifice of intellect* [*Verbal Inspiration? Language and Revelation in Classical Islamic Theology*, lecture given on 21 November 1994 at the plenary session of the annual conference of the Middle Eastern Studies Association (MESA) and published in S. Wild, *The Qur'ān as Text*, pp. 180, 184–85].

This is not the place to comment upon these two quotations from the perspective of the epistemological commitments of reason in the domain of religious studies in general and that of Islamic studies in particular. The possibility of having a commitment and the way of defining this territory will be clarified in the remainder of this essay.

From the perspective of a kind of research which is always accompanied by a critical return to procedures, a process of cutting and pasting, theoretical constructs, explanations and meaningful results, it can be concluded that the Qur'ān is only one among a number of objects of study that have the same level of complexity and the same abundance of meanings, such as the Bible, the Gospels and founding texts of Buddhism and Hinduism, all which have already experienced and may yet experience still more historical growth. It is necessary to ask what would finally serve to distinguish the religious corpus just mentioned from the vast Platonic and Aristotelian corpus with all its different forms in Islamic and later European contexts, or from the corpus of the French Revolution or that of the October Revolution of 1917 (cf. the works of F. Furet). It is nevertheless clear that the invocation of a religious dimension of all religious texts, which is often the object of reductionist interpretations, should be more respected as such by the analyst who uses the principles and methodology of deconstruction. This attention given to avoid reductionist approaches ought not lead to ignore the other side of the problems raised by what 'believers' use and qualify straightfully as 'Holy Scriptures', while discourse analysis would show that the claimed holyness is, in fact, the result of a complex process of sacralization through time. In other words, any analysis of religious discourse should integrate the curiosity and the problematisation of historical psychology.

By way of concluding these introductory remarks, it will be helpful to ask whether scholarly experience, as amassed by Orientalist scholarship, enables us to move on into a new phase of Qur'ānic studies. What would then be the epistemological orientations, the methodological choices and the appropriate programmes for this new stage? Such new fields of scholarly investigation of the Qur'ānic phenomenon must obviously meet two requirements:

1. More and more Muslim scholars should be urged to contribute to the new approaches to the religious texts, by increasing the possibilities and places for the exchange and confrontation of thoughts, in order to make progress in what is bound to be a long-term enterprise with the ultimate goal, indeed, of thinking, knowing (*la noèse et la gnoséologie*) and acting;

2. Room should be given to previous and contemporary scholarship of Muslim believers. But which scholarship? What positive knowledge, independent of theological requirements, can be derived from it? Will it be possible, from this heterogeneous, but undivided reality that is, in the same time, the Qur'ān as oral delivery, the Qur'ān as liturgical recitation, the Qur'ān as text, the revealed Word of God, to separate data that can be declared 'objective' from psychological burdens and the content of faith, which believers attach to the Qur'ān in their daily use and which are still experienced as the ultimate revealed Truth? Is it necessary to classify all Muslim (or Christian or Jewish) discourses as prior or alien to the modern critical reason, as merely documentation for psychological and historico-sociological inquiry? This would lead to the placement of an entirely artificial scientific

goal next to the exuberant and effervescent product of history by the strong dialectical exchange between human faith (itself the result of the interaction between the social imaginary, the imaginal, reason activities and collective memory) and the forces of social, political upheaval.

I shall attempt to answer these questions under the following subheadings: 1) priorities and limitations of historical-anthropological interpretation; 2) linguistic, semiotic and literary interpretation; 3) religious interpretation; and 4) final proposals

2.1. *Priorities and Limitations of Historical-Anthropological Interpretation*

Important contributions to Qur'ānic studies have been published recently. They offer a concrete basis for a reassessment of the methodological and epistemological debate on the approaches applied to the religious discourse in general, to the particularly significant example represented by Qur'ānic Discourse in particular. All the titles mentioned in the Select Bibliography deserve an in-depth discussion, but each would require an entire monograph if justice is to be done to them. In the following paragraphs, I shall concentrate on the following titles: Herbert Berg: *The Development of Exegesis in Early Islam*, Curzon, 2000; Jacqueline Chabbi: *Le Seigneur des tribus*; Issa Boullata: *Literary structures of religious meaning in the Qur'ān*, Curzon, 2000.

The monograph by H. Berg has the merit of synthesizing in clear and objective terms the two opposing schools of thought concerning *ḥadīth* criticism from I. Goldziher and J. Schacht, N. Abbott and F. Sezgin to M. Cook, N. Calder, C. H. M. Versteegh and others. The two schools are called 'early Western scepticism and renewed scepticism' on one side and 'the reaction against scepticism and the search for middle ground' on the other side. After a carefully detailed analysis of the main arguments and positions, Berg insists on two points which consolidate my own position regarding this discussion and the solution that is eventually offered by Berg himself. The level of discussion between the two opposing positions is described in the following terms:

> *... that these two positions are diametrically opposed is evidenced by the vehemence and at a times condescending exchanges between scholars. Schacht has characterized Islamicists who would undermine the insights of Goldziher as being guilty of 'intellectual laziness'. Motzki speaks of Calder's 'prejudice ... against the isnāds and riwāyas', 'wild speculation without sufficient proof', and lesser sophistication (compared to Shoeler). Motzki also demands 'Let us abstain from speculation and restrict ourselves to the facts'. More disturbing are the ad hominems directed at sceptics. For example, Azami condemns Shacht's work as filled with 'inconsistencies', 'unwarranted assumptions', 'mistakes of fact', 'ignorance', 'misunderstandings' and 'unscientific method of research'. Abdul Rauf dismisses as 'unfair and unscholarly' those who 'just pass sweeping judgements in the name of objective scholarship'* [Berg, p. 222].

The condescending attitude of classical philologists towards Muslim scholars who have no idea of the discipline called philology and historicist criticism is well known. This disdain would have been fairer, had the illustrious scholars handled the delicate matter of their research with less passion and dogmatic certainty. I have written and observed that Western scholarship on Islamic studies, apart from its fragile results, has often left Muslims with a field of ruins, without caring about their intellectual responsibility for any damage caused. I do not know of any of them, even today after all the ideological polemics on Orientalism, who would have raised the issue of the psychological, ethical, existential impact on Muslims suddenly faced with the collapse of their inherited traditional acceptance of 'revealed Truth' and 'divine Law'. We know how intellectuals, scholars, believers and non-believers, handled the same situation created for Christianity in Europe by reason of the Enlightenment and the historicist positivist cognitive system. Kant, Hegel, Bergson, Max Weber, R. Bultman, E. Troelstch and so many other thinkers, each responded in his own way to the same field of ruins generated for Christian tradition. Orientalists, with their intellectual arrogance, shook to the foundations a 'sacred' tradition, knowing that no-one from inside the community would take up the cudgels and propose new horizons of meaning to those that had been dismissed, closed up by a scholarship which turned out to be so unfair, fragile and subjective in its both options. What had been held to be indisputable theory on the authenticity or the total apocryphal nature of the *ḥadīths* on which all exegetical, historiographical and *sharī'a* works are based, is presented today with plausible objections as an 'impasse'.

> *There is no middle ground,* writes Berg, *rather, I have sought to help resolve the impasse one way or another by drawing on the methods of both, but not on either of the assumptions that underlie their circular reasoning ... My method of constructing stylistic profiles ... allows us to break the 100 A. H. barrier and test the authenticity of materials which claim to come from the very first decades of Islam. However ... my method cannot determine the authenticity, chronology or provenance of any single ḥadīth ... So to the questions 'did someone named Ibn 'Abbās ever say anything about the Qur'ān? And if he did, is any of it preserved or discernible?' the answer must be: we do not know and we may never know* [pp. 226–30].

This is not the place to discuss the relevance and the results of the method chosen by Berg; I have underlined the very last sentence of his book, for it expresses exactly the position I have been defending since 1970, not only in relation to Qur'ānic studies, but about all religious traditions, more especially the monotheistic traditions based on the leaps from oral to written regimes of constructing and transmitting truth, true meanings, true law, etc. In all the construction processes of each tradition, there is a **myth of origins** for scriptural exegesis (Bible, Gospels, Qur'ān) similar to the one built on the mythical figure of Ibn 'Abbās. On this indisputable basis, we can agree on the hierarchy of scholarly tasks, namely, the search for authenticity, chronology and authorship. It is certainly useful to identify the myth of origins and its functions; but this search is subservient to a much more decisive one, not only for Islamic tradition, but for all historiographical memories in oral cultures and in the most modern, critical cultures of contemporary secularized societies. This anthropological perspective is followed and enhanced by a philosophical assessment about the **regimes of truth** at all times and in all cultures. It is the only way for scholarship to rid itself of the ethnographical approach reserved for non Western thought, culture and Judaeo-Christian religious tradition. The resistance of dominant scholarship since the nineteenth century to the adoption of this cognitive posture translates clearly the ideological basis concealed in all the formal attributes of safe, universal, reliable knowledge.

This having been said, I am the one who has also pointed systematically to the pioneering Western researchers in the field of Qur'ānic studies and Islamic thought in general, to a point where I am accused by Muslim colleagues of ignoring or excluding Muslim contributors to the field. There is no doubt that Muslims cannot cross the boundaries of the creed based on the **myth of origins** which remains for them the greatest unthinkable. In the generic name Muslims, I include not only practising believers, but also the many individuals who make claims upon a culture, a sensitivity, a spirituality, in other words an Islamic *ethos* without confining their thought to the dogmatic confinement of a single orthodoxy. Mention will be made of the Muslims' contribution to Qur'ānic studies in the third part of this chapter, though it is fitting to state here that no arbitrary boundary has been drawn; the epistemological criterion used here is open to debate, provided that the essential distinction between the cognitive attitude of belief and critical reason be respected. While no claim can be made for the superiority of one over the other, important differences separate the two states of cognition in terms of function, choice, aims, interests and results. Furthermore, the confrontation between these two attitudes and their respective products is necessary for a fuller awareness of the dimensions of cognition.

The criterion is as follows: the object of research is a collection of initially oral utterances put into writing under historical conditions that are not yet elucidated. These utterances have then been elevated, by the industry of generations of historical figures, to the status of a sacred Book which preserves the transcendent Word of God and serves as the ultimate and inevitable point of reference for every act, every form of behaviour and every thought of the faithful, who themselves are to be considered as communally interpreting this heritage. In this framework of study, a number of operative concepts and problems exist and still await a sufficiently objective, well-thought out and inclusive elucidation, so as to appeal not only to the community of scholars and thinkers, but also to those believers who consider themselves practising and orthodox. This is a crucial point if one intends to overcome the arrogance of scientific reasoning which provides believers with no opportunity to speak out and which interprets, cuts and pastes, categorizes and judges, without actually elucidating the mechanisms, omnipresence, results and significance of belief for every human being. The task of the **scholar-thinker** is to include in his or her field of investigation and analysis all that has been said, experienced and constructed and which emerges within the confines of dogmatism. To refuse today to enter these laboratories, so full of energy and significant events, which have become societies torn apart by so-called religious revolutions, would be to deprive the social sciences of essential data with which to renew their theoretical positions and strategies of intervention.

It will be seen later how belief can be integrated while also being submitted to critical analysis of the most fruitful kind. In a spirit of equity, it is necessary to mention something of the still relevant achievements of orientalist scholarship. In my *Lectures du Coran*, I presented three comparative tables which clarify the relationship and the differences between the Muslim approach as synthesized by al-Suyūtī in his *al-Itqān fī 'ulūm al Qur'ān*, the Orientalist approach as summarized and followed by A. T. Welch (*Encyclopaedia of Islam*) and the approach, still in the process of development, of the social sciences which are themselves subject to the elusive challenges of a comparative history of religions, conceived and written as an '*anthropology of the past*' and an '*archaeology of daily life*'(G. Duby, J. Le Goff, Alphonse Dupront). Although not without problems, the theoretical research project proposed by this last category of approach ought not to be too hastily dismissed. For example, the synchronic, linguistic exploration of Qur'ānic discourse, combined with an anthropological analysis, was recently used in an rich monograph to be discussed later (Chabbi, *Le seigneur*). The third approach is made possible by the progress of the social sciences and the cumulative achievements of Orientalist scholarship.

The taboo that Muslim orthodoxy has always placed on Qur'ānic studies was more easily lifted during the period of historical-philological positivism than it is today.[1] The euphoria of

1. It is appropriate to mention in this context the attitude of my colleague, the Tunisian historian Muḥammad Talbi, who gained a worldwide fame as one of the most open-minded, tolerant, cultivated Muslim. I know him since 1956 when I was myself a student and he, the Director of the Tunisian Student Residence in Paris. I thought we were friends, understanding each other, sharing the same endeavour to modernize Islamic thought, although we use two different epistemological postures. It has been very difficult for me to master my revolt and disappointment when he aggressed me in a so wild manner that noone of the so-called fundamentalist Muslims had ever done with me. A large audience of more than one hundred persons witnessed an authoritarian *imām* passing the judgement of excommunication against a 'hypocrite so-called Muslim working to serve the West' (he could not say 'Zionist' because the chief Rabbi Samuel Sirat was chairing the session during which I delivered my paper). I insist on the fact that Talbi has trained generations of students in historical criticism, and he received recently an Award for Tolerance by the Agneli Foundation. I would not have been able to mention this extremely significant event if Professor Talbi had not confirmed what he did in a written form, which I quote without any further comment, except my full recognition of the 'Model of tolerance' for having provided me with such a relevant illustration of the 'unthought and the unthinkable', as displayed by a famous Muslim 'modern' intellectual:

> *Salah Stétié exerce donc son 'droit à la réflexion libre' dans la transparence, et sans cette rage avec laquelle certains désislamisés* (sic) *qui préfèrent tactiquement l'ambiguïté, s'acharnent sciemment à déconstruire la figure de Muhammad le Prophète et à déconstruire son Coran prétendument*

scientific reasoning was boosted by colonial rule. Hence the battle for a critical edition of the text of the Qur'ān, including most notably a chronological ranking of the *sūrāt* is not as persistent as it was in the period between the writings of T. Nöldeke and those of R. Blachère. All the same, this subject has lost nothing of its scientific relevance, since it implies a more reliable historical reading, less dependent upon suppositions, hypotheses and the quest for the plausible (despite the trust she puts in her methods, J. Chabbi cannot avoid writing in the conditional mood). Unless more revealing manuscripts related to the history of the text are found, which is still possible, it seems better to draw the conclusion that an irreversible situation has been created by the systematic destruction of precious documents or by the lack of interest of people today in all that has become essential for modern historical knowledge. This field of research does not seem to have broadened its horizons or inquiries, if one is to judge by three collections of articles bearing carefully chosen signatures: *Approaches to the History of the Interpretation of the Qur'ān*, ed. Andrew Rippin, *Approaches to*

et faussement révélé. Leur modèle et leur maître à penser est sans conteste Mohamed Arkoun qui, tout en refusant la transparence, sans dire jamais clairement s'il est, oui ou non, Musulman, consacre pas moins le plus clair de son temps à démolir le Coran comme authentiquement théandrique, ipsissima verba, *parole entièrement divine à la source, à l'amont; et entièrement humaine, 'en une langue arabe claire' (Coran, 26:195), à l'arrivée, à l'aval. A la troisième rencontre de la Faculté de théologie itinérante des religions du Livre (Troyes, 17–20 mai 2000), il a consacré sa communication à la 'déconstruction du* Mushaf*', c'est-à-dire de la vulgate coranique. Je ne rentre pas dans l'intimité des cœurs et je ne fais de procès d'intention à personne, Mais Mohamed Arkoun ne peut quand même pas s'exclamer: 'Attention! Je dis toujours texte* dit révélé*; je ne dis jamais texte révélé;' ajouter: 'Ceci, je le dis ici, peut-être en Tunisie, mais pas ailleurs;' s'indigner: 'Et voilà que maintenant on fait remonter la mise par écrit du texte au Prophète lui-même!' et ne pas nous faire douter de son appartenance à l'Islam, appartenance dont il se laisse créditer sans protester, cultivant ainsi sciemment l'ambiguïté. Je lui demandai, pour la clarté du débat, de se situer clairement. Il préféra garder le silence. Manque de courage? Double langage? Ou plutôt ambiguité entretenue à dessein?* ['L'intelligent', in *Jeune Afrique*, no. 2122, 17 September 2001]

the Qur'ān, ed. G. R. Hawting and Abdul-Kader A. Shareef, and *The Qur'ān as Text*, already cited above, the title of which does not fulfill its promises, as its editor, S. Wild, has admitted. Each contribution seems to be limited to verifying the continuity of historicist issues, philological analyses and peripheral curiosities. This syndrome, clarified by J. van Ess, is apparent in the work of each of the researchers contributing to these collections, although they consider themselves to be experts in a well-defined domain. Yet the researchers never reflect upon the subject of this knowledge that requires specific intervention on all levels and in all possible ways of the production and propagation and assumptions of meaning. All of this includes those involved in the collections in question as well as those produced by the writing of the researcher and those which circulate among the community interpreting its heritage (*la communauté interprétante*). The problem must be reiterated: we are dealing with a corpus of which the primary constitutive function of its linguistic articulation is to express the true meaning of human existence – the objective, ideal, intangible, insurmountable norms that must be strictly observed in order to keep this existence in line with its true meaning. We are also dealing with secondary corpuses derived from the first, of which the linguistic articulation has functioned similarly throughout its long history (the *yaqūlu-llāhu* of the exegetes and of current discourse or *jā'a fī-l-ḥadīth* perpetuate, throughout the long course of history, the illusion of a continuity experienced between revealed norms and meanings and the accumulated interpretations and plans used by the living tradition of the community of believers. We are thus dealing with an existential structure translated into multiple, developing existential realities. Is the researcher permitted to systematically sever knowledge of marginal facts from the critique of **prophetic discourse** as a discourse of existentiation (the Arabic term, *ījād* renders the causative function more explicit) which gives shape, content and orientation to the actual existence of the believers? This is the problem toward which the **scholar-thinker** directs his or her sights, as a reaction against the dominance of academic reasoning which imposes its manner of cutting and pasting the heritage, not on the basis of an intellectual authority which might create a *debt of meaning*, but by the mechanisms of academic power that are intertwined with and dependent upon the political philosophy of modern states, just as the clerics[1] who create and guard religious orthodoxies were intertwined with these state powers before the advent of the secular revolution.

The concepts introduced here, as well as those used previously, are likely to put off quite a number of readers or even researchers who are unfamiliar with the discourse used in the social sciences and in a Christian theology that is aware of the challenges of the modern criticism of religious thought. Doubtless in deference to the pioneering theologians, J. van Ess leaves to Muslims the responsibility of accomplishing the same theological tasks. There remains, however, an objection on the epistemological and gnoseological level. The advances of critical approaches, as brought to light by the example of the Qur'ān, would certainly benefit from the recent attempts to diversify the methodologies and enlarge the scope of a compared history of religions, coupled with the elaboration of an anthropological frame of understanding.

It is now appropriate to say something about J. Chabbi's contribution before analysing it in greater depth later on. In brief, it is a welcome example of historical analysis of the Qur'ān which illustrates the possibility of crossing an epistemic and epistemological threshold in the progress towards the desired disposition of scholarship. The author traces the insurmountable boundary between the normative code of the profession of historian and the domain of thought and knowledge of the believer, while still incorporating this methodologically separate domain into the field of historical inquiry. The result is genuine progress, not only in historical writing as such, but first and foremost in the elucidation of the linguistic and historical processes which generated this belief, nourished it until it has become the inexhaustible source and ever powerful force of all the combined efforts and mental projection for

1. As we have seen with the eloquent example of Muḥammad Talbi quoted above, the clerics are not exclusively the '*ulamā*' specifically devoted to the maintenance of orthodox belief in every society.

understanding the inaugurating moment (*moment inaugurateur*) and its mythological, ideological, semantic and semiotic ramifications and expansion, as well as the intellectual, institutional and artistic creations which are still developing into something increasingly complex. By using anthropological categories such as myth and social imaginary, the historian can assemble under the same critical approach transformative dialectics reflected in Meccan enunciation, carefully restored to their context and hence liberated from the overly specific meaning which subsequent religious readings have expanded. As such, one can retrace the inchoative manifestations of a supra-tribal rationality and the formation of a nascent conceptual framework in linguistic usage, the beliefs and the narratives of the limited social group (*nās, 'ashīra, qawm*) that was meant to be the *addressee* and gradually became the dialectical protagonist and the involuntary agent of an historical transformation which had been fought, refused and denied in Mecca before imposing itself in Medina, through a doubly armed Prophet who added the weapon of revelatory speech to military might. The religious interpretation of these events, which historians and anthropologists reconstruct through archaeological investigation, was later transformed into a succession of idealized figures in a vast and long-lasting foundation story of opponents in Mecca and helpers in Medina (the *kāfirūn, munāfiqūn* versus the *mū'minūn, muhājirūn, anṣār* in orthodox terminology). This also requires the same kind of archaeological investigation to distinguish between historical and sociological reality and the subsequent mythical expansion of the religious imaginary.

It now becomes possible to see how one might step out of the scientific rigidity of the historist critical method which, since the nineteenth century, has imposed its judgments, chronologicalist order and thematic categories, divisions of reality and objects of study, etymologism and quest for origins and the filiation of ideas and narratives to link it with biblical, Hebraic or Christian sources, to the detriment of its literary and spiritual creativity which transforms language and thought dynamically from the dual standpoint of fundamentally utopian thoughts and concrete action with the intention of actualizing them in history. J. Chabbi is not entirely successful in escaping all those shortcomings which she criticizes sharply; she has not succeeded either in clarifying the anthropological problems, such as the tribal and political organization often used as key references for her impressionistic interpretations, but not analysed on the level required by her ambitious theorising. The philological concern is still unavoidable, but can now be enriched by the contribution of linguistics, so as to give place to the distinctive characteristics of the oral enunciation (*l'énonciation orale*) in relation to written accounts (*ènoncés écrits*) and to replace etymologism by the reconstruction of semantic fields and networks of language connotations, through patient micro-analysis which combines archaeological excavation with vocabulary, ethno-linguistic inquiry and ecological, sociological, cultural and political re-contextualization. All this is attained by using sources known for their precariousness and insufficiency as well as a number of literary procedures, such as disguise, selection, transfiguration, sublimation, transcendantalization, essentialization, sanctification, mythologization and, currently, gross ideologization. This is not the place to specify the significance for the historical method of this set of concepts, which I have intentionally grouped together and often used to indicate the substitution of a principle of reading texts respectful to social dialectics and their effects on the relationship between language and thought, a principle that is at one and the same time rigid and ignorant of these dialectics, with a tendency to turn developing ideas, contingent representations, the assumptions of truth, precarious power relations and functional or arbitrary categories into eternal essences, intangible substances, ontological and transcendental truths, and ethical and legalistic norms, immune to every form of human intervention.

The principle of reading for the Qur'ānic text should be applied equally to all sources with the same set of requirements: the *ḥadīth* collections, the works of exegesis, the biographical literature, the expanding biblical-Qur'ānic imaginary in mystical experience, the *Isrā'iliyyāt*, the lives of the prophets, the integration myths of the symbolic founding figures, such as Abraham in the pantheon and

Arab rituals associated with the *Ka'ba*. These rich sources can be reviewed and reinvested in an archaeological excavation, now writ large, where the question does not arise of quarrelling over the sources, the authenticity and the truth of positive facts, liberated from the superstitions of the straightjacket of legends, popular stories and the ramblings of a pious imagination. This is what historicism has long done, reinforced by dialectic materialism, at a time when Marxist rhetoric made its prejudice of rationality prevail in all fields of knowledge. The great classical commentators are no longer consulted – as many orientalists have done and still continue to do – as reliable authorities in clearing up the semantic contents of Qur'ānic vocabulary. All commentaries are treated as corpuses which must be read within the changing contexts of their production, acceptance and reproduction.

It is useful, in this context, to elaborate on Chabbi's monograph since it furnishes a relatively convincing illustration of the methodological priority and limits of the historical-anthropological approach, as applied to a corpus which lays the foundation of a religion. The limits are those which the historian imposes upon himself when judging himself to have completed the work of scrutinizing and using the documents. One can see clearly that, regarding the question of contemporary critical practices and the Qur'ān, the historian ends up with an extreme tension between two different attitudes of the human mind, that of limiting knowledge to theoretical and practical pieces of information artificially constructed by scholarly disciplines or that of recognizing the reliable and potentially universal teaching of these disciplines, while also creating space for a policy of hope (a concept which enables the integration of theological developments on the history of salvation, the quest for salvation and eschatological hope into historical psychology and religious sociology).

To clarify: if the present resources of historical inquiry allow it to be established, in accordance with a scientifically acceptable manner, that the Qur'ān, when viewed in the ecological, ethno-linguistic, sociological and political theatre of 'tribal' life in Mecca and Medina at the beginning of the seventh century C. E., cannot but change its cognitive status, a whole new field of work will be possible. This raises the question of whether an historian can do justice to two clearly differentiated statuses of cognition, that of a Meccan Qur'ān restored to its 'concrete' historical and linguistic reality as distinct from the Medinan corpus as well as from the universal corpus later imposed under the name of *Muṣḥaf*, and that of this *Muṣḥaf* which would be more aptly named the **Official Closed Corpus** which the interpreting community has accepted and will continue to accept for the foreseeable future as a *tanzīl*, a revealed given (*donné révélé*) that abolishes through interpretation and in experience, i.e., in the course of history, the status of the corpus as analysed by historians.

One cannot beg the question by saying that this is the concern of believers because it is the historian who uncovers the new status of belief, to the extent that his or her achievements as an historian are recognized as being intellectually compelling. A first answer would consist in expanding the same inquiry, by applying the same deconstructive procedure to the entire history of societies into which this *revealed given* has been received, interpreted and translated into ethical, legalistic, political, semantic, aesthetic and spiritual codes. I have proposed the concept of **societies of the Book-book** (*sociétés du Livre-livre*), including the Jewish and Christian examples, in order to integrate the *revealed given* into the productive forces of the history of these societies before it was disqualified, marginalized and even eliminated by scientific and political revolutions. It is possible that the historian's refusal – by leaving to the theologian and the philosopher a task that lies within the sphere of responsibility of the historian – of enlarging the working domain, reflecting a philosophical commitment to the *fait accompli* of the eighteenth century political revolutions in Europe and America. This would explain the difficulties of dialogue between historians, anthropologists, theologians and philosophers on these delicate subjects.

One should not forget that these battles and debates take place within the historical trajectory of European thought as it has developed since the sixteenth century, i.e., with the first challenges to the mediaeval heritage by the Reformation and the Renaissance. Within the Islamic context, these questions are still suppressed and considered unimaginable. One can see the disarray in the human mind wherever there is a failure in the indispensable work assigned to philosophy and anthropology, of taking charge of the domains of thought left in ruins by the social sciences which limit themselves to working on divided fragments of an undivided reality.

2.2. Linguistic, Semiotic and Literary Interpretation

These disciplines have produced far less seminal or innovative work than the historical approaches. Semiotics and 'new literary criticism' became fashionable in France between 1960 and 1980 with the support of A. J. Greimas, R. Barthès, G. Genette and a number of their disciples. A relatively small number of doctoral theses on the Qur'ān have seen the light in France, although it has not been possible to publish any of them, whereas studies on the Bible and the Gospels abound and were quickly published. Linguistic approaches, especially in the domain of discourse criticism, are not well represented either. Nevertheless, studies of Arabic linguistic history have flourished in the last twenty years of the twentieth century. One can see this as clear proof of an intellectual timidity, itself nourished by the researcher's prudence in refraining from the study of the Muslim sacred text. At the Sorbonne, many have preferred to renounce subjects which had aroused their intellectual curiosity, but also their fears of rejection in their countries of origin. C. Gilliot has been willing to work on the 'common Islamic imaginary as displayed in al-Ṭabarī's (d. 310/923) commentary', although limiting himself to the classical scholarly track to which he continues to make substantial contributions.

As for the literary approach, there is nothing equivalent to N. Frye (*The great code*), without even mentioning the abundant research which has enriched and renewed biblical studies. I personally planned to discuss the use of the metaphor in the Qur'ān in order to correct an intolerable shortcoming which has lasted since the mediaeval battles over accepting or totally rejecting the metaphorical dimension in the interpretation of God's word. A book by Ibn Qayyim al-Jawziyya (d. 751/1350), bearing the eloquent title of *al-Ṣawā'iq al-mursala fī-l-radd 'al-jahmiyya wa-l-mu'aṭṭila*, clearly sets out the stakes in the debate over the theology of revelation. I did not abandon such a rich project; but the terrain left to be cleared is immense and the few works available on the subject did not incorporate the most significant debates among linguists, rhetoricians, psychoanalysts and philosophers of language. Muslims are themselves scandalized at hearing of this shortcoming and refer with pride to Abū 'Ubayda (d. 203?), Al-Sharīf al-Rāḍī (d. 406/1016), al-Jurjānī (d. 403/1013), al-Bāqillānī (d. 471/1078), Fakhr al-dīn al-Rāzī (d. 606/1210), al-Ṣakkākī (d. 629/1231) and to the immense *i'jāz* literature of which the apologetic dimension still weighs heavily on contemporary works (e.g., Mustafa Ṣādiq al-Rāfi'ī, Sayyid Quṭb, Muḥammad Shaḥrūr, et al). They fail, however, to mention the current hostility to metaphor and the fact that the doctrine of the uncreated Qur'ān (see *createdness* in the *Encyclopaedia of the Qur'ān*) has prevailed since the Caliph al-Qādir's decree (fifth/eleventh century). Literary approaches are accepted along the lines illustrated by the works of M. S. al-Rāfi'ī and more durably and significantly Sayyid Quṭb's *tafsīr*. Studies of Arabic rhetoric and literary criticism are quick to scrutinize the positive and negative consequences of where the rich intuitions expressed in *al-Taṣwīr al-fannī fīl-Qur'ān* (1945) and *Mashāhid al-qiyāma fīl-Qur'ān* (1947) are fully developed and systematized.

The intervention of Sayyid Quṭb in this field raises an important theoretical debate. Faith based on oral, liturgical, ritual reception of **prophetic discourse** as is the case of Quṭb and the majority of Muslims, leads to subtle intuition, enlightening interpretation and lyric emotive writing which are missed by scholars who use intellectual training and discursive devices in order to decipher the same discourse. At the same time, faith works with postulates, assumptions accepted as iron-clad certainties; not only does it evolve within the confines of dogma, as shown through the engaged and engaging *Tafsīr* of Quṭb, but the literary talent added to the powerfully inspiring acceptance of God's Truth strengthens and perpetuates the dogmatic cognitive framework as much and as surely as **prophetic discourse** did and continues to do within its own mythical, symbolic, metaphorical, aesthetic devices internalized and adequately reactivated, using a way of thinking and a style untouched by the philosophy of suspicion. I am not opposing an intellectual objection, or a 'scientific' methodological critique to Sayyid Quṭb and all those who display such an undeniable talent in his literary analysis; I am merely raising a serious psychological issue in the hope that scholars will consider it as subject worthy of more inquiry. The success of Sayyid Quṭb in the literary field, like the intellectual impact of Ibn Taymiyya on contemporary Muslim thought, enhance the purport of the issue. Does this success mean that the social, cultural, imaginative and linguistic framework in which **prophetic discourse** is received is still alive and supportive to the cognitive, literary, semiotic articulation (what is called *naẓm al-Qur'ān* by ancient and contemporary readers/receivers) used in the first enunciation of the prophetic discourse? Or should we suspect both the interpretations of the commentators – believers and non believers alike – and the intrinsic organization *(naẓm)* of the prophetic discourse in its first enunciation? This question affects the current scientific attitude expressed by the word '*approaches*' used in several recently published titles. The key postulate commanding the whole reading of Quṭb is that the Qur'ān has a coherent unity, a unitary message, as has each *sūra*. This coherence is served with the same strong unifying *naẓm*, diversified in its literary, stylistic, rhetorical devices, but pursuing the same goal (*hadaf*) which is the imaginative representation and simultaneous conceptualization of human existence (*al-taṣawwur al-islāmiy*, to use the Quṭb expression). Although this postulate is defended by the attitude of the faithful, it can be agreed as a fruitful heuristic hypothesis not only for the readings of the Official Closed Corpus, but also for the acceptance of the oral discourse in the context of oral cultures. The 'approaches' commanded by each discipline are methodologically acceptable and even necessary; but no one 'specialist' should ignore the complex problems raised by the cognitive status of what I call **prophetic discourse** in order to stress the need for complexification as the only way to avoid simplifications and reductive interpretations.

Among the positive results of this complexified issue, is the possibility of enjoying, at one and the same time and with the profound attention of an undivided conscience, the spiritual emotion, ethical beauty and aesthetic pleasure of the oral or written discourse. It is one of the distinctive characteristics of **prophetic discourse** to bring together these three values acting as psychic forces – the true, the good and the **beautiful** – in order to draw the human subject more surely to the salvational utopia. That is precisely what Greek literature did before the intervention and victory of Aristotelian logocentrism. Additionally, there remains the simple fact that the foundational texts of religions never lose their initial status as oral/aural enunciation. Thus do the faithful identify with them through liturgical recitation, ritual conduct and quotations in current conversation (Graham, *Beyond*; see '*Recitation of the Qur'ān*'; '*Ritual and the Qur'ān*'; Everyday life and the Qur'ānic quotations in the current conversations).

It is therefore important to consider the possibilities offered by new literary criticism to adequately decipher all of the components of religious discourse in general. Beyond **prophetic discourse**, what status should be assigned to the immense corpus left by Ibn 'Arabī and other mystics who have reached the same stature? These spiritual, poetical amplifications of the prophetic discourse can help to perceive the as yet unknown creative power of prophetic discourse. Religious and literary qualifications do not allow for an account of the exceptional richness and dimensions of all written texts of which the exact status has yet to be defined.

How to take up these 'scientific' challenges without neglecting any of their cognitive assets? It is not enough to denounce the shortcomings of apologetics and the repression of innovation by the guardians of orthodoxy. To take one case, Naṣr Abū Zayd, the first Muslim scholar to face the Arabic world directly by writing in Arabic while teaching at Cairo University, tried to break the many taboos which prohibit the application of the most relevant achievements of contemporary linguistics to the Qur'ān. Before him, Muḥammad Khalafallāh tried to apply literary criticism to the narratives in the Qur'ān; and in spite of its modest scientific scope, his essay caused a major upheaval. The works of Naṣr Abū Zayd contain nothing revolutionary if one places them within the context of scholarly output of the last twenty years, since they explain quite straightforwardly the conditions necessary for applying the rules of defining and analysing a text to the Qurān, whatever text it may be (*mafhūm al-naṣṣ, falsafat al-ta'wīl, al-ittijāh al-'aqlī fī-l-tafsīr)*. Once more, the violent reaction to attempts whose purpose is merely to popularize knowledge long since widely accepted, underlines the area in contemporary Islamic thought of what cannot be and has not been thought.

2.3. The Religious Interpretation

The concept of an **interpreting community** leads to a wide range of possibilities for the use of speech that has become text and of a text that was laid down in the **Official Closed Corpus**, but which is still invoked and experienced as speech. These range from the most learned exegesis to daily liturgical recitation and the spontaneous quoting of verses or *ḥadīths* in current conversation, in controversy or at joyful or sombre events. Qur'ānic studies were mostly interested in scholarly exegetic readings offering historical information, cultural insights or grammatical and lexical explanations which could enrich the understanding of the text as given in the **Official Closed Corpus**. Insufficient account has been taken of the cognitive status of every religious approach as interpreted by and for the interests and expectations of the community. There are two major reasons for this. *Firstly*, all approaches and all appropriations are confined within a **dogmatic enclosure**; and *secondly*, the great commentaries which made themselves authoritative over the historical development of the living tradition are used as orthodox instances of authority in order to reproduce the fixed inherited interpretations. Not only are believing Muslims imprisoned within this dogmatic enclosure, Orientalist scholarship has also long contented itself with transferring to European languages the ideas of the dominant Sunnī Islam before doing the same with Shīʿī Islam. This practice gained more credibility and official approval in the colonial contexts, and when recent political threats of fundamentalist Islam enabled political scientists to dispute the supremacy of expertise needed by official administrations. Those, for example, who attempted to tackle the question of the authenticity of the prophetic tradition used this material to prop up artificially constructed historical 'explanations' of Muslim attitudes, claims and behaviour. In so doing, they are careful to protect their scholarly status with certain rhetorical techniques: 'according to Muslim tradition,' 'according to Muslim faith,' etc; and thus does the dogmatic enclosure remain untouched and free to operate without restraint.

The concept of **dogmatic enclosure** applies to the totality of the articles of faith, representations, tenets and themes which allow a system of beliefs and unbeliefs to operate freely without any competing action from inside or out. A strategy of refusal, consisting of an arsenal of discursive constraints and procedures, permits the protection and, if necessary, the mobilization of what is uncritically called 'faith'. It is well known how scrupulously the profession of faith (*ʿaqīda*, see creeds) is translated and described, but no green light has ever been given to a deconstruction of the axioms, tenets and themes that hold together and establish the '*adventurous cohesion*' of every faith. The point is not to demonstrate the scientific validity or the irrationality of the articles of faith, but to trace their genealogy from Nietzsche's perspective of the criticism of values, as well as their psychological functions and decisive role in the formation and upbringing of every human being. All this is a matter for historical psychology with its curiosity and inquiry which has, as previously mentioned, not yet been integrated into historical-anthropological methodology and the research agenda. An example of this direction of research is greatly desired and could proceed by exploring the shared Islamic imagination as represented in the great interpretative corpuses such as those of al-Ṭabarī, Fakhr al-Dīn al-Rāzī, Muḥammad Ḥusayn al-Ṭabaṭabā'ī and M.T. Ben Achour, amongst so many others. As long as faith and spirituality are the object of simple narrative and descriptive accounts – be it with the remote detachment of the gnostic (in the style of H. Laoust) or with the warm and exhorting empathy of the believer (in the style of J. Jomier or Kenneth Cragg) – Qur'ānic studies and, more generally, the comparative history of religions, will be unable to accomplish the exhaustiveness and relevance expected from them.

The religious interpretation, as applied to foundational texts, is also the place in which creativity of meaning, assumptions of meaning, representations and mythological or ideological constructs emerge and erupt in accordance with the cultural context of different social groups. This is equally true for mediaeval approaches now considered sacred and obligatory classical reference works as well as for contemporary approaches. The functional relation between the **Official Closed Corpus** (including the *ḥadīth* corpuses) promoted to the rank of primordial foundational, normative Text and the interpretative corpuses to which the **Official Closed Corpus** gives rise, does not differ as far as religious corpuses are concerned, as in the societies of the Book-book, or secular corpuses, from those of modern political revolutions. The latter, however, benefit from historical clarity and tools of analysis which exclude any possibility of resorting explicitly, as do the first, to the enchanted world of mystery, the supernatural, transcendence and the miraculous, where the operation of sanctification, mythification, sublimation, transfiguration, ontologisation and even mystification rests. Still, the historian has to determine the various forms of reasoning used (grammatical, theological, legalistic, historiographical or philosophical) as well as the kind of rationality, imagination and modes of intervention and creative imagination employed, as in the case of al-Hallāj, al-Tawḥīdī, Ibn 'Arabī, Molla Ṣadra Shīrāzī, Sayyid Quṭb, et al.

On the basis of these propositions, it can now be seen how the integration of religious interpretation into the expanded domain of the historian might enrich historical knowledge while introducing less speculative criticism focused on religious reasoning that, as demonstrated here, is only a modality of the reasoning used in all plausible discursive constructions. At the same time, it has been shown that the various kinds of interpretation discussed here lead to the same acknowledgment, namely that the progress of Qur'ānic studies has depended on Orientalist scholarship of the nineteenth century (the term 'scholarship' is used to underscore the Orientalists' refusal to epistemologically commit their accumulated knowledge to a criticism of religious reasoning that would include all known examples in the societies of the Book-book). The refusal of the historian, anthropologist, sociologist, psychologist, literary critic and semiotician to identify and answer the challenges of prophetic discourse and the logic of existential feelings and emotions (*al-manṭiq al wijdānī* , to use Quṭb's expression) it generates, will maintain the gap between the 'reductive, positivist' scientific posture of mind and the 'dogmatic', 'subjective', 'emotional' attitude of religious mind. As for Muslim scholarship, it continues to inflict upon itself limitations, mutilations and prohibitions that only accentuate the dependency and backwardness of Qur'ānic studies compared to the recent innovative works mentioned in the bibliography. What it has produced since the nineteenth century has more of a documentary interest for a history of religious psychology and the expansion of the imagination of religious discourse, especially in the domain of politics, than any intellectual and scientific merit that could enrich our knowledge of what I called the **Qur'ānic fact** or **phenomenon** and of the **Islamic fact**, these being used as eloquent examples to reach a more relevant, encompassing, explicative theory of the religious phenomenon in general. The recently published essay by Muḥammad Shaḥrūr, *al-kitāb wa-l-Qur'ān*, has had a success that bears witness to both the intolerable pressure of dogmatic control over Qur'ānic studies and the limitations within which every discourse with hopes of innovation must be pursued.

2.4. Final Proposals

A project has been initiated by the publishers, Brill, under the academic supervision of Professor Jane McAuliffe to publish an *Encyclopaedia of the Qur'ān* conceived and produced with respect for the critical order of rational processes. This project is long overdue. It confirms this chapter's position on the historical and epistemological discrepancy between philosophical and scientific reasoning as practised today in the West and elsewhere, and Islamic reasoning as it asserts itself in its positions on Islam as well as in political action, codexes of law, educational systems and individual and collective behaviour under the leadership of political 'élites' who are clearly not prepared to initiate and guide a policy of intellectual and cultural shifts. As long as the Islamic logic of existential feelings and emotions prevail over the intellectual responsibility of human mind, there will be a place for an 'Islamic' *Encyclopaedia of Islam* and, even more so, an 'Islamic' *Encylopaedia of the Qur'ān*. 'Islamic', in this context, means the legitimate features of a long, rich, specific historical experience, more or less mixed, conditioned by the subjective, mythical, ideological driving forces inherent in each collective memory. The task remains to produce an Encyclopaedia which would help to reconcile the requirements of critical knowledge and the legitimate irreducible ethos of a culture, postures of mind and existential styles of human expression. The *Encyclopaedia of the Qurān* project is a scholarly, intellectual, scientific and hopefully spiritual answer to the ideological theory of the 'clash of civilizations'. It should offer a reliable databank that will undoubtedly, like every work of emancipating scholarship, be subject to discussions, additions and revisions. It will, however, be impossible to ignore, in particular by people who pursue the cognitive project of understanding the religious phenomenon in a comparative, universal perspective.

To sustain the project within that perspective, it would be helpful to conclude with the following proposals. It is necessary to open up the Qur'ānic fact by situating it in a comparative approach, not only within the three monotheistic religions, but also within a historical anthropology of the religious phenomenon in its geo-historical and geo-cultural ambiance that, for the time being, could be qualified as Mediterranean. The historical phase of what historians explore under the name of the Near East should always be kept in sight, although not in order to rediscover the so-called origins or to reconstruct linear filiations of ideas, representations, linguistic forms and rituals of expression. The aim should be to deepen our knowledge of constituent elements common to the monotheistic religious conscience in its global historical genesis and strategies of differentiation in order to preserve its exclusive vocation to receive, interpret and transmit the revealed Truth. This requires more than an accumulation of names, facts, dates and titles of major works; it needs a deconstructive analysis of the organizational themes common to the monotheistic consciousness, the inaugural moments of spiritual history, the new departures from cultural codes that engender logical existential systems, dogmatic enclosures, societies of the Book-book, elected communities committed to salvation, in contrast to anonymous groups destined to stray and be damned; in brief, it is a matter of deepening our knowledge of all these historical formations that the ethnographic view imprisons in so-called identities and encloses in equally unconfirmed regions, traditions and cultures.

The concept of the Official Closed Corpus provides a good example of the comparative approach that will enable Muslim readers of the *Encyclopaedia* to better assess the stakes in a scientific problematization of orthodox vocabulary inherited from a theological theory of values resistant to every critical examination. The Jewish and Christian traditions have similarly experienced a before-and-after in what has been called the *fait accompli* of the Official Closed Corpus. Christians today are willing to read the apocryphal writings that the church omitted between the fourth and the sixteenth century (cf. their publication in the *Pléiade* series by F. Bovon and P. Geoltrain). The fundamental texts do not function in the same way in each tradition, before and after the triumph of an Official Closed Corpus. Scholarly research without the burden of dogma creates more favourable conditions for historical re-readings of the texts selected as sacred and thus untouchable. One can thus understand why the concept of an Official Closed Corpus is more effective for a comparative history of the religious phenomenon in its prophetic trajectory.

Two more gaps that must be mentioned. The theological and philosophical attitudes of reasoning in the societies of the Book-book, should be the subject of the same comparative historical approach within the perspective of a critical historical epistemology. Tackling such a task requires constant vigilance, not only in checking the use of all conceptual frameworks that have been protected from the critique of deconstructionism but also in introducing and refining more inclusive concepts which are more productive from the perspective of a critique of religious reasoning, beginning with its formulation by Jews, Christians and Muslims.

As regards the Qur'ān more directly, it is clear that what is called for here is a protocol of interpretation that is free from both the dogmatic orthodox framework and the procedural disciplines of modern scholarship which is, it must be admitted, no less constraining. It is an interpretation which wanders, in which every human, Muslim or non-Muslim, gives free rein to his or her own dynamic of associating ideas and representations, starting out from the freely chosen interpretation of a corpus whose alleged disorder, so often denounced, favours peripatetic freedom and unbridled creativity. This approach is able to extricate itself definitively from every kind of arbitrary rhetorical, artificial and allegedly logical reconstruction, and deluded 'coherence' later imposed by legal, theological, apologetic, ideological and fantastic interpretations. One potential model here is, of course, the creative freedom of the likes of Ibn 'Arabī; but in this case the desired freedom is more subversive, since it would include all forms and experiences of subversion ever attempted by mystics, poets, thinkers and artists.

TWO

Belief and the Construction of the Subject in Islamic Contexts

The wandering Arabs say: We believe. Say (unto them, O Muḥammad): Ye believe not, but rather say 'We submit,' for the faith hath not yet entered into your hearts. Yet, if ye obey Allah and His messenger, He will not withhold from you ought of (the reward of) your deeds. Lo! Allah is Forgiving, Merciful.

Qur'ān 49, 14.

Thus, it is the 'for me' and the 'for us', if it is believed, that constitutes the true faith and distinguishes it from every other faith which is content with hearing about the deeds. It is this faith alone which justifies us, without the law and good works, for the mercy of God manifested in Christ.

Martin Luther

C'est donc de la doxa des Grecs qu'il faut partir.

Paul Ricœur

... le sujet n'est pas un être, mais un travail, un mouvement de l'acteur sur lui-même par lequel il s'efforce de construire son expérience et de lui donner sens. 'Empiriquement', le sujet ne peut être perçu que par ses effets sur le travail de l'acteur, car moins il est transcendant, plus il ne s'incarne que dans cette activité même.

Ainsi, la notion d'expérience peut-elle remplacer celle d'action, de la même façon que les mouvements sociaux ne se donnent à voir que dans leur éclatement, dans une tension interne qui est la marque même du sujet.

F. Dubet, in *Penser le sujet autour d'A. Touraine*, p. 120.

1. Problematizing Belief

As soon as we decide to put in historical and philosophical perspective any key problems of Islamic thought, we are confronted with all the difficulties inherent in the historical gap that separates the Islamic from the European frames of thought. These two adjectives, 'Islamic' and 'European' already contain a gap that is not only temporal but, more substantially, notional and cognitive. On the one hand, any cognitive statement must create for itself a place in a connotative and conceptual network strongly marked by the categorizations and the semantic structure of the religious discourse. On the other hand, we are sent back to a trajectory and procedures of thought enriched uninterruptedly from classical Greece and Rome legacy down to the present day by an intense educative dialectic between what I would call the rights of critical, independent reasoning which claims intellectual responsibility and those of religious reasoning, commanded by dogmatic postulates, principles and foundations. Thus, P. Ricœur, like several other thinkers, forces himself to start from the Greeks and retrace the successive and philosophically differentiated fields for a present-day critical re-examination, of the crucial question of belief (cf. *Encyclopaedia Universalis*, article *croyance*).

Usual practice requires that in order to examine the same question in an Islamic context, we must necessarily start from the Qur'ānic data complemented by that of the prophetic Tradition, the teachings of the *salaf al-ṣāliḥ* (Pious Ancestors) and the reforming doctors included in the profession of orthodox faith (*'aqada*) peculiar to every community (*ahl al-sunna wa al-jamā'a, ahl al-'iṣma wa-l-'adāla*, etc). Thus, the articles of faith adopted by orthodoxy are excluded from any critical work, in the sense in which the philosophical, then historicist, sociological and anthropological thought in Europe has continued, since the thirteenth century, to submit the contents of the Christian faith to increasingly radical interrogation and revisions. This is the meaning of the famous scholastic formula *fides quarens intellectum*. One can even go back to the Evangelists and the earliest apostles such as Paul, to retrace the long, uninterrupted history down to the present day, of an educational tension between the postures and categorizations of Greek thought on the one hand, and religious semantics and the symbolic capital of the Semitic tradition on the other hand. Jesus of Nazareth in effect, expressed himself in Aramaic within the synagogue and the already long and strongly crystallized tradition in the Hebrew Bible, whereas the Evangelists, accepted as reliable transmitters of the Christian message, expressed themselves in Greek.

Islamic tradition is characterized, on the other hand, by a remarkable linguistic – hence cultural – continuity in the transmission and usage of the fundamental sacred texts (at least until the eleventh century, in the case of the doctrinal literature entirely written in Arabic after the Qur'ān) and an increasing discontinuity of the cultural, political and intellectual fields that contain all the problems that had been thought or suppressed, related to what I prefer to call '*believing*' in order to propound, in the very choice of the concept, the theme which theologians of the three monotheistic religions have long developed and defended under the name of '*faith*'. To explain this choice, it should be recalled rapidly here that the most harmful discontinuity, not only for religious thought, but for the general evolution of societies linked to the Islamic fact,[1] as essential referent of law, politics, ethics and social issues, is the rejection to the point of the lasting

1. The concept of *Islamic fact* which I have often used makes it possible to better develop the concept of *Qur'ānic fact* and to differentiate Islam as the instance of the religious *(instance du religieux)* and Islam as a set of determinant factors at work in the general historical evolution of societies that converted to this religion.

elimination of the philosophical attitude after the death of Ibn Rushd (1198). The disputatio (*munāẓara*) sustained by him with al-Ghazālī (d. 1111) at 80 years' distance remained, as we know, a dead letter on the Islamic side, whereas Christian Europe, from the thirteenth to the sixteenth century, enthusiastically welcomed what became Latin Averroism. The discontinuity gradually came to affect theological thought, exegetic practice, the elaboration (*istinbāṭ*) of legal qualifications (*aḥkām*), political thought and historiography. Efforts made by liberal researchers and intellectuals, particularly of Arabic expression, between 1830–1940, have been too ephemeral, fragmented, often polemical and apologetic, intellectually limited and scientifically inadequate to be capable of simultaneously tackling the internal weakness of Muslim scholarship, the weight of neglected oral cultures and the challenges of a modernity mediated by an arrogant colonial regime that rejected, dismissed and alienated a large part of Muslim scholarly productions. It is under these historical conditions that the post-colonial national states promoted a process of (re-)building 'national' identities. The intellectual, cultural and spiritual history of all societies freed from colonial domination in the years 1950–60 remains not only to be written in a critical and factual manner, as well as to be considered in a long-term perspective and with the most appropriate tools and methodologies of historical psychology and sociology.

It is to this complex task, that is so lengthy, hence necessarily collective, that I am trying to contribute since I have asked the question about humanism in the Arab-Islamic context (see my *Humanisme arabe au IVe/Xe siècle*) and that of a plural, open rereading of the Qur'ān (see *Comment lire le Coran?*, text published in 1970, reproduced in *Lectures du Coran*). In tackling today the question of believing, I would like to provide a new illustration of the programme of a critique of Islamic reason, including a central problem already discussed in the Qur'ān, with the illuminating distinction between *īmān* translated as 'faith' and *islām* denounced in *sūra* 49 as superficial submission, or even applied to norms and external conducts of adherence to a group of Muslims in formation (*sūra* 49). Since this problem has become a discriminating, theological point *(maṭlab, mas'ala)* from the first doctrinal confrontations, I will try to reactivate an old discussion in a framework of thought and with the theoretical objectives required by the current practices of critical knowledge. The possibility could be mooted of either of a re-foundation (*i'ādat al-ta'ṣīl*) of the classical discipline of the Sources-Fundamentals (*'ilm al-uṣūl*) in both their aspects, theological and legalistic), or of a re-working of what is obviously a contribution to the philosophy of the religion, using Islam as an example that has hardly been considered until now. At this stage, I would prefer to avoid speaking of an Islamic theology, for reasons which I shall specify later. I will certainly not go through the completion of such an enterprise in this essay. I will take the first indispensable steps along a path to which other researchers-thinkers will venture, I hope, to contribute supplements, additions, readjustments, confirmations and even invalidations. I have already explained in the introduction, the theoretical aims I had in mind when I confronted the three competing and conflicting postures of reason: the religious, the scientific and the philosophical. The confrontation is **historical**, and in no way normative. I avoid any value judgements, asserting the superiority of one posture over the other; which is why I suspend, rather than ignore or eliminate, as an historian, all of the theological, dogmatic assessments of orthodox or heretical belief. It is more enlightening to evaluate the cognitive consequences of the exclusive use made of one posture, while totally ignoring the necessity to consider the relevant teachings proposed by the others. I know how impatient believers as well as the defenders of the secularized culture of disbelief are to affirm their strong certitudes. When confronting each other, both sides are intellectually arrogant. That is why I am defending a pluralistic, open epistemology that goes beyond the contradictory debates on the one-sided truth, or the right of each individual to hold on to his 'difference', without caring about the ideological dimensions implicit in each 'difference', or 'identity' currently based on emotional ties. Pluralistic epistemology will lead to a new approach to what is called fundamentalism. The latter attitude of mind is not generated only by religious reason; it can also be found in classical metaphysics practised in the name of philosophy, or in modern ideologies defended by a so-called scientific reason. As I have said in several contexts, I wish to illustrate and employ an emerging reason that is capable of emancipation from all forms, levels, types of institutionalized ignorance.

2. Itineraries

In an original version of this essay written for the colloquium on *Le Musulman dans l'histoire* at the Abdul-Aziz Foundation in Casablanca (25–27/3/1998), I thought I could confine my inquiry to the problem of faith-belief within the framework of the Islamic tradition. But the reactions raised by my presentation at the colloquium led me to expand the scope of my reflection, especially after reading or rereading new books recently published on several themes (see the Bibliography).

At first sight, the literature that I consulted might be thought to be too external to the subject matter. What connection is there between believing in Islamic contexts and an anthropology of the political and the religious spheres in Islam (J. Dakhlia), the civil war in Algeria, the approaches of social history applied essentially to Western societies, or even a dictionary of theology explicitly reserved for the Christian model? In fact, strong links can be found between the books I have explored and the question of the subject and belief on which I am focusing in this chapter.

My first strategic option is to subvert, in the cognitive and intellectual sense, the religious field as it continues to be monopolized contentiously by fundamentalist theologians, political entrepreneurs who manipulate the religious-political beliefs and options to mobilize individual imaginary and collective national forces. Such a subverting task also concerns the social sciences as far as they continue to practice either an ethnographic description of religious rituals and beliefs, or reduce religious reasoning to its fundamentalist exercise. Examples of this subversion are provided in the works of P. Gisel and P. Evrard,

P. Ricœur and A. LaCoque, J. Y. Lacoste (to a lesser extent) and many others who should be mentioned, even in Islamic studies like Uri Rubin, J. van Ess, A. Neuwirth, M. Lecker and many others mentioned in the Bibliography. These works enrich the exploration of the religious field while confronting with rigour the most recent and fruitful contributions of different currents of thought which have continued since the nineteenth century, to discuss, criticise, correct and challenge the prevailing approaches. We know how all the works of P. Ricœur aim at putting together again, re-articulating, and re-appropriating domains of reflexive thought and knowledge accumulated by the social sciences such as history, sociology, linguistics and anthropology. P. Gisel forms part of the same critical dialectic of influence, which incorporates all the currents of thought likely to stimulate research and radicalize the theoretical advances on the subject of believing, finding its roots in the experiences of individuals and societies. However, P. Ricœur tries to appear as a philosopher, whereas P. Gisel, professor of theology at Lausanne University, adheres explicitly to this discipline. *Le dictionnaire de théologie* by J. Y. Lacoste is, in this respect, an eloquent sign of the progress made towards an interactive practice of theology and philosophy, which is very new and very promising, both recognizing humbly to be indebted to social sciences, whereas these latter less easily renounce a sovereignty which is still inadequately established, particularly in respect of anything relating to the interpretation of religious phenomenon.

It is true that the subversion of the religious field in order to restore it to its own determinants and irreducible functions, cannot be conducted properly without the intervention of the social sciences when they consent, in return, to integrate in the same interactive practice, the questioning and the resistance of theology and philosophy. We will convince ourselves of the relevance of this requirement by reading the work, which is both a manifesto and a programme, edited by the late B. Lepetit, one of the initiators and brilliant practitioners of an '*alternative social history*'. The normative, edifying speculations of the theology of belief would be ineffectual if they failed to integrate the methods of sourcing and the levels of manifestation of beliefs in the institution and society as expounded by the historian J. Revel in his contribution to the book in question.

Two objections of unequal importance ought to be considered here. The first, apologetic and ideological in nature, deserves to be raised because it comes from a sociologically important current of militant Muslim demands for an '*Islamisation of the sciences*', or, according to the title of a recent work by the Moroccan Abdessalam Yacine, an '*Islamisation of modernity*'. The founding idea is that Islam is not only a system of static beliefs and non-beliefs, dogmatically received and applied; it is also a thought provided with all the principles, methodologies, discursive procedures and conceptual tools of investigation and control for establishing and re-establishing, whenever necessary, the validity and legitimacies of all the orders of existence of man. This whole, recapitulated, duly transmitted and correctly instrumentalized in the great, living Islamic Tradition, is irreducible to any other and cannot be influenced, conditioned or deviated from by any other. Nevertheless, all the cognitive systems and models of historical action produced by modern Europe to promote and legitimize the hegemony of the West over the rest of the world have sought and continue to seek the destitution and eventually the elimination of the irreplaceable Islamic tradition of thought and action. There is no simple mimetic rivalry in these arguments for constructing a hegemonic model in opposition to that from which one seeks to free oneself, then protect oneself. There is the claim of an ontological privilege which establishes the intellectual, scientific, ethical, political and legal validity of all the products of history acknowledged by Islam.

The instigators of this militant attitude do not give themselves the means of perceiving and avoiding the obvious amalgamation which they make between a historically legitimate struggle against a real situation of subjugation and an operation of validation which rests entirely on a believing itself to be exempt from all scientific and philosophical examination. This is an excellent example of a subject of research that begins to take charge of the new social history in the Western sphere, but which is abandoned to the narrative and factual reporting of political scientists in the case of 'radical Islam' The concept of ontological privilege finds numerous applications in all religious communities and even, with the correctives imposed by the secularization of thought, among modern utopian movements such as scientific socialism and Communist salvation by the proletariat. The reference to God, guarantor of ontological privilege, is in fact taken from the traditional institutional, theological and spiritual contexts in order to be adjusted to fit the structures of a social imaginary constructed with constant amalgamation between a scientific rationality that has been cobbled together and a belief system rooted in the unplumbed depths of an eventful, polymorphic, savage religious belief.

This situation is caused by the lack of a guiding hand of authority. All this should be retained as a not yet duly explored historical, sociological, anthropological and psychological domain of realities, because social sciences as applied to Islamic studies, too often remain dependent on the categorizations, the periodizations and problematizations of classical Islamology.[1] The second objection is more difficult to deal with because it comes from recognized researchers who occupy positions of power in prestigious academic institutions. It is pointless today to go back over the reluctance, and even open resistance shown yesterday by classical Islamicists and political scientists. Better to devote one's attention to the efforts of the few researchers-thinkers who try to detect the methodological shortcomings and the implicit or explicit ideology involved in the erudite accumulation of knowledge. It is well known that a large part of the narrative and descriptive literature about classical and contemporary Islam, is too dependent upon the written documents used to present what is given the all-embracing name of ' Islam'. For this reason, this type of erudition contributes to the maintenance and spread of ideology implicit in the primary texts that are

1. As I have shown in 'Transgresser, déplacer, dépasser', in 'L'œuvre de Cl. Cahen', *Arabica*, 996/1, revised and expanded in my forthcoming book *Penser l'Islam aujourd'hui.*

used without being deconstructed with the tools and procedures of critical discourse analysis. This implicit ideological solidarity between a type of scholarship and current expressions of Muslims as protagonists in society, is particularly evident in the material recently produced on the subject of so-called fundamentalist Islam. I include in these remarks the writings of Muslim scholars who add their own political or religious gloss on the shortcomings of erudite Western descriptive scholarship.[1]

I will content myself with pointing here to the Maghreb as a relevant example to illustrate the previous observations. I have retained the works of F. Colonna and of J. Dakhlia (see the Bibliography) because they are recent and their authors are very much involved in the epistemological and methodological approaches, writing, problematiztions and cognitive options which have become emblematic of the masters of the EHESS. I

---

1. This observation can appear excessive, even polemical. If I am given the time, I will establish with all the necessary documentation, the epistemological and cognitive differences between works of Muslim scholars on the field I am exploring myself, namely history of Islamic thought. I have in mind the works of M. Talbi, H. Djaït, A. Laroui, H. Ḥanafi, R. al-Sayyid, A. al-Jābiri, N. Naṣṣar, A Bayḍoun, F. Zakariyā and many others. The generation of A. Charfi, Moncef Benabd al-Jalīl, 'Abdou Filali Anṣāri and their younger disciples are more clearly incorporating the perspectives I am defending under a general *Critique of Islamic Reason*. The contributions made by the *'ulamā'* to the same field should be classified as orthodox management of belief, using classical sources as intellectually and spiritually constraining for an immutable expression of the true faith, without caring about the deconstruction of this faith which I am proposing. I do not claim to have personally completed all the operations of deconstruction required by the founding texts called Holy Texts; I am merely opening up some perspectives and developing tools and issues, in order to initiate a complex work of research depending upon many teams of excellent scholars. I think, however, that I have taken the first steps, defined programmes and opened up perspectives which deserve to be discussed, extended and put to good use by young researchers. It remains for others to grapple with the massive corpus of Sunnī and Shi'ī *ḥadīth* and with the canonized corpuses of jurisprudence schools. See my 'Critique de la raison juridique en Islam', in *Penser l'Islam aujourd'hui*.

have myself been won over by this innovative school of *Annales*, because it has provided many decisive illustrations of a successful combination between erudite research, pluralist methodology, historical epistemology and constant critical reassessment. The history of thought in the Maghreb region of North Africa has not yet sufficiently benefitted from the type of scholarship represented by the school of Annales and the general history of this particular area also remains rather neglected so that it is difficult to explore what I have called since 1976 'the modes of presence of Arabic thought in the Muslim west' (in *Critique de la raison islamique*, Paris, 1984; see also 'Langues, société et religion dans le Maghreb indépendant', in *Les cultures du Maghreb*, L'Harmattan, Paris, 1995).

The questions of conjuncture, scale, modalities, processes of expansion, assimilation, oblivion and elimination, so essential in the works of social history are only partially and incidentally applied to the study of belief in connection with the learned frameworks of religious thought which are in constant interaction with the oral cultures in Berber, as well as in Arabic expression. Generally speaking, much that pertains to theology and religious law is not dealt with as object of social history and cultural anthropology. Where it is , it is for the purpose of repeating the orthodox categorizations and definitions, without prior deconstruction of the dominant Malekite orthodoxy in its learned formulations and diverse appropriations in the popular forms of lived 'religion' (which needs redefining each time in a microsocial history).[1] I will return elsewhere to dwell at greater length on the works of J. Dakhlia and F. Colonna which contribute useful elements to an investigation of the horizons and limits of thought in the Maghreb. I note in passing that there is not yet any comprehensive presentation of a critical history of thought in the Maghreb which takes into account the Latin, Arabic, Berber and French expressions of thought. The nationalist option only retains the line of development of Arabic expression, without resolving the problem of the Maghrebian appropriations of the themes, problems, fields of reality and disciplines dependent

1. See, for example, a personal episode that I have described in 'Avec Mouloud Mammeri à Taourirt-Mimoun', in *Awal*, 1991.

on this line. It is clear that any such investigation in a particular historical, linguistic and cultural area, could make an important contribution to the issues of belief in Islamic contexts.

3. Appropriations

It will have been noted that my title links two major themes that are usually treated separately – belief and the construction of the human subject. 'Believing' is the gerund of the verb 'to believe'; like any noun based on the infinitive, it refers impersonally to the action intended by the verb and the state resulting therefrom. It is important to retain the dynamic processes engaged in any act of believing. The subject solicited by a phenomenon, an event or a proposition accepts or rejects its assent and thereafter conditions the maintenance of this assent in relation to the effects of truth and falsehood, and the success or failure that produced the believing. This latter is rooted in the institutions, social relationships and everyday experiences of the subject. In this sense, it cannot be dissociated from the ecological environment, the memory of the group, cognitive frameworks and social structures in which the human subject emerges, is constructed and deployed.

Believing thus defined has the advantage of encompassing all the types and levels of belief and, in particular, this modality called 'faith' that is more narrowly linked to the assent required by the self-referring discourse which is transformed into fundamental texts and canons of the Scriptures (I prefer to use the term 'Official Closed Corpus') of the great religions. Since the concept of faith is already developed in founding texts such as the Bible, the Gospels and the Qur'ān, I think it necessary to place it at critical distance with the help of a more comprehensive concept which makes it possible to place faith among all the modalities and levels of believing. This is what also fashioned Islamic thought, as will be demonstrated, with the concepts of *i'tiqād* distinguished from *īmān*. In the Christian domain, there is the recent example given by P. Gisel who, in a very stimulating book, preferred to reflect on what he calls *L'excès du croire* (Paris, 1990) where the concept of faith intervenes incidentally, each time to be consolidated theologically. My objective is different, because I do not seek to use the expanding field of analysis of believing in order to reconstruct an Islamic theology by submitting it, as in the classical period, to interactivity with philosophical reflection and the repeated challenges of the social sciences. I have said that the existence of an Islamic theology remains problematic, not only because the very notion is disputed from outside, but because I have long been trying to open a debate in the framework of a comparative approach to the three so-called revealed religions.

Before beginning this discussion, it is necessary to examine the possibilities of appropriation of French terminology strongly marked by philosophical and historical criticism and Arabic terminology with its strong orthodox Islamic system of connotations. A philological investigation into the words themselves will not suffice. It is essential on the Islamic side, to specify the protocols of reading the founding texts on the one hand, and the orthodox doctrinal literature on the other hand. It is on this point that my views vary as much from the traditional protocols which continue to establish themselves in the believing community as from the historicist and philologist approaches of Islamicists who declare that they stand by the exercise of a cold erudition, indifferent to the social constructs of all belief. Clearly, it is not easy to name the second category with precision. The dividing line does not, in effect, separate Muslims from non-Muslims; Muslims who would, needless to say, be believers and Orientalists or Islamicists who would be non-believers, even hostile to Islam according to the heresiographical perception conveyed today by ideological classification. We know of the active role of Christian Islamicists and Jewish believers who, epistemologically, share with the Muslims the theological premises of defence of 'faith' in a same God, a revealed given, the same exigencies of obedience to the Law supported by the same hope of salvation. There is thus a third category which has not yet received any particular denomination, or a fully recognised place in the institutions of the administration of activities peculiar to the believing communities on the one hand, and the secularized, academic world on the other. I dare not speak of researchers-thinkers, because all researchers are supposed to accompany their activities with an accumulation of learning and of critical and interrogative thought. Nevertheless, I do not think it would be unfair to point out the multiple and very significant differences between the intellectual postures and the writings of researchers-thinkers such as Paul Ricœur, J. Le Goff, Cl. Geertz, P. Bourdieu, J. P. Vernant and others, and those of erudite historians such as J. Van Ess, B. Lewis and W. Madelung, to mention only a few well-known names.

3.1. The Protocols of Reading

Since religious belief finds its first articulation in the prophetic utterances transformed into Scriptures or the Holy Book, it is appropriate to redefine the cognitive status of this essential reference by integrating two given elements that must be addressed, namely, the rights of the 'believing' reading and those of the critical reading. There is open tension and conflict between the two readings which is why I speak of the rights of the one and the other. Getting these rights recognized is tantamount to overcoming the dividing lines of an ideological nature that have been obscured for centuries by considerations of imagined notions like divine Truth, eternal salvation, the sacred, transcendence, revealed law, intangible values, orthodoxy necessary for orthopraxy.

The 'believing' reading has given birth to numerous corpora of belief, diverse and rich in historical content. Its theological posture ought to be restored in its options, procedures, and historically determined horizons as well as in its works of culture and civilization. It is in this work of linguistic, historical, sociological and anthropological restitution that the rights and intellectual responsibilities of the critical reading intervene. It is necessary to accept as objects of history, psychological analysis and historical anthropology what the 'believing' reading calls God, prophetic function, the revealed and revealing Word, the sacred, retribution, prayer, trust in God, and so on. Historians have already used all this religious vocabulary; but they have presented it in a scientific culture based on a prejudice in favour of rationality which has long been that of Aristotelian categorization, continued and restored by the reason of the Enlightenment whose strategies, argumentation and themes aimed precisely at the substitution of its 'scientific' sovereignty to that of religious reason under the institutional figure of the theological *magisterium* of clerics (bishops, pastors, rabbis, imāms). We have to deal with a bone of contention in which not all the files are open; those which are open are awaiting a more equitable instruction. This is the initial stage of the work which falls to the researchers-thinkers. Defining the cognitive status of religious discourse and the type of human subject which it is constructing, firstly requires an unlearning of the biased teachings of the culture based on the prejudice of rationality. This will be done by restoring to the culture of the marvellous its place and functions before they are dismissed under the precepts of Aristotelian science (the triumph of the logocentric tradition) and completed by nineteenth-century scientist and historicist positivism.

Beyond the two protocols of reading which continue to prevail concurrently, I have already pointed out in the Introduction to what must to be a third way which fully integrates the most fruitful exigencies of the historico-anthropological and linguistic approach, the practices and productions of 'believing' reading treated as objects of cultural and social history; the whole coming to sustain and establish a new interactive practice of philosophy of the religious fact, a comparative theology within the monotheistic framework open to subsequent expansion, and social and religious sciences. One of the strong and promising points of this orientation is the opening up of a cognitive field in which Judaism, Christianity and Islam would be dealt with on an equal footing, using the considerable resources already gathered by historians of the ancient Near East (biblical studies, semitic studies, societies, cultures and civilizations, always including the Arab and Islamic dimension with all the Judeo-Christian, Semitic and Greco-Latin legacies, as well as with all the theological schemes and frameworks which continue to be practised and reactivated under the pressures of contemporary political violence, as systems of self-foundation and self-promotion of various communities. It is here that I am going to let J. Y. Lacoste speak who, in the foreword to his *Dictionnaire* abovementioned, justifies the field that theology must cover in the following terms:

> *Ceci d'abord est un dictionnaire de théologie, par quoi l'on entend, en un sens restrictif qui est aussi un sens précis, le massif de discours et de doctrines que le christianisme a organisé sur Dieu et sur son expérience de Dieu. Il est sur Dieu d'autres discours, et la théologie fut souvent le première à défendre leur rationalité. En réservant donc un terme pour désigner une pratique (historiquement circonscrite) du logos et un appel (historiquement circonscrit) au nom de Dieu [my emphasis], nous ne prétendons pas nier l'existence et la rationalité d'autres pratiques et d'autres appels – nous pensons seulement d'user de 'théologique' pour nommer les fruits d'une certaine alliance entre le logos grec et la restructuration chrétienne de l'expérience juive [my emphasis]. De ce que le philosophe parle lui aussi de Dieu, il s'ensuit rarement que son intérêt soit théologique, au sens fixé. Parce que le judaïsme a pu nouer ce qu'il avait de plus riche à dire sans piller l'héritage théorique de l'Antiquité classique, il est également improbable que ses doctrines aient besoin d'être dites théologiques. Et on admettra encore que la (sic)* kalam *Islamique obéit elle-même (sic) à des règles de structuration assez originales pour qu'il soit inutile, sauf à admettre un certain règne du flou, de la baptiser 'théologie Islamique'. Quant à l'étude comparée rigoureuse de tous les discours où intervient le signifiant 'Dieu' (que son intervention soit celle d'un nom ou d'un concept, ou autre), elle en est encore à l'état d'enfance.*[1]

I would be the last to describe this position as apologetic, particularly after having read the whole of the work. I retain on the contrary, the heuristic incentives of a definition which deserves to

1. I prefer to keep the French original text, because the translation might generate misunderstandings.

be taken seriously by historians of philosophical and theological thought in what I have long been called the Greco-Semitic sphere and which I prefer to call today the cultural Mediterranean space. With this geo-historical concept, as developed by F. Braudel, we can develop a retrospective strategy to reread and rewrite the entire history of thought without excluding or putting aside the important contributions of classical Islamic thought. This approach would not only reassess our fragmented presentation of the history of philosophy, theology and sciences, but it would change the contemporary ideological climate in which the so-called 'Islam and the West' are opposed, and the Mediterranean area more and more marginalized with its various contributions to the shaping of European thought since Middle Ages. As an historian of Islamic thought, I agree with J. Y. Lacoste that theology as 'an alliance between Greek logos and the Christian restructuring operation of the Jewish experience' differs, in effect, from the line followed by Jewish thought as well as that developed by Islamic thought which cannot be reduced to *kalām*. This discipline cannot be correctly evaluated if it is excised from what has been called religious sciences (*'ulūm dīniyya*) especially exegesis, the sources of religion and the sources of law (*uṣūl al-dīn* and *uṣūl al-fiqh*), historiography and even *adab* in its specific dimensions during the classical period.[1] Where *kalām* has been driven towards a polemical defence of the emerging Islam facing the already established religions such as Manicheism, Judaism, Christianity, and the promoters of Greek philosophy, it is right to present it as a 'defensive apology' to use L. Gardet's expression; but major works – especially the massive contribution of Joseph van Ess on *Theology und Gesellschaft im 2 und 3 jahrhubdert Hidschra* – have totally changed the old interpretation adopted by J.Y. Lacoste. By so doing, this author confirms two observations: like many Christian authors, he prefers to use an obsolete literature on *kalām* to strengthen the uniqueness of Christian theology compared to Jewish and Islamic developments of the same

1. Many references can be mentioned here; the last book devoted by G. Makdisi to Ibn 'Aqīl is particularly relevant to this context. See also my forthcoming book, *Combats pour l'humanisme en contextes Islamiques.*

discipline; in his desire to throw down the intellectual gauntlet, he supports my former call for a new reading of history of thought in the wider, encompassing perspective of Mediterranean area.

The truly important question to be considered in this context is to find out to what extent the required conditions for the development of a modern Islamic theology are available today and if not, what should be done to introduce Islam into the philosophical, ethical, spiritual and scientific debates which govern any relevant attempt to bring Islamic life and thought up to the level of the contemporary challenges. There is a discipline called *'ilm al-kalām* whose specialists are known as *mutakallimūn*; but its field has remained narrow, and its subject contested by philosophers on the one hand and by the strongly traditional scholastic trends on the other, especially the Ḥanbalī line which imposes faith without asking how (*bilā kayf*). Some authors have preferred to use the expression 'sources of religion' (*uṣūl al-dīn*) to link the discipline to another, less negatively connoted and called 'sources of law' (*uṣūl al-fiqh*). Muḥammad 'Abdu attempted to reactivate a theology named *tawḥīd* in his essay on *The oneness of God* (*Risālat al-tawḥīd*). The term *lāhūt* whether preceded or not by *'ilm*, allows the formation of the adjective *lāhūtī* but, as coined and used by Christian Arabs, it could not be retained by Muslims for obvious reasons of contamination by Christian ideas. We are thus faced with a conceptual field that is considered suspect, distorted by religious science and awaiting a sufficiently strong, innovative and relevant conceptualization in order to receive a declinable name and indisputable scientific status. The expansion of the *fatwā* genre – a jurisprudential consultation on miscellaneous cases – to which several contemporary *'ulamā'* owe their fame, underlines the loss of relevance in current Islam to theological activity, even in its classical form. The contrast is striking with the exuberant, historical continuity and the intellectual and spiritual fecundity eminently attested to by the *Dictionnaire* devoted by J. Y. Lacoste to Christian theology.

This author appears to have needlessly succumbed to a normative temptation in his restrictive definition of theology. However, I retain it because the summarizing and well-documented articles of the *Dictionnaire* impose the undeniable oneness of a historical course of thought in Europe. I only regret the weakness of the contributions on the theology of religious pluralism and the lack of interest in the comparative approach of the three monotheist religions which emerged in the ancient Near East. Recognizing all this and without any mimicry or idea of reproducing a model, I will put forward the following heuristic propositions for the possibility of an Islamic theology which would put an end to the reservations which it has raised among Muslims and non-Muslims, and impose its irreducible pertinence in the current debates on the functions of religion and the re-creation of religious believing currently in operation everywhere:

3.1.1.

The possibility of an Islamic theology is, first of all, linked to responses which will continue the discussion already engaged in the Middle Ages between philosophical reasoning and religious reasoning, as the latter defined itself in the three religions of the Book. This discussion was taken over in the 1930s, in the context of the philosophical and historical reasoning, in relation to the possibility of a Christian philosophy. Two contradictory positions were defended by E. Bréhier (against) and E. Gilson (for). The same question was raised and remains open of the possibility of an Islamic philosophy. The debate was widened considerably in the context of confrontations between modernity of the classical age in Europe itself and the currents of post-modernism and liberal philosophy. Christian theology turns towards the practice of an interactive reflection where it proceeds to agonising revisions, but obliges the philosophical partners and practitioners of social sciences to integrate the irreducible dimensions of religious fact. In the current climate that has prevailed since the emergence of the ideological postulates combined with those of belief in the so-called Islamic Revolution, Islamic thought has refused to assume and even to take note historically of its cultural and intellectual discrepancies, discontinuities, issues left unthought and those declared unthinkable – not allowed to think of – under the treat of political violence.

3.1.2.

The problematization of the cognitive and spiritual relevance of the common axiology of the religions of the Book for the construction of the human subject, is a second prerequisite which conditions the possibility of all theology open to the exigencies of emergent reason. By common axiology, I mean the totality of principles, postulates and definitions related to the great themes that constitute religious belief: revelation, the Word of God, creation, the Covenant, or the Alliance (*mīthāq, 'ahd*), prophetic mission, prophetic discourse, holy Scriptures, the Book, the Canon of the Scriptures, faith, loving obedience to God, trust in God, man in the image of God, Divine Law, justice, worship, resurrection, eternal life, immortality, salvation, and so on. This vocabulary, that is already used in the fundamental statements, constitutes the matrix of the representations and the contents of believing which have been defined, codified and imposed in the course of a gradual action of self-on-self of the believing communities. This action has sustained what these communities call 'the Living Tradition' whose formation has been marked by mechanisms of mimetic rivalry between protagonists developing in the same socio-cultural and political arena in the Mediterranean historical space.

3.1.3.

The difficulties peculiar to theology in this task of problematization, are due to contradictions and tensions between the risks of the intellectual drift in the effort of theorization of the religious fact and the apologetic temptation to safeguard at all costs, the contents of faith which cement the social bond, consolidate the spiritual ethos and nurture the hope of salvation in every member of the community. Recognizing the existence of a common axiological structure underlying the contingent historical constructions, sites of belief peculiar to every Community; deconstructing this structure perceived as original in order to show its material and historical contingency, is re-treading in reverse the course followed by classical theologians and metaphysicists. The operations of absolution, sacralization, mythologization, spiritualization, transcendantalization, in the context of a culture of the marvellous and enchantment, will be replaced by analyses which will generate relativization, desacralizaion, demythologization, demystification, historicization, despiritualization. It is an historical fact that theologies of communities, or rather advocating communities, have caused the apologetic concern for preservation and maintenance to prevail through all the climates of what they call 'the Living Tradition'. The intellectual responsibility to submit this Tradition to criticism is costly, but it revives scientific knowledge. The history of theologies is very much marked by their resistance, in the name of a dogmatic belief, to the most fruitful currents of thought.

3.1.4.

Resistance continues and tends to win some political victories in the Islamic domain, notably as a result of the rapid disintegration and ideologization of traditional belief. The chances of an Islamic theology capable of managing simultaneously a weighty scholastic heritage, profound discontinuity, conceptual amalgams and semantic disorders of 'revolution' without revolutionary thought, seem to weaken. The problem is then to know whether the disintegration of the religious function under the impact of the forces of globalization and defensive-offensive, reactive attitudes of communities which claim to be 'believing' communities, is going to become a *topos* of cognitive and philosophical relevance for the new theology defended in the columns of the *Dictionnaire.*

3.1.5.

The identification and new themes (*topoi*) of relevance will be conditioning to an ever greater extent the intellectual legitimacy, cognitive validity and functional bearing of theology as an interactive scientific discipline dealing with an irreducible domain of human reality. In this perspective, it appears fair to me to accept that if Islamic theology continues to accumulate very damaging delays, it will share with Christian and Jewish theologies, the same mental obstacles and cognitive difficulties of rethinking radically the question of fundamentals in order to rebuild the entire common axiology. Then the apories of orthodoxy, orthopraxy, authority and power, fundamentalism, and foundationalism re-emerge. In other words, one disregards, once again, the great heuristic doubts raised by the emerging reason about the functioning of the 'great narratives' on which are rooted the believing in the past, as well as the ideological 'certitainties' of today. In the matter of believing, one cannot, for example, overlook the hypothesis of Cl. Lévi-Strauss concerning the construct of subject, whereby individuals and groups would only have a limited self-constructive power; they are bound to use more or less complex and productive combinations in a list of possibilities – themselves variable according to historical circumstance and the socio-cultural environment – *proposed in a closed world* (cf. *Anthropologie structurale*, Paris, 1958). There we have a point of relevance which theologies cannot ignore. They can invalidate or consolidate the hypothesis of the anthropologist by re-examining the doctrine of man created in the image of God, receiving thereby the power to construct oneself as a person called upon to fulfill one's terrestrial and spiritual destiny through devoted obedience to the revealed Law.

3.1.6.

I have purposely left aside the case of Jewish theology because it would require a special consideration for its two-sided historical trajectory in the Arab-Islamic contexts and in European Christian contexts. I prefer to leave it to Jewish thinkers themselves to express themselves on two decisive limitations imposed on the Jewish effort to appropriate the theological and ethical axiology, which defines equally, for all three communities, the historical condition imposed upon minorities humiliated and persecuted for so long and the problems raised by the struggle to establish and legitimize the state of Israel.

Those who criticize me for giving more place to the setting up of theoretical and methodological frameworks than to substantial monographs can measure to what extent Islamic studies suffer from weakness, rather the absence of theoretical and epistemological debates fitting, of course, into concrete historical, sociological and anthropological frameworks. We are well aware that the accumulation of scholarly knowledge (which remains, as I have said, an indispensable step) does not necessarily generate critical, inventive, liberating thought. I consider, as regards belief in Islamic contexts, that constructive criticism would go further and reach more reliable conclusions if the basic tools were available, such as a scientific *encyclopaedia of the Qur'ān*, a reliable *historical dictionary of the Arabic language*, historical lexicons of the theological, philosophical, legal, historiographical and linguistic terminologies. We still lack critical editions with reliable indexes of outstanding works, such as the commentaries of the Qur'ān, the large collections of the *ḥadīth*, the *Mughnī* of 'Abd al-Jabbār, the *Iḥyā'* of al-Ghazālī, the *Kitāb al-umm* of al-Shafi'ī, and so on.

That is not all. To these major obstacles peculiar to the situation of Islamic studies which one hopes is temporary, may be added all the difficulties linked to the global forces at work in our history since the apparent triumph of the free market culture legitimized by liberal philosophy. More than ever, the culture of disbelief (cf. Stephen Carter, *The Culture of Disbelief: How American Law and Politics Trivialise Religious Devotion*, New York, 1993), everywhere imposes its pressures to the extent of making derisory and obsolete all the efforts for a critical appropriation of the culture of belief. What is now called a 'knowledge society' in the sense of information technologies, has replaced industrialised-industrialising societies. The forces linked to tele-techno-scientific reason determine more and more closely the exercise of critical reason in the field of the human and social sciences which should normally keep throughout their practice, the responsibility of expressing the constraining rights, obligations and ethical rules for individuals, citizens, communities, civil societies and states. We speak more currently on human rights than on moral, civic, intellectual responsibilities; it is difficult to point out either to the ethics of responsibility or to the ethics of conviction, according to Max Weber's distinction. How all these pressures and changes affect believing and how the weakening process of believing strengthens the impossibility to articulate any constraining ethical discourse?

3.2. Disintegration or Re-composition of Believing?

Sociologists and political scientists interested in current expressions of the religions, speak of re-composition of believing under the pressure of several factors. The choice of the term 're-composition' can indicate either a decision of neutrality in relation to all normative evaluations of the more-or-less ephemeral forms, levels and functions of the new believing, or a purely mechanical concept of the processes of formation of any type or level of believing. In the latter case, faith as a religious modality of a believing regulated by a doctrinal *magisterium* and all the paths of institutionalization of the religious, would be reduced to ordinary believing, commanded by an incontrollable play on diverse mechanisms. If, to avoid this theoretical drift, I speak of disintegration of believing, I run the opposite risk of reintroducing surreptitiously the normative exigencies of a theological *magisterium* whose limitations and timeframe I have just defined. Disintegration presupposes the prior existence of an integrated and integrating, instituted and instituting state of believing. At the same time, what distinguishes emerging reason from religious reason and sovereign scientist reason that is particular to classical modernity, is that it tries to identify and clarify all the objectivist, or reductionist drifts for better operating the new points (*topoi*) of relevance mentioned above. Since the study of metamorphoses and statuses of believing has been linked to that of the construction of the human subject, it will be useful to specify further the theoretical stakes of the discussion which we have just introduced.

Is the project of an adequate knowledge of a social programme and mechanisms of production of any society compatible with the assertion of an independent, critical subject capable of knowledge of self? The social sciences always call upon anthropological assumptions which they attempt to cover with a veil of objective pseudo-science, just like the religious discourses which they had dismissed were covering all the norms, beliefs, values, with a sacred veil by means of which all the norms had been internalized by the believer as proceeding from divine commandments. This critique of the hidden ideological role of the social sciences does not abnegate the positive knowledge which they continue to accumulate. It aims to underline the urgency of a radicalization of the theoretical reflection and the broadening of the historical, sociological and anthropological scope of their investigations to avoid the exclusive focus on the example of Western societies; an urgency made greater still in the present context of globalization decided, planed and guided exclusively by the Western systems of thinking, knowing, judging and acting. The self-promoting West does not even integrate in its geopolitical strategies the imposition of its world vision and 'universal' values, to counter the negative or positive perceptions other peoples and cultures are developing towards its policy.

All the so-called metaphysical postulates are hard to determine if at all; for this reason, they cannot operate as they did for centuries in all traditional cultures. In democratic contexts, a group of privileged protagonists elected by universal suffrage, chosen for their expert achievements, or following the secret interplay of influences, exercise the monopoly of competence-decision in the determinant spheres of political, economic, and monetary matters. Only the laws of the marketplace, calculation of national interests, and geopolitical strategies of competing protagonists can deflect the sense of justice or greater oppression, the short-term or medium-term choices. It will be noted, in effect, that the forces of globalization at work hardly leave any room for the planetary debate on the choices of civilization. These latter are reduced to the opposition of 'values', removed from the generalized critical resumption and put forward in discourses of identity, produced concurrently by the protagonists of dominant societies and by those in search of emancipation.

It is true that in the social sciences one also observes increased interventions to reactivate and enrich the debate on the question of the 'subject' (see bibliography, *Penser le sujet: Autour d'A. Touraine*). It is a matter of containing the pretensions of conservative religious movements, closed to the achievements of intellectual modernity, as well as of the various groups and communities struggling for identity, nationalist and religious rights. If religions have to make a return to history, they will have to take into account all the achievements, intellectual and scientific conquests of modernity and secularized culture and law since the first political revolutions in Europe. They will not monopolize again, as the so-called Islam used by the post-colonial states is doing, the control of institutions and instances in which the construction and destiny of the human subject are decided independently. Any subject, any society builds itself through a complex dialectal play of social mechanisms under the governance of a rule of law. This is the most precious product of modern philosophical, political reasoning, prior to the eighteenth century no religious system of belief and ethical values had ever achieved what the Enlightenment did in Europe until today. Yet not all contemporary societies and cultures have fully benefitted from this conquest. The given sociological, cultural and political facts are not seriously considered by those hegemonic Western societies which are conducting the process of globalization according to their own historical pace. The conceptual and theoretical matrix constructed in Europe during the classical age of modernity should be revised and up-dated with regard to historical action, social agents and the interaction between each social agent and the prevailing system of historical action. This revision should be extended to each contemporary society with its specific political regime. Action is the product of norms and values internalized by the group and, to various degrees, by every member (person/individual/citizen) according to the dominant theology or political philosophy. Through institutionalization, these values become roles, patterns or models of **perception-action-judgement.** The social order proceeds neither exclusively from divine decree, nor from the social contract, but flows from the levels of internalization of representations specific to each group of protagonists. Thus, classical sociology, from Durkheim to Parsons, is a social philosophy which imposes a representation of the protagonist and modern morality. God is no longer outside of us, but in each individual who will be all the more independent if he can master the norms, thus escaping from the control of the group (which he will try hard to convert, in fact, to his particular norms). Depending on whether the protagonist defines himself as an individual citizen or a person with a spiritual vocation, there will be an individual/person/society dialectic in the space of citizenship regulated by the laws in force, or between the person and the spiritual community in the framework of what I call the societies of the Book-book. This protagonist exists insofar as modern society exists as such, that is to say, as a system of inequality more or less regulated in a spirit of justice and dignity of the citizen; a system in which the beliefs, conduct and positions of class are defined by their effectiveness (pragmatism, functionality).

It can be seen how classical sociology and its current outcomes have exposed social mechanisms and systems of norms and representations which construct the subject in interaction with social groups. At the same time, this sociology has substituted for the ancient idea of fate or destiny, those of necessity and hazard which in the long run, govern all human existence. Man understands himself as an individualized, historical subject who acts and thinks only within the limits of compulsion objectified by linguistics, sociology, psychology and history. We spoke of disintegration or re-composition of believing. Now we understand better why it is preferable to leave this theoretical difficulty open. As long as there is an obvious need to perform other analyses, and incorporate new questions, we will suspend any leap into an untenable choice. We will return to the examination of the metamorphoses of believing in Islamic contexts that have so long been postponed and begin by applying to the Qur'ān in its received version as the Official

Closed Corpus, the protocol of reading proposed for all founding holy Texts as well as the secondary texts derived therefrom. We will question thereafter the current practices of societies in which the two competing models of control of belief and subsequent production of history confront each other.

4. From Emerging Religion to Corpora of Belief

I return to the Qur'ān not in order to rediscover the founding origins and authentic expressions of Islamic believing, but to illustrate the effectual relevance of the concept of social and psycho-linguistic construction of believing. The investigation is not, first of all, theological. It is historical, provided that it includes the interrogations of historical psychology and anthropology. The theological moment can be considered only after this methodological investigation which should restore to the text, that which we read today in all the characters of the primary oral enunciations before the creation, diffusion and reception by all Muslims of the Official Closed Corpus, called the written down volume (*Muṣḥaf*). This is to free the primary oral enunciations from all doctrinal constructs and mental retro-projections accumulated by the interpreting Community (in fact by the *'ulamā'* and learned individuals promoted to the rank of religious authorities (*al-a'imma-l-mujtahidūn*) after the Pious Ancestors (*al-Salaf al-ṣāliḥ*) who memorized and transmitted the whole Revelation during the first four centuries of the *Hijra*.

Chronologically, the dividing line before and after the Official Closed Corpuses or collections of traditions can be traced with the help of the following dates. The four founders of Sunnī schools of *fiqh*: Abū Ḥanīfa (d. 150/767), Mālik ibn Anas (d. 179/795), al-Shāfi'ī (d. 204/820), Ibn Ḥanbal (d. 241/855); the authors of the biography of Muḥammad (*Sīra*): Ibn Isḥāq (d. 150/768), Ibn Hishām (d. 219/834); the authors of the six collections of *hadith*: al-Bukhārī (d. 256/870), Muslim (d. 261/875), Ibn Māja (d. 273/886), Abū Dāwūd al-Sijistānī (d. 279/889), al-Ṭirmīdī (d. 279/892), al-

Naṣā'ī (d. 303/915); the professions of faith such as those of Ibn Baṭṭa (d.387/997), al-Barbahārī (d. 329/941); Qur'ānic exegesis and historiography: Ṭabarī (d. 310/923). The Imāmī Shī'ites have their own collections with Kulaynī (d. 329/940): *al-Kāfī*; Ibn Bābūye (d. 381/991): *Man lā yaḥzuruh al-faqīh* and *al-'aqīda al-imāmiyya*; Abū Ja'far al-Ṭūsī (d. 460/1068), al-Shaykh al-Mufīd (d. 413/1023) author of the *sīra* of the twelve Imāms in *Kitab al-irshād*; the two sharīfs al-Rāḍī (d. 404/1014) and al-Murtaḍa (d. 437/1045). For the Ismā'ilī branch, we will recall al-Qāḍī al-Nu'mān (d.363/974) author of the *Da'āim al-islām*.

The dates-limits are 150/767–437/1045. We will note the chronological priority of Sunnī jurists and theologians in relation with the demands of the Umayyād, then 'Abbasid state; the *fiqh* defined by Ghazālī as *qānūn al-siyāsa*, the Canon of the conduct of every faithful submitted to legal responsibility (*mukallaf*) towards himself, his family, his city, his community and finally God, will also receive a primacy as Instance of spiritual authority (*ḥukm*] differentiated from the instance of power (*sulṭa*), to assure the doctrinal *magisterium* (*martabat al-ijtihād*) and control of orthodox believing. It is this Instance linked to the caliphate in place, but independent of it in law, which decides on the integration or rejection of schools, movements of thought such as Sufism, Mu'tazilism and branches of Shī'ism. The Imāmīya succeeded in imposing its particular collection with a slight historical time lag; the Ismā'ilī Shī'a have the advantage of Fātimid support for establishing the contents of their believing. The Sunnī *magisterium* eventually incorporated a moderate Sufism which was within the limits laid down by the Qur'ān, the *Sunna*, the *ijmā'*, three Source-Foundations whose appropriate usage is defined by two normative disciplines, the *uṣūl al-fiqh* inaugurated by the *Risāla* of al-Shāfi'ī and the *uṣūl al-dīn* with al-Ash'arī (d.324/935) and Abū Manṣūr al-Baghdādī, (d. 429–1038).

But the crucial moment for the composition and diffusion of the secondary corpora established as the second *aṣl*, Source-Foundation of the Islamic Instance of religious authority, is situated between 855 and 923 for the Sunnī, and 940–991 for the

Imāmiya. Al-Ṭabarī. is an even more decisive reference because it represents the culmination of an evolution which terminates with him and the point of departure of a scholastic knowledge which continues to establish itself down to the present day for that which affects religious thought and orthodox control of believing.

Let us specify a crucial point. The composition, diffusion and consecration of the written corpora have allowed the setting up of a supreme Instance, from which, from every community, learned *'ulamā'* draw intangible definitions of the ideal conduct and means of validation and reactivation of orthodox believing. There have thus come into being over a period of time a continuity of the normative field embodying Qur'ānic statements, episodes of the exemplary life of the Prophet (*sīra*) and his Companions – in particular 'Alī and the twelve (or seven) imāms) for the Shī'ites – and teachings which form the *ḥadīth* or prophetic Tradition. In situations of everyday life, and in frequent conversations, believers invariably cite Qur'ānic verses, *ḥadīth* compiled as short accounts and fragments of the life of the great symbolical Figures integrated into the greater Corpus of belief. This means that the believing experienced ignores the distinctions of the historian, sociologist and psychologist analyst between the Qur'ān as chronological series of oral statements, then as the Official Closed Corpus, the secondary corpora elaborated by the interpreting communities for the purpose of integrating into the relatively open Corpus of belief everything that appears as innovation, heterogeneous conduct (*bid'a*) imposed by historical evolution or socio-cultural diversity. The discipline of *uṣūl al-fiqh* codified the formal techniques of this integration of profane history into the Corpus of belief in which there appear only orthodox knowledge, individual and collective conduct, duly legitimized, that is to say linked by a common determinant (the famous *'illa* of theological-legal reasoning) to the categorizations of all human experience perceived as divinely rooted (*al-aḥkām al-shar'iyya*). That is why the *corpus juris* which grew into the essential referents for the exercise of justice in the believing city, eventually brought a 'reasoned' confirmation to the entire Corpus of belief. This latter functions, in fact, as the receptacle of a continuous collective work of construction and validation of believing. This receptacle, static in the number of texts collected, remains alive, indefinitely productive as to the existential usages which the protagonists make of it to reinterpret their profane experience in the sense of devoted obedience (*ṭā'a*) to the divine Law. One uses for this purpose discursive techniques of integration, or better, cancellation of concrete and profane historicity in order to vest it in the framework of History of Salvation. These techniques, well analysed by P. Ricœur in *Temps et récit*, are in operation in the founding narratives using literary devices for the accounts of transfiguration, appropriation, insertion of the profane in the sacred.

We are thus placed before four corpora differentiated by the analyst, namely, the Qur'ān in its two aspects oral and textual, the *ḥadīth* in its Sunnī, Shī'ī and Khārijī versions, both oral and textual, the *corpus juris* and the great common Corpus of belief. But in the experience of the believers, these four function in an indivisible, convergent and interdependent manner as a totalizing system of norms, references and representations which cement the unity of every community in a shared *true* believing. It must not be forgotten that committing the texts to writing never abolishes a return to oral usages in ritual performances, in everyday conversation and educational practices. Under such conditions, how should a critical approach be conducted of every corpus differentiated without reducing the practical functional bearing of what can be called, like for other religious traditions, the living Islamic Tradition? I think we can avoid this methodological pitfall by maintaining a constant toeing and froing between the overall Corpus of belief as we have just defined it and the corpora which sustain it and perpetuate its religious *ethos* which is inseparable from the historical dynamics of the societies of the Book-book.

4.1. A Believing in Process of Emergence

Provided with all these definitions of a historical and conceptual framework of investigation, we can return to the founding corpus, initiator of all the others – the Qur'ān as collection of oral enunciations. The committing to writing of an indeterminable number of verses at the time of the Prophet does not change anything in regard to the strictly linguistic relevance of articulation of meaning in the oral communication situation. The problem which any hermeneutic, placed before a word (*parole*) transformed into text, must resolve, is precisely how to take charge of all the differences between this first enunciation that is irreversibly lost and the relevance peculiar to the discourses derived from the interpretation of a written text which continues to have a historical career in the cultural system of orality. These problems are widely discussed by linguists, semioticians, psychologists and anthropologists (see particularly the works of J. Goody). I must stress to Muslim readers, but also classical Islamicist colleagues, that my distinction between a **before** and an **after** of the Official Closed Corpus has nothing to do with either the problems of authenticity of the 'Uthmānian *Muṣḥaf*, or with those of an opposition of theological nature between divine authenticity of the primary statements which must be saved at all costs as such, and degradations of the transcendental meaning of the latter with the intervention of various commentators and users, believers and non-believers. Ultimately, the problem of the linguistic genesis of meaning in the two systems of orality and textuality, reflects upon that of the philosophical status of meaning, distinguished from the effects of meaning (*effets de sens*).

At the stage of the primary statements, it is not possible for us to proceed to an exegesis of the Qur'ān by the Qur'ān (*tafsīr al-Qur'ān bil-Qur'ān*) as this would be recommended as the surest way, after the availability of the Official Closed Corpus, with its arbitrary chronological arrangement of the *sūras* and verses. The historical reading restores the real conditions of the contemporary situation in which the addressees reacted on successive statements in a chronological order whose reconstitution remains uncertain. It is thus difficult for us to locate the stages and mechanisms of the reading and construction of a believing in a process of emergence. The non-historical, even non-theological, would permit to differentiate *īmān* and *islām* from *sūra* 9 where it is said: '*But God has endeared the Faith (īmān) to you, and has made it beautiful in your hearts, and He has made hateful to you unbelief, wickedness, and rebellion*' (Verse 7). *Islām* is a term difficult to translate, because it is subjected to a conceptual effort which historians limit to the period after the *Hijra* (see my article *Islām* in the *Encyclopaedia of the Qur'ān*). It happens that *sūra* 49 is classified as 114 in modern attempts at chronological classification. It thus reflects on the final state of the conceptual work of the two notions *īmān* and *islām*. In the current state of the discussion, it is only possible to put forward remarks suggestive of a plausible progression of the construction of believing in the twenty years of Qur'ānic preaching. When testing the three classifications of the standard Egyptian edition of 1925, by Nöldeke-Schally, and R. Bell, N. Robinson followed the development of two themes, namely, the female companions of the faithful admitted to paradise and the names Allāh and Raḥmān. In the twelve occurrences of the former theme, some speak of young virgins with firm breasts and large black eyes, others simply of purified spouses (*azwāj muṭahhara*). The Egyptian edition does not make it possible to establish any development of this theme. Nöldeke-Schally and R. Bell stress that the first description only occurs in the Meccan *sūras*, and the second in the Medinan. The same applies for *Allah* and *Raḥmān*. For 'Lord' in all the early *sūras*, the name used is *rabb*; whereas *Raḥmān* and *Allah* are used concurrently in the second Meccan period; afterwards, *Allah* establishes Himself progressively as the only one addressee of believing and obedience to the exclusion of all other designations.[1]

Respect for chronology of the Qur'ānic enunciations makes it easier to reinforce recurrent polemics against numerous opponents and the social and political positions of the groups involved. The current Arabic lexicon has been thoroughly revised in the direction of what will subsequently become a Qur'ānic **axiology** whose commanding power over thought and action, continues to establish itself under diverse historical, socio-cultural and

1. For the exact statistics of the occurrences in the three classifications, see N. Robinson, *Discovering the Qur'ān*, London, 1996, pp. 87–91.

psychological forms. I will come back to this concept of Qur'ānic axiology which I have already defined without linking it sufficiently to the historical and sociological contexts of its reception and the changing impact on the local forms of believing (see my *Islam: Morale et politique*, UNESCO, 1986, pp. 23–45). The vocabulary applied to groups of protagonists in rivalry, conveys the genesis of a historical paradigmatic drama. These are, as in any story, oriented towards the quest for a highly desirable result, auxiliary protagonists and opponent protagonists. The primary Meccan statements define, firstly in visionary terms, the ultimate object of the quest and the situation for the purpose of transforming: a 'Lord of the tribes' (*rabb al-ʿālamīn*)[1] progressively restored as transcendent partner, creator, active, protagonist and protector of man (*al-insān*); a community of well-guided believers (*umma*), personally bound by a pact of devoted obedience (*tāʿa*) only to the Commandments of the *rabb*, transformed into Allah, and of Muḥammad ibn ʿAbdallah who became the Faithful Messenger of Allah. The opponents of this quest comprise the category of *kuffār* (ungrateful, deniers of the bountifulness of the Lord, later opposed as infidels in the highly elaborated pair: *kāfir/mū'min* in which the conduct of infidelity serves to emphasise pure, warm, staunch faith (*īmān*), on any account, of the true believers (*mū'minūn*); the category of *munāfiqūn* dissimulators, hypocrites who adhere by calculation to the group of the auxiliaries; the category of *Aʿrāb*, Arabs of the desert, who refuse openly to join the Cause of God and His Messenger, thereby displaying the most arrogant infidelity (*ashaddu kufran*); the category of *mushrikūn*, associators, polytheists, that is to say the Arabian religion which is the subject

1. I am using the translation chosen by J. Chabbi as the title of her recent book which proposes a strictly historical and synchronistic reading of a corpus treated at the same time as group of statements attested in the texts of what she continues to call the Qur'ān. I cannot discuss here the numerous problems linked to this translation, that are exegetically very fruitful, for a redefinition of believing, and hence the status of religious truth, as I am attempting to elaborate it in the present essay. See the explanation by J. Chabbi, note 645. See also the two diagrams on pages 98 and 99.

of all the Qur'ānic enterprise of redefinition, transformation and reorientation towards what became *dīn al-islām*, the religion of Islam; the category of *ahl al-kitāb*, Peoples of the Book, previous recipients of the bountifulness and guidance (*hudā*) of God and the Messengers, but who persist in denying the final initiative of God to re-establish in His eternal Truth, the Covenant, which they had betrayed and broken.

As regards the auxiliaries, the form *ṣaḥāba*, Companions, first disciples, does not appear in the Qur'ān. This category will be later constructed and expanded upon. It is about the *muhājirūn*, the early converts who renounced their former parental and clan solidarities in order to follow Muḥammad to Medina; 'those who have received the faith' (*al-ladhīna āmanū),* distinguished, as we have seen, from those who showed an external, revocable adhesion to Islam. It can be said that at all the stages of its development and in all circumstances, the Qur'ānic discourse designates the new believing which will decide the immediate fate and the final salvation of all the protagonists invited or summoned depending on the case, to listen, open their hearts, recognize (*ta'qilūn*) the convincing, speaking signs which give rise to thinking and contemplating (ā*yāt bayyināt*) and which are proposed to them. The introduction of intrigue underlines the dramatic tension of the confrontation and uncertain result – at least before the return to Mecca – of the battle between good and evil, error and salutary knowledge (*'ilm*), straying and divine guidance with, at the end of the trajectory, the inevitable, irrefutable final judgement determining the eternal damnation or salvation of every soul (or 'person' as we would say today).

This analytical presentation of the semiotic structure which underlies all Qur'ānic statements must not cause one to lose sight of the progressive construct of believing by repeated touches, additions, corrections, radicalizations, concessions and ruptures right down to firm, victorious, discriminating and prescriptive proclamations of the *sūrat al-Tawba* classified 113 or 114, and *al-Mā'ida* classified 112 or 116. We will retain a decisive feature of the rhetoric and semantic work of the discourse: temporal, spatial, factual and personal designations are systematically avoided. The groups of protagonists are transformed into protagonists of a **spiritual drama.** The political and social situations and what is actually at stake are sublimated into paradigms of conduct and recurrent choices inexorably involving the ultimate destiny of every soul (person) confronted at the same time with temptations, constraints and solidarities of the immediate life (*al-dunyā*, or 'society' as we would call it today) and with the exigent internalized look of a God whose self-presentation and self-attestation are already so insistent and so diversified within the limits of the founding discourse that will undergo expansion and metamorphoses that are difficult to determine.

Before proceeding to the examination of the orthodox Corpus of belief, let us dwell further on *sūra* 49. Its chronological place already allowed contemporary users to refer eventually to the previous verses memorized, as it established itself after the formation and circulation of the *Muṣḥaf*. We can thus get an idea of the stage of construction and functioning of belief after some twenty years of teaching and action in order to promote the *umma* of the 'brothers' in God.

It is interesting to note that at this stage, the working of the concepts of *īmān* and *islām* is far from being complete. That is why it is difficult to translate the two terms. The firmly established usage is to translate *īmān* by faith and *islām* by submission to God. But the English terms, as much as the Arabic terms, convey contents which owe much to the doctrinal workings and religious experiences lived as much in Christian and Jewish contexts prior to the Qur'ān as in Muslim contexts after the Qur'ān. Before deciding, let us allow *sūra* 49 to speak.

Of the eighteen verses, five begin with the frequent formula *yā ayyuhā-l-ladhīna āmanū*: 'O you who believe'! directly appealing to the category of *mū'minūn*, translated as believers. R. Blachère feels he must be more explicit in translating *īmān* in the verse 15 by 'ceux qui ont reçu la foi' (those who have received the faith). Several distinctive features of *īmān* are specified:

Never to anticipate – by making one's particular initiative

prevail – over the instance of God and His Messenger; not to raise the voice or raise the tone before the Prophet as one usually does with ordinary associates; not to interrupt the Prophet from outside, but wait at his door should he wish to come out; to mistrust false information insinuated by the wicked; to take into account the presence of the Messenger as an enlightened guide and not to expect him to follow the hazardous decisions of everyone; to know how to reconcile two factions among the believers who are at war; to eventually fight the one who transgresses until they return to the order defined by God; the believers can only be brothers and restore peace among them; not engage in malicious conjectures, mocking comments, malicious gossip either among men or among women; not to claim to give lessons to God on what religion is; not to remind as a favour extended to the Prophet the act of obedience to Islam (*aslama*). To all these imperatives of social ethics and personal control, are added definitions of greater religious and political significance in the verses 13, 14 already cited as an epigraph and 15:

> *O mankind! Lo! We have created you male and female, and have made you nations and tribes that ye may know one another. Lo! the noblest of you, in the sight of Allah, is the best in conduct. Lo! Allah is Knower, Aware* [49:13].

> *The (true) believers are those only who believe in Allah and His messenger and afterward doubt not, but strive with their wealth and their lives for the cause of Allah. Such are the sincere* [49:15].

We understand clearly the tension between a vision of man and society which resists change and a pedagogical, patient, benevolent work of improving what we would call today the human condition. I am aware that this concept may be anachronistic for the historical stage of the two modes which clash in this emergent Islam. However, how can it be denied that beyond a new ethico-political code of social bond, verses 13–15 take the first sure steps, easily identifiable for subsequent developments of a spiritual theology of the human person and even of a philosophical subject, if the philosophical attitude had not been eliminated from the Islamic field of thought? In the background of the encouragement addressed to the believers, we also guess that the new *ethos* of the human subject which the prophetic discourse seeks to implant in hearts, will remain for long an emancipatory utopia which will later sustain the nostalgic quest for a lost Inaugurating Moment, or, today, the revolutionary assertion of an Islamic model of civilization superior to all others.

If we accept this historical reading of *sūra* 49, we can translate *īmān* as the act of loyalty to a pact that binds two parties, and *islām* as the act of obedience to a socio-political and religious body in the process of institutionalization. The verbal form *āmana* means to guarantee security against any turnaround, or renunciation of an engagement undertaken. This meaning is better expressed by the concept of *tawakkul,* entrusting oneself to God, as a mark of confidence in a being not only reliable, but worthy of all the marks of devotion, recognition and devoted obedience. However, one should not lose sight of the fact that faithfulness thus defined is not constructed directly and exclusively in relation to a God who is still Himself in the process of self-attestation. This refined representation of faith will only establish itself much later after the gradual working of sublimation of the 'Word of God' through mystical experiences; codification of the professions of faith, definition of legal qualifications, all concurring in the cancellation of the historicity of Qur'ānic discourse and given to be recited, read, and experienced as the eternal Word revealed by a transcendent God.

Sūra 9, also late (classed 115), shows the taking root of *āmana*, in the security sought in a pact. *Barā'atun min Allahi wa rasūlih* is a denunciation of accord (*'ahd*) with the unconverted tribes (*al-mushrikūn*, designation of religious exclusion) to whom a delay of three months (*al-ashuru-l-ḥurum*) is granted for performing the act of obedience (*islām*) or they run the risk of being fought against (verse 5, of the sword). The term *tawba,* retained as one of the two titles of the *sūra*, is translated as repentance, returning to God, whereas on the social terrain meant by *sūra* 9, it is a matter of surrendering matched by a tactical delay (the well-known *dahā'*) which makes it possible to exercise a power henceforth acquired under the attributes of the authority which wins hearts. It will be remembered that this definition of a discourse which acts on the sociality of the protagonists in order to transform it, while incorporating into its semantic, rhetorical and semiotic articulation, the structural data of this sociality. One cannot speak of disguising of reality to construct a crude ideology of struggle (as is the case with modern ideological discourses). As has been seen, the believing under construction transforms the condition of a small group by opening it to the horizons of meaning and action whose historical productivity is widely illustrated by spectacular expansions and recurrences. The work of Islamisation of history will be different on this major point from the work accomplished by what one can now call **prophetic discourse**, for what I have just said about *sūras* 49 and 9 is found in the Bible and the Gospels. The discourse of the different religious sciences and the Islamic institutionalization of the religious will, trap the protagonists in a mimetic escalation for conquering and retaining the monopoly of the administration of the codified Islamic model as will be seen in the orthodox Corpus of belief.

Let us conclude this discourse by recalling that the French term *foi* – from the Latin *fides, fidere* – went through the same developments with Christianity. At the Qur'ānic stage, we retain the word 'faith' provided we do not project on to it all the expansions and definitions which were spread afterwards by the different users of the prophetic discourse and which became dispersed, fragmented and decontextualized texts while being collected in the Official Closed Corpus. It is for this reason that we shall come back to the word and the concept of believing. It alone will make it possible to give the modalities, levels of expression, and types of actualisation of what the terminology will call *īmān* and *i'tiqād*, their rightful place, the first being supposed to refer to the contents and attitudes of faith required by God, the second insisting further on the distinction between what the faithful is considered to accept as true (*l-iqtisād fi-l-iʿtiqād* of Ghazālī as well as all the professions of faith which dogmatically define the articles of faith) and what pertains to a condemnable credibility either by critical reason or the managers of orthodoxy.

4.2. The Great Orthodox Corpus of Belief: Expansion, Codification and Dispersal of Belief

It is impossible to monitor here the geo-cultural expansion of belief as it would have been internalized by the first Muslims setting out to conquer the many populations who were unfamiliar with the Arabic language, Arab culture and Arab society in the setting of *Jazīrat al-ʿarab* and in the even narrower setting of Ḥijāz, the real cradle of nascent Islam. It must be admitted that the inspirers and the promoters of the conquests had at least assimilated what could be termed 'the structure relating to the protagonists' which allowed the articulation and the early acceptance of Qur'ānic belief. In effect, the same educational processes and techniques of persuasion – even after violent conquests – had to be created before pagan, animist, Manichean, Zoroastrian, Jewish, Christian, then Buddhist, Hindu, and Confucian opponents who sought to retain their respective beliefs and institutions. Much has been written about the military, political, administrative and cultural conquests, but the available documentation hardly makes it possible for us to know exactly either the levels or the content of belief of the conquerors and the conquered, or the interaction between the processes of Islamization and the mechanisms of survival and resistance available to the local cultures, in their customs and religious beliefs. I have already indicated the importance of the cultural, anthropological and linguistic area that is collectively known today as the Maghreb. The progressive effacement of the separate identities of these North African countries and their ideological transformation into a purely Arab Islamic 'identity' from the time of the Arab conquest until modern times were radicalized in a systematic negation of the various Berber (*Amazigh*) peoples in which local, pre-Islamic religious beliefs have been always mixed with the Islamic belief as it codified in the great 'orthodox' Corpus. This case is not peculiar to the Maghreb, of course; all the post-colonial Jacobin, nationalist states have used religion to 'unify' the nation on the model that had been created in Europe in the ancient monarchic regimes. This means that after the original emergence of Islamic belief as described in the Qur'ānic discourse, one cannot rely exclusively on the official written corpora developed by the various factions or communities that emerged in the great number of ethno-cultural groups that existed throughout the former Muslim Empires and in the modern Muslim world, as they do in the Maghreb. There is a need for a historical sociology of belief and the education of human subject in each group that uses a distinct language, one which relates explicitly to its distinctive memory that integrates as adequately as possible its adherence to the great Islamic corpus. Nor should it be forgotten that this great corpus is restricted to a belief in the Qur'ān as the manifestation of the Word of God, transmitted by his messenger Muḥammad, the biography (*sīra*) of Muḥammad and the eschatological vision that controls the personal life of each believer. This common corpus of belief is, as we have indicated, diversified through time and space, into derived corpora specific to communities called factions and schools.

The approach I am defending is different from what has been done so far by means of a strict division of labour between ethnographers or ethnologists specializing in the description of 'societies without writing' according to the Levi-Strauss definition and learned elites in control of orthodox belief. My contention has been always that the historical development of both oral and written cultures is dominated by a dialectic tension between two organized structural forces opposing the state (the political centralizing force) with writing, learned elites and orthodoxy (religious and political) on one side and fragmented societies (tribes, clans and patriarchal families), oral 'dialects' and cultures, 'heterodoxies' condemned by the learned managers of the sacred on the other. This dialectic can be correctly observed and adequately interpreted only if the tools and methodologies of history are merged, using written documents and ethno-sociology, local dialects and investigation of all these groups with their specific collective memories. There are very few works in which the boundaries of specialization are truly merged in order to completely change representations and interpretations of belief and the teaching offered to the believer. On the contrary, macro-theories on the clash of cultures presented by political scientists are currently overwhelmingly successful all over the world, despite the fact that they spread a dangerous, ideological polarization of backward, obscurantist, anti-humanist cultures and religions that threaten enlightened, advanced, humanist 'values'.

To these difficulties of ideological nature are added all the obstacles inherent in the documentary resources available to any historian who has been converted to the approach to belief that I am proposing, one which combines the curiosities of historical sociology and psychology. These obstacles include the voluntary destruction of valuable documents such as the incomplete *Muṣḥafs* of the Qur'ān, in order to ensure the triumph of a single Official Closed Corpus, or all those writings that are considered heterodox; the oblivion generated by the ideological pressures of selection and accidental loss and the great number of manuscripts dispersed throughout the world that have not yet found competent scientific editors. There are also published texts but they are in a form that makes them unusable for scholarly research and delays in research due to scholastic conservatism, indifference, caution and the taboos that still surround the critical study of belief. This situation has contributed to an expansion of the extent of the unthought that has accumulated in the oral and written expressions of Islamic belief while these same various political and social forces have manipulated belief in both its popular, oral and learned, written expressions. The content of belief has become more and more politicized, remote from the spiritual and ethical values inherited from the past. For the last thirty years, new channels of information, school education programmes and official political discourse have supported forms and functions of belief which could be described as being simultaneously 'revolutionary', conservative and ritualistic. The best interpretation of this radical transformation is provided by the anthropologist Claude Geertz, as opposed to any from an

'Islamicist', neither a classical Islamicist working on major classical texts nor a so-called expert in political, fundamentalist Islam. In his *Islam Observed* first published in 1967 that was only translated into French in 1992 under the title *Observer l'Islam: Changements religieux au Maroc et en Indonésie*, Claude Geertz expounded on the issue of belief while exploring two regions at opposite ends of the geographical spread of Islam, Java and Morocco. Little has been done to follow his example and it is worth indicating the epistemic and intellectual reasons for this fact, though I cannot embark on this direction in the present work.

4.3. Towards a Historical Anthropology of Belief

In this respect, I must begin with a recent study by M. Cook of those who opposed the writing down of the Tradition in early Islam. This study was one of the papers read at the colloquium entitled *Voix et calame en Islam médiéval*, published in *Arabica* 1997, 3–4, booklet 4, pp. 437–530, for M. Cook's contribution). *Voix et calame* is another way of referring to orality or even *orature*, to use the term coined by P. Zumptor, as opposed to the written word. The author begins with the observation made by Ibn al-Jawzī (d. 597/1200) about the exceptional achievement of those Muslims who memorized the Qur'ān and the prophetic Tradition and continued to transmit it orally in a reliable manner. All other nations have transmitted their traditions in writing, without naming the authors and the transmitters (437). He then examines the question of the origins and significance of the opposition expressed to writing down the Tradition in a society that was becoming ever more inclined to the written word. In addition to the question of the origin of this attitude, Cook provides an opinion on the much-discussed question of the authenticity of the Tradition. Here are his conclusions:

> *The view behind my own reconstruction is more or less the following: traditionalist literature substantially preserves authentic materials from the second half of the second century; handled carefully, it can tell us a good deal about the first half of the second century but*

> *it is not, in genera,l usable as evidence for a period prior thereto; which is not to say that much of it may not, in fact, derive from such a period, and can on occasion be shown to do so. This view is reasonably close to that of Schacht; it is considerably, more conservative than that of Wansbrough, somewhat more radical than that of Van Ess, and very much more so than those of Abott and Sezgin* [p. 490].

After having examined 'the Jewish parallel' of hostility to the writing down of the oral Torah, the author concludes:

> *In sum, Rabbinic Judaism and early Islam are unique in sharing the same general conception of an oral Tradition which exists alongside a written scripture; and within this general framework, they share not just hostility to the writing of the oral, but also a specific pattern of ascription. Accordingly, it seems unlikely that these are parallel phenomena that just happened to coexist in that part of the world in the same period* [p. 512].

Besides the use of primary sources to continue to open up a thorny domain, the author allows me, by the very importance of his contribution, to better characterize two complementary approaches to the same subject of study, namely, orality and writing in the transmission of religious tradition. It will have been noted that Cook clearly fits into a long line of scientific authorities who share his position on the subject of the dual problem of authenticity and the question of influence, and thus the origin, of one tradition in relation to another. It is certainly valuable to consolidate, as he does here, the idea of the shared cognitive space of the rabbinic tradition and the Islamic tradition. However, as I have often repeated since the writing in the 1960s of my book *L'humanisme arabe au IVe/Xe siècle,* one should not remain mired in this treatment, which is helpful albeit historicist, of the question of orality and writing when the fecundity of the issues and analyses of social and cultural anthropology are well-known. I prefer to clarify here the connection between the question treated by Cook and believing as an object of historical, sociological and anthropological investigation. What is the meaning of the shared insistence of the two traditions, Jewish and Islamic, on the specific status of the Qur'ān and of the written Torah preserved in written corpora and the fact that the oral Tradition should not be written down or, '*it could fall and cause to fall into the wrong hand?*' Cook lists several plausible reasons for this hostility. There is the fear of the *ahl al-ra'y* that the free development of legalistic reasoning would be stopped, resistance to efforts by the Umayyads to fix the Tradition in writing, persistence of '*a remnant of the barbaric (sic) past of the Arabs of the Jāhiliyya*' (pp. 491–8). Historicist reasoning cannot include the question of belief as one of the important signposts in the system of thought commanded by orality to the system governed by writing. All that I have said about the concept of the 'societies of the Book-book' reveals its relevance to the continuous struggle between orality and writing at several levels of social, political and cultural life. I have linked together the *Book* 'the Heavenly well-preserved Book' spoken to audiences by the voice of the Messenger and fixed thereafter in writing in a codex (*maṣāḥif*) and, inseparably, the *book* as a material invention of civilization supposing technical progress to produce paper, to improve the alphabet, to edit the works, etc. There is also the intervention of the state with its needs for archives, historiography, codes of law, the learned elites who would assume the control of the language, and the transmission of learning, hence the orthodoxies.[1] This is really what happens with the rapid emergence of the imperial state and its expansion with the 'Abbasids. Belief, which had just been provided with its most general statements in the prophetic discourse, cannot escape the increasingly unequal struggles between two systems of thought, that is to say of production and social control of the 'true' meaning. The importance of meaning, of symbolic capital,

---

1. On the concept of *kitāb* in the Qur'ān, see the strictly linguistic and historical definitions and, above all, the theological stakes, in Jacqueline Chabbi's book, op, cit. This is the same line of analysis that I have long been developing in my concept of **societies of the Book-book** of which historicist historians cannot make use.

of spiritual authority and of political power implied in the struggle between the '*savage mind*' ('*la pensée sauvage*') and domesticated civilized written culture, are already developed in the Meccan and Medinan Qur_ān under the opposing concepts of *Jāhiliyya* and '*ilm*, polytheistic false knowledge and true religious knowledge. This anthropological dichotomy has spread throughout conquered societies and is still spreading through the fundamentalist discourses and ritual expressions of 'Islam'. The main issue is to explain the development of belief from its expressions in traditional societies from the thirteenth to the nineteenth century, and then during the initial impact of modernity on Muslim society prior to 1940. The most brutal shift took place in the second half of the twentieth century and lead to the present clashes in several places between the two forces which has been termed *Jihād versus McWorld*. These historical stages will be reviewed in all the necessary detail, focusing on the sociological expansion and the psychological expression of belief, especially in the contexts of the wars of liberation against colonial rule (1950–1967) and the policy of the post-colonial regimes.

4.3.1

The long period of Ottoman, Safavid and Moghul Empires is characterized by the systematic use of Islam by imperialist states. Shi'ism became the official religion of the Safavids in the Iranian sphere of influence, Sunni Islam was monopolized by Ottomans and the Moghuls; both chose a single official school of law to replace the doctrinal pluralism of the classical period with the supremacy of a single school. This affected learned expressions of belief in the sense that theological debates between the different schools disappeared; the '*ulamā*' were limited to the learned repetitions of professions of faith and the system of laws already established in the officially recognized school (Ḥanafī, Shāfi'ī, Mālikī, Ja'farī) according to the regions covered by the central state. I call this 'the period of state-imposed Islam' (*étatisation de l'Islam*).

Despite this official written, 'learned' Islam, a popular Islamic culture developed under the leadership of many local saints who were able to share the dialects, beliefs and customs of the various ethnic groups which the remote government was unable to control politically. An ethno-sociological survey is needed of this neglected but exuberant Islam, so often condemned as 'superstitious' and illiterate by the official 'orthodox' Islam concentrated in the urban, social classes. It is true that popular belief was based on the culture of miraculous, the imaginary representations of supernatural powers, invisible beings such as those called *jinnis* (genies or *djinns*) in the Qur'ān, the cosmic forces. There was even a clear-cut dividing line between the language and culture transmitted by women through their daughters and those of the menfolk who were reluctant to share what was labelled as 'childish' belief. I can bear witness myself of what was being taught by men and women in Kabyle society in Algeria until the late 1930s and the 1940s. The most significant, noticeable fact is that everywhere, popular Islam was taught as an animist, naive, ritualistic system of belief, overlaid with superficial elements of the Islamic creed. It was entirely devoid of any kind of theological thought or intellectual rationalization. Sociologically, this form of religious life was far more widespread and dominant than the learned level described and studied by historians who pay no attention to that other 'Islam' that is left for the ethnographers to deal with.

During the period under consideration, the intellectual field in the whole Muslim area has been shrinking, even in the urban contexts in which some scholarly activities were carried on in the line of the religious sciences practiced during the classical period of Islamic thought. Historians used to speak of the decay and ankylosis of this entire period; they paid greater attention to political and military history than to intellectual and literary production. That is why scientific information about the historical process of disintegration, impoverishment and underdevelopment of religious and cultural life in Muslim societies until the nineteenth century is so sorely lacking, and as far as Islam as a spiritual and ethical legacy is concerned, this could be said to remain true even today. Islamic thought has been isolated from the richest intellectual and scientific achievements of the classical period; it has remained indifferent, suspicious, if not clearly hostile, to all the revolutionary discoveries, inventions and intellectual shifts in Europe in the name of modernity. Even during the period known in the Arab world as the Renaissance (*Nahḍa*) that lasted from 1830 to 1940, intellectuals and scholars failed to introduce and spread a sustainable sense of the spirit of modernity; the most significant improvements and writings produced at that time were to be forgotten, condemned and rejected as the result of 'intellectual aggression' (*al-ghazw al-fikri*) of colonialism when the national struggle for liberation began post-1945.

4.3.2 From 'Socialist' Revolution to 'Islamic' Revolution

This paragraph is devoted to the intellectual history of Islamic thought during the crucial period that began at the end of World War II and extended its dramatic consequences to the present time. This history has never been written. A plethora of commercial literature has accumulated concerning fundamentalist, radical, political Islam and focusing on the threat of 'Islam' to the West, the failure of political Islam, the expanding idea of *Jihād.* Yet, at the same time, so many voices or peoples remain silent or have been silenced both by the prevailing political regimes in each country and by the selective attitude of the Western media. They remain ignored, marginalized and are mentioned only rarely and incidentally by certain authors, lumped together under the name of *Liberal Islam.* 'Islam' is mentioned everywhere, linked to every event, every country, every political movement, every trial, every scandal. It has replaced the name of Allah in his various attributes; it is the origin of all those generally negative initiatives; it is responsible for terrorism all over the world, for the worse violence against Muslims themselves in several ongoing civil war. The failure of the peace process since Oslo is exclusively related to Islam; the military totalitarian regimes in 'Islamic' countries are supported by Islamicist fanatical movements ... A powerful worldwide imaginary of a threatening, omnipotent, historical force called 'Islam' has progressively been constructed since the murder of the President Anwar Sadat, the rise of Iranian Revolution with Khomeini, the Gulf War, the terrorist atrocities committed in in France, the spread of Islamic militants all over Europe and America, Chechnya, the Balkan wars, and so on.

It is true that the majority of Muslim intellectuals, artists and scholars have remained silent. Few of them have participated in the heated ideological debates that take place at an international level. Those who dare to declare their position in the face of so many tragedies express a preference for the discourse of victimization rather than of self-criticism extended to the whole history of Islamic thought, as I am trying to do in this book. No one author has ever thought of choosing as a subject a long-term retrospective examination of the cultural, social, linguistic and political genesis and consequences of the *Unthought in Contemporary Islamic Thought*. Many intellectuals share with the conservative '*ulamā'* the apologetic response that claims that Islam is spiritually, ethically, legalistically, intellectually, scientifically and culturally self-sufficient; there is room for any type, any level of the unthinkable or the unthought. It is pointless to compare the historical development of Islamic thought to the rapid progress into modernity made in Europe in all fields of thought and knowledge or to maintain that a particular aspect of modernity should be 'islamicized' in order to make it relevant to the specific principles and values promoted by Islam since the Qur'ānic Revelation ...

The idea of devoting a chapter to belief and the shaping of the human mind has been forced upon me by the civil war in Algeria that has been continuing for ten years at the time of writing. The explicit 'arguments' used by the promoters of such a collective tragedy to 'legitimize' the assassination of so many innocent victims are related to 'Islam'. My point is not to discover the identities of the real perpetrators responsible for what are clearly crimes. This point is frequently discussed among the protagonists. The more urgent task is to identify the roots of the mental shift which has so adversely affected Algerian society. What I call the 'mental shift' is the subject of research which needs still to be defined and made acceptable to scholarship as currently applied to Islamic studies. The **irrational** dimension of human psychology, both on the individual and the collective level, is not incorporated, as such, in any programme of multi-disciplinary research. This means that contemporary societies are raising unprecedented issues, outside the scope of academic rationalization of individual and collective psychology. My contention is that all the events that have taken place in so-called Muslim societies cannot be 'explained' or made comprehensible on the basis of what is currently known, taught, claimed and disseminated about 'Islam'.

I promised to return to the subject of Qur'ānic axiology, of which there are two types with two different functions. The first can only be defined with the help of a comparative analysis of the prophetic discourse in its three manifestations: biblical, evangelical and Qur'ānic. It seeks to define the cognitive status of this discourse and its commanding functions of thought and conduct of believing protagonists in societies of the Book-book. This is what I have attempted in the work already mentioned. The second forms part of literature of which the corpus of belief consists. Several works by Ghazālī come into this category, especially '*The Jewels of the Qur'ān*', *Jawāhir al-Qur'ān*. It is an eloquent example of spiritual sublimation of the Qur'ān transformed into text, while being restored by faith to its theological status of the eternal, vivifying Word of God. It is no longer a question of historical reading of the verses in their first oral delivery, nor grammatical, lexicographical and historical exegesis for theological, legalalistic or simply linguistic ends, nor of projective readings in which volatile or militant subjectivities are scattered. It is a matter of the methodical bringing together of the totality of verses to identify fragments, places, themes, objectives and subtleties of meaning which must act as supports to spiritual exercises to bring the faithful nearer to God. It is this sort of school textbook which will sustain and guide the religious pedagogy of the founders and heads of brotherhoods of local saints entrusted with upholding an Islamic *ethos* of popular religion through the centuries. The selected verses from the *sūrat Yasīn, al-Ikhlāṣ, al-Fātiḥa, āyat al-kursī* (the verse of the Throne) are called jewels because they give to think, to meditate, to elevate the soul, to strengthen the conscious of the human subject. They are all most known, and most frequently recited and invoked in popular devotion down to the present day. We can thus dismiss speculative theologies and doctrinal confrontations that have been more or less infiltrated by procedures of syllogistic reasoning, rhetorical tournaments and abstract argumentation so remote from the oral culture and popular ritualization of believing. The well-known *Iḥyā' 'ulūm al-dīn* of the same al-Ghazālī is a more extensive work going in the same direction of stabilizing an orthodox believing deliberately oriented towards a spiritual Islam. The Malkite *fuqahā'* of Andalusia and the Maghreb condemned it, thus taking a step towards scholastic, ritualist and Maraboutic Islam which predominated until the emergence of *salafī* reformation and nationalist movements.

4.3.3 Psycho-linguistic Mechanisms

There remains a more crucial problem, at least in the perspective of our deconstructive approach, namely, that all the precedents for defining two rarely mentioned levels of construction and functioning of believing: the level of *competence* of the religious subject and that of its demonstrated *performances* or realizations. By borrowing the pair of concepts – *competence* and *performance* – used in generative grammar, I want to suggest that the generative relationship which connects the organizing representations of faith internalized by the religious subject and the conduct produced by this faith, are inseparable from the wider and more comprehensive relationship described by psycho-linguists and socio-linguists, that lies between competence and performance. This relationship has been raised in Islam to the rank of a theological dogma which assigns to the Arabic language a privileged status of the language in which the Word of God is embodied. We are aware of the protests and discomfort of Christians before Latin was substituted by the vernacular for celebrating mass. Just as the child produces from the ages of 7–8 years, phrases of a grammaticality which comply with learning skills already acquired, similarly, he begins at this same age, to imitate ritual conduct, postures of the body and formulas of integration into the believing community. This means that religious believing works simultaneously on the individual body by introducing it in powerful dispositions, the social body by enrolling it in the paradigmatic matrix of the corpus of belief and the configuration of the faculties of the mind (tensions between rationalizing consistencies, representations of the fideist imaginary, and drifts of credulity in a culture of the marvellous, constraint of places of memory which define the 'specific' identity of the community). The irreducible status of religious believing is often claimed by believers, but the psychoanalysis of this status is still in discussion. Whereas one finds similar functions in believing generated by the great, rousing ideologies in the context of modernity, believing and learning form a pair. They condition themselves mutually in all contexts. If we add that any community is, simultaneously, instituted by the memory which it constructs for itself of its qualifying tests in time and instituting by the imperatives of believing that which perpetuates it in its Tradition, we will have the most open and the most critical problematization of believing and the construction of the subject.

4.4. Shifting Without Surpassing Believing

In the article 'Croyance' already mentioned, P. Ricœur has given a concise, clear and at the same time critical exposé of the principal stages of a philosophy of belief, carefully distinguished from a theology of faith that is essentially Christian. I will retain for my purpose here the importance of the stages whose educational significance for the human mind has remained little or not yet known by Islamic thought (I consider that the Greek stage had been partially and inadequately known and implemented by mediaeval philosophers of Arabic expression. It remains to ask oneself what, in this implementation, pertains to the field of simple historical curiosity and what would perhaps present a philosophical relevance today for a redefinition of the cognitive status and the role of believing in the construct of the new emergent human subject).

There are the stage of English pragmatic philosophy with J. Locke (1632–1704) and David Hume (1711–1776); that of the critique of Kant (1724–1804), Hegel (1770–1831), Marx (1818–1883) and Nietzsche (1844–1900); that of Husserl's (1859–1938) phenomenology, enriched by M. Merleau-Ponty (1906–1961); that of the human and social sciences in which the more or less viable and promising success of emergent reasoning becomes established.

In his *Philosophy of Human Nature*, D. Hume deserved credit for shifting the question of belief from the field of philosophy of the voluntarist, rational subject to that of philosophical anthropology and a moral theory of conduct. The English concept *belief* receives a more positive and comprehensive extension than that of its corresponding French *croyance*:

> *Le belief voisine avec l'impression qui désigne l'événement constitutif de la vie de l'esprit avec l'aide qui dérive de l'impression, avec l'habitude ou coutume qui joue le rôle d'un principe général d'ordre, en particulier dans l'instauration des idées abstraites et des règles générales.* (P. Ricœur, op. cit.)

Kant also introduces a decisive step into the integration of faith-belief in the *Critique of Pure Reason* and practical reason. He shifts the point of relevance of faith towards the universal ethical imperative in order to free it from a dogmatic theology which establishes the existence of God with 'proofs' that are too weak. This task is pursued in a text whose title heralds a new horizon of intelligibility: *Religion in the Limits of the Simple Reason* (*La religion dans les limites de la simple raison*). The frontiers between religious faith administered by the doctrinal *Magisterium* of the Church and the faith-belief object of philosophical critique, become clearer, while rich possibilities of reciprocal exchanges and fertilization open up. The German concept of *glauben* covers the compound faith-belief, whereas French continues to separate them. Much later, still in Germany, Ernst Troeltsch integrates the challenges of philological historicism in a theology of '*la religion dans les limites de la conscience historique*' (cf. Pierre Gisel, L'institutionnalisation moderne de la religion, in *Revue de l'histoire des religions*, 1997, 2, pp. 153–82). It is interesting to observe the differences which thus become apparent between European intellectual sensibilities driven by the same spiritual and cultural given, but with different political practices; and one must observe the fate of these significant differences in the new political space of the European Union now in process of construction.

What happens to these philosophical advances on the status of faith-belief in our context of a 'sur-modernité' (to use the expression coined by M. Augé) which generates more and more disposable thought, like the gadgets sold in supermarkets? We saw how Christian theology takes control of this question. In Islamic contexts, there is not yet a rethinking of faith-belief and the construction of the subject, nor have functional alternatives been proposed to models of historical action advocated by indistinctly political and religious entrepreneurs. The masters of power display an Islamic believing that claims to be more 'enlightened' than that of their opponents who pretend to follow a more original, more authentic, more legitimating believing. However, the two types of protagonists are historically, theologically and spiritually at equal distance from a faith-belief re-examined in the perspectives and with the exigencies which I am proposing here. People who are receptive to this type of investigation amount to few isolated individuals, without the power of decision and without the means of intervention to take over, at least in relatively informed circles, the elementary contributions of the social sciences and the philosophical revival of the religious fact. When A. Touraine explains that the human subject of modernity is '*the secularized descendant of religion*' (*Critique de la modernité*, p. 249), Christians and lay people find issues to debate and motivations for sharing the strategies of the author aiming to elucidate the games and stakes of secularization in rivalry with the religion of yesterday and today. The same proposition is without historical, cultural and sociological significance in Islamic contexts that are dominated by fantasized forms of the political and religious believing, the status of the person, the individual citizen, the state, the community, civil society and several themes

I am considering in this book. The small minority of researchers, teachers, writers and artists who could adapt the proposition to the particular situations of their respective societies, constitute a socio-cultural enclave which communicates more easily with the audience of A. Touraine than with those whom it ought to reach first.

Let us recall briefly that western Christianity had been at the same time a source, a protagonist, a beneficiary and an opponent in the modern adventure of the human subject in Europe. This latter produced three fundamental novelties in the construction of the subject-protagonist, protagonist-subject of history: 1) the revolutionary fact conjugating the philosophical conquest of the independence of the subject; 2) the promotion and protection of this conquest by the institution of a legally constituted state with a civil society as contractual party (democratic pact founding the social bond); 3) involvement of a state and a bourgeois class of entrepreneurs in the economy. The national fact mobilizes the **civic faith** of individual citizens in an imaginary of progress made credible by scientific and technological conquests, thus substituting the hope of immediate liberation of the human condition in the eschatological hope of traditional religion. The postulate of **rational man**, sustained by classical metaphysics, operates concurrently with theologies already heavily influenced by widepsread Greek philosophy, illustrated by the social sciences which have accompanied the strategies of expansion and development of bourgeois conquerors taken over by protagonists of liberal economy on global scale.

We know in what brief historical circumstances and under what pressures of ideology of development/underdevelopment, free world/communist world/third world, the revolutionary fact, the national fact and the postulate of rational man were introduced in non-European cultures regulated by other religions. We would need a new Max Weber, benefiting from all the theoretical discussions raised by the famous thesis on the links of cause to effect between Protestantism and the rise of modern Europe, to set out to analyse in a wider and better documented historical and anthropological perspective, the connections between religious fact, as source of **ideation** and tool of production of history on the one hand, and on the other hand, the imperatives of development according to competing models of 'scientific socialism' and liberal capitalism from 1945 to 1989. Material as well as intellectual modernity, long dominated by the desire for power of the two superpowers, has still not been subjected, outside its places of birth and continual deployment, to adequate appropriations to make cultural and religious traditions fruitful in depth or deliver them from their obsolete ideological burdens. In this historical and philosophical perspective, it can be said that neither Christian thought, nor modernity with universalist assertion have risen to the dignity of privilege which current opinion attaches to the religious and secular axes of the European exception. And it cannot even be said today that liberal philosophy, triumphant since the collapse of its Marxist rival, shows more eagerness to take charge of tragedies caused outside Europe and in Europe itself by a modernity which contents itself with preaching about the conditions of its passage to post-modernity, as it has done since the nineteenth century on its mission of transmission of a so-called humanist civilization of progress to the colonies.

It can be understood that contemporary philosophy refuses or confesses effectively the impossibility of thinking of the truth as being ontologically, logically and conceptually based or founded. It ventures to defend the idea that truth remains a fundamental question, because all the work of the human and social sciences – to say nothing of upheavals introduced by biology in the very definition of the human person – tends to dissolve all the fundamentals used by theologies and philosophies in all traditions of thought. Henceforth, neither believing, nor its most defended modality, faith, can claim to rest on indisputable fundamentals as they did easily before the passage to an epistemology that rebelled against all **foundationalist** thought and hence, necessarily dependant on hermeneutical strategies. Dissolution of the foundations, relativity of values and subjectivity of interpretations are so many constraints which orient thought towards the production of **disposable** explanations, ideas and theories which last the time of a political majority installed in power by a popular sovereignty, itself volatile, changing with the passions of the moment when it is invited to cast a vote. Backward peoples and primitive cultures are required to convert to this representative, elective democracy while they are experiencing a **serious crisis of legitimacy that affects all the domains and levels of believing**. There is a belief in what works perfectly, that is to say produces all the expected results within a given period of time. This pragmatic believing is gradually invading faith in even the most remote regions or societies in the world. Can resistance to the continuous disintegration of the subject organize itself into what sociologists redefine under the old name of 'mystical' that which simultaneously encompasses the experience of great witnesses of spiritual life and a new problematization of the subject? Here is a programme definition which, if taken seriously, would bring about a redistribution of urgency in the research programmes of the social sciences and a more relevant radicalisation of their theoretical constructs:

> *La mystique en tous ses états, en tous ses âges, en toutes ses amplitudes, oeuvre patiemment à l'érosion du régime référentiel – elle ne convoque Dieu en toute créature que pour anéantir l'un en l'autre, au bénéfice seul d'un sujet enfin habilité ...; il convient de déchiffrer en tout mouvement mystique, l'instance de désagrégation du sacré, d'extinction d'un principe d'économie où le rapport au divin et à l'institution qui prétendait l'énoncer au monde, donnait à toute opération sa valeur propre – péché ou perle de salut*[1] [D. Vidal, in *Penser le sujet*, op. cit., p. 131].

It remains for us to examine the very possibility of '*a subject*

1. I could not reach a relevant, immediately intelligible translation of this subversive definition of the '*mystic in all its substantive dimensions, all its ages ...*' Actually, throughout this book, I have experienced, suffered from the impossibility to jump from Arabic to French and English logospheres, and vice versa. I hope the readers will share with me this enlightening experience.

finally habilitated' and if the answer is positive, we must verify the relevance of avenues offered at the beginning of the twenty-first century, to the emergence of such a subject. As always, we must evaluate the gaps which, in Islamic contexts, will further delay the full participation in the global work of authorization of the subject, which means his emancipation from the mechanical solidarities imposed by the Islamic fact in its current expressions since 1945.

4.5. A Subject Finally Habilitated

It is clear, from all the preceding analyses, that religious believing, even in the form of a faith with the support of divine enlightenment, does not escape from the constraining impact of historical change and social priorities on the genesis and deployment of the human subject. This is also the first time in history of thought that the subject is in a much better position to emancipate himself from alienating forms of knowledge which are no more than mystifying, mythologizing, transcendantalising, sacralizing mechanisms made possible by credulity confused with believing and faith. We can thus understand the evocation of a subject that is finally promoted to the capacity for self-determination enlightened by self-criticism. This 'finally' cannot mean the jubilation of a hope that is totally and definitively fulfilled after it has been so greatly nurtured and diversely expressed, either through traditional eschatological discourse or the more recent scientific imaginary of progress, yet so continuously denied by concrete history. Deconstructive reason cannot be compatible with new messianic expectations. It rather measures the long errancy, detours, ruses, failures, perseverance, ephemeral success and illusory solutions, as well as the decisive conquests of reason to free itself from chains and illusions which every time it has constantly recreated, reassessed and reincarnated in 'reformed' institutions. This recurrent mythological activity of reason would not have been possible without a deeply rooted psychological disposition for believing. Instructed by the denial regularly inflicted by history on the certitudes grounded in religious as well as 'scientific' knowledge, reason tries new procedures, new hypotheses and new critical means in order to rehabilitate the continuously failing and renascent subject. The claim of religions to rehabilitate the spiritual vocation of the human person in an attempt to achieve the Absolute of God, after the obvious failure of modern secular ideologies of hope, illustrates the repeated activation of reason on the same uncritical beliefs and collective imaginaries.

It is true that we are just beginning to rethink in the same time the cognitive status of traditional religions and the limits of scientific knowledge. We dot that under the pressure for many, the total indifference of many others, while millions of peoples reduced to penury and excluded from the increasing comfort provided by the new economies, are either driven to despair or to a reactivated hope and belief that only traditional religions or even new sects can liberate them or alienate more dangerously their mind. The World Bank has just published a detailed report on the various social and psychological consequences of the increasing effects of poverty on human dignity through the world (see *The voice of the poor*, 2000). The inquiry covers 60 countries and 60,000 individuals who have expressed their own experience of poverty: dislocation of families, selling of children, alienation of abandoned women with small children, absence of social security and isolation of the élites who are more oriented towards the prosperous societies of the West than to solidarity with their own people. Entrepreneurs invest their money outside their own countries because many regimes do not secure the required stability and confidence for important economic projects. The *Realpolitik* of the richest and most powerful nation-states are doing more to unbalance the situation than prevent or correct it.

Under such pressures and political indifference, there is no place for positive functions of religious believing. Rather, religious references are used by many social and political protagonists to legitimize violence against all those groups and decision-makers who preach democracy without democratic culture and modernity without modern intellectual tools and frameworks of constructive criticism. In this perspective, the theoretical discussions about the elimination and return or the rehabilitation of the human subject are totally irrelevant for all the poorest societies neglected by their own states, abandoned by their own élites and deprived of their own historical memories and cultural traditional systems of values. This does not mean that it is useless for those thinkers who contribute from the viewpoint of each cultural tradition to the protection and emancipation of the human condition facing new threats and challenges through this phase of globalization.[1]

My ambition in presenting the evolution of believing in Islamic contexts is precisely to show how the contemporary philosophical trends and the practice of social sciences are more closely related to the specific concerns of western hegemonic societies than to the urgent needs of the marginalized cultures, the dominated societies, the excluded peoples. The paths indicated by liberal American philosophy (Ch. Taylor, Mc Intyre, R. Rorty, J. Rawls) certainly provoke interesting questions relating to practical issues such as justice, multi-cultural education, immigration, cultural clashes, human rights and oppressive regimes ... But the hegemonic position of the USA in relation to the rest of the world including the European Union, is not yet accepted as a decisive issue for scientific research and the philosophical quest for meaning, and not only for the world political, economic, financial order. Research and thinking are conducted as if the rest of the word has either to follow, to learn and contribute to the solutions, the results agreed upon in the hegemonic role of western civilization, or to remain unconcerned and doomed to decay and domination. It is here that, for many Muslims, the doctrine of *jihād* compensates by its political mobilization the weakness of its theology. This important aspect of the ongoing globalization leads us to the question of Violence, Sacred and Truth. Undoubtedly, violence is reaching an unprecedented intensity and scale in all contemporary

1. Catholic and Protestant Christianity might have more opportunities and intellectual resources to enhance their spiritual message for a culture of peace and politics for hope. But both should invest more decisive efforts to adapt their theology to the undisputable clarifications and horizons of intelligibility proposed by what I call the emerging critical reason.

societies, rich and poor, highly developed and underdeveloped, democratic and oppressive. How this phenomenon is related to the disintegration and the re-composition of believing? Does it favour a positive reassessment of traditional religions, or does it accelerate the rejection of religious references more than it ever did in the time of the 'religious wars' supported by the sanctifying doctrines on the 'just war' or 'holy war'? As far as Islam is concerned, we have shown in several essays that it is more threatened in its spiritual future than Christianity, because very few thinkers are devoting relevant intellectual and scientific attention to limiting the negative impact of the large political manipulations imposed by the ongoing struggles for power in all Muslim societies. The will to power is more than ever delaying, disturbing and falsifying the critical quest for an uncertain and unreliable contingent meaning.

THREE

Logocentrism and Religious Truth in Islamic Thought

The Example of al-I'lām bi-Manāqib al-Islām

It is impossible in a discussion to bring in the actual things discussed: we use their names as symbols instead of them; and therefore we suppose that what follows in the names, follows in the things as well, just as people who calculate suppose in regard to their counters. But the two cases (names and things) are not alike. For names are finite and so is the sum-total of formulae, while things are infinite in number.

Aristotle, *On Sophistical Refutations*

Surely in this there is a sign for men of understanding.

Qur'ān, 16:67

It would be impossible to tackle exhaustively such a difficult subject in the short space of the essay that follows. The main aim is to establish a point of departure for long-term research with the ultimate objective of making possible a new reading of the Qur'ān, and more generally all the major texts of classical Islamic thought. It will no longer be considered sufficient to highlight the documentary – and, in some cases, literary – value of a text through a discussion of its content and modes of expression in order to make them comprehensible to a modern reader. This task, while still necessary but restricted to explicit statements, will be extended to include analysis of the **implicit** information contained in any discourse. This is a step towards an integral history, since an understanding of the implicit content will be more informative as to the cognitive structures and the way in which they function in a given cultural context. History, sociology, ethnology, anthropology and linguistics share and exchange their areas of interest and their methodologies; with the mind following its bent for an interactive disciplinary science.

The text chosen for this first essay is an *Exposé of the Eminent Qualities of Islam (al-I'lām bi-manāqib al-islām)* by Abū-l-Ḥasan al-'Āmirī (d. 381/992) a philosopher to whom an earlier study was devoted.[1] The reasons for this choice will become apparent. By way of introduction, it would be useful to provide some clarifications on the importance of logocentrism. Let us concentrate on the predominant ideas that will direct the reading of the *I'lām*.

1. Writing, Text, Reading

The many meanings of the ancient Greek word *logos* include one to which philosophy has given a long and eventful history, that of the Word as the reasoned articulation of thought. Arabic perfectly expresses this ambivalent unity with *nuṭq* meaning word that is articulated, therefore intelligible. This link between word and reason is confirmed in *manṭiq*: logic, or domain of reasoned discourse; and in *nāṭiq*: speaking and rational (being).[2]

Thus, all the initial difficulties of expression (speaker), acceptance (hearer) and the search for meaning (thinking subject) are to be

1. The conquest of Happiness according to Abū-l-Ḥasan al-'Āmirī, in *Essais sur la pensée Islamique*, 3rd ed., Paris, 1984, which contains the essential bibliographical details.
2. See also the concept of the 'spoken' [*verbum* or verb] developed by Thomas Aquinas: cf. E. Gilson, *Linguistique et philosophie*, J. Vrin, 1969, p. 18.

found concentrated in the concept of *logos/nuṭq*. Aristotle reflected at length on these difficulties, and there are many references to them throughout his philosophical discourse. '*With him, the logos ceases to be prophetic; the product of human art and a tool for social intercourse, it is defined as dialectical discourse, whose highest form will be at best the professorial discourse (the one which pays least, though some, attention to the conduct of the listener).*'[1]

This substitution of professorial discourse for the **prophetic logos** was to heavily influence thought and the quest for meaning, especially in the Middle Ages. There can be no question here of describing a lengthy and meandering process whose decisive moments cannot even be identified with desirable precision.[2] The main fact, from our point of view, is that despite triumphant professorial discourse based on rigid conceptualism (Aristotle's ten categories and Porphyry's five voices served to classify all realities, including God) and formal dialectic, the Word of God continued to forcefully raise everywhere, the mysteries of the origin, function and purpose of the plenary *logos*. The resulting confrontation was replaced by efforts at harmonization and also generated polemics and apologias, eventually leading to intellectual rifts. The argument centered on a cluster of conceptual dichotomies amply covered by the historian of ideas: reason/faith, essence/existence, soul/body, spirit/matter, heaven/earth, understanding/feeling, Good/Evil, incorruptible/corruptible, etc. As a result, for some hundreds of years, the physical world, and writings about it, were interpreted on the basis of the categories accepted by all who (consciously or

1. P. Aubenque, *Le problème de l'être chez Aristote*, P.U.F., 1952, p. 115.
2. It is true that even in the Christian West, the role of, say, Thomas Aquinas, is viewed differently by historians with a variety of initial options. In the case of Islam, the orientation imposed on thought and language by the movement still called (for lack of a better term) *Mu'tazilism* remains poorly defined, despite the existence of studies – new in many respects – from J. Van Ess and others. The work of Fārābi, for example, has not yet been satisfactorily edited in its entirety: See the examination of two texts edited by M. Mahdī, in Arabica 1971/2. See also Hans Daiber's recent *Bibliography of Islamic Philosophy*, 2 vols, Leiden, Brill 1999.

unconsciously) were under Aristotelian influence as a universal, immutable and infallible given. There was a strong awareness of the difficulties that exist in describing the world, let alone Being, and thus in progressing from the morphological and syntactic articulation to the ontological order. Within the Arabic language, however, the route that had led Aristotle from the linguistic basis of the Greek tongue to the categories of thought was not really retraced. There was a transposition of ideas, but they were not approached or arrived at independently.[1]

This is the route that philosophers, and more generally historians of ideas, are compelled to retrace today, in order to become simultaneously aware of the content of a given discourse as an act of knowledge and of our own situation, as readers, in relation to that discourse. To put it another way, if we want to make use of a document dealing with the history of ideas, we have to resurrect the relationship between writing/text/reading in all its complexity. Any text, once written, escapes from its author and takes on a life of its own, whose richness or poverty, expansion or desiccation, oblivion or revival, will henceforth depend on its readers. Only rarely does the reader comprehend a text in all the meanings intended by the author. Very often it is something he recites in order to free himself from his own internal discourse. In this case the text is being exploited as an excuse, rather than used properly as a channel of information. It becomes the setting for an intense dialectic between reader and author. The relationship is complicated by the fact that every author is originally a reader, while not every reader is an author. All these movements, exchanges and interactions help determine the life of the *logos*, in other words the mind embodying itself in a language and giving birth to many

---

1. This judgement may be nuanced by a closer study of texts such as *Kitāb al-ḥurūf de Fārābi,* (ed. M. Mahdī, Beirut, 1970) and the *Radd 'ala-l-manṭiqiyyīn* by Ibn Taymiyya, Bombay, 1949. It should be noted that the mystical discourse has poetic status and, as such, requires a different approach from the one applied here to 'scientific', logical discourse. It would make a most interesting study to evaluate the linguistic gap between these two discourses which were vying for supremacy in the period covered here.

languages. Each language, in turn, can remain at the stage of the spoken word or extend itself into writing.[1]

The following is a diagram representing all these distinctions and relationships:

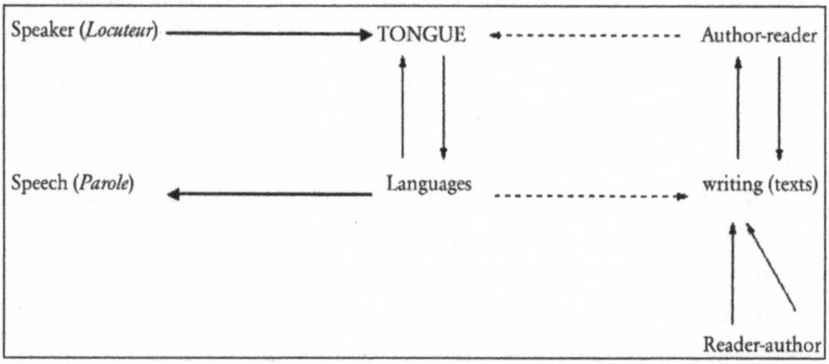

It can be seen that the speaker – especially when he is a prophet – can draw on the spoken language in order to enrich the breadth of expression of his own language, whose modifications resound back into the spoken language as a shared heritage. Authors – especially poets and great thinkers – do much the same thing.

This complex of interconnections occurs within what could be called the logocentric enclosure.[2] In its most general sense, this

1. The distinction between the spoken word and writing is crucial for any reading that seeks the full meaning of a text that has been fixed in writing after being uttered and transmitted orally. Plato distinguished clearly between the logical word, judging and thinking in positive and negative terms (contradiction and third possibilities excluded), and the artistic statement, the 'supreme degree of inextricability', simultaneously imposing the possible and impossible, the imaginary and the real, the imminent and the transcendent, being and non-being, etc., in time and space. See *Sophiste*, analyzed by J. Brun in *Platon et l'Académie*, P.U.F., 1960, pp. 57–63. Rhetorical writing accentuates the rigid character of the logical word and can divert poetic writing from its primary function which is to suggest the plenary character of the living word. Cf. E. Gilson, op. cit., pp. 239 et seq. Saint Augustine's impassioned question (p. 243) can also be asked of the entire Qur'ān, so variably written and manipulated by readers of all sorts.
2. On the application of this concept to Western thought, see J. Derrida, *De la grammatologie*, Editions de Minuit, 1967.

expression designates the inability of reason to manifest itself either to itself or to another without the intermediary of language in an internal, external or written word. This does not mean that the limits of language coincide exactly with the limits of thought. Thought remains a free activity, permanently able to extend the scope of language and increase its effectiveness. This is still happening today in the various branches of learning, as it did at the birth of Greek thought, or of modern science. It is the privilege of a contemporary historian to be in a position to help attempt[1] a departure from this sort of historically constituted enclosure, after exploring and describing the successive distances covered by it up to the present day. This is precisely the sort of methodological and epistemological attitude that we would like to see prevailing in the study of classical Islamic thought. The object would be to put an end to the repetition of a given form of writing after making a detailed study of its limitations, describing its internal mechanisms, evaluating its role and tracing its correlations. The analysis should show the extent to which, in classical literature, the **thing**, as Aristotle says, is just as much not signified as signified; and how, as a result, the realities of life, life itself, are transmuted into rhetoric. The ultimate objective of this work is to free the mind of these rhetorical figures, not simply to imprison it in some new type of enclosure, but to lead it back to a conscious desire for difference as the essential starting point of any quest for truth, along with rejection of the explicit or implicit repetition of the values and intellectual procedures born, amplified and perpetuated in a given cultural tradition.[2]

It is easy to show how the whole of Islamic thought,[3] in its

---

1. In fact a total departure is out of the question, as in practice would mean inaugurating a different itinerary: This is a feature of our condition as speaking, political and historical animals. All we can do is strive to keep the mind's eye fixed on the near side and the far side of language.
2. Cf. G. Deleuze, *Différence et répétition*, P.U.F., 1968. It is necessary to grasp the concept of difference as it is elaborated in this major work.
3. See M. Arkoun, Introduction to Classical Islamic Thought, in *Essais*, and *La pensée arabe*, P.U.F., 5th edition, 1997.

anxiety to represent fully and faithfully both revealed truth and the sapiential[1] Greco-Persian tradition very rapidly walled itself up in a logocentric enclosure principally delineated by the decisive concept of *aṣl* (source, root, origin, foundation). *Aṣl* means referring from the outset to the **Inaugural difference** (the revealed given) which must be endlessly consulted to verify the legitimacy of any human endeavour and of the discourse that expresses it. But the mind loses touch with the **difference** when engaged in the search for logical coherence. Consequently, while maintaining the requirement for a return to the roots (*uṣūl*), reason has, in practice, enclosed *ijtihād* within the rigid confines of a scholastic methodology (*uṣūl al-fiqh*). Al-Ghazālī, who devoted much thought to this situation, defines it perfectly as follows:

> *'Observe that which is brought down to you from your Lord and follow no other masters besides Him' (Qur'ān, VII, 2). In its obvious sense (ẓāhir), this verse tells us to refer only to the Book. But the Book itself has indicated that we should follow the Tradition (sunna), this being unanimous agreement (ijmāʿ), while the Book itself is based on reasoning through analogy (qiyās). All of that is definitively revealed; that is what is to be followed, to the exclusion of the utterances of creatures.*[2]

Any attempt to know the truth (*al-ḥaqq*) therefore consists in practice of total submission (*taqlīd*) to the authority of the Qur'ānic text whose linguistic pre-eminence is inevitably confounded with the transcendence of God's will. The confusion reaches its lowest point in the work of a *mujtahid* who, following the line spelt out by al-Ghazālī, deploys endless ingenuity in connecting profane reality with revealed Truth by procedures of analysis, reduction

1. The description 'sapiential' is more exact than 'philosophical', for *falsafa* had developed much more as a body of learning than a quest for truth. See M. Arkoun, *Contribution à l'étude de l'humanisme arabe au 4e/10e siècle*, J. Vrin, 1982 (abbreviated to *Humanisme* in later quotations).
2. *Al-Muṣṭafā*, II, p. 122.

and reasoning rooted entirely in the confines of logocentrism. The *mujtahid* misleads himself and the faithful by perceiving reality exclusively through the prism of the literal meaning of a Text held to represent the original, pre-existing Word. The Mu'tazilites were aware of the problem and tried to overcome it, but the notion of an Arabic language sanctified by the fact that God had chosen it as the vehicle by which to address humankind was too powerful. Henceforth, correct usage of the grammatical and lexical rules of Arabic is sufficient to ensure the permanent validity of the meanings.[1] The difference between the independent scholar (*mujtahid*) and the reproducer (*muqallid*), now consists only of the former's claim to provide proof (*ḥujaj*) of the veracity of his opinions, the latter simply receiving commands without claiming any justification (*bilā kayf*.) Both, in fact, recognize the primacy of God's Word, while allowing themselves to enter into human, more or less rational, discourse on the subject of this Word. Thanks to the distinction between imminence and transcendence of language that escapes him, al-Ghazālī thinks he can refute the assertion of the *ḥaṣwiyya* and the *ta'līmiyya* in claiming that 'the way to knowledge of the true is imitation (*taqlīd*)'.[2]

Ijtihād is a partial response to the perception of the need for reasoning in order to adapt to the regulating and constraining principles of Greek science. That is why the science of the sources-foundations (*'ilm al-uṣūl*) is a setting in which the disciplines of logic, linguistics, theology and ethics – studied essentially in the aftermath of the *falsafa* – converge. But the faculty of reason has to pay for the satisfaction obtained from these exercises by accepting the role of handmaid to the revealed Text; its sole function is to shape, bend and systematize reality in accordance with the ideal meanings it recognizes[3] in God's 'signs'.

1. Hence the 'linguistic' introductions to works of *uṣūl al-fiqh*.
2. See *al-Muṣṭafā*, II, p. 123. On *ḥaṣwiyya* and *ta'līmiyya*, see H. Laoust, *Les schismes dans l'Islam*, Paris, 1965.
3. This is the true meaning of the verb *'aqala* in the Qur'ān, as we will try to explain in an essay currently in preparation. It conveys the idea the mind 'reflects' – in the literal sense – truths that are already given or revealed, not those that might be found at the end of a gradual search,

The singularities that abound in the world, in history and human life, must all be linked to the Origin, incorporated into the images of the Same, the Identical, the Analogous. At this level of operation, the rationality deployed in the religious sciences and Aristotelian-Platonic corpus become synonymous: each celebrates a regressive learning pivoted on Imitation as accurate reproduction (*taqlīd*) of the Archetypes supplied by the Revelation or Ideas. This type of learning is appropriate to the mythical consciousness that prevailed in the Islamic cultural context until the nineteenth century.[1]

From the observations made so far, the following characteristics of logocentrism can be listed in the Arab-Islamic case:

1. All activity involving thought is ruled by the dogmatic notion of a reason being capable of advancing towards the Supreme Being (God), and thus in affinity with the eternal True-Good-Beautiful. The ultimate motivation of all thought is not scientific in the modern sense, but aesthetic, ethical and emotional. By defining man as a creature gifted with intelligence, by appointing him 'the Vicar of God on earth' (*ḫalīfat Allah fī-l-arḍi*), the Qur'ān (following Judaeo-Christian thinking and in accordance with the Greek philosophical tradition) establishes that sovereignty of the subject and that identification of the Ego, which will receive a more 'methodical' formulation in the Cartesian Cogito.[2] This ego, invested with a divine mission and thus promised to immortality, is to supervise the faculties of the mind in their function of re-cognition (*ya'qil*) (in dreams, take-offs of imagination, rational speculation, meditation) of the *True-Good-Beautiful* as opposed to the *false-bad-ugly*.

---

let alone a speculative quest. The intelligence is focused on what is already stated and/or experienced, not on the as yet unformulated and/or yet to be experienced.

1. See M. Arkoun, *Humanisme*, pp. 366–9.
2. Descartes is invoked for historical and critical reasons: historical, to indicate the parallels between mental structures in the Arab-Islamic and Latin-Christian settings; critical, to outline the limits of the enclosure within which sovereign reason has been deployed both in the 'Orient' and in the 'West'.

2. The function of Reason/Intelligence (*'aql*) illuminated by intellect, itself God's creature, or possessed by ideas, is the recognition of the One-True-Original-Being, the original Creator.[1] This is what explains the interrelation between metaphysics, theology, ethics and jurisprudence, and eventually their convergence. The re-cognition of these values, followed by their communication, take place within and through a language based on common sense, that uses constant references to the usual, the sameness, the common sense, to guarantee the conformity of opinions and proposed solutions to the axioms of Reason along with techniques of representation and expression. All these discursive operations help to keep the discourse within a well-worn path along which intelligibility is immediate for everyone.
3. The modes of operation of Reason in its task of 'climbing back to the foundations'[2] consist essentially of stating relationships of identity, analogy, resemblance, implication or opposition from the starting point of universal definitions, primary substances and immutable essences.
4. In order to acquire the means to the desired end – the definitive edification of a science functioning as a security system for the human being – reason raises simple empirical data to the level of the transcendental by projecting the 'dreamed' structures[3] of the transcendental into them. This is particularly apparent in physics, anthropology and cosmology.[4]

Among dogmatic theologians (*mutakallimūn*) and jurists (*fuqahā'*) whose main aim is precisely to actualize the mark of the transcendental in the concrete world and history,

1. Each of these denominations, both current in mediaeval literature, corresponds to a specific language and religious sensibility. They have been brought together here to emphasize the concept of Reason mobilized by the idea of Oneness and unity as opposed to multiplicity.
2. A felicitous expression coined by J. Berque.
3. Dreamed in the sense used by G. Bachelard.
4. See M. Arkoun, *L'humanisme arabe*, Chapter VII.

reason resorts to the most arbitrary procedures in pursuit of its objective. It rejects embarrassing facts as unorthodox and creates axioms along such lines as '*a Companion of the Prophet cannot lie*'; '*the (Muslim) Community cannot be in agreement about an error*'; '*everything is true during the period of prophecy* (*nubuwwa*); *the Companions know every detail of the life and teaching of the Prophet*'; '*a contradiction between the Qur'ān and the Sunna can only result from the alteration of a text by human agency*'; and so on.[1]

5. The religion, culture and the state that constructed within the logocentric confines, become its supports and constitute regulating and unifying forces. These forces tend to predominate over the forces of differentiation: ethnic differences, heresies and the customs, beliefs and folk traditions of minority groups, excessively independent individuals, etc. Instead of favouring attempts to find a way out of the enclosure, religion and culture are transformed into codes and institutions that apply themselves to the defence of an 'official' legitimacy. The quest for meaning is then reduced to a simple repetition (*taqlīd*) of meanings already established and assimilated into a specific type of discourse.

6. The speaking individual becomes free of the constraints and limits of logocentrism only through the experiences of love and death.[2] For it is through love and the confrontation of death that a feeling of a genuinely ineffable truth is created, one that asserts itself in an internal, singular and incommensurate space and that cannot be projected into the linguistic space coded and defined by the rules of grammar and the resources of the lexicon. This is the setting for the ultimate struggle between a spontaneous

---

1. This attitude still persists, see G. H. Juynboll, *The Authenticity of the Tradition Literature*, Brill, 1969.
2. Art, through which humanity expresses '*the stubborn desire to endure*' (*le dur désir de durer* of Apollinaire), could be added to the list. However, the status of artistic activities in Islam will have to be explored when more is known about the various branches (painting, music, architecture and so on).

internal discourse, coinciding fleetingly with the feeling of a different, original truth, and the external, conventional discourse which, to ensure effective communication, enforces the mode of repetition. In Islam, as in the Judaeo-Christian tradition, this struggle is illustrated by the examples of prophets, mystics and certain poets on one side, by the 'logocentrists' – theologians, philosophers, jurists, moralists and essaysists – on the other. It is a distinction that throws light on the meaning and scope of all the conflicts that punctuate the history of religious and philosophical thought.

It is now appropriate to attempt corroboration of all these observations by showing how the discourse of *al-I'lām* is inserted in the logocentric enclosure whose characteristics have just been defined. By the same token, it can be understood why the modern mind may approve of al-'Āmirī's objective – making a strict formulation of religious truth – and why it can nevertheless serve this objective anew only by moving into another mental space.[1]

2. Islam as Eminent Truth

Let us begin by identifying the role of historical circumstances in the conception and the writing of the work. Like most intellectuals of his time, al-'Āmirī sought to display his abilities as a means of getting close to the high rulers. It is thus very probable that he composed the *i'lām* at the request of a Samanid vizier. The dedication expands on Abu Naṣr's[2] love of wisdom and the high regard in which he held all that '*throws light on the superiority of*

1. Something that many Muslims, Jews and Christians still do not realize. That is why we are striving to promote a problematic that goes beyond the mere pleasure of erudition to make history fulfil its cathartic function, that of freeing minds from the functional, but subjective representations of the past, and thus making it possible to focus in detail on all the factors contributing to any production of meaning.
2. On the identity of this Abū Naṣr, see the editor's introduction to the *I'lām*, p. 13.

the original true religion (*al-milla al-ḥanīfiyya*) *over other religions*' (p. 74). The work is thus a product of the important cultural movement then under way in Buḫāra, earning its rulers the approval of Muqaddasī.[1] In fact, al-ʿĀmirī never departs from a serene and 'objective' tone. Although working on a theme then current in polemical and apologetic literature, he always retains the measured tone, the moderation and sense of rational investigation, that identify philosophical writing. He capitulates neither to the militant fervour of Shīʿite missionaries (*duʿāt*) nor to the simplistic dogmatism of the Sunnī sermonizers (*wuʿʿāẓ*). These are precisely the merits which make the *Iʿlām* a privileged document in which the relatively emancipated reason of the *falāsifa* is brought to bear in an investigation of religious truth. It represents a valuable test case on the level of effectiveness of philosophical reason in dealing with the complex problems posed by the clash of several religions, each one claiming with equal assurance to have the monopoly of Truth.[2]

As we stated above, every text puts the analyst in front of a type of writing practised by the author and a type of reading chosen by the reader or receiver. Our own reading of the *Iʿlām* will consist in finding the constituent elements and mechanisms of such writing, then with the principles of reading such product.

2.1. *Philosophical Writing in the Iʿlām*

Modern studies in stylistics draw a very enlightening distinction between collective style or writing and individual style. In the sociology of literature, the concept that corresponds to collective style is that of the collective or trans-individual subject.

1. See A. Miquel, *La géographie humaine du monde musulman*, Mouton, 1967, pp. 316 sqq.
2. Which is why what we are saying about the *Iʿlām* could apply, with appropriate adjustments, to all of the immense literature inspired by the Islamic-Jewish-Christian polemic. Studies in this area seem generally unaware of the reasons for deconstructing the systems of thought that govern apologetic and heresiographical discourse, and are generally unaware of the method for doing so.

> *Of course there is no question ... of a collective consciousness situated outside individual consciousnesses, and there is no consciousness other than that of individuals. It is just that some individual consciousnesses in relationship with one another are not intersubjective, but intrasubjective, and thus constitute the subject of all thought and action of a social and cultural nature ... It is always important to remember the fundamental assertion of genetic, structuralist sociology that the signifying (which means collective) coherence of works of art, far from being more individualistic than that of the thinking or writings of average individuals, achieves a much higher degree of socialization.*[1]

Reference to a collective subject is all the more relevant in the case of the *I'lām* in that it is not a work of art at all,[2] but a text aimed at making a coherent formulation of representations and convictions broadly shared by a vast community. Al-'Āmirī's text looks very like '*an act of historic solidarity*',[3] a résumé of the cultural and religious values of an expanding social group, the group of minds educated in philosophical *adab* and convinced that the philosophical sciences would make it possible to bypass all the divisions that were splitting Muslim polity.

As will be seen, the writing of which the *I'lām* is an example, draws on a vocabulary and cultural models already constituted, assimilated and collected in manuals which provide clear evidence of its degree of expansion. The *Mafātīh al-'ulūm*, the *Fihrist* and the *Kitāb al-ṣinā'atayn*, are not merely collections of terminologies, definitions and technical disciplines to be consulted individually by specialists; they reveal a new approach to language and culture by an entire generation. This approach aimed at achieving a

1. Goldman, L., *Marxisme et sciences humaines*, Gallimard, Idées, 1970, pp. 104 and 110. On the concept of collective style, see P. Guiraud, *Essais de stylistique*, Klincksiek, 1969.
2. While L. Goldman's position on the subject of artistic creation is much disputed, the subject and aims of the *i'lām* make it possible remain on the sidelines of that debate.
3. According to R. Barthès's definintion in *Degré zéro de l'écriture*, Editions du Seuil, 1953, p. 24.

broader coherence between lines of thought, cultural traditions and social forces that, in the fifty years between 350 and 400, had fallen into virulent conflict.[1] Like many other works of the period written by run-of-the-mill authors, the *I'lām* expresses (and up to a point achieves) this widely felt need for consistency. In the process, it makes it possible to confirm the predominance of collective, over individual, subject and style. Here as in many other cases, it would be erroneous to think in terms of 'originality' and 'personal' input. All that can be attributed specifically to al-'Āmirī is the organization of discourse, a type of comparison between current ideas and problems, a way of ordering values and solutions often mentioned in other contexts. By doing this, he maintains many 'intrasubjective' relations not only with his contemporaries, but with all Arabic-speaking Muslims who can absorb directly, and who themselves practise, the type of writing we have been discussing.[2]

To illustrate these observations, we are going to examine the usage the author makes of (1) a lexicon, and (2) a culture.

2.2. *Usage of a Lexicon*

The editor had the excellent idea of assembling a detailed index of the technical terms used in the book. In total, it lists 672 occurrences of words or expressions in alphabetical order.[3] Examination of the resulting vocabulary suggests a number of observations.

First and foremost, one is tempted to assess the level of opposition or of harmonization achieved between the two tendencies even mentioned in the title. A scientific statement (*al-i'lām*) on the subject of religion (Islam). In fact, the vocabulary of scientific-philosophical significance and the vocabulary of religious significance are fairly evenly balanced. Among the terms most

1. Even in the twentieth century, Muslims still attribute currency and intellectual credence to works which, like the *i'lām*, pursue and attain a certain level of consistency. See the editor's conclusion.
2. See M. Arkoun, *Humanisme*, pp. 161 sqq.
3. It has been shown why listing roots in alphabetical order is preferable in this kind of abstract: see 'Contribution à l'étude du lexique de l'éthique musulmane, in *Essais sur la pensée Islamique*, op. cit., pp. 319 sqq.

frequently employed are *'aql* (40 occurrences), *'āqil* (14), *'ilm* (46) and *ṣinā'a* (in the sense of scientific technique) (49). In comparison, the terms used by al-'Āmirī, are *dīn, adyān* (43+55*), milla, milal* (17), *'ibāda* (32*), i'tiqād, i'tiqādāt* (24), etc. The opposition between reason and faith, science and religion, is not pertinent, because it is secondary. It arose after the expansion of philosophical culture in the context of the Qur'ān (or the Gospel in the case of Christianity); by means of differentiated discourses (mystical, theological, fundamentalist [*uṣūlī*], philosophical), it expresses an intrinsic opposition between the Qur'ānic disourse of mythical structure[1] and logocentric discourse or, in other words, between metaphoric, symbolic expression, rich in all sorts of literary suggestive forms, themes, meaning, and conceptual formulation linked to a rational meaning.

To show how this opposition works, here is an analysis of two conceptual nuclei around which all the other terms listed in the index are clustered. By conceptual nucleus, we mean a group of words used to express a consistent theme in a given text. It implies that the links created between the words have arisen in a new cultural context and owe nothing to etymology.[2] For example, *'aql, ṣinā'ā, siyāsa, sabab, 'illa, iḫtiyār.* on the one hand; *dīn, milla, ḫabar, ḥadīth, ijtihād, taqlīd* on the other, are not derived from a common origin; but as they are used in the *I'lām*, and more generally in philosophical and theological writings from the eleventh century of the Hegira onward, each group constitutes a well-defined constellation of meanings. Thus, on the one hand, there is a Reason (*'aql*) which, through the independent practice of scientific techniques (*ṣinā'āt*) accessible to a small number of minds (*ḫāṣṣa*), can obtain guidance and guide (*siyāsa*) others (*'āmma, ra'āyā, sawdā, dahmā, sūqa*[3])

1. See 'How to Read the Qur'ān' in M. Arkoun, *Readings of the Qur'ān*, 2nd ed., Tunis, 1991.
2. This finding confirms the teaching of modern semantics in contrast to that of Aristotelian linguistics which held that comprehension of the essence of a thing begins with the etymology of the word designating the thing (*étumos logos*: knowledge of the 'true'): see P. Guiraud, *L'étymologie*, P.U.F., 1964.
3. Various expressions applied to the anonymous ignorant masses in Medieval literature.

by discerning (*tamyīz*) cause *(sabab, 'illa*) and effect (*ma'lūl*) and by choosing the best side (*iḫtiyār*) in every situation. On the other hand, there is a religion (*dīn*), a confessional group (*milla*)[1] fixed in a corpus of information (*ḫabar, ḥadīth, āthār, sunna, matn, turāth al-rasūl, kitāb*[2]) that one must struggle to understand (*ijtihād*) in order to make one's conduct (*taqlīd*) conform. Between these two nuclei, reason assumes the more or less appropriate role of mediator. It is put to work both in the religious sciences (*'ulūm milliyya*) and in the sapiential sciences (*ḥikmiyya*). This is where reason most seriously misunderstands itself. It is advanced as a power *(quwwa*) producing truth (*ḥaqq*) and certainty (*yaqīn*), as the sovereign arbiter of truth and falsehood (*ṣawāb/ḫaṭa'*) even in matters of faith; it is defined as the explicit (*ṣarīḥ*) pure reasoning (*'aql mujarrad*) of the mind; it asserts that '*science is the exhaustive apprehension of the thing as it is, without fault or error*' (p. 84); it classifies things in three categories as rationally compelling, possible or deniable (p. 103) and asserts the absence of any contradiction (*'inād*) between truth established by demonstrative argument (*burhān*) and truth imposed by the true religion (*al-dīn al-ḥaqq*) (p. 87); it knows 'that to acquire mastery of the sapiential sciences is to acknowledge the benefit of possessing three assets (*marāfiq*): (1) certainty of reaching perfection in human virtue by grasping the essential truths of beings *(ḥaqā'iq al-mawjūdāt*) and by becoming capable of exercising authority over them; (2) discovery of the seats of wisdom, the true knowledge (*taḥaqquq*) of causes and effects and of all there is to know about the wonderful Order, the harmonious symmetry of the various aspects that the Artisan (*Ṣāni'*) has given to creation; (3) uphold, in the quest for demonstrative arguments (*burhān*), the traditional affirmations and insure against the opprobrium attached to the 'servile reproduction (*taqlīd*) of weak doctrines' (p. 87).[3] All this enables the following sequence of postulates to appear at the beginning of the first chapter:

1. On this important concept, see Fārābī's work *Kitāb al-milla*, ed. M. Mahdī, Beirut, 1968.
2. Respectively: information, prophetic tradition, traditions, usual practice and Tradition of the Prophet, text, legacy of the Envoy, book.
3. The editor makes a modernising commentary on this passage (introduction, p. 28) which denotes that type of reading devoid of epistemological, critical distance.

'Faith (*imān*) is true, certain belief; its seat in the soul is the power of reason. Unbelief (*kufr*) is lying belief, deprived of certainty; its seat in the soul is the power of the imagination (*al-quwwa-lmutakhayyila*). It may happen that the power of the imagination is good; but the power of reason cannot lend itself to a lying belief' (p. 83).

Reason is thus predestined to the truth; if the rules for logical deduction and the construction of propositions are correctly applied, it cannot make mistakes. This means that it does not itself have to initiate the elaboration of the truth with which it is already filled; on the contrary, its whole activity consists of reciting authentically, clarifying, explaining, classifying in a discursive formulation, all that the language of faith – the immutable Word of God – has laid down in a mode both simple and inexhaustible. Thus, reason grants itself all the conditions necessary for the completion of its mission for and in the name of the faith. At one moment, it can be trumpeting its will to power, claiming a monopoly of demonstrative argument, sweeping aside false beliefs in all sovereignty; at another, on the contrary, it can be admitting its weakness, recognizing 'in the matter of possible meanings (*al-ma'ānī-l-jā'iza*), the need to await the intervention of the commandment (*amr*) from on high, owing to its inability to attain truths by itself and its need, in many such cases, to resort to matters coming from outside' (p.104). In the matter of serving the Lord (*ḫidmat al-mawlā*), 'the share of imitation (*taqlīd*) has greater value than that of reason, in the sense that the former expresses obedience (*ṭā'a*) while the latter only provides eulogy and approval.' (ibid.)

This use of reason conforms perfectly to the expectations and requirements of a linguistic awareness attuned to the conceptual material contained in the *Mafātiḥ al-'ulūm*. It generates a discourse whose functional truth is as apparent to minds resistant to *falsafa* as to those of its adherents. Statistical analysis reveals a pattern of selection in the philosophical terminology: the terms most often used are those borrowed from ethics, politics and logic that have gained currency in the religious sciences. Examples include *'āqil* (14 appearances), *'ilm* (46), [*burhān*] (9), ra'y (5), rawiyya (5), *muqaddamāt* (6), *yaqīn* (6), *i'tiqād* (24), *ḥaqq* (21), *ḥaqā'iq* (6), *ma'rifa*

(9), *ma'ānī* (15), *ṭabī', ṭibā', ṭab'* (3, 4, 5), *aḫlāq* (14), *faḍīla* (22), *siyāsa* (11), *riyāsa* (9), *sulṭān* (10) and *malik* (31), among others. However, there is a very limited use of more specialized words such as awwal (a single instance), *ta'alluh* (1), *falsafa* (1, against 19 for *ḥikma*), *sabab* (3) *'araḍ* (1), *ḍidd* (2), *idrāk* (1), *jins* (3), *iḫtiyār* (1), *ustuqussāt* (1), *anjum thawābit* (1), *mukawwanāt* (1), etc. On the other hand, the vocabulary of the religious sciences themselves is quite widely used: *fiqh* (13), *kalām* (13), *mu'āmalāt* (13), *sharī'a* (8), *al-kutub* (13), *ḫalīfa* (15), *al-amr* (14), *nabiyy* (9), *nubuwwa* (11), *rasūl* (6), *akām* (12), *'ibāda* (36), *taqlīd* (8), and so on.[1]

All these terms are used with the emotional and conceptual baggage that each has accumulated in the course of a long history. This is one of the constants of reason which regards language as a writing of the soul. When a definition is proposed, it lays down a postulate or series of postulates that involve a large number of implicit presuppositions. This is always particularly true in the case of religious concepts.[2] But what might seem to be a source of ambiguity, obscurity, contradiction and empty verbiage, functions in the discourse of the *I'lām* as 'a discursive training', a language with an effectiveness all of its own, not despite, but because of its abstraction, its generality and syncretic nature, the linguistic platform resulting from a selective use of the lexicon solicits the reader's loyalty through frequent reference to all the religious, historical, psychological, scientific, political and ethical projections that haunt each collective consciousness.[3] It is a type of writing appropriate to a particular type of reading: the psychological setting in which the acceptance or rejection of an oral or written message takes place is the affective memory that broadly conditions the deployment of analytic or critical intelligence. A discourse is

1. For translations of the terms cited, see *Contribution to the Study on the Ethical Lexicon*, op. cit.
2. See analysis of *creed*, below.
3. The concept of collective consciousness (see *Humanisme*, pp. 176 sqq.) is essential in order to understand how the same word in the same language can have different connotations and specific internal reverberations, according to whether it is being perceived by a Christian, Jewish, Zoroastrian, Sunnī, Shī'ite or other sensibility.

most accurately absorbed, then recited, when it is consonant with a religious sensitivity and an eschatological vision.[1] Formulae such as *al-dīn al-ḥaqq, al-dīn al-ḥaqīqiy, al-ḥanīfiy, al-ṣādiq, al-ṣaḥīḥ, al-milla-l-ḥanīfiyya, al-'aql al-ṣarīḥ, al-mujarrad, al-ṣaḥīḥ,* propositions such as 'religions always aim to promote the general interest' (p. 105), 'the quiddities (*mā'iyyāt*) of religions are rational; nor is it permitted to neglect them so long as this world below continues to be filled with human nature' (p. 102); 'all that reason holds to be necessary is accepted as obligatory; all that it rejects is abandoned as tainted; all that it declares possible is left without definition (*ḥukm*) until such time as it is found among the intelligibles (*ma'qūlāt*) that which will make it possible to decide for or against' (p. 103),. To summarize, this is a whole collection of the modes of representation, the mental habits and attitudes revealed when studying a culture or a creed, that affect the mind of the author-reader by virtue of their impressionist efficacy and absolutely not through the strength of their cogency. It is here that the expression '*intellectual dreaming*' takes on its full meaning. Philosophical-religious discourse works like poetic discourse, by replacing concept with metaphor, dialectic with evocation, the slowness and deliberation of exegesis with the spontaneity of cries of pain or rapture. The philosopher-theologian and the fundamentalist theologian (*uṣūlīy*), like the poet, succumb to the lyrical pressure of a universe of meanings concentrated into a vocabulary and grammar that perpetuate the substitution of a dreamed (but coherent) world for the real one.[2]

A deeper analysis could be made of the ways in which lexical material functions in the *i'lām*. It would be useful, in particular, to complement the synchronic analysis with a diachronic one

---

1. The vision developed by al-'Āmirī includes the resurrection of souls and bodies, see pp. 135–7.
2. The use of vocabulary and grammar (subject/object structure; logic by implication and inference; stylistic techniques) described here is especially interesting since it is still current and even predominant in contemporary Arabic writing, the main difference being that references to Revolution (socialist ideology) now obscure the unchanging theological thought structures behind a vocabulary and a dialectic wrongly described as 'modern'.

by showing the extent to which the philosophical vocabulary is detached from its origins, how this disconnection occurs, and how the religious vocabulary locked into discussion of the statutes of the *'ilm*, and thus of the truth, is cut off from Qur'ānic usage. There are two reasons for refraining from expanding the present study in this direction. Firstly, we still lack the monographs that would be essential if we wanted to disassociate ourselves from the usages that tended to predominate in the fourth century among the great translators and, through them, those applied to Greek texts which are themselves many-layered; secondly, unlike ourselves, readers of philosophical and religious literature in the fourth century attached little importance to the sedimentary layers of semantics. For them, meaning was determined essentially by the associations, correlations, axioms, and oppositions active in current usage. We must therefore continue the study in a synchronic direction if we are to be able to evaluate the extension of 'discursive training' that can be seen in the *I'lām*.[1] We should complete this evaluation by describing the workings of the culture which the study of vocabulary has only hinted at.

2.3. Usage of a Specific Culture

The reason why we have chosen the *I'lām* for working out a problem applicable to the whole of Islamic thought and even, with adjustments, to Western thought,[2] is that it purports to deal with religious truth by reference to what was most rationally advanced in Arab-Islamic culture – *falsafa*. It is neither a vehement, exclusively polemical defence of Islamic religion, nor a pretentious, imperialist intervention using philosophical scholarship. What one finds, rather, is a recapitulation of the essential problems and procedures for achieving Arab-Islamic culture in the form that emerged from four centuries of practice. By analyzing these procedures, it will

1. See notably texts by Bāqillānī, 'Abd al-Jabbār, Ibn Bābūyê, al-Tawḥīdī, parts of the Ikhwān al-Ṣafā', etc., *Humanisme*, pp. 184 sqq.
2. This is performed by practitioners of the new criticism, historical psychology, the 'archaeology of knowledge', etc.

be possible both to locate the major problems that haunt Islamic consciousness and to trace the outlines of the mental arena in which a particular mode of human existence has been deployed.

The *I'lām* presents us with an essentially written culture resting on:

1. a technique of exposition;
2. a criteriology;
3. a creed.

Let us examine each of these points.

2.3.1. *A Technique of Exposition*

Compared to he *Kitāb al-sa'āda wa-l-is'ād,*[1] the *I'lām* seems a solidly composed work. It conforms to the system of classical rhetoric as it includes, according to the editor's presentation, an introduction, a development over ten chapters and a conclusion. In fact, as is always the case with writings of this sort, the plan followed is not dictated by a quest for analysis and synthesis, a wish to string ideas together and arrive at an acceptable conclusion; it expresses, rather, that kind of formal rigour that consists in stating, in an exhaustive and orderly manner, all of the learning – objections, refutations, quotations, received ideas, and so on – relating to a specific theme. The nomenclature, the classification, the divisions and sub-divisions are exposition procedures characteristic of a method of learning that concentrates on presenting the sum total of knowledge already acquired. Simply skimming the list of chapter headings is enough to give an idea of the artificial and disparate character of the divisions laid down. '*Introduction on what it is necessary to know*' and the first chapter '*On the quiddity of science*' both deal, in fact, with the same subject, namely, science, its purpose, its definition and its methods. Chapter II ('*The nobility of the religious sciences*') and Chapter III ('*The superiorities of the religious*

1. See M. Arkoun, 'La conquête du bonheur', in *Essais*, op. cit.

sciences') can be combined under the single heading of: '*Superiority of the religious sciences*'. Chapters V–X are really just subdivisions of a general chapter on the superiority of Islam according to criteria laid down in Chapter IV. Finally, the conclusion lists the doubtful matters (*shubuhāt*) which have not found a place in the foregoing scheme, and which detractors of Islam enjoy referring to.

The result of this method of exposition is that the text projects an impression of clarity at the cost of dissipating the material. The organizing and guiding concepts of thought are drowned in incidentals, refutations or assertions in arguments dominated by arithmetism and geometrism.[1] Thus, the author announces that his comparative study will cover the six religions mentioned in verse 17 of *sūra* 22 ('*As for the true believers, the Jews, the Sabaeans, the Christians, the Magians and the pagans, God will judge them on the day of Resurrection*'); the teaching of each of these religions is based on four main areas: dogma, worship, social relations and interdictions; and each of these four areas consists, in the end, of five basic supports, 'which shows that the primary supports of the six religions are twenty in number' (p. 125).

The magical allure of numbers and counting is all the more significant here in that the only religions actually examined are Judaism, Christianity and, to a lesser extent, Zoroastrianism. The effects of this arithmetism upon the general structure of the work and the validity of its comparisons is also apparent: Although al-'Āmirī states two essential rules for any comparison,[2] he fails to perceive the arbitrary nature of his own approach which is to judge the other religions in terms of the major supports defined in works of the *fiqh*.[3]

These observations are important but have to be understood

1. This method of composition is common to the major works of theologians and jurists such as Māwardi, Ghazālī, Ibn Taymiyya, etc. See M. Arkoun, 'L'éthique musulmane d'après Māwardi, in *Essais*, op. cit.
2. Comparison should only be made between facts of the same sort; it should not attribute to a whole group a defect displayed by some of its members.
3. See the remarks on *creed* below.

properly. They are not made in order to stress the weakness of the plan, the formalism of the composition or the inconsistency of the arguments by the standards of a twentieth-century reader, but to draw attention to a hierarchy of procedures deployed in a specific cultural context for the purpose of 'organizing" a discourse in order to ensure communication. When we use apparently deprecatory terms (arithmetism, geometrism, arbitrary and so on) it is solely to stress the distance between these techniques of exposition and our own. This should be borne in mind when comparing the analyses that follow.

2.3.2. A Criteriology

Whether they produce the illusion of a very clear plan or whether they carry 'disorder' to extremes, mediaeval Arabic texts share an adherence to a rigid criteriology. They do not contain any statement that is not also an implicit or explicit judgement in terms of objective or subjective criteria. The term 'objective criteria' is used to mean all of the truths received through 'common sense' which underpin identity and thus recognition of all reality, and 'common sense' refers to that which regulates the workings of the mind in a given space-time. Thus, all of humanity influenced by monotheist teaching posits the existence of one God, a Revelation, angels, prophets, souls etc.; and the necessity for Resurrection, for a distinction between true and false, good and evil and thus for a fundamental schism between believers and non-believers. These convictions underlie the presuppositions of any mediaeval act of intelligibility, and continue to this day to underlie all theological research.[1]

To these criteria, common to all 'peoples of the Book-book', each community tries to add a specific content with the aid of other criteria, also presented as objective despite their particular

1. One might also include a large proportion of research in the humanities. The undemonstrable presuppositions underlying some structuralism and some historical philosophy reduce the scope of contemporary science.

historical determinants. This is the major significance of the advent of Christ, then of the Qur'ān, in a context that is more or less shaped by biblical texts. Each revelation reactivates a demand for universality in the awareness it influences; but at the same time, it endorses a split by over-valuing the language, random events, circumstances and traditions that belong to a particular group of individuals. This ambivalence has led, most noticeably in the immense polemical literature, to the pious substitution of subjective certitudes for objective criteria.

Al-'Āmirī cannot avoid this necessity. He admits that the six religions considered, all make the same claim to put forward a collection of beliefs, a form of worship, institutions (*awḍā'*) concerned with social relations and rules (*rusūm*) laying down what is forbidden (pp. 123–4). But he adds that 'the reasonable man' (*al-'āqil*) should carefully verify the superiority of the four areas of the religion he accepts over the ones he rejects: and not by following in the footsteps of the ancients, but by observing the requirements of pure reason. It is an occasion for meditation on the words of the Almighty: '*Thus, whenever, before you, We sent an apostle to forewarn a nation, those who lived in comfort said: "This was the faith our fathers practised; we are merely following in their footsteps."*' (43, 22). Any 'reasonable man' is thus expected to be responsible for determining the best religion, which he will then have to follow. This task, as al-'Āmirī sees it, consists of a validation of Islamic criteria by means of 'rational' criteria. These are the aphorisms or postulated definitions listed at the beginning of each chapter, whose demonstrative value is stressed by expressions such as 'it being the case that …; it being established that …; it being recognized that …; we should return to the subject of our exposé …; we hold it to be certain that … Aphorisms were, in fact, a form of expression much relished, especially in the fourth century, by a public fascinated by the idea of '*timeless wisdom*'. They expressed the moral values established by '*the experiences of the nations*' and reinforced with the authority of the prophets, sages, mystics and great princes who had given them incisive formulations. In them and through them, the moral implications that are so easy to verify in daily life are confused with positive knowledge. The aphorism is both an axiom and something that ensures the mental convergence characteristic of Wisdom (*ḥikma*). The aphorisms/axioms are filled with mixed inputs from religion, ethics, politics, metaphysics, the sciences and so on. They initiate a cumulative form of learning and postulate an undivided consciousness that accepts a statement as a strict truth.[1]

Here are a few of the statements on which al-ʿĀmirī relies, and which could not be effectively refuted by a Jew, Christian, Zoroastrian, Shīʿite, Sunnī, etc:

> '*To acquire learning is to develop the heart*' (p. 99); '*Receiving instruction with docility is what helps most to awaken the intelligence*' (ibid.); '*Only a man devoid of respect for others follows the path of attacks on men of science ...*' (p. 109); '*The finest quality of eminent men is to avoid boasting of what places them above the masses*' (ibid.); '*The truth is accessible to him who wants it and desires to state it*' (p. 123); '*On the path leading to God, there are manifest signs and clear indications (shawāhid)*' (ibid.), and so on.[2]

The linkage of an Islamic criteriology with these generalities represents the crucial moment of the demonstration but this moment cannot be ascribed to that which is wholly internal and affective. This is the reason for mentioning non-demonstrable presuppositions whose obvious truth is felt, but not spoken or written. By making simultaneous use of aphoristic and systematic writing – the first fragmentary, discontinuous, suggestive and open; the second full, continuous, specific and closed – the text of the *Iʿlām* has the advantage of underlining a split between two competing intellectual approaches that are nevertheless complementary. We

---

1. On the aphorism, see remarks on readings of the Qurʾān below.
2. The aphorisms correspond closely with the ideas developed in each chapter, which strengthens their value as criteria validating and signaling the intention of 'scientific' discourse. The process is part of what we have called elsewhere 'the construction of wisdom' (*Humanisme*, p. 243).

are thus invited to compare the genre of the anthology in which the aphorism-axiom predominates and the essay or treatise genre (*kitāb*, *muḫtaṣar*, *risāla*) in which the explicit, logical statement predominates. Without making this comparison, one cannot understand the subtle dialectic that governed intellectual life in the Middle Ages. Al-ʿĀmirī and his contemporary, Miskawayh, who composed both anthologies and systematic works, are particularly representative of this area.[1]

The quest for appropriate criteria to establish the superiority of Islam takes us back to the classical discussions between that various schools of thought that differed on the subject of Truth. Compelled to make his way using the formulations and procedures of the *falāsifa*, which had become classics by then, and those of the fundamentalists, the author strives to reach balanced positions on the three criteria that determine all Islamic thought: the epistemological, the methodological and the historico-ethical.

a) The epistemological criterion emerges from the classification of the sciences. It confirms the well-known opposition between the philosophical sciences and the religious sciences (*ʿulūm ḥikmiyya/milliyya*), one using logic, the other language, as its instrumental science (*āla*). The ordering of the different disciplines can be presented as follows:

1.On the anthology as a form that responds to both socio-political and aesthetic needs, see *Humanisme*, pp. 146 sqq.

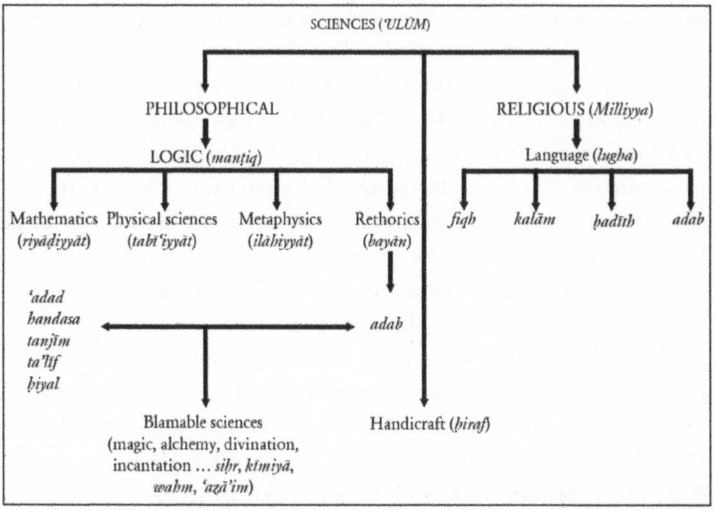

What criteria does this classification imply? Apparently, the table shows the coexistence of three clearly separated orders of activity. One is ruled by logical reasoning; one is linked to language and then there is the handicraft activity reserved for the masses and essentially practical (p. 85). The blameworthy sciences are placed beside philosophy to which they seek attachment, though in vain, since they do not conform to the standards of logic. Close examination of the commentaries given on each science, discloses an illustration of the rivalry, so vigorous in the fourth century H., between mythical awareness and metaphysical awareness. By emphasizing that the *fiqh* and the *kalām* are produced by reason, by insisting on the importance of *adab* – conceptual discourse (*bayān*) on one side, literary discourse (*kalām manẓūm, muntabi'*) on the other – the author reveals his adherence to a purely scholastic classification that confuses tidy listing, a taste for symmetrical arrangement and minute descriptions of the curiosities and procedures of each science, with a genuine search for their foundations. Al-'Āmirī tries, however, to bypass certain contradictions that were obstinately kept alive by various Religious political parties. The *ḥashwiyya,* who considered that the philosophical sciences 'consist only of big words, brilliant denominations set about with syncretic notions to mislead the unwary ignoramus, to bog down the inexperienced man-about-town', are put in their place with the reaffirmation that 'the foundations and the parts of these sciences give birth to doctrines conforming to pure reason, confirmed by correct demonstration in accordance with the teaching of the religious sciences' (p. 87). Some theologians influenced by these *ḥaswiyya*, distrusted a logic in which they could discern only 'an obscure terminology, strange denominations'. The refutation here is more insistent, and helps define a basic criterion of all knowledge:

'Logic is a rational instrument that enables the reasonable soul fully to distinguish the true from the false (*ḥaqq/bāṭil*) in speculative matters, and good from evil (*khayr/sharr*) in practical matters. To those souls that use it, it occupies a place that is very close to the criterion (*mi'yār*) of justice which enables us to assess knowledge. It is logic that stresses the importance of question and answer, objection, contradiction and the sophistry of refutation (*mughālaṭa*). Furthermore, it is this that enables us to resolve ambiguities, to expose sophistries (*tamwīhāt*) and other habitual notions while in the process of verifying statements. Apart from that, logic procures, for those who use it, a pure intellectual pleasure; from it, the soul derives such confidence in learning that it becomes in itself a force calling for the acquisition of wisdom, not to earn the praise of others but to enjoy the blessing of arriving by this route at the truth and the very spirit of certainty (*rūḥ al-yaqīn*) (p. 95).

Presented in these 'limpid' terms, acceptable to any 'reasonable man', the role of logic, and through it, the philosophical sciences, appears decisive and irreplaceable. In any case, al-'Āmirī calmly concludes that the reason why he has expanded on the classification of the sciences, was to produce a method (*minhāj*) for studying the religious sciences and displaying their superiority (*rujḥān*) (p. 97). In other words, the philosophical sciences have methodological priority and the religious sciences have teleological primacy.[1] Here

1. 'Religious science can become the foundation on which the construction of other sciences takes place.. whereas no other science

we have a perfect illustration of the medieval mode of intelligibility. What is being put forward, in a tone of compelling certainty, are precisely those frames of reference, concepts, definitions, analytic and expository techniques that are rejected by those to whom the demonstration is addressed. And what is held up as the source of truths, as a method of reflection, as a means of communication, is exactly what transforms truth into personal conviction, reflection into dogmatic repetition and communication into soliloquy.[1]

Thus, the passage quoted uses essential concepts (reasonable soul, true/false, good/evil, verification, intellectual pleasure, etc) derived from the construction of the sort of wisdom that was revered in fourth-century intellectual circles. It is here that all the difficulties of a demonstration of the superiority of Islam are concentrated. One is reminded of grammarians such as al-Ṣīrāfī, Rummānī or al-Fārisī reading or hearing the eulogy of logic, and still more of the Jewish and Christian philosophers who, with the same conceptual apparatus, the same methodological framework as al-ʿĀmirī, 'demonstrate' the superiority of Judaism or Christianity.[2] One can understand why a collective reflection on schism was impossible in an intellectual climate in which people assumed the *a priori* existence of substantial immutable realities, accessible to reason but inflated, in practice, with very variable content by that same reason. The act of knowledge involves a fairly long and rigorous path taken within a discipline that has been thoroughly mastered, and which consequently procures either the 'praise of others' leavened with material advantages, or the 'pure intellectual pleasure' so avidly pursued by true sages. It is essential, in a study of historical psychology, to note that a definition of logic is completed by recalling the affective motivation that impels the individual soul to develop this sort of learning.

---

could ever become so powerful that religious science could be founded upon it' (p. 106). Also see below on the concept of revelation, p. 223.

1. See *creed* below.
2. See P. Sbath, *Vingt traités philosophiques et apologétiques d'auteurs arabes chrétiens*, Cairo, 1939; and, more generally, the valuable bibliography assembled by C. G. Anawati in *Polémique, apologie et dialogue islamo-chrétien*, Rome, 1969.

What al-ʿĀmirī says about language enables us to evaluate even more fully the importance of the affective criterion in the act of knowledge. He is not unaware that the linguistic sciences – grammar, lexicography, literary criticism, etc – here termed '*adab*' or *ādāb* – are the instrument of the religious sciences, the space in which they are constructed. He enters a defence of this '*adab*' against 'a group of devotees' who see it as the futile pastime of worldly people. 'Having an extensive knowledge of the language,' he writes, 'does not imply that one is capable of expressing oneself with ease and purity (*faṣāḥa*); rather, it means achieving a natural use of language, for example, in poetry, in speeches, epistles or proverbs. Each of these forms, in fact, contains resources – such as well-turned maxims, or astonishing comparisons – which are used to sharpen intelligence. That is why these maxims and comparisons are immortalized in books and why it is said of them that 'they are living language'. In fact, anyone who has reflected on their beneficent effect upon assemblies in remedying division, their powerful efficacy in removing hostility and discord, in winning the hearts of great kings and making them want to be associated with the noble acts and fine declarations we expect of them, is certain that being so bold as to deny this is taking the risk of showing contempt for something important. By learning them and passing them on, we encourage higher souls in the direction of greatness (*al-maʿluwa*), and impel the man who likes hearing them to amass enough of it to attract good renown' (pp. 96–7).

Al-ʿĀmirī expands upon the literary use of language when replying to those who criticize the Qur'ān for lack of clarity. 'The cases in which there is expressiveness (*ġaraḍ*) in the poetic discourse', he writes, 'are three in number:

1. A statement is made using symbol (*ramz*) and enigma (*laghz*), and avoiding explicit designation;
2. The construction is general and concise, by which I mean that a large number of meanings is contained in few words;
3. The meaning of the statement cannot be grasped in itself, being

perhaps linked to premises (*muqaddamāt*) that need to be stated in advance. There is no doubt that those attached to knowledge of form have a different conception of the value of clear exposition (*bayān*) to those attached to profound knowledge ...' (p. 198).

When reading these comments on the expressive resources of the language, one cannot help recalling the extensive literature on the *i'jāz* that, in the fourth century in particular, developed in the wake of the critique of the 'twin arts' (*al-ṣinā'atān*) of grammar and rhetoric and of logic. However, al-'Āmirī juxtaposes two theoretical discourses on logic and language, rather than comparing them and looking for common criteria. Here again, he displays an approach typical of classical Arabic culture. On the one hand, logic is presented as a universal language of reason focused on eternal intelligibilities; on the other, language is conceived and practised as the instrument for achieving and communicating the most nuanced, the most profound and the most unexpected meanings. By referring to the importance of the symbolic, allusive, enigmatic aspects of language – to put it in more general terms, the language of mythic structure – the author reproduces one of the most pertinent objections raised by the grammarian al-Ṣīrāfī against the logician Abū Biṣr Mattā: that the statement (*nuṭq*) has a number of aspects that logicians do not perceive.[1] Finally, this constant juxtaposition of the theoretical priority of the logical criterion and the practical efficacy of the linguistic criterion points to the crucial, but hidden, mainspring of every discourse: the logical discourse itself operates in the framework of a grammar, a lexicon and a rhetoric from which it acquires probative force. As al-Ṣīrāfī says, logic alone has never succeeded in healing a divergence between two individuals, in proving that God is the third 'person' of a trinity, that One is more than one.[2] It is at the level of the linguistic statement with its double load of meaning, simultaneously affective and discursive,

1. See the famous controversy cited by al-Tawḥīdī in *al-Imtā' wal-mu'ānasa*, I, pp. 108–28; and Muḥsin Mahdī in *Logic in Classical Islamic Culture*, Wiesbaden, 1970, pp. 51–83.
2. *Imta'*, p. 125.

that indefinable but effective the criterion (or rather criteria), of demonstrative communication is attained.[1]

The Methodological Criterion

While the epistemological criterion seeks to fix a method as 'a definable direction regularly followed by the mind', the methodological criterion is concerned with what technical procedures to employ to arrive at the desired truth.[2] One of the interesting aspects of the *I'lām* is that it shows how the fundamentalist methodology *(uṣūl al-fiqh)* is defended and applied with the help of an initial philosophical option. This is an aspect of the real conditions under which Islamic thought was exercised that is still poorly understood.[3]

Here again, al-'Āmirī initially appears conciliatory. He refutes certain theologians who have attacked the *ḥadīth*, and – inversely – traditionalists who denigrate theology; and he answers 'a category of Imāmites and a group of Ḥanbalites' who are critical of the use of personal opinion (*ra'y*) and reasoning by analogy (*qiyās*) in the *fiqh* (pp. 111, 116). In other words, each of the four religious sciences – *ḥadīth, kalām, fiqh, lugha* – is presented not only as a complete science, but as a necessary attainment answering a need for truth in theory and practice. They are to be studied in the order dictated by their subject matter and purpose: the *ḥadīth* supplies the material (*mādda*) needed for the construction of *kalām* and *fiqh; kalām* defends holy religion and enables the individual to join an élite

1. This proposition could be amply developed with the aid of the literature on the *i'jaz*, see *Encyclopédie de l'Islam*, 2nd ed., under *I'jaz* (article by G. E. Von Grunebaum).
2. On this distinction, see *Humanisme*, pp. 195 sqq.
3. One is reminded in particular of the first mu'tazilites and the early *falāsifa* in this area. It is also important to appreciate the role of *adab* as illustrated by Jāḥiẓ and writers of the fourth century. Rather than continuing to examine the theological, juridical, philosophical and literary 'fields' separately, it is necessary (as we can see) to use the term Islamic thought to cover all intellectual activities in the language through changing historical and socio-cultural contexts.

that can reject or approve a thing with total clarity of vision (*baṣīra*); *fiqh* is as it were 'an intermediary between the *ḥadīth* and *kalām*' (p. 111), consisting in an effort of reflection (*ijtihād*) to distill from the texts those standards without which no royalty (*mulk*) is possible; and language, finally, is (as we have seen) the instrument used in these practices (pp. 111 *et seq..*).

We will return later to the historical-ethical criteria used to establish the hierarchy and validity of these sciences. Let us dwell for a moment on the most disputed points in the methodology that are shared by the *uṣūl al-dīn* and the *uṣūl al-fiqh* (the foundations of religion and law). We note that al-'Āmirī sides squarely with the Ḥanafites. He quotes and discusses a remark made by Abū Ḥanīfa:

> *Someone questioned him on the subject of qiyās: ought it to be abandoned, when it has a tradition going back to the Envoy? 'Yes', he replied. Ought it to be abandoned when there is a saying by one of the Companions? 'Yes', he replied. Ought it to be abandoned when there is a saying by one prominent among the Followers? 'The Followers are men and we are men,' he said.*
>
> *He made a distinction between the Companions and the Followers because he knew that the former had had the good fortune to be witnesses to the circumstances of Revelation and also to the conditions in which the Envoy's sayings and actions took place ... and we do not doubt that a witness to all of that could discern true meanings in it which would not be apparent to people who were not there. Furthermore, the Followers were in a situation similar to that of virtuous men (ṣāliḥūn), since they too were ignorant of the inferences (dalā'il) made accessible by the circumstances described* [p. 120].

These lines add nothing new to the external history of *fiqh*; but they are most enlightening to anyone trying to define a mode of intelligibility and the horizons of a culture. Al-'Āmirī's adherence to the Ḥanafite methodology cannot be explained solely by a wish to please his Sāmānid masters.[1] His extensive borrowings from Greek logic and politico-ethical ideas prove that his choice is governed more by a wish to validate the religious sciences with the aid of the philosophical sciences. In this context, the quoted passage implies the following consequences: the Qur'ānic text and traditions dating back to the Prophet and the Companions impose obedience and exclude all research (*ra'y, qiyās*). This means that the Qur'ānic exegesis and critique of the *hadīth* must be correctly absorbed. In listing the rules for this critique (pp. 120–1), al-'Āmirī (like many others) merely compensates for a practical impossibility – that of setting up an authentic corpus that would be accepted by all believers – with an excess of theoretical requirements; except for the Companions, *ijtihād* is a permanent necessity. In effect, 'however large the number of traditions passed down to us may be, there is a limit which cannot be exceeded. But the events that occur in the created world are potentially infinite, and if *ijtihād* is forbidden to the muftis, there are only two possibilities open to them: either an infallible Imām has to be proclaimed, as the Duodecimians did; or everything that reason judges good has to be permitted, as al-Naẓẓām recommended. So far as the infallible Imām is concerned, his whereabouts will not be known and it will not be possible to consult him when events occur; and as for relying on what reason judges good, it is the gravest innovation (*bid'a*) according to the Ḥanbalites and the Imāmites. So we are compelled to connect the application (*far'*) to the foundation (*aṣl*) by holding to the practice (*sunna*) of the greatest Companions'[2] (p.118).

In trying to make critical and rationalist standards prevail in the religious sciences, the philosopher has in fact allowed himself to be taken over by the mythic mentality: gaze fixed on the inaugurating

1. As indicated by an editor's note on p. 120.
2. This passage is a good illustration of the very blurred distinction between historical awareness (inevitability of change resulting from time or even progress on some level: pp. 102, 104–5) and mythical awareness (return to the time of foundation). Thus, *falsafa* emerges as a dynamic force, but is itself subjected to the myth of origin and, more generally, to the historical-transcendental theme that survives in European thought to this day.

Time of Revelation, the need for *qiyās* as a method for controlling history through a limited number of teachings related to the past, adherence to *ijtihād* in principle but submission to the authority of the ancients in practice, and so on. So the attempt to make religion into a science has actually transformed science into religion.

The Historical-ethical Criterion

The philosophical attitude comes into its own, up to a point, in the context of history and ethics. We know that these two disciplines, practised together, made it possible to transcend the Arab-Islamic horizon in time and in space.[1]

The notion of history that predominated from the Sassanid period onwards, is governed by a principle tirelessly repeated by authors of every stripe: 'the place of religion in relation to royalty (*mulk*) is that of the foundation in relation to the building; and the place of royalty in relation to religion is that of guardian of the supports' (p. 153). The author further elucidates this principle when he writes: 'the virtues of man will only be perfect if spiritual conditions are mingled with temporal conditions, the motivations of that other life interwoven (*ishtibāk*) with those of this life' (p. 158).

This concept presupposes four essential criteria which govern reflection in the *i'lām*, and in Islamic thought in general:

1. Criterion of choice of a leader (*sā'is*);
2. Criterion of the ethical-political conduct of the leader and the led (*sā'is/masūs*); criterion of the ethical-juridical standard;
3. Criterion of the superiority (*faḍl*) of a specific religion, a specific political space, a specific personality (the whole subject of the *i'lām*);
4. criterion of valid knowledge and useful action (*maṣlaḥa*)

1. See M. Arkoun, 'Ethique et histoire d'après les *Tajārib al-umam*', in *Essais*, op. cit., pp. 51 sqq.

On the choice of a leader, al-ʿĀmirī states a criterion which, while legitimising the power of his protectors, adopts in political philosophy a position solidly inspired by Greek and also Shīʿite ideas. He begins by recalling the Prophet's exemplary practice in one of those passages characteristic of historical-ethical writing: sufficiently general in tone not to single out any individual, but pointed enough to give all holders of power food for thought. 'In all his attitudes, the Prophet was attached to the image of a creature totally given over to love of his Lord' (p. 157); he was thus able to give the 'struggle for God' (*jihād*)[1] the special content required by 'the simultaneous pursuit of the prophetic mission and of royalty', through 'recourse to force where it is indicated and to teaching when the time is ripe' (p. 156). The *jihād* thus waged differs from civil war (*fitna*) and from banditry (*taṣaʿluk*); it is 'defence of the religion and preservation of the order maintained by the agents of development of the lands and the leaders of men' (ibid.). And 'as the Muslim religious Law was founded by the Prophet on the basis of this praiseworthy practice, it is well known that whoever, after him, assumes charge of important matters of politics and royalty, necessarily becomes the Guide (*Imām*) of his contemporaries, the glory of all his descendants ... from the moment that he acquits himself well of this task and conforms in all that he undertakes to the practice of the Prophet' (pp. 157–8).

With this prudent formulation, the criterion of the choice of leader can fall on every 'reasonable man'. All he has to do is make the distinction between 'the true institution of Islamic royalty' (*al-awḍāʿ al-ḥaqīqiyya*) and real history, made up of accidents which are often unhappy (*āfa*) but which 'do not justify criticism of the original true religion' (p. 158). This is where logocentrism asserts its supremacy: true history is the one that is defined, stated and represented inside the enclosure of the logical discourse; it dominates and judges real living history, which may on occasion reflect some aspect of 'the true institution' but which in the main is contemptible.

1. As al-ʿĀmirī's analysis of the notion of *jihād* clearly shows, the translation 'holy war' is inadequate and dangerous.

The three other criteria are just corollaries of the first. Broadly speaking, the good ethical-political conduct of the leader and the led, the validity of the ethical-juridical standard stated by the *mujtahid* and the superiority of one religion, one state, one personality, are functions of the extent to which the double action of the Prophet is actualised in the person of the Guide. In practice this means the recognised pre-eminence of the Companions, the strong and unconditional link established between true knowledge and useful action, made manifest in the conduct of each sage (*al-ʿilm bi-l'amal, al-ʿamal bi-l-ʿilm*[1]), the correlation between the superiority of Islam and the liberation of the human individual. This last feature is, in al-ʿĀmirī's view, one of true history's more successful projections into real history. He notes that 'human dignity (*al-sharāf al-insīy*) was linked by the Persian kings with ascendancy, for they prevented their subjects from rising from one rank to another ...'; with Islam, this dignity at last depended on the 'reasonable soul' (p. 160). One can see how the criteria are used to enrich the logocentric apparatus: real history is perceived objectively from one side, but only so that the Image of true history can be superimposed from the other.

2.3.3. *A Creed*

While the writing of the *Iʿlām* can be called philosophical, by reason of the inflected use of vocabulary, from the importance of rhetoric in the organization of the thesis to the criteriology guiding its reflection, it will be seen that it also has some characteristics peculiar to religious writing. In effect, rhetoric and criteriology are only formal requirements put forward by the philosophical *adab*, to systematize and impose a creed (the word 'creed' is used to refer to the collection of convictions that govern sensibility, perception, thought and action). Under this definition, a creed encompasses the articles of the traditional profession of faith, but in combination with other elements derived from experience of urban life and an eclectic cultural tradition. To put it another way, we are witnessing

1. A constant theme throughout classical Muslim ethics, linked to the ruling principle of the general interest (*maṣlaha ʿāmma*).

a re-arrangement of specifically Islamic convictions to make them appropriate to new socio-cultural requirements.[1]

These elements of Islamic conviction are not analyzed or developed in themselves; they only appear in the course of the essay in the role of indisputable truths underlying the argument. They can be distilled into the following major affirmations:

1. There exists a true Artisan (*ṣāni' ḥaqq*) who is known to us through His successive revelations to the prophets of the Bible and, in the last instance, Muḥammad; He is the true primary One, the Lord and source of creation and Commandment (p. 105 and passim);
2. Divine Revelation cannot be affected by any doubt; it is the chink of light (*mishkāt*) to which the first foundations of all speculative science refer (p. 106);
3. The Qur'ān is the Revelation that completes and replaces all preceding ones; it founds the true religion that can never be abolished (p. 172 and passim);
4. Muḥammad is the Envoy of God to show the Truth and the right Way, to teach the Book and Wisdom, to order Justice and the Good and to prohibit turpitude and evil ... (p. 173 and passim);
5. Muḥammad, founder of the *Umma,* is the exemplary spiritual and temporal Guide (pp. 156–8 and passim); the *ḥadīth* is the record of his teachings and historical practice, piously assembled by his Companions.

Islamic dogma teaches the happy medium in everything: the oneness of God as opposed to the anthropomorphism of the Jews, the Christians' Trinity, Manichean dualism and pagan polytheism; a prophetology which does not fall into the exaggeration of the Christians or the inadequacy of the Jews: the prophets are servants of God chosen by Him and infallible; a healthy conception of

1. On the *falsafa* functioning as a creed, see *Humanisme*, pp. 195 sqq. passim.

angels: 'they are but his honoured servants. They do not speak till He has spoken: they act by His command' (Qur'ān 21, 27–28); respect for other writings despite the superiority of the Qur'ān; a rational approach to eschatology when dealing with metempsychosis, or to principles of light and darkness representing reward and punishment; God will restore souls to their original bodies and all creatures will recognise the good and bad acts committed here below (pp. 130–7).

The five pillars of worship – prayer, fasting, *zakāt* (religious charitable contribution), *jihād* (struggle for God), and pilgrimage[1] – express the same sense of measure and concrete rationality; they make it possible, in effect, to deploy the activities of the soul and the body under optimum conditions, in the threefold domain of individual, family and political life (pp. 140–50).

The strictly religious scope of this profession of faith is largely obliterated by the superimposition of undemonstrable presuppositions drawn from the fourth-century philosophical creed.[2] Revelation is virtually reduced to the Qur'ānic text made partially explicit through the historical action of the Prophet. 'Human' reason, equipped with specific examples of grammar, rhetoric, logic, physics and metaphysics, would intrude upon this text, to worry at it with ceaseless references to the following presuppositions:

1. There is a human nature (*jibilla baṣariyya, ṭabī'a insiyya*) whose improvement and well-being are functions of the authority exercised by the reason (cf. *Makārim al-aḫlāq*);

2. Reason restrains bad instincts; it ensures right and salutary action by imposing the true religion; it thus asserts itself as a power (*quwwa*) capable of recognizing all the truths that are consubstantial and coeternal with it in conformity with the creative Will of God;

---

1. Note that *jihād* is given a place, while the profession of faith (*shahāda*) is not mentioned.
2. This explains the tension between philosophical creed and 'orthodox' creed as asserted by the ash'arites and even more radically by the Ḥanbalites. See Laoust, *La profession de foi d'Ibn Baṭṭa*, Damascus, 1958.

3. There exists an ideal political space and an ideal historical period, both materialized in Arabia by Muḥammad; a space extended to the central part – essentially Iran and Iraq – of the inhabited world (*ʿumrān*), and a period extended by the action of worthy Successors;

4. Reason, like religion, is not focused on individual interest but on the general interest (*maṣlaha, ʿāmma, kulliyya*);

5. The need to perpetuate the ideal state – in other words to safeguard the general interest – implies the need to know the true religion; the need to know implies, in its turn, the need to learn and teach (*taʿallum, taʿlīm*), to have knowledge and to act (*ʿilm/ʿamal*).[1]

We will return to this interpenetration, this reciprocal conditioning of religion by history and history by religion. Al-ʿĀmirī goes as far as to regard as excessive the fact that 'Christianity is founded solely on the effort to resemble God' (*ta'alluh maḥḍ*) (p. 145), while Islam defines the happy medium between an exclusive spirituality and an excessive attachment to this world. Many other factors already noted or yet to be encountered point in the same direction. The creed that emerges from the *Iʿlām*, and that will eventually impose itself on all Islamic thought, has a function that is civilizing (*taʿmīr, ʿimāra, ʿumrān, ḥarakāt al-ʿimāra* ...) at the same time as it leads towards salvation.[2]

2.4. Principles of a Reading

The principles of a reading are not always closely connected with those of a writing, which is why it is appropriate to examine them separately. We shall see, however, that the type of reading practised by al-ʿĀmirī makes it easier to understand why, in his case, it is more accurate to talk in terms of a collective rather than individual style.

---

1. Many texts can be found using the index accompanying the *iʿlām* under *ʿilm* and its derivatives; *maṣlaba, 'mr* (derivatives).
2. See M. Arkoun, 'Lexique de L'éthique musulmane' and 'Ethique et histoire', in *Essais,* op. cit.

Reading is envisaged here as the sum of the reverberations caused by a text on a consciousness and, subsequently, the attitude of that consciousness to the text. The quest might be for proof, argument, explanation or emotion, depending on whether it is haunted by a theory to be established, a system of ideas to be developed, conduct to be illuminated or a sensibility to be satisfied.

It could be said that all these different requirements coexist – although certainly in variable degrees – among all readers of sacred or philosophical texts in the Middle Ages. All of these texts give a broad role to aesthetic-ethical emotion, either in support of a demonstration or as a persuasive lever. As has just been shown in the case of the *I'lām*, reason feeds the illusion that it verifies, chooses and supervises in the context of a creed based on the expectation of eternal salvation, the hope of a just world.

In al-'Āmirī, the reading is utterly confident, reason and emotion coinciding: moderately critical or prudently interpretative, depending on whether it is dealing with philosophical texts, texts of *kalām* or *fiqh*, or sacred texts. It has been seen how the philosophical disciplines have to be assimilated to serve as the framework for a 'reflective' reading of works of religious science. We have yet to identify the direction in which this need to 'reflect', in terms of specific norms, affects the reading of sacred texts and, through them, the way in which history is perceived.

Let us begin by noting the clear disproportion between the number of quotations from the Qur'ān and those taken from other religious texts. According to the index compiled by the editor, the Qur'ān is quoted by name 18 times (the number of verses quoted is much larger); the Gospels, 6 times; the Torah, 6 times; the Psalms, once; the Synod, once. To see this difference as indicating an apologetic intention would be to adopt a purely external view of the author's thinking. It should be seen rather as an application of the postulate described above, concerning the ultimate character of Qur'ānic revelation. This revelation would thus constitute the decisive argument (*dalīl qaṭ'īy*) on all issues; in other words, it is a constant principle of the reading. The rationalzing attitude is permanently inflected by the posture of faith, but this does not mean that it is necessarily subservient thereto. On the contrary, reason takes on greater maturity when the Qur'ān is being read; it takes elements of psychology, language, history, economics, physics and other learning into account in order to underline the precise purposes or wishes of God. The procedure is too well understood to need further explanation. It will be noticed, on the other hand, that when this same reasoning is applied to the reading of other Writings, it always does so to separate them from Qur'ānic Truth, or to expose their imperfections, lacunae or backwardness in comparison with Islamic teachings and institutions. In one case, the reading tends to be comprehensive, because it is striving to connect a given event or solution to the verse or verses through projection and deduction; in the other, it is simply literal and particularizing.

There are numerous examples illustrating this disparity in the *i'lām*. One of the most significant appears in Chapter 10 which deals with the 'superiority of Islam in terms of learning'. It includes the following declarations:

> *The Jewish institutions are restricted to what is written in the Torah. The Christians have a book they call 'the synod' which contains the rules of the church and other practices. The Zoroastrians have a book bearing the name Avesta, with commentary in two other books entitled Zen and Bā-zend. These books contain indications useful to the lives of the faithful; but these last have not acquired the habit of deducing new ways of applying them. Their religions rest solely on acceptance of the established doctrine (taqlīd); the doors of rational scrutiny are closed to them, and they cannot go outside the text in doctrinal development (istinbāṭ) ...*
>
> *Among the Muslims, by contrast, the bearers of tradition have applied themselves to gathering information on the Envoy of God – blessings and salutations be upon him – and his Companions and their followers, with the anxious care of men afraid to miss the smallest detail ... They have learned everything about all the transmitters, their names, their surnames, their genealogy, their ages, the chronology of their times, the date of each one's death,*

> *the number of masters of which each has been the disciple and companion and whose teaching he has received, the number of Traditions each has handed down. Theologians, jurists, linguists and litterateurs (udabā') did much the same in their own respective disciplines. Moreover, Muslim intellectuals have had the benefit of access to translations of works by celebrated Byzantine, Persian, Hindu and Greek sages ... If the faithful of other religions possessed such extensive knowledge, such developed sciences, their books would be seen in their hands and would not pass unnoticed by those who sought to know them. Those who opposed them would not be ignorant of their titles and content, just as they have not been ignorant of the books translated into Persian and Syriac. And let no one object that most of the translators practised Christianity and Sabaeism, for they did this work only because they had perceived the power and greatness of Islam. Their goal was to seek favour with the Caliphs who firmly maintained the duties and the foundations of Islam*[1] [pp. 182–3].

This passage, which we have had to shorten but which is well worth reading in its entirety, confirms the working of the creed; it traces with great precision the horizons of Islamic thought when it was at its peak. Horizons that are open and circumscribed at the same time: open to everything tending in the direction of a harmonious, integrated reading; limited to the outlines traced by a divine message already linked to a historical achievement: that of the civilization and culture known as Islamic. The works of that civilization and that culture are interpreted and experienced as an expansion of the truth of Islam. The fertility, the effectiveness and dynamism of these works, are signs of the superiority of the religion taught by the Qur'ān and Muḥammad. Inversely, this religion is seen as the indispensable source and setting for any exemplary historic achievement, ensuring man's salvation on earth and in the heavens. Consequently, all reading and all writing will necessarily have to be done within this confine, in which a

1. It is interesting to see what their contemporaries perceived as the real motives for the cultural activities of these 'protégés'.

religion demonstrates its trueness and greatness by referring to temporal successes and a civilization perceives and projects itself as an extension of the 'true religion'. This means that reading and writing involve an idealization of the culture, to put it on the level of its religious purpose, and a 'secularization' of the religion to make it serve worldly existence. Any attempt to emerge from this confine results in loss of direction (*ḍalāl*).

Fundamentalist teaching has certainly always stayed within it.[1] This is also what explains the fragmentary reading of the Qur'ān and the *ḥadīth* practised by al-ʿĀmirī along with all Muslims. It is a reading favoured by the type of discourse used in the Qur'ān and in collections of *ḥadīth*,[2] an aphoristic discourse in which each fragment suggests several meanings, unlike the logical discourse found in treatises and 'composed' works.[3] Each verse or *ḥadīth* functions as an aphorism, a short formal unit rich in different meanings which emerge in response to different life situations. Reading (or quoting) a verse, *ḥadīth* or aphorism involves the re-actualization of a situation that has already been experienced, a meaning that has already been tested, to appropriate it to a new (or reiterated) fact. The reading is comprehensive in the context of a given verse (or *ḥadīth*) coupled with a given event, but fragmentary and partial at best in the context of the Totality of the Qur'ānic text – or the anthologies – on one hand, or of a long period of history on the other.

It seems surprising that al-ʿĀmirī, along with those who, like him, discerned the symbolic character of the Qur'ānic

1. From this point of view, the thought of the *falāsifa* of the prophetic philosophy is as fundamentalist as Sunnī thought. The intellectual idealism of the first and the cross-historical vision of the second are both directed towards the dynamization and guidance of concrete history through supreme values (God, Revelation, Prophet, Imām). Among the Sunnīs, however, a certain way of using the Qur'ān, the *ra'y*, the *qiyās* and the *ḥadīth* tends to ensure a meretricious and nit-picking form of control (see the literature of legalistic ruses or *ḥiyal*) rather than the activation of history.
2. And, of course, in the anthologies that have been mentioned.
3. This distinction was well developed by Julia Kristeva in *Recherches pour un sémanalyse*, Editions du Seuil, 1969.

discourse, nevertheless resorts to the opportunistic use of verses to 'demonstrate' some theory or other. He makes shrewd stylistic observations to refute those who denounce the capacity of the Qur'ān to prove anything at all, given that sects of all descriptions quote it in support of the most diverse opinions (pp. 186, 198–9). But he is not above using the procedure himself (pp. 14, 117, 124 and passim). What this means is that the impressionist reading along the lines of the *i'jāz* and the logocentrist reading are in permanent competition. Even when logical formalism appears to be triumphant, the reality is that emotive attachment and references to subjective certitudes underlie every act of reading. However, that did not prevent intellectuals in the Middle Ages from believing in the independence, the permanence and the completeness of judgement based on reason.[1]

Conclusion

What have we gained from our own reading of the *I'lām*? Essentially, an evaluation of the practical efficacy and theoretical inadequacy of philosophical writing in the fourth century H./tenth century. This writing is effective in the sense that it succeeds in emphasizing the role of Islam as the driving and regulating force of a culture and civilization which, in the period we are considering, were undoubtedly the most glittering and powerful in their world. The value of al-'Āmirī's demonstration resides in the solid links he manages to establish between Revelation and history. The first is perceived as a body of teachings adapted to the nature and political conditions of humanity; the second presented as the setting in which the Divine wishes were being fulfilled, along the lines of the first successful applications achieved by the Prophet. History, in consequence, is the decisive criterion that makes it possible to measure the distance between the models fixed by the true religion and human behaviour in practice. However, the setbacks

1. The entire literature of Qur'ānic commentaries up to the present day should be examined from this angle.

and misfortunes encountered in history cannot detract from the validity of the Message itself.

This reading of the texts and their historical projections is made possible by an unconditional acceptance of the logocentric tradition. The status and operating conditions of the religious sciences are defined using the schematic Platonic and Aristotelian features of philosophical learning. Reason thus asserts a methodological supremacy, but only to subject it to the service of a creed. Hence the arbitrary treatment of religions that are incompatible with Islam. Overall, the type of culture whose workings and function are demonstrated by the *I'lām* conforms to the modern definition, according to which culture starts with the interdiction of established desires. We have seen that the discourse deployed is exclusively ethical-religious because it concerns the repression of primary human drives in order to prepare for the advent of the perfect man. So, like the literary discourse, logocentrist discourse embodies a displacement: instead of pursuing a reconciliation with the inevitable in the human condition, it seeks to compensate for the failings of that condition with the promise of future Felicity. If our reading has succeeded in showing the need for this deciphering, it will have attained its goal of freeing us from ancient thought processes and persuading us to re-examine repeatedly the meaning and scope of all cultural action.

FOUR

Authority and Power in Islamic Thought

O you who believe! Obey God and obey the Messenger and those of you who are in the position of decision making; If you have a dispute concerning any matter, refer it to God and the Messenger if, indeed, you believe in God and the Last Day. That is better and more seemly the good option.

Qur'ān 4:59

Neither legal relations nor political forms could be comprehended whether by themselves or on the basis of a so-called general development of the human mind, but that on the contrary they originate in the material conditions of life.

K. Marx, *A Contribution to the Critique of Political Economy*

La personne, tout en faisant partie de l'Etat, transcende l'Etat par le mystère inviolable de la liberté spirituelle et par sa vocation aux biens absolus.

J. Maritain, *Christianisme et démocratie*

My main concern in this chapter is not to describe once again the historical developments of different doctrinal elaborations on the concept of authority (*ḥukm, ḥākimiyya*) in Islamic thought, since this has been done in several books and articles. However, the most recent studies are, in fact, focused more on power (*sulṭa, sulṭān*) in its political expression through the state than on authority.[1] The Orientalist approach to the subject remains more narrative and descriptive than critical, while the Muslim presentation is still dominated by the ideological, apologetic claim to restore the 'authentic' *Madīna* model in the traditional framework of what is currently presented as the regime of religious law (*siyāsa shar'iyya*) for Sunnīs and the supreme legal authority (*marja' al-taqlīd*) for Shī'ītes. For these reasons, it becomes urgent to initiate a critical evaluation of authority in Islamic thought in the historical and anthropological perspectives I have proposed in several books and articles since my *Humanisme arabe au 4e/10e siècle, op. cit.*

Before we start our exploration, it is necessary to consider some basic facts. Are there authors, texts or periods which could be considered as more relevant to a critical evaluation and decisive assessments than others? Is it possible to discover an hierarchy or a thoughtful articulation between levels of authority as is presented in Islamic thought during its classical and contemporary periods? We shall try to answer to these difficult questions and, beyond that, to propose a new analytical framework through which to rethink the tensions and connections between authority and power in Islam.

1. Problems of Conceptualisation

The first obstacle to be identified is the vocabulary used by ancient as well as by contemporary thinkers or writers in dealing with religious phenomena in general. Unsuch as many historians of Islamic thought, we need to distinguish from the beginning between two irreducible frameworks of analysis, conceptualization and theorization, the one known as political theology and the other emerging in the context of European modernity under the name of political philosophy. These two frameworks existed in the classical

1. See La notion d'autorité au Moyen Age: Islam, Byzance, Occident, G. Makdisi, J. and D. Sourdel (eds), PUF, 1982. See also the article 'Autorité' in J. Y. Lacoste, Dictionnaire de théologie, PUF, 1998.

Islamic period. Philosophers used the Greek corpus to define '*The virtuous city*' (al-Fārābī's *al-Madīna-l-fāḍila*) according to Plato's and Aristotle's views, while theologians and jurists turned their attention to the definitions given in the Qur'ān and the prophetic Traditions (*sunna, ḥadīth*). Although philosophers in classical Islam contributed to the enrichment of political thought, they did not initiate a cognitive shift from their Greek sources and higher authorities. Aristotle, in particular, was promoted to the rank of 'first master', Fārābī being the 'second'. Intellectually, they used the same attitude of *taqlīd* as theologians and jurists, if we understand *taqlīd* as the active intellectual search for identifying among the known respected authorities in a field of knowledge, the most stable, reliable sources of authority.[1] I have shown in my *Humanisme arabe* how this intellectual convergence on the problem of authority is one of the distinctive characteristics of the mediaeval mindset and cognitive practice.[2] For this reason, we cannot confuse the mediaeval political philosophy that was not yet emancipated from theological categories and modern political philosophy that has deliberately strived for full emancipation from any concession to theology. After the thirteenth century, Islamic thought eliminated all references to its own philosophical legacy, except the existential, theosophical metaphysics maintained by Shī'ī Imāmī thinkers; but both trends, Sunnī and Shī'ī thought, never paid serious attention to the modern European development of philosophy until the nineteenth century. The recent expansion of the fundamentalist interpretation of Islam shows that modern philosophy remains totally alien to contemporary Islamic thought. The slightest reference to this philosophy is rejected as irrelevant to the authentic, self-sufficient conceptualisation provided already by the Qur'ān, the *ḥadīth* and the orthodox authorities in what is received as the divine Law governance (*siyāsa shar'iyya*) for Sunnī Islām, the governance of the theologian jurist (*wilāyat al-faqīh*) for the Imāmī Islam.

1. Jackson, Sherman A., Islamic Law and the State: The Constitutional Jurisprudence of Shihāb al-Dīn al-Qarāfī, Brill, Leiden, 1996, pp. 80–112.
2. See what has been said already in Chapter 3 on Logocentrism.

How should we proceed, then, if we want to rethink the concepts of authority and power, not only in the light of the theoretical framework and the concrete practice bequeathed to us by the living Islamic Tradition, but more decisively, in the light of what I call emerging reason? Would it be relevant to the present political and cultural situation of 'Muslim' societies to reactivate the classical dialectic tension between *ijtihād/taqlīd* and remain within the cognitive limits of religious reason in general and of Islamic reason in particular? If we consider religious reasoning, we should stress the difference between its evolution in Christianity – the Protestant, Anglican and Roman Catholic sects since the Renaissance movement and Lutheran Reformation in the sixteenth century – on one side, in Islam with its three living traditions – Sunnī, Imāmī and Ismā'ilī – on the other side. Christian theology had to cope with the challenges and political revolutions initiated by a dynamic capitalist bourgeoisie and the efficient alternatives offered by reason of enlightenment. Islamic thought missed, and is still missing more than ever, these two historical forces through its development since the thirteenth century which is also the beginning of the expanding European hegemony. Christianity is even presented by some theoreticians such as Marcel Gauchet, as '*the religion of getting out from religion*'; by others such as René Girard, as the only one religious answer which succeeded, in the sacrifice of God incarnate, in transcending violence coupled with the sacred as the two operating anthropological forces in human societies. On the contrary, Islam as a religious experience and an historical force that still remains a prisoner in the anthropological triangle traced by **Violence, Sacred, Truth** (*dīn al-ḥaqq*). This theological statement is reinforced by sociologists and political scientists who focus their interest on the fundamentalist expressions of political Islam, neglecting or undermining other expressions less visible, often silenced, but significant in the present context. While political scientists provide a wider audience for an arbitrary selected manifestation of what is presented globally as 'Islam',[1] they

1. See the coming book of Fedwa Malti-Douglas, *Medecines of the Soul: Female Bodies and Sacred Geographies in a Transnational Islam*, University

do not offer any positive intellectual contribution to enhance the interpretation of the religious phenomenon and its function in all contemporary societies. For this reason, I have concentrated my critical search on the most radical issues, such as authority and power and the cognitive status of revelation, reformation or subversion of the *salafī islāḥī* framework of perception and interpretation.

It is vital to show that contemporary sociological and political Islam ignores and dismantles what classical Islamic schools of thought have achieved and bequeathed concerning authority and power. Consequently, the so-called *'ulamā'*, who claim to be the reliable spiritual authorities for contemporary believers, are unable – even in terms of classical *ijtihād* and *taqlīd* – to point to the intrinsic limitations of the whole legacy on the subject we are examining here. Moreover, those *'ulamā'*, (*mullah* or *ayatollahs* for Shī'ites), have clearly manifested, as did the *salafī* reformers from 1850 to 1940, in which sense and to what degree the issue of authority and power thus far remains the unthought of contemporary Islamic thought at the different stages and trends in its recent development. I know that this contention is refuted by scholars, *'ulamā'* and militant believers who are unable to grasp historical reasoning about the changing epistemological postures of reason in each given culture and at each stage of a long historical development. When we come to the so-called revolutionary leaders who claimed, at the same time as did Khomeini, to fulfil the function of the supreme legal authority (*marja' al-taqlīd*), coupled with political leadership as the 'legitimate' head of the state, we know how relatively free are intellectual confrontations based on the well-established rules of the mediaeval *disputatio* (*munāẓara*), become impossible today under the pressures of two forms of arbitrary censorship. One is imposed from above by the state which has monopolized the control of what is officially called everywhere 'religious affairs'; the other comes from below with the fundamentalist defenders of the 'true Islam'

---

of California Press., Berkeley, 2001. The author refers correctly to what she calls 'the contemporary Islamic textual corpus' including an Islamic revival along with Islamic fundamentalism.

against its 'enemies' inside and outside. As far as religious issues are concerned, more specifically the problem of authority and power, this lack of free, critical, duly documented debates prevails in all contemporary so-called Muslim societies. I call 'documented debates' those conducted by historians who are well informed on both political theology and philosophy in Islam, Christianity and secularized Western developments from the Middle Ages until the contemporary confrontations about democracy, the rule of law, civil society and religious authority.

These are the vital questions and the currently operating forces that I am going to consider in the present essay. I shall focus on the two interrelated levels of authority:

Firstly, the authority intrinsic to the Holy texts given to recite, read, interiorize and understand as a supra-human source and foundation from which derive and on which rest all the legal qualifications and categorizations (*aḫkām*) articulated and collected by the body of authority or doctors of Law (*'ulamā'* or *a'imma mujtahidūn*). It is currently contended that these authorized *'ulamā'* are theologically independent from any type or level of political power; they can have access to the function of a judge (*qāḍī*) who is more specifically responsible for the judicial affairs (applying the law to acts of devotion and all the transactions between individuals: *'ibādāt* and *mu'āmalāt*); but recent discussions among historians tend to establish the idea that this privileged theological status of *'ulamā'* in the Sunnī version of Islam is the result of a long struggle of *'ulamā'* as a social category against the caliphate which has been the representative of God (*ḫalīfat Allah*), not of the Messenger of God (*ḫalīfat rasūl Allah*) from the rise of Umayyād dynasty (661) to the fall of al-Ma'mūn and the reign of Mutawakkil (848). We shall come back to this important historical aspect of the battle which throws light on the distinction between authority and power in all times and all societies.

Secondly, the level of power (*sulṭān*) exercised by institutionalized 'authorities' named caliph, imām, sulṭān, emīr (today there are kings and presidents who have a different status in law). The word 'authorities' refers to a combination of a power backed up by a more or less legitimate authority. The Qur'ānic expression *ūlū-l-amri minkum* contains this ambiguous combination. Theoretically, in the classical system after 848, these are the protectors – not the interpreters and implementers as representatives of God – of the divine Law (*sharī'a*), to be distinguished from positive legal norms (*fiqh*); their competence is limited to the strict enforcement of the intangible divine Law through the judges appointed by them, but independent from them in their judicial activity. Legal norms are developed by those learned men authorized for *ijtihād* (*a'imma mujtahidūn*). Authority circulates from God in the heaven to those human agents – called social protagonists by modern sociology – who are qualified to explain in theological, juridical, ethical terms the normative rules (*ḥukm, aḥkām*) which every believer, including the head of the polity, has to obey. Authority, power, legitimacy, legitimization, law, legal rules and ethics are interconnected, inseparable primary concepts, constantly disputed, revised, reassessed by theoreticians and social protagonists in all historical contexts. My contention is that Islamic thought has initiated an interesting approach since the first great dispute called *al-fitna-l-kubrā*, and sustained a rich theoretical and practical debate in the dialectic, pluralist, dynamic context which prevailed until the political split between Sunnī-Shī'ī schools on one hand and the elimination of philosophical reason and culture on the other. To show this complexity which ended with poor, restricted, dogmatic, local discussions and views after the thirteenth–fourteenth centuries, I shall quote the following texts as significant landmarks in the long historical march of Islamic and modern thought on authority and its related concepts.

2. Islamic Framework of Cognisance and Interpretation

I am quoting here the al-Khū'ī text on the authority of the Qur'ān as the ultimate constraining reference for every cognitive statement, more specifically in the domain of ethics and law. As has been seen in Chapter 2, all schools came to a common agreement on this point.

2.1.

> *It behoves a true Muslim – rather every thinker – to apply himself to understanding the Qur'ān, clarifying its mysteries and acquiring its enlightenment; for it is the Book that guarantees the establishment of peace, happiness and order for human beings, and promotes their prosperity and helps them attain it. The Qur'ān is, moreover, a reference book for the lexicographer, a guide for the grammarian, a competent authority for the jurist, a model for the man of letters, a goal of persistent search for the sage, an instructor for the preacher and aspiration for the moralist. From it are derived the social sciences and public administration; on it are based religious sciences; its guidance makes possible the discovery of the secrets of the universe and the laws of nature. The Qur'ān is the eternal miracle of the everlasting religion. It is the exalted and lofty order for the equally exalted and lofty sharī'a [sacred law].*[1]

Until al-'Allāma al-Ḥillī (726/1325), the Imāmī doctrine on authority rejected *ijtihād* and *qiyās* as sources for law because they lead to the mere personal opinion of the jurist, and the *akhbār* transmitted from the 12 imāms have a more revelatory value than any opinion (*ra'y or ẓann*). Al-Ḥillī succeeded in imposing *ijtihād* which was recognized as a probative force for the majority represented by the non-scholarly community submitted to *taqlīd*. In the seventeenth century, the theory of al-Ḥillī began to be challenged by the important *akhbārī* school or trend initiated with Muḥammad Astarabādhī (1036/1626) and amplified by many others, mainly Yūsuf al-Baḥrānī (1186/1792) and Muḥammad al-Bihbahānī (1206/1792). These were recently studied by Robert Gleave in *Inevitable Doubt. Two theories of Shī'ī Jurisprudence*, Brill 2000. I shall comment on the significance of the resurgence of *Akhbārī* school in the seventeenth–eighteenth century Imāmī contexts for the general debate on authority and power in Islam in general.

1. Al-khū'ī, *The Prolegomena to the Qur'ān*, translated with an introduction by A. A. Sachedina, Oxford University Press, 1998, p.26.

2..2.

About the living Tradition of the Prophet (*sunna*), the Ḥanbalī Aḥmad Ghulām Khalīl (d. 275/888), among many other authors, states:

> *The Sunna is the foundation on which the Community is built. (The models to be followed) are the Companions of Muḥammad, the people of the authoritative sunna and the Community (ahl al-sunna wal-jamā'a). Whosever fails to follow them, errs and commits innovation (bid'a) . . . Whosoever alleges that there is any matter in Islam for which the Companions of Muḥammad do not suffice, has lied about them and launched a slanderous attack against them. He is an innovator, he goes and leads astray, and introduces into Islam that which does not pertain thereto. Know that there is no qiyās (inference from analogy) in the sunna, nor can any comparable rules (amthāl) be formulated for it or any fleeting emotions followed with regard to it. It is the recognition of the Prophet's models (left traces, āthār) without a why? or a how? (raising questions for qualification or explanation). To discourse, polemicize, dispute or argue is an innovation that raises doubt in the heart, even if one hits upon the truth and the Sunna (in this fashion).*[1]

2.3.

According to Ibn Khaldūn (d. 808/1406), Islamic jurisprudence (*fiqh*) is:

> *the knowledge of the rules of God which concern the action of persons who admit to being bound to obey the Law respecting what it declares to be obligatory (farḍ, wājib), forbidden/illicit (maḥẓūr/ḥarām), recommended/liked (mandūb/mustaḥabb), reprehensible/disliked (makrūh), indifferent/merely permitted*

1. Quoted by G. V. Grunebaum in op. cit. pp. 109–110.

> *(mubāḥ). Such knowledge is acquired from the Book (the Qur'ān), the Sunna and such arguments as the jurists may deduce for the necessary comprehension of the laws contained therein. It is the body of rules derived from these laws that is called fiqh.*[1]

2.4.

Al-Qarafī (d. 684/1285) on the *madhhab* and the conditions to refer to it as an authority, or *taqlīd*:

> *What is the meaning of 'Mālik's madhhab' and the 'madhhab' of other aphorisms in which it is permissible to follow them via taqlīd? ... If you say 'that which they say which is true and correct concerning religious matters, including those things of which the lawgiver has commanded, in which we should acquire knowledge', this statement would be invalidated by the cases of uṣūl al-dīn and uṣūl al-fiqh. For while these include matters concerning which the lawgiver has commanded that we acquire knowledge, it remains, nonetheless, forbidden to perform the taqlīd of Mālik or anyone else regarding these things. If you say Mālik's madhhab and the madhhab of other scholars who are followed via taqlīd consists of branches of positive law (al-furū'), I respond: if you mean all the branches of positive law, your statement is invalidated on the grounds of those branches which are known, necessarily, to be a part of the religion, such as the obligation to perform prayers, the fast of Ramaḍān, the prohibition on lying, fornication, stealing and the like For there is no place at all in these matters for taqlīd, because their status is already known by necessity ... If, on the other hand, you mean only some branches of positive law, how, then, is this portion to be determined? Moreover, even if you clarify the manner in which this portion is determined, you will still not have achieved your goal. For your definition will remain non-inclusive in that it will not comprise the legal causes (sabab, asbāb) and prerequisites (shurūṭ) in which you follow the scholar via taqlīd. Indeed, legal causes and legal prerequisites are*

1. *Al-Muqaddima*, quoted by R. Levy in *The social Structure of Islam*, Cambridge, 1957, p. 150.

not the same as legal rules (aḥkām). For this reason, the scholars have said: 'Legal rules belong to that portion of God's address that is prescriptive (khiṭāb taklīf), while legal causes and prerequisites belong to that portion that is descriptive (khiṭāb waḍ'). And it is because of questions such as these that we find hardly any of the lesser legal authorities able to respond definitively when asked to define the madhhab of their Imām whom they follow via taqlīd. This applies equally to the followers of all the madhhabs.[1]

2.5.

Ghazālī (d. 1111) on the necessity of a ruling institution, be it a caliph, an *imām*, an *emīr*, a *sulṭān:*

There are those who hold that the imamate is dead, lacking as it does the required qualifications. But no substitute can be found for it. What then? Are we to give up obeying the law? Shall we dismiss the judges (quḍāt), declare all authority to be valueless, cease marrying and pronounce the acts of those in high offices to be invalid at all points, leaving the populace to live in sinfulness? Or shall we continue as we are, recognizing that the Imamate really exists and that all acts of the administration are valid, given the circumstances of the case and the necessities of the moment? The lesser evil is relatively speaking the better, and the reasonable person must choose the latter possibility.[2]

To all these categorical, dogmatic Islamic texts (only one belongs to a contemporary Shī'ī authority), I add one signed by a well known Islamicist to show with which epistemological posture classical Orientalism handles basic disputed issues in Islamic thought in general, in matters related to what modern thought practices as the philosophy of Law which is different, of course, from what Islamic tradition teaches as *Uṣūl al-fiqh*.

1. Jackson, Sh. A., op. cit., pp.115–6.
2. Ghazālī, *al-Iqtisād fī-l-i'tiqād*, quoted and translated by G. V. Grunebaum in *Medieval Islam*, 1953, p. 168.

2.6.

Ann K. S. Lambton: *State and Government in Medieval Islam*, OUP, 1981, introduction, pp. XV–XVI:

> *In* Islam, *the antithesis between the* individual *and the state or government is not recognized, and no need is therefore felt to reconcile and abolish this antithesis.* Islam knows no distinction between church and state. *The parallel between Islam and Europe in the Middle Ages, when church and society were one is, perhaps, close. In Islam, there is no doctrine of the temporal end which alone belongs to the state and the eternal end which belongs to, and is the prerogative of, the church; no balance between the two; each equal to the other when acting in its own sphere; each equally dependent on the other when acting in the sphere of the other and no tension between the historic community and the church as custodian of the universal common elements in human existence. The state is 'given', and it is not limited by the existence of an association claiming to be its equal or superior, to which it can leave the preaching of morality and the finding of sanctions for its truth. It has itself to repress evil and show the way to righteousness; there is no clear-cut boundary between morality and legality. In practice, temporal power was often usurped and there was a* de facto *separation between the spiritual and the temporal, but there was no* ideological *separation; no ruler, however much he may have violated the law, challenged the principle of its universal application. The lack of any formal doctrine of such powers had important consequences in the field of* individual freedom. *It contributed to, if it was not actually responsible for, the creation of a situation in which power was arbitrary and exercised by the last despot who had usurped it. It also had important consequences for the attitude towards civil war and internal unrest.*

We can recapitulate all the constraining principles and definitions in what I called the Islamic framework of cognisance and interpretation in the two diagrams presented by Robert

Gleave in his recent book, *Inevitable Doubt*, (pp. 185 and 199). The explanations of the two diagrams are to be read in Chapter 4 of his book, under the title 'Rationalist Morality'.

RATIONALIST MORALITY

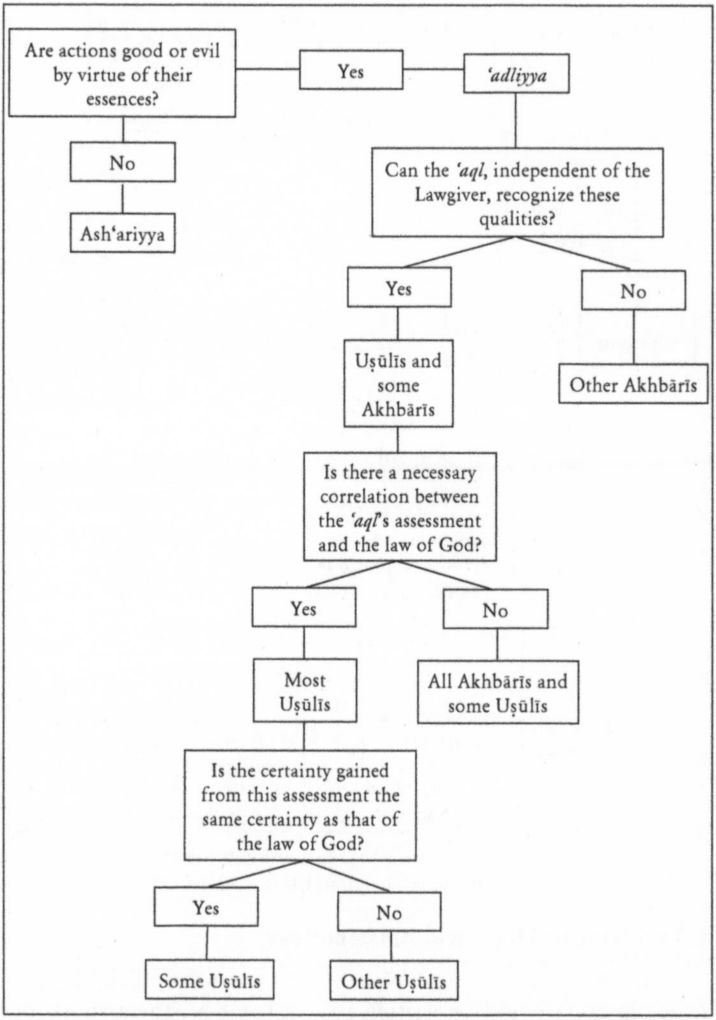

Diagram explaining the positions of different sects over the relationship of reason and revelation as depicted by Muẓaffar Riḍā.

RATIONALIST MORALITY

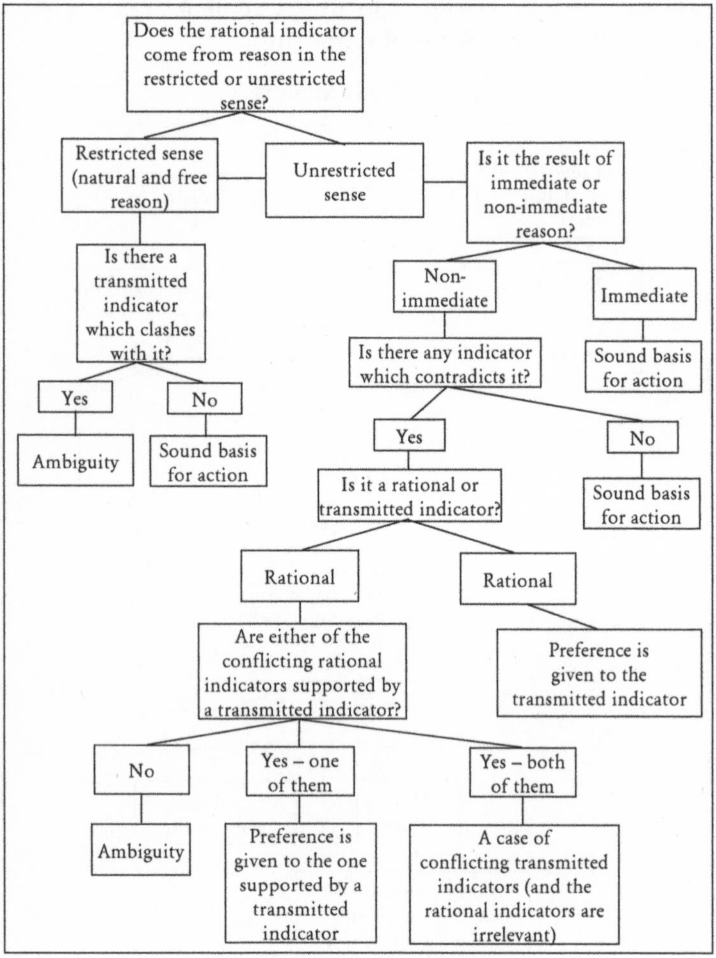

Diagram examinig the relationship between reason and revelation in Baḥrānī's M10.

3. Problems of Historical Epistemology

A whole book could be written to comment on these short, but authoritative texts. I shall not repeat what is already well known about their explicit content; for my critical strategy applies to all systems of thought, ancient and modern. It is much more important to illustrate the as yet unconsidered concept of **historical epistemology**. For doctrinal texts and the texts interpreting them it is essential to unveil the implicit, hidden axioms and prerequisite postulates which command each explicit proposition. Let us read the six texts one by one.

Al-Khū'ī restates the strictly orthodox theological teaching shared since the tenth century by the whole Community about the Word of God as the 'revealed given' transmitted in the Book called the Qur'ān. This is the supreme, transcendental, absolute Authority recognized, obeyed and venerated by all Muslims. The author has a classical statement which could have been made by any other Muslim belonging to any of the numerous competing schools and fractions (*firaq*) about orthodoxy. Two remarks are in order about al-Khū'ī position:

1. The Imāmī community agreed on the Qur'ān as the revelation of the Word of God through Muḥammad, but it discussed problems relating to the collection of the Qur'ān up to the fourth/tenth century and developed its own exegesis based on a different corpus of traditions as is shown recently in two majors contributions;[1]

2. There are deep discrepancies between *Sunnī, Shī'ī* and *Khārijī* communities about the living Tradition as the second supreme source, or foundation (*aṣl*) of authority. Each community developed its own **collective memory**, collected in separate Official Closed Corpuses. As in all such dogmatic, theological statements, al-Khū'ī's presentation of the Qur'ān is axiomatic: each proposition is true in itself and cannot be discussed; a number of deductions can safely be made without any need for verification or argument. One could expect a thinker who

1. M. A. Amir-Moezzi: *Le guide divin dans le shī'isme originel: Aux sources de l'ésotérisme en Islam*, Paris, 1992; English translation: *The Divine Guide in Early Shī 'ism*, New York, 1994; Meir M. Bar-Asher: *Scripture and Exegesis in Early Imāmī Shi'ism*, Brill, Leiden, 1999.

spanned the nineteenth and twentieth centuries (November 1899–8 August 1992) to make some historical, scientific remarks on the necessity of reassessing the cognitive status of the Qur'ān in a comparative and critical perspective; on the contrary, we see how the main issues relating to this conservative 'orthodox' presentation, can illustrate the vast unthought in the thinking of a supreme theological authority (*marja' al-taqlīd*) of Imāmī Islam. This raises the problem of epistemic and epistemological continuity in Islamic thought to which the periodization of European thought does not apply. The intellectual and scientific **regime of the truth** as articulated by al-Khū'ī, does not and should not differ from that inherited from venerated authorities of Middle Ages: we shall see what effect this historical fact has on modern life in the so-called Muslim societies (political, cultural, linguistic, scientific, educational and intellectual life).

The statement on the *sunna* obeys the same fixed, inherited epistemic pattern: the reference to *ahl al-sunna wal-jamā'a* is one of the strongest postulates which shaped and continues to command, consciously or unconsciously, the reasoning not only of Muslim believers, but of pre-modern religious reason in general. Historians, ancient and modern, do not pay attention to the issue of postulates underlying the explicit discourse; they use the vocabulary of Muslim historiography and its narrative framework which have been fixed, *post facto,* in the ideological 'Abbāsīd context, the 'orthodox' representation of the split of the *umma* into competing communities since the so-called great *fitna* (656–661). *Fitna* itself is a theological concept which covers the real forces and agents of the struggles and what was at stake, and is more closely related to tribal sociological mechanisms and cultural codes than to the theological definitions that were introduced much later on.[1] The

1. Many examples can be given of so-called modern scholarship, in which the concept of the imaginary representation of the past *post facto* is never used to differentiate between the positive, critical history of the emerging 'Muslim' societies and 'Islamic' rule on one side from the mythical construct of this historical moment transfigured into the Inaugurating sacred Age of Revelation and Prophetic Model.

debate on the so-called 'rightly guided caliphs' (*khulafā rāshidūn*) in Medīna (632–661) has continued in terms of a back-projection of the theological construct of a *Sunnī, Shī'ī, Khārijī* Ideal Type of a sacred-sanctifying instance of authority, to which should be referred all the legal procedures of allegiance (*bay'a*) to the legitimate caliph, imām, sulṭān (king today). Theology is, in its essence, political, but in its style of articulating a meaningful existence, it uses a mythological framework and impressionist literary devices. It might refer to chronological facts, but its gaze is fixed on the eschatological horizon of salvation, or what H. Corbin described as the *hierohistory* = spiritual and sacred-sanctifying history. This raises a major problem of methodology to which we shall refer again in the discussion on Lambton's text. We shall need to differentiate two levels of knowledge which interact constantly in religious life and discourse. The level of **imaginary** representations and the level of discursive logocentrist articulations of what is called, without further precision, truth. In all cultures, Truth with capital T, refers to the Truth imagined, constructed, articulated and projected back by the historiographical literature produced *post facto* under the pressures and the specific needs of several social, ethnic, competing groups, as is clearly shown during the Umayyād and 'Abbāsīd rule. Each group defends and promotes its own 'orthodox Truth', using the same literary device of projecting back to the same Inaugurating Time when Revelation, or a revelatory discourse attributed to ancient wisdom in 'non-revealed' religions, occurred. This collective process of building the supreme instance of Authority is repeated everywhere through history and is also present in the secular theory of popular sovereignty on which is based our democratic legitimacy.

Contemporary Muslims are continuing to refer to this instance of Authority as it has been crystallised, especially in the writings of Ibn Taymiyya. The prophet Muḥammad taught clearly and with the most desirable accuracy what to believe, what not to

---

See Khalid Yaḥya Blankinship, *The End of the Jihād State: The Reign of Hishām Ibn 'Abd al-Malik and the Collapse of the Umayyāds*, SUNY, 1994; Hichem Djaït: *La grande discorde*, Gallimard, 1989.

believe and how to behave according to the revealed standards. His Companions memorized every sentence, every gesture, every attitude they heard and witnessed from the Messenger of God and transmitted all of that sacred tradition with a scrupulously pious sense of authenticity. *Ahl al-sunna wal-jamāʿa*, currently called Orthodox Muslims, are exclusively those believers who follow this authentic, purifying Tradition; all other groups claiming a different constructed orthodoxy are rejected out of the 'Community promised to Salvation' as 'sects', heretics and erring groups.

The orthodox literature that is well represented by the texts we have selected, never points out to the **hidden psycho-literary process** of projecting back the founding existential Truth which nourishes and sustains 'spiritually' – a concept to be reworked – ethically or mythically the faith of each believer; a faith which cannot itself exist without the support of the competing **collective living memories** that emerged and are still emerging today under the name of fundamentalist or revivalist movements, or national identities through accelerated historical pressures. All these groups obey to what can be described as the **Islamic Paradigm**. As I have just presented its literary, historical genesis, this Paradigm is neither a theological nor an ethical, or purely mythological concept; it is a psycho-sociological, historical, anthropological construct articulated in a typical, appropriated *literary genre* with specific rhetoric and semiotic devices.[1] Because of this complex combination of levels of human existence with the corresponding devices of expression, creativity and self affirmation, the Islamic Paradigm, once internalized as such through individual ritual performances and collective celebrations within each self-promoting community, operates in all historical contexts as the supreme transcendent, sacred, intangible, founding, superseding Authority.

Again, I must point out here that we are using two different levels of conceptualization relating to two different epistemological postures and resulting in two different cognitive strategies. This must be clearly grasped by each reader in order to avoid the

1. Well described in Fedwa Malti-Douglas, op. cit.

misleading current emotional reactions and irrelevant objections of all those who feel disturbed in their inherited system of beliefs and non-beliefs, supported by the traditional theological, historiographical framework of 'knowledge'.'Islamic Paradigm' is a concept used to recapitulate the results of the historical, anthropological, linguistic and conceptual deconstruction of the collective memories called living Tradition by each community. The reader should notice that the deconstructive operation relies on what I would call **progressive-regressive method** which goes much beyond the factual, descriptive, narrative presentations of classical historiography. With the progressive-regressive method, we can identify the ideological options and the mythological constructions of the social imaginaries. We look back to the past (regressive process) not to project on the sacralized, sacralizing texts used as sacred and foundational, reliable in all times and all places, the demands and needs of the present-day Muslim societies – as has been done precisely since the formative period of Islamic thought. We can look back, however, with the modern archaeological cognitive project which gives priority to the discovery – removing the cover or unveiling – of the axiological hidden discourse commanding the explicit discourses not only of the various disciplines practised in the past, but also the Holy Texts used as the transcendent Sources-Foundations (*Uṣūl*) of the normative Law, ethics, politics and semantics. We are then in a position which would better enable us to evaluate the historical epistemologies used in each given historical context in which a cognitive paradigm prevailed through a long time and a large space, without projecting back irrelevant 'modern' criteria or value judgements which would mean reverting to ideological interpretations. The regressive analytical, deconstructive approach is simultaneously a progressive process used to liberate contemporary Islamic thought from obvious, heavily ideological, mythological manipulations of the dismantled collective memories in the present context of modernisation and globalization. This critical inquiry is also designed to contribute to the programme of emerging reason, namely, providing our present thinking with a new dynamic, more relevant intellectual tools and flexible procedures that are constantly being revised, re-appropriated theoretical frameworks to reassess on more reliable basis, the articulation of authority and power.

The paragraph that has just been read is a concrete illustration of the progressive-regressive method specially required by all the religious living traditions and currently used by the collective living memories of the communities as a **supra-historical space of mental projection and spiritual validation of the ideal, eternal, divinely rooted 'values'**. I have interrupted my regressive analysis to insert it into the present needs and expectations, not only of Muslim readers, but of all religiously motivated readers and beyond them, anyone interested in the development of a multicultural, anthropologically and philosophically based humanism. If a more concrete historical example is required to support all of the 'abstract' analyses I have presented, I would refer to the ongoing struggle between Jews, Christians and Muslims concerning the control of Jerusalem, a city that is claimed by all three religions as 'their' irreplaceable 'sacred' place. The competition is obviously political, using the most reprehensible ploys – killing, destroying, negating the dignity of the human person, denying elementary justice through several conflicts involving international responsibilities – in the name of uncriticized Truths, the unthought, the sacred, unchangeable divine Law and redefined authority for all three protagonists. The most depressing aspect of this tragic experience of the divine leading to the use of the most terrible violence, is that neither the custodians of the sacred, nor the leading democratic, modern nations have been able so far to articulate even a relevant analysis of this case study, to say nothing of defining a solution which would be constraining for the human mind, nor for an international law whose total absence or inadequacy is precisely established by the historical genesis since the destruction of the Temple, the construction of the Dome of the Rock, the substitution of an Islamic sovereignty for the previous Christian one, the battles of the Crusades and, last but not least, the Sykes-Picot agreement! We can really speak of the defeat of human mind.

To return to our archaeological inquiry, two important remarks are in order. The first concerns the concept of **Paradigm,** with a capital P. The anthropological, historical, linguistic and mythical dimensions of the Islamic Paradigm can also be identified in the Jewish, Christian, Hindu and Buddhist examples. The relevance of the concept can even be extended to secular contexts, as is clearly shown in the case of the French Revolution which became the '*laïc*' Paradigm of the French Republic.[1] The second refers to the concepts of Truth and authority. Viewed from the critical, deconstructive analysis we are proposing, this Truth and the authority attached to it and derived from it are not declared wrong, or dismissed; they are recognized with their specific content and psycho-ideological functions in all the historical contexts in which it operated and it is still claimed as a non-superseded model. This is what we continue to study and have lived with until now as the 'ontological, substantial, essential, unchangeable Truth', postulated by theological and metaphysical reason for many centuries in the monotheistic and the Greek patterns of thought. At the same time, we have displaced this Truth to another space of intelligibility in which veiled functions are unveiled, hidden postulates are questioned and old controversies rekindled between 'orthodox' believers and 'free thinkers'.[2] The single absolute Truth becomes a truth with a small t as one of a plurality of truths; but it continues to exist and compete with all the other forms, levels or regimes of truth. In our democratic, liberal regimes, truth as well as authority are trivialized in the name of 'democratic identity' which recognises differences between human beings , as well as human rights and 'ethno-cultural justice'.[3] We shall come back to this crucial debate carried on since the late eighties in North America, extended to Europe since the pressure of migrants and refugees is affecting the

---

1. See F. Furet, *Penser la révolution française*, Gallimard, 1984; and Pierre Nora, *Les lieux de mémoire*, 7 vols, Gallimard, 1954–92.
2. As they are recently presented with well balanced re-definitions by Sarah Stroumsa: *Free Thinkers of Medieval Islam. Ibn al-Rāwandī, Abū Bakr al-Rāzī and their impact on Islamic thought*, Brill, Leiden, 1999; see my review of the book in *Arabica*, 2000/2.
3. See Sylvie Mesure and Alain Renaut, *Alter ego: Les paradoxes de l'identité démocratique*, Aubier, Paris, 1999.

political balance of forces in all democratic, liberal societies.

According to psychoanalysts, sociologists, anthropologists, social imaginary receives and activates mental representations promoted with semiotic, mythological, ideological manipulations, to the cognitive status and functions of substantial, indisputable, irreducible truths. This is another intellectual and political regime of producing, recognizing and activating truth. Religious definition of truth refuses to consider this regime, as it has refused since the Middle Ages, to account for the fundamental role of the metaphor and metonymy in the revealed word of God. Both facts are intellectually subversive to the orthodox religious conceptualization of the Truth. Consequently, religious reasoning cannot incorporate a new and powerful rival form of the fundamentalist Truth which also has the power to sacralize, mythologize and ideologize ordinary, profane social protagonists, current events, human discourses and contingent norms. The problems, hopes and needs of the new marginalized social classes are projected into the revolutionary programmes mixing between the eschatological Salvation promised by traditional religions and the political emancipation promised by the 'modern' leaders. This model is incarnated by several leaders since the nineteenth century by both the Mahdīs and Imāms in Muslim contexts and by secular leaders in the ex-communist, fascist European regimes.

This psychological, social and historical mechanism has an anthropological dimension because it applies to the structural functions of the social imaginary developed by all social groups. The objective reality is always represented, experienced and expressed through the complex interactive contributions of reason, imagination, imaginary and individual and collective memories.[1] We see all we can learn from the progressive-regressive analysis. Without it, the concept of orthodox Islam with its subsequent heresiographical vision of sects, true and false religions, believers and non-believers, Islamisation of knowledge and foreign, western knowledge, will continue to obscure and alienate the critical,

1. See my study 'Imaginaire social et leaders dans le monde musulman contemporain', in *Arabica*, 1988, vol. XXXV.

creative, emancipating use of reason. Once we discover that Sunnī, Shī'ī, Khārijī and any other sectarian orthodoxy is built on emotional devotion to beliefs and non-beliefs, on self-entitlement to the possession of the Truth leading to Salvation, we are obliged to rethink the whole scale of values and legitimacies founded on the authority of the revealed Truth, or the 'modern' secular Truth used to mobilize the imaginary of scientific progress and ultimate liberation through the bourgeois or proletarian revolution. Self-entitlement to Truth is evidenced in all historical contexts in which a leader assisted by a group of disciples, succeeds in gaining the emotional adhesion of masses to a politics of hope.

The texts of Ibn Khaldūn and al-Qarāfī help us to gain an in-depth critical evaluation of the aspect of authority called *taqlīd*. In his recent book, *Contingency in a Sacred Law* (Brill, 1998), Baber Johansen has convincingly shown how a Law perceived, taught and lived as sacred for fifteen centuries has actually been fully submitted to historical, social, human *contingency*. He describes the intellectual, social and political devices, but not the linguistic, cultural and psychological tools and processes which transform positive legal and ethical norms into divine, sacred, unchangeable qualifications (*aḥkām*) of human thoughts, acts and institutions. Even for those theologians – mainly Mu'tazilite – who recognize the deliberate action based on the will and the human capacity to act, the authorship of the act and the capacity to act is still ascribed to God. Ibn Khaldūn, so highly praised as the initiator of historical criticism, adheres to the orthodox, legal framework in which human acts and intentions are legally and ethically defined without any question as to when, why or how this framework, which was obviously set up by jurists, exegetes and theologians, imposed itself until his time as the divinely inspired eternal definition of Law. We learn more from this attitude about the historical, continuous process which has allowed the unthought to accumulate in Islamic thought until today. In his *Ibn Khaldūn, An Essay in Reinterpretation*, London 1982, p. 104, Azīz al-Aẓmeh makes the following observations which corroborate our line of explanation:

> *The didactic classification of sciences presented in the Muqaddima starts with the positive sciences. Positive and religious sciences of peoples other than Islamic, are ignored, not only because the author was concerned with giving an account of those sciences prevalent in his age. They are ignored because the religion of Islam and, by implication, all the sciences that give it support and articulation, stands to other religions of the Book as the Qur'ān stands to other Holy Books and as the prophecy of Muḥammad stands to the prophecies of his predecessors. This is one described by the term naskh, which denotes abrogation without invalidation and hence has the sense of supersession (my emphasis), the best equivalent in a European language being the German 'Aufhebung' in its Hegelian acceptation. Ibn Khaldūn cites the Qur'ānic injunction to neither believe nor disbelieve what is stated by the peoples of the Book (Qur'ān 2, 87–88). The positive sciences have thrived and reached a very consummate level of development. The first to be discussed are the sciences of the Qur'ān.*

The essential idea to grasp, in this context, is the substitution entailing *supersession* in human relations as well as in the history of cultures and ideas. In the traditional theological presentation of the three 'revealed' religions, Christianity supersedes Judaism, Islam supersedes Judaism, Christianity and, needless to say, all other religions and systems of thought. Muslim scholars feel they can dispense, as Ibn Khaldūn did, with any need to point to other traditions of thought and knowledge. This cognitive posture is expressed today in a more arrogant style by those who endeavour to *Islamise Modernity*. With this attitude, the tradition of thought is doomed to miss all enabling opportunities in order to avoid accumulating false knowledge and an increasing number of epistemological obstacles.

Al-Qarāfī leads us to another illustration of the unthought in a given tradition of thought. First, we are invited to revise a wrong interpretation of the concept of *taqlīd* by leading historians of 'Islamic' law such as J. Schacht. The author explains clearly that *taqlīd* is not a lazy, pious imitation, obedience to the norms defined, fixed by former authorities in a given school of innovative doctors of law; it is a dynamic, critical exercise to determine the right criteria which can justify the acceptance of an authority in the field of theology and law, because both are actually related to each other. The first task of an active, accurate *taqlīd* is to identify an authority, a doctor recognized for his ability to practice a correct, productive *ijtihād*, not just a solution for a given legal case. The only difference between *ijtihād* and *taqlīd* is that the first consists of an effort of intellect applied directly to the holy texts to produce a divinely-inspired legal qualification (*ḥukm*) or to extrapolate it (*taḫrīj*) using the devices of *ijmāʿ* or *qiyās* for those who accept it. For the second (*taqlīd*), it is sufficient to identify the reliable authority that conducted the search correctly, so that there is no point to repeat it. Here, we have undoubtedly a restrictive, uncritical definition of authority. Moreover, in describing the steps to be followed by the *muqallid* to fully control the reliability of each level of authority, al-Qarāfī, like all *ʿulamāʾ* until today, stops at a decisive point which is the self-entitlement of each founder of a school to mediate for all the believers on the ultimate intent of the Lawgiver in His revealed Word. The concept of ultimate intent of the divine Law (*Maqāṣid al-sharīʿa*) has been fully elaborated by the jurist al-Shāṭibī (d. 790/1388). It is indeed a powerful example of what I would call today a critique of legalistic reason in Islam; but this critique could not cross the theological boundaries of mediaeval religious thought.

What do we learn in this perspective from the text of Ann K. S. Lambton? Mainly a clear confirmation of the epistemological posture of classical Islamology since the nineteenth century. The concept 'Islam' is never deconstructed; it is used in the sense imposed by classical Islamicists, received and heavily strengthened in our ideological context of opposing 'Islam' and the 'West', by political scientists. It is indeed an eloquent example of *taqlīd*, transferred to modern scholarship devoted to Islamic studies. 'Islam' is constructed as a substantial, unified and unifying body of beliefs, non-beliefs, institutions, customs, stabilized theological, legal and ethical doctrines, recurrent practises and representations.

All these features are to be found at any time and in any society. They have shaped an Ideal-type of what E. Gellner singled out as the '*Muslim society*'. Fundamentalist contemporary discourse has, of course, strengthened and extended this ideological construct which is acting, prohibiting, commanding, approving, condemning, explaining, and refuting in the same way that Allah acts and organizes the whole grammatical, semantic structure of Qur'ānic discourse. 'Islam' is the ultimate Authority which replaces actual protagonists in all the normative functions normally shared by institutions, political leaders, civil servants, etc. It is indeed an **ideological monster**, constructed and currently used by all types of protagonists, Muslims and non-Muslims alike. In spite of all these confusions, this complex, obscure, active entity is the antagonist counterpart of the 'West' constructed since 1945 in the conflictual contexts of the Cold War, the colonial wars of liberation, the Israel-Palestinian tragedy, the geopolitical strategies of the Seven major powers (G7) to submit the whole world to the universal Law of the Free Market. The European Union as a geopolitical unit is clearly differentiated from the two ideological conflicting poles 'Islam' and the 'West'. Islam as an ideological construct should rather be compared to the church as a clerical institution which was also identified with the whole of organized society until the modern European revolutions (Britain, American, French) imposed the secular, liberal alternative. From that historical point of view, all the discourses based on implicit or explicit comparisons between Islam and the West entail anachronistic representations which shaped the two conflicting collective imaginaries called 'Islam' and the 'West'. This polarized opposition is the result of mutual perceptions developed since the nineteenth century by Muslims about Westerners and Westerners about Muslims on the basis of colonial struggles and equal ignorance institutionalized on both sides, a process that continues today.

It would be interesting to trace back the historical process through which Islam has substituted Allah as the omnipotent Agent and ultimate source of authority. The process started in the Middle Ages, when divergent collective memories developed their respective retro-vision of the symbolic Figure of Muḥammad for the Sunnīs,

'Alī and the chain of infallible (*ma'ṣūm*) Imāms for the Shī'ites. With al-Shāfi'ī (d. 204/820), the Sunna of the Prophet is elevated to the rank of the second, indispensable source of authority; some authors will even accept that the Sunna can supersede the Qur'ān. This is a significant step in the downgrading process leading to the dispersion of the holiness, sacredness, transcendence of the Word of God; in the same time, the downgrading of transcendence, ontology as stated in the Qur'ānic discourse, is compensated by the upgrading – which I have called transcendentalization, sacralization, ontologization – of the collective voice that expressed itself through the social, cultural and political construct of the 'living Islamic Tradition'. Paradoxically, the downgrading-upgrading mechanism has been most effective during the last fifty years with the 'promotion' of Islam to the highest function of the supreme Authority, encompassing, and even confusing, the cognitive status of the Qur'ān, the empirical, historical and collective dimension of the Sunna (and Imāms) and, last but not least, the systematic ideological manipulation of the whole religious sphere by two different collective protagonists, both deprived of any significant competence in religious thought. Above, there is the state agency with its large number of servants who '*monopolize the full exercise of legal violence*' (as Max Weber put it); below, there is the populace, the masses, uprooted from their rural, traditional, cultural codes and obliged to seek refuge and some hope in what I call populist expressions of a politicized Islam.[1]

With all these explanations, it can be understood to what extent and how, the discourse of classical Islamology contributes in his own way to the downgrading-upgrading mechanism without paying attention to its negative effects, or at least recognizing the scientific necessity of deconstructing it and offering an alternative intellectual posture to surpass the disintegrating forces operating in the so-called Muslim polity and society.

1. See 'L'Islam actuel devant sa tradition et la mondialisation', in *Penser l'Islam*, op. cit. Actually, there are intellectuals, scholars, scientists who share the same uncritical religious beliefs with the lay people who have no access to learned culture.

Ann K. S. Lambton has so deeply integrated the substantialist, omnipotent concept of Islam that she has built her argument on a widespread anachronistic reasoning about Islam and Europe, using the ideological paradigms forged by reason of enlightenment since the eighteenth century. Jumping from Middle Ages to Modern times in Europe, she traces an arbitrary comparison to show that 'Islam' did not develop the principles, distinctions or concepts which emerged in Europe after the seventeenth–eighteenth centuries. 'The antithesis between the individual and the state', 'the clear-cut boundary between morality and legality', 'the separation between the spiritual and the temporal' are, as usual, mentioned to build a negative image of a temporal Islam contrasting with the positive representation of a Modern Europe in which all these emancipating principles and values have been clearly stated and implemented. It is undeniable that no formal doctrine of separation has been proposed by a Muslim thinker and taken up seriously by a large, influential social class to implement it in durable institutions as the capitalist bourgeoisie did in Europe. Today, we can even say that we witness regressive teachings and claims of Muslim militants who reject even the very idea of democracy in its Western form. But these facts and many others need to be examined and reinterpreted in the new historical context of globalization which requires a more relevant cognitive strategy and a wider perspective on the interactive developments of cultures in the emerging multi-cultural societies.

My philosophical contention is that the epistemological posture, the conceptualisations and the methodologies used so far under the authority of the reason of enlightenment, which replaced the *auctoritas* of the theological-legalistic reason that prevailed for centuries in Christianity and Islam, this whole cognitive system is obsolete and irrelevant to the emerging multi-cultural, multi-ethnic societies. An emerging reasoning is following up these emerging societies; an emerging reason that has to struggle for its specific tasks which are different from the pragmatic, empirical, technological tasks assigned to **tele-techno-scientific reason.**[1] Since the highly

1. In the whole of this book, I am using the concept of reason in its well-known contents in history of thought, not only of philosophy in its

symbolic year 1492 (Jews and Muslims expelled from Spain, discovery of America and the Atlantic route, beginning of European expansion and hegemony), all societies more or less related to an Islamic authority, had either to catch up with the new European Model of historical action or to stay far away from satanic innovations and hold on its respective ethno-cultural religious codes. The Ottoman Empire tried for a while to challenge European ascension with purely military might; after the eighteenth century, the '*sick man of Europe*' – a nickname given in Europe to the Ottoman regime – had to await its final death in 1924. The history of the whole Mediterranean area has not yet been written in the critical, encompassing, emancipating perspective of the new emerging disciplines called historical anthropology, historical sociology, historical psychology, religious anthropology, social and political anthropology. Islamic studies still lag far behind this promising scholarship coupled with a relevant, creative, diversified philosophical search. This is the only way to put an end to a cold, distant, formalist scholarship which says Islam is a given, just as theologians repeat Revelation is given, or A. Lambton avers 'the state is given'. This kind of given can challenge reason, fire the imagination, enhance contemplation, meditation, admiration and pleasure, but it should never be worshipped, used as a device for alienation, oppression or a just war; it must remain the object of constant inquiry, accurate criticism, radical reappraisal and re-appropriation.

4. Authority in Classical Thought: A Historical Survey

The expression 'classical thought' refers to two different levels

---

European trajectory from classical Greece to contemporary 'western' thinking, but in the whole Mediterranean area, including all the Medieval discussions on Intellect and reason in the Arab logosphere. I have noticed that current pragmatic English would say 'reasoning' where the whole, old concept of reason is at stake. My purpose is to deconstruct all rationalities, all types and levels of reasoning in the *history of thought* as I practise it since my *L'humanisme arabe*, published in 1970.

in the historical development of Islamic thought: the level of a creative intellectual and scientific activity aiming exhaustiveness, coherence, accurate criticism and perfection in all accessible fields of knowledge. The corpus of knowledge accumulated according to this ambitious concept became a model, especially in religious thought, for subsequent generations who looked back to a time they termed the Golden Age (*circa* 750–1400). The second level is the acceptance and the use made of the classical corpus by Islamic thought from 1400 to the present time. This long period is dominated by the attitude called *taqlīd*, either in the sense defended by al-Qarāfī, or as a mere narrowing, lazy, literal reproduction of scattered elements selected from some texts of the classical corpus and totally de-contextualized. We have also mentioned the reactivation of the Akhbārī school in Imāmī Islam since the seventeenth century. Even during the so-called Renaissance (*nahḍa*), when ephemeral use of fragments of Modernity became possible, the *taqlīd* attitude prevailed, in the necessity to refer back to classical authorities. In the late 1930s, the Muslim Brothers movement began its struggle for a more radical *taqlīd* of the founding 'authorities' in the time of the Prophet. This attitude was to be long-lasting and is today manifested in the well-known, fundamentalist, radical, political Islam. The sense of accurate criticism and the philosophical dimension of classical thought as well as the positive conquests of modern thought in Europe are equally denied and categorized as the unthinkable – that which should not be allowed to think of or with– in this recurrent, 'authentic' line of thought. These definitions and views cannot be ignored or undermined in our critical historical survey on authority and power. Without dismissing totally the chronological stages of evolution fixed by historians so far, we shall propose a more inclusive framework of critical deconstruction and conceptualisztion of all the texts relating to authority and power.

4.1. Searching for a Framework of Analysis

To introduce this search, I shall use the example of the concept of God's caliph as it is developed and discussed by P. Crone and M. Hinds (*God's Caliph: Religious Authority in the First Centuries of Islam*, C.U.P., 1986).

The thesis defended in the book is that the common pattern of religious authority developed in ancient sources and received as 'the conventional Islamicist view of the caliphate', is historically sustainable. It is not correct to repeat that:

> *political power passed to a new head of the state, the caliph; but religious authority remained with the Prophet himself or, to put it differently, it passed to those men who remembered what he had said... But though the fourth caliph ('Alī) was also a Companion and more over a kinsman of the Prophet, he failed to be generally accepted, and on his death, the caliphate passed to men who had converted late and unwillingly (the Umayyāds), so that the happy union of religion and politics now came to an end. Caliphs and 'ulamā' went their separate ways, to be briefly reunited only under the pious 'Umar II* [pp. 1–2].

Relying on early *ḥadīth*, letters of al-Walīd II, Yazīd III and court poetry, the authors contrast the view constructed by the 'Ulamā' through their struggle for status as the supreme instance of authority with the function of the caliph as the representative of God (*khalīfatu-llāh*), not merely the successor of the Prophet (*khalīfat rasūli-llāh*). Caliphs are the legatees of prophets (in the plural) in the sense that they rule a society with their own authority and their verdicts count as sacred law. Umayyād legal practice is the start of what was to become Islamic Law. Law is always God-given; the prophets acted as adjudicators with divine authority; '*early ḥadīth reflects a stage at which God-given Law was formulated by God-given caliphs*' (p.50). A number of scholars appear as specialists in caliphate law, not as bearers of a prophetic tradition. Until the time of al-Ma'mūn, the title *khalīfatu-llāh* could be stated on coins along with Muḥammad *rasūlu-llāh*, although the canon of caliphate law had been closed by the time of Hārūn al-Rashīd. The failure of al-Ma'mūn to intervene in the debate on the issue of created Qur'ān is a benchmark of the balance of forces between the caliph and the *'ulamā'* concerning the expression of authority and political power in political theology (*siyāsa shar'iyya*); with the caliph Mutawakkil (848), the status of *'ulamā'* as the legatees of the prophets (*warathatu-l-anbiyā'*) in Sunnī Islam and of the Prophet and the Imāms in Shī'ī Islam, will remain an undisputed, established, intellectual and spiritual privilege. This does not mean, however, that the class of *'ulamā'* would enjoy a totally effective independence from the head of the state. Some strong personalities gained a significant level of independence, but the majority of them had and continue to have more than ever to negotiate their status with the state that monopolizes the full exercise of legal violence.

The point made concerning the status of God's caliph remains open for discussion regarding two aspects not fully considered by the authors, namely, the new Islamic paradigm incarnated in *God's given Law formulated by God's given caliph* which is presented as a definite, irreversible conquest against the *Jāhilī* paradigm based on the socio-political mechanisms of the *'aṣabiyya*. We know through the same corpus of texts used to establish the historical evidence of the emergence of God's caliphate authority that the *Jāhilī* system was still alive and operative in all the competing social groups, no only during the Umayyād period, but throughout the history of what we describe as 'Islamic'. The struggle between the Sufyānid and Hāshimī clans continued under the guise of an Islamic vocabulary and references. Other clans and tribes through the vast empire conquered by the Umayyāds and the 'Abbasids continued to obey to the well-founded, ethnological background which was supposed to be replaced by the Islamic paradigm. Instead of inquiring about the continuous interaction between the ancient and the new paradigms, modern scholarship has thus far preferred to reproduce the ideological viewpoint and political practice of all established states. Only the population that is more-or-less integrated into the official institutions and legal codes have access and a place in written historiographical archives; the rest of the population is merely mentioned as 'the masses' *('awāmm)*, the peasants, the Bedouins, the popular condition of life. This ideological categorizations is confirmed by the religious, political, economic and intellectual élites everywhere and in all times; in the emerging Islamic paradigm, social distinctions had already been made between the *muhājirūn*, the *anṣār*, the *ahl al-bayt* and the *mawālī*. Chronological criteria were even added to introduce a hierarchy of dignitaries (*afḍaliyya*), based on the earliest date of conversion. The criteria is presented as purely Islamic, beyond the old kinship solidarities but, in fact, we know how these solidarities continued to play a carefully concealed role, hidden behind an Islamic vocabulary and criteria powerfully worked out in the Qur'ānic discourse, early *ḥadīth* and the vast body of poetry.[1]

I am not supporting those ethnologists and sociologists who remind us of the persistence of the ethnographic institutions and oral culture in societies standardized uniformly as 'Islamic'. I rather prefer to introduce a methodological shift in the reading of all the ancient texts including the Qur'ānic discourse. I have taken the example of God's caliph book because both authors are known to classical Islamicists for their keen historical criticism but, in this particular case, both remain in the old philological framework limiting the discussion to the opposition between authentic/apocryphal texts. This discussion remains relevant; but we know that it did not overcome the opposite interpretations of the sceptical hypercritical school and the supporters of the traditional definition of authenticity. For this reason, I have for many years been defending a third posture relating to this methodology: because we know that we shall never have enough documents to bring proof that is convincing enough to put an end to the two opposite attitudes ultimately based on subjective conviction, especially where religious belief is at stake, we should go beyond the limits of the philological discussion and displace the concerns to another space of critical analysis and intelligibility. If we aim to contribute to an anthropological approach of the

1. For the early poetry corpus, we now have a very precious tool with which to study the vocabulary in the perspective I am defending here; see Albert Arazi and Salman Masalha, *Six Early Arab Poets*, new edition and concordance, Jerusalem, 1999.

religious phenomenon through the example of Islam, we should pay more attention to the heuristic hypothesis that a new emerging religion is always a linguistic, literary, psychological, ritual, social and political process. I use the term **'a heuristic hypothesis'** to leave room to the well-established theological definition of a new religion as a God's given revelation, perpetuated by a regular succession of God's given legitimate deputies (called caliphs, Imāms, Popes, elected communities, saints worshippers close to God, 'ulamā', rabbis, bishops , etc.). To serve the heuristic hypothesis, all texts produced, preserved and interpreted by the interpreting communities, through a continuous living tradition, from the founding Official Closed Corpuses to the subsequent literature of narrations, biographies, commentaries and professions of faith, should be submitted to the deconstructive critical, archaeological procedures of discourse analysis as I have shown in the chapters of this book and elsewhere. With this approach, the relevant framework of analysis will not be only chronological, as is the case in all disciplines applied to Islamic studies, but more anthropological and ultimately philosophical. Instead of showing only the chronological evolving process '*from Caliphal to Prophetic Sunna*', we shall first consider a more inclusive superseding issue which is the form, type and purport of **meaning** generated before and after 1) the full elaboration of the Official Closed Corpuses; 2) the extensive spread of the founding Official Closed Corpuses. It should be clearly understood that this methodological approach leads to a totally different combination and use of the disciplines required for the inquiry. The cognitive system imposed so far by the foundational strategy of traditional disciplines (*uṣūl al-dīn* and *fiqh*, or theology and divine law) is methodologically suspended, but not ignored, marginalized or arbitrary dismissed; it is suspended in order to permit research and critical thinking from any interference of dogmatic postulates and interpretations, both in Muslim scholarship and Western philological erudition. The centrality of the Official Closed Corpuses lies in the anthropological difference between the oral and the written regimes of what is called truth, orthodoxy, legitimacy/illegitimacy, divine law/positive, natural law, legal/illegal (*ḥalāl/ḥarām*), sacred/profane, mythical/historical, ritual/practice, and so on. There is a shift from the formalist transcription of the doctrines as articulated in the texts – whichever the text – to a linguistic, anthropological disclosure of the different layers of meaning and ideological stakes which are different in what I call the oral and written regimes of meaning and 'truth'.

In my critical analysis of the historical discourse exemplified in the important work of Cl. Cahen, I have shown how all Islamicist discourse implicitly endorses, not only the general theological options of the global Islamic discourse, but also its Sunnī, Shī'ī, Khārijī and Ḥanbalī versions, because it has rarely integrated the strategies of discourse analysis in order to unveil and problematize the mental tools and conceptualisation procedures of basic disciplines such as theology, *fiqh*, exegesis, historiography, biography, and so on.[1] I shall not repeat here what I have already written concerning the Prophetic discourse and all the discourses derived and produced therefrom in changing contexts from the end of Prophetic experience (632) to the present day. I shall just add some observations on the problems caused by the articulation of the historical results accumulated thus far by classical scholarship (regardless of the religious background of each scholar) in the new interpretations expected from the cognitive strategy which I have proposed in this paragraph.

According to our previous definition of the progressive-regressive method, we cannot read the Qur'ānic discourse and the historical experience of Muḥammad with only one of the two established cognitive frameworks, either the hagiographic, apologetic, theological one used by the orthodox Islamic tradition after the triumph of an Islamic state; or the modern positivist, historicist, scientific one defended by the classical school of historical criticism. In our perspective, both need to be deconstructed to unveil their implicit epistemological options; both are to be read as historical documents for a history of self-representation pursued by each

1. I shall be developing all these important positions with more nuances and bibliographical references in a coming book on *Penser l'Islam aujourd'hui*. See also the general bibliography at the end of this book.

community through the building process of its collective memory under the pressing needs of its present history. This means that we can neither reduce the Qur'ānic discourse and the Islamic living tradition to their immediate, linguistic, sociological, historical, anthropological content, nor accept the religious sacralization and ontologization achieved in these documents to use them as sacred, ontological, legitimate sources according to the orthodox paradigm of the believers.

Sociologically, it is not possible to trace any rigid frontier between what the Qur'ān called *Jāhiliyya* on the one hand and Islam on the other. This ideological confrontation continues to operate to the present day as a political slogan under the guise of theological vision. 'Islamic' state and Islamic Law have also translated this opposition into two categories of jurisdiction, the Territory of Islam and the Territory of War (*Dār al-islām* and *Dār al-ḥarb*). Outside the major cities, popular cultures and languages, ancient beliefs and customs have always dominated as an area of resistance to the central administration. The Islamic orthodox paradigm has never exercised its full impact on all groups and sectors of what we label currently as 'Muslim' societies. We know that E. Gellner has even reduced the cultural, linguistic and ethnic diversity of so many groups and societies labelled as Muslim to a substantive, paradigmatic, single *Muslim Society*. His well-known book with this title is a striking example of a scholarly, well-constructed imaginary hypostasis or archetype. Thus, social and political scientists converge with theologians in constructing the same archetype in spite of all the differences and discrepancies demonstrated by social and political sciences.

Chronologically, it is difficult to fix a date separating the end of Arab polytheist society and the full conversion of the state and the 'Muslim society' to the constructed Islamic paradigm. Bedouin and peasant societies continued to exist with their customs, social structures, languages, cultures, systems of beliefs and non-beliefs and collective memories until the demographic and urban revolution that occurred in the last forty years under the voluntarist centralizing, Jacobin 'national' states. The Prophetic discourse inspired and influenced at different levels, groups and societies 'converted' to Islam; but it has also been appropriated and distorted in the cultural, anthropological and historical frameworks of so many collective memories. It is true historically that Muḥammad spoke and behaved as the 'lord of tribes' in the strictly historical, anthropological meaning presented by J. Chabbi in her recent thesis.[1] When the Qur'ān says 'O you, people' (*ayyuha-l-nās*), or uses the word translated as 'individual' or 'human person' (*insān*), the form of address is certainly directed to the group present during the initial delivery, or more often to the members of the clan or tribe. Linguistically speaking, however, the same expression fits and is used in its initial Arabic form in all social contexts to communicate, not only any type of message, but the paradigmatic grammatical structure sustaining the whole Qur'ānic discourse. This does not mean that the general conceptualization of the discourse has a universal philosophic purport, but in all Islamised contexts in which the Islamic paradigm is more or less present, the expression *ayyuha-l-nās* and the word *insān* are received as having a universal spiritual purport.

Statecraft practice has shifted the cognitive status of Qur'ānic discourse from its initial creative function – articulation of a new framework of thought, belief and historical action – to an empirical, positive, legalistic function clearly defined by Ibn al-Muqaffaʿ who expressed in his *Risāla fī-l-ṣaḥāba* the urgent necessity of providing the state with a unifying code of laws as required by the new status of God's caliphate authority, before the triumph of a so-called Islamic Authority monopolized by the *'ulamā'* as we have said. In other words, the Umayyād state simultaneously introduced a shift and an apparent continuity in the concept and use of authority, a shift in the sense that the charismatic status of the Prophetic discourse is *institutionalized* in a state run by a dynasty of rulers self-promoted to the dignity of God's deputies; a continuity, because there is an arbitrary claim that every 'caliph' acts in the name of God to interpret, protect and apply through his representatives

1. *Le Seigneur des tribus: L'Islam de Mahomet*, Paris, 1997; see the introduction.

– governors, judges and the state apparatus – God's given Law! Concretely, we know that the self-promoted caliphs belong to the Banū Sufyān clan who used all the deeply rooted agnatic solidarity *('aṣabiyya)* against their rivals, the Banū Háshim, in order to break the action of Muḥammad b. 'Abdallah. Many problems arise here which I shall explain more fully than classical scholarship has done in its philological historicist framework of intelligibility.

Which specific objective differences – beyond or outside any theological consideration – can be retained between the status of Muḥammad during his teaching and leadership activities and the status of the self-promoted God's caliphs? How can the status of the so-called Right-guided caliphs be redefined between these two types of protagonists and how can the whole status of 'Alī and the subsequent developments of the *Imāmī, Khārijī, Mu'atazilī, Ḥanbalī* political theology be rethought? To avoid any theological interference at this historical and anthropological stage of discussion, we should suspend all the vocabulary currently used as given, even by critical historians who think that they have to 'respect' the way Sunnī and Shī'ī Muslims present themselves at a point that they speak as orthodox believers. All the protagonists defend positions commanded by their respective collective memories and their strategies in order to promote what would today be called their 'identities'. During the socio-historical process of shaping the status of the Prophet or Messenger of God (610–632), we should consider Muḥammad b. 'Abdallah only as one leader among other actors, one who was engaged in a struggle to gain the attributes and the full function of a prophet. He pursued this endeavour in a social and political environment in which there was no organized ruling state; he could not use any constraining institution or codified law to impose either an institutionalized authority or a recognized obedient political power. These tasks lay ahead of him. Even his clan and patriarchal family could not subscribe to the discourse he started to utter not in his own name, but as a message articulated grammatically by a personal independent 'author'. The political, religious and social clash between the *'aṣabiyya* polytheistically based Arabian society and the new discourse was total, immediate and uncompromising. It was doomed to end in military clashes.

All these are the concrete conditions through which one leader among other potential rivals, emerges as a prophet, speaking and acting on behalf of a God who is himself obliged to define his person, his attributes, his uniqueness in the socio-cultural arena in which the paradigm of prophethood and God's revealed word were familiar, but disputed for many centuries, namely the area known today as Middle East. The most specific feature of the prophetic status is that he gains authority over his listeners first and foremost with a discourse itself structured linguistically with particular grammatical, semantic, stylistic, rhetoric and dialectic devices. I describe this as the prophetic discourse illustrated in the three well-known holy Books, the Bible, the Gospels and the Qur'ān. It is true, nevertheless, that at the stage of Muḥammad's predication and socio-political action, the authority of the discourse he was articulating was not yet commonly, fully received as the word of God himself, a word called revelation, *waḥy*, or the descending address (*tanzīl*). I have shown in other essays[1] how the religious concepts of God (named Allah), revelation, the Word of God, Prophet, Messenger, human person, community, truth as right, right as truth (*ḥaqq*) and so on, are worked out and have received a specific, substantial, conceptual content through the development of the Qur'ānic discourse itself. The grammatical structure of the communication and the semantic shifts introduced in the current Arabic lexicon, literary genres and rhetorical devices have been simultaneously used with the clear intention of **subverting** the deep linguistic and cultural structures commanding the interactive mechanism of language and thought in the Arabic logosphere.

The originality of the emerging process of prophetic authority lies in the exceptional combination of successful political, social and cultural action and its **sublimation** into a specifically religious discourse using an organized system of metaphors, parables and symbols. The followers of the 'Prophet' (the quotation marks mean that I am not using a received theological concept, but the one I am

1. In my *Lectures du Coran* of which I am preparing a third revised and enlarged edition.

re-elaborating) were engaged in creative movements and uplifted by the rich symbolism supporting the goals of every initiative. The impact of any civilization is proportional to its capacity to symbolize human existence. Prophetic discourse achieved a great deal in this direction; its permanent influence on successive generations right up to the present day, can be explained by the richness of its symbolic expression to the existential vicissitudes and hopes of the human condition. In spite of all this, there were groups of Bedouins (*aʿrāb*) who continued to refuse to obey the 'Prophet', participate in the *jihād* and pay the *ṣadaqa.* This means that charismatic authority needs time, repetition, ritualization and a long process of internalization as a system of 'transcendent' norms by all members of the community produced by and producing this tradition. We must insist on this point. Originally, the authority of the 'Prophet' was directly affirmed and perceived through his charismatic historical action and the semantic, syntactic and rhetorical structure of the Qur'ānic discourse. After his death, this integrated representation of living authority broke up into two processes of development. The Qur'ān and the *ḥadith* were collected, transmitted, registered and interpreted, ending in large corpuses of scriptural Tradition. The state, on the other hand, used this facet of authority to legitimize its political, social and legal powers, paying special attention to maintain a fiction of authority incarnated in God's caliph without the charisma and all the attributes specific to the prophetic status as described.

There is another significant point to be emphasized in the emergence of authority from the perspective of God's revealed word. We have paid much attention to the texts as material documents to be used by historians; but very few consideration have been given to what literary criticism calls the *aesthetics of reception*, meaning how a discourse – oral or written – is received and interpreted by listeners or readers according to the semantic system of connotations specific to each individual speaking a given language. This question refers to the conditions of perception imposed in each culture, or, more precisely, each level of culture corresponding to each social group in every phase of historical development. The succession of diverse exegesis and interpretations of the Qur'ān provide a good example for studying the aesthetics of reception of a religious discourse. One could say that these are very trivial remarks; since everybody knows that it is almost impossible to read any text – especially symbolic, mythical religious texts – without projecting on to it, adding to it postulates, problems and values specific to the dominant culture of the reader or the receiver. But even if this psycho-linguistic mechanism is currently recognized, we have to confess that the history of perception peculiar to each socio-cultural group is much less taken into consideration than the **general rationalized standard definition** of the prevailing national and religious systems of thought and culture. I have illustrated this point with my study on the marvellous in the Qur'ān (see my *Lectures du Coran*, op.cit.). The discussion, generated by this unusual reading of the holy text, showed clearly how the prejudice of rationality which commanded the pious as well as the modern historical reading of holy founding texts, has eliminated the marvellous as the anthropological dimension of the type of knowledge produced and expanded by imagination interacting with reason. This dimension opens rich possibilities for a more inclusive psychology of religious and poetic knowledge beyond the prevailing irrelevant opposition between reason and imagination. The respective dimensions and mechanisms of mythical and historical knowledge in Islamic thought are still maintained in the domain of the unthought; but we observe the same phenomenon in other religious traditions more concerned with rationalizing moral, civic and practical teaching than with a critical evaluation of the philosophy of knowledge underlying this traditional, conservative teaching. In Chapter 2, I point to another tension between reason and imagination which is present in all systems of thought and at all times, including the increasing gap in our current history between a hegemonic tele-techno-scientific reason, philosophical reason and the new cognitive horizons of human mind.

These epistemic and epistemological considerations are even more in order when we deal with *ijtihād* as theologians and jurists understood it and practiced it. Opposing *ijtihād* to *taqlīd* as we do currently without further questioning many of the aspects involved in the two activities is just deleting the decisive issues raised by the interactive development of authority and power at the stage of Qur'ānic discourse, the formative period and subsequently, all the later stages until today. In other words, *ijtihād* and *taqlīd* cannot be considered as purely intellectual activities linked to devotional intentions. Both have political and jurisprudential considerations, involving the concrete use of authority and power at all levels of social, political and legal life. These levels already exist at the stage of prophetic discourse when a structured, centralizing, imperial state is not yet settled; but as soon as a state emerges with its leadership, bureaucratic servants, legal codes and judicial organisation, the levels are more intricate and the use of power supersedes the reliance on authority in everyday life. The ordinary language does not reflect clearly this inversion of the hierarchy between authority and power; it rather hides it when those servants of the state who monopolize the exercise of legal violence in the society, are called 'authorities' in several languages (*ḥukkām*). This questioning on the practical articulation of authority and power under the state control supersedes all the doctrinal debates to which we reduce the approaches of Law (*sharī'a*), authoritative rulings (*aḥkām, fiqh*), legitimacy, judicial institutions and practices, status of the state, and civil society . . .

Biographical and historiographical literature contributed to the discursive transformation of the actual power monopolized by the state and its servants into authority. The literary device has been applied in the *sīra* of the prophet, 'Alī, the so-called right-guided caliphs, the Companions, the followers of the Companions and more generally, to the imāms, mahdīs, saints, friends of God, *'ulamā'* and all those who are presented as the hairs of the Prophet. All societies need these symbolic, sanctified and sanctifying figures to project on them the ideal type of authority, justice, truth and guidance. Breaking the continuity of charismatic authority would mean the end of living tradition and the breakdown of the Community. The chain of authorized transmitters in the *ḥadīth*, the succession of reformers (*iṣlāḥ, muṣliḥ*) who lead the Community back to the founding Time of the Prophet's/Imāms' charismatic authority, are good illustrations of authority as the supremely constraining reference for all levels and types of institutionalized power. The psychological forces at work in this constant re-articulation of power to authority are represented by social images and the search for pragmatic more than speculative rationalization. Imagination and reasoning are the two interacting mental activities displayed in Qur'ānic discourse for recognizing (*ta'qilūn*) and keep in the heart (*qalb*) the meaning intended in each verse called a sign (*āya*). The psychology of knowledge at the historical stage of Qur'ānic vocabulary is not yet accepted as a particular field of study; I have introduced it in my contribution as *Le merveilleux dans le Coran*; but the example has not so far inspired any follow up, although this approach is essential to understanding how a new religious belief is a psycho-linguistic and social construct.

4.2. The Formative Period

W. M. Watt, J. van Ess and many others have traced the main lines of this period. More recently, substantial monographs have increased our knowledge about the formation of the Twelver Shī'ī and Sunnī schools and doctrines. I mention particularly those titles which are relevant to the subject:

Melchert, Christopher, *The Formation of the Sunnī schools of Law, Ninth–Tenth Centuries*
Brockopp, Jonathan E., *Early Mālikī Law: Ibn 'Abd al-Ḥakam and his Major Compendium of Jurisprudence*
Bar-Asher, Meir M., *Scripture and Exegesis in Early Imāmī Shī'ism*
Newman, Andrew J., *The Formative Period of Twelver Shī'ism Hadith as Discourse between Qum and Bagdad* (see the Bibliography).

For our purposes, we need to concentrate on the new conditions of perception and thinking created by the Umayyād and the first 'Abbasid state. The relevant point here is the inversion of the process described for the Qur'ān and the charismatic presence of Muḥammad. Priority was given to the definition, expansion and internalization of authority as coming from God who inspired, guided and supported the Prophet in all his initiatives, decisions and teachings. Authority preceded chronologically and ontologically any exercise of power (the predication in Mecca was focused on authority of divine commandments and teachings). Traditional sources suggest that during the period of the 'right-guided' caliphs, the exceptional individual memory of the *ṣaḥāba* and their scrupulous devotion to the new religion contributed to preserve the Word of God in the authentic form enunciated by the Prophet, the new hierarchy of values and the practical actions performed by the Prophet in the name of God. But the struggle developed between the well-rooted beliefs, institutions and solidarities of *Jāhilī* society on one hand, the new ethical, political and legal vision of an authority progressively introduced by Islam, on the other. The fact that 'Umar, 'Uthmān and 'Ali were all assassinated is sufficient to refute the concept of the 'Right-guided' caliphs and all the retrospective visions accumulated by historiographical literature to oppose an Islamic Utopia to the real social, political and ideological forces at work in all social groups that were more-or-less converted to what is globally called 'Islam', the Qur'ān, the *ḥadīth* and *sharī'a*. All these instances of authority were in the process of development in the '*sectarian milieu*' described by John Wansbrough, J. van Ess and many others. The purpose is to control the natural violence of man by the ethical and spiritual sublimation of his desires. Bloody and structural violence during and beyond the Arab conquests of several Mediterranean societies; ethnic, cultural and religious clashes with the new expanding Umayyād and 'Abbāsīd state have been reported and described in the theological framework opposing the light of Islam, its Law and right beliefs and non-beliefs to the darkness of *Jāhiliyya*, meaning all societies and peoples before Islam. We have indicated clearly that the Qur'ānic discourse used the same linguistic device to avoid mention any date, place, event or proper name and using only a religious, moral vocabulary to categorize concrete social groups, protagonists and events, attitudes of obedience or rebellion to

God and his Messenger (*kāfirūn, munāfiqūn, mushrikūn, muhājirūn, anṣār, mū'minūn* . . .) Theologians and jurists have systematized and expanded this theological categorization and introduced the well-known heresiographical vocabulary of Sunnī, Shī'ī, Khārijī, Zaydī, Rāwāfiḍ, Mu'tazilī, Ibāḍī , etc.

The State established by the Umayyād and 'Abbāsīd dynasties is the result of a military conquest combining bloody violence and a discourse of authority inspired by many verses, especially the ninth *sūra* called *Barā'a*, the rupture of a previously agreed pact (see above in Chapter 1). The new social, political and legal order is always fixed and 'legitimized' by the victorious group. The State, as a constraining and controlling legal power, will use God-given authority as a necessary reference for legitimizing a temporal power presented as originally lacking any intrinsic authority of its own.[1] Thus, official ideology can be said to impose an image of legitimate power by misrepresenting the actual military genesis (*jihād*) of the state. There are two constant characteristics of the official ideology. One misrepresents the real historical genesis of the legal state in order to gain and maintain the loyalty of the people to an idealized image of legitimacy. The ideological construct of the legitimate state that attempts to politically control the masses is different from the Prophetic discourse that seeks only the symbolization and a type of rationalization of authority as long as there is no other way of expressing a will to power through an established state. With the state, the discourse of authority becomes the legally constraining system of orthodox beliefs and non-beliefs fixed by theologians and jurists and enforced by judges. Orthodoxy – in its various versions defended by 'sects' competing for the control of the State – is no more than the official religion, receiving increased support from the by appointed '*ulamā'*. The shift from caliphate to prophetic *sunna* is the result of the struggle by the *'ulamā* to control the sphere of influence through *ijtihād* activity required by the development of

1. In fact, political anthropology shows that '*savage mind*' (*la pensée sauvage*) has its own coherence and intrinsic authority. In that sense, Qur'ānic discourse is necessary polemical to dismiss the 'wrong values' of *Jahīliyya*, and replace it by the True divine knowledge (*'ilm*).

divine Law. This struggle reached its climax when al-Ma'mūn tried to reconcile the status of God's caliphate authority with the Shī'ī political theology concerning the charismatic Imām. The *miḥna* ended with the victory of *ahl al-'ilm*, the doctors of religious Law as they were represented by the resistance of Ibn Ḥanbal and the theoretical work of al-Shāfi'ī who stated that 'the ultimate arbiter is the consensus of the entire community: the caliph counted only in so far as every member of the *umma* did' (*God's Caliph*, p. 93).

At this point in the historical survey, we must turn our attention to the Shī'ī line of debate and struggle for authority and power. We know that the Shī'ī and Khārijī lines and their numerous subdivisions received their own expression through the repression of the Umayyād state, pursued in a different style by the 'Abbāsīd caliphs until the failure of al-Ma'mūn who attempted to unify the *umma* on the basis of the Shī'ī-Mu'tazilī alliance (see A. J. Newman, op. cit., pp. 2–11). Even contemporary scholarship viewed these social, doctrinal developments through the heresiographic theological framework imposed by Sunnī Muslims who claimed to be the true defenders of Orthodox Islam, the Shī'ī and Khārijī movements being rejected as sects responsible for the breakdown of the true *umma* who were promised salvation. Small groups of Ibāḍī Muslims have survived until today in Oman, Jabal Nefusa (Libya) and Mzab (Algeria). Ismā'ilī Muslims were at their political success with the Fatimid dynasty (909–11), but today they remain a very dynamic community under the guidance of the Imām Karim Aga Khan. The Twelver Shī'a gained their own political hegemony with the emergence of the Safavid dynasty in Iran under the long reign of Shah Ismā'il (1501–1524). This enabled the Imāmī community to organize its clerics along a comparable vertical line which prevailed in the Roman Catholic church, rather than in emulation of Sunnī *'ulamā'*. These clerics became the representatives of the Imāms in relation to the community, as was recently witnessed with the Khomeini experience.

The text-oriented Imāmī tradition can be traced back to 'Alī ibn Abī Ṭālib, the legitimate heir of the charismatic authority incarnated in the person of Muḥammad during his prophetic mission. This is not the place to discuss the problems of authenticity raised by the textual tradition built through the succession of twelve Imāms, who ruled mainly in Qum which was a Shīʿī city-state between 874–1067. The main anthologies which became the Official Closed Corpuses, in the same way as those of the Sunnī tradition, are: Aḥmad ibn Muḥammad al-Barqī (d. 274–80/887–94): *al-Maḥāsin*; Muḥammad ibn al-Ḥasan al-Ṣaffār (d.290/902): *Baṣā'ir al-darajāt*; Muḥammad ibn Yaʿqūb al-Kulaynī (d. 329/940): *al-Kāfī fī ʿilm al-dīn*; Ibn Babūyè al-Shaykh al-Ṣadūq (d. 381/992): *Kitāb man lā yaḥzuruhu-l-faqīh*; Muḥammad b. al-Ḥasan al-Ṭūsī Shaykh al-Ṭā'ifa (d. 460/1067): *Tahdhīb al-aḥkām* and *al-Istibṣār fīmā-khtulifa fīhi min al-akhbār.*

Since the purpose here is to compare authority and power in the various doctrinal constructs of Islamic thought, inquiry will be limited to the following remarks:

Before Twelver Shīʿa became the official religion of the Safavid dynasty, the community lived in cities such as Qum, Najaf, Karbalā, within a larger political territory ruled by a Sunnī state. The community was widely scattered, but religiously unified with a strong, living collective memory nurtured by the Imām's traditions focused on matters of doctrine, practical aspects of daily life, the miraculous and supernatural and the achievements of the mythologized symbolic Figures of the Imāms. Esoteric doctrines of early Imāmism, as described by M. A. Amir-Moezzi (in *The divine Guide in Early Shīʿism*, SUNY, 1994), are preserved as a constituent part of the religious imaginary and a cultural background in which spiritual, ethical and legal norms could always be perceived as being derived from God's revelation and the charismatic authority of the Imāms. The difference from the Sunnī doctrinal literature is that charisma is limited to the Prophet, although the right-guided caliphs, rejected as illegitimate by all Shīʿī communities, are also credited with charismatic virtues. More generally, local saints are elevated to the same supernatural status to fulfil their function of spiritual guidance. This is an anthropological dimension of all pre-modern systems of thought, knowledge and belief.

The most interesting point to consider in the perspective of the unthought in contemporary Islamic thought, is that the issue of authority and power remains inherited at the historical stage, from all forms and levels of political theology developed in the complex ideological climate by competing ethnic, cultural and religious groups. These groups are still presented as religiously driven, totally cut off from their specific historical and cultural memories, as well as their sociological, concrete and constraining solidarities, beliefs, norms and all economic and ecological factors. The so-called parallel traditions developed by so many groups categorized as heretics and sects acting against the unity of an elected Islamic *Umma*, followed the same pattern of sacralization, mythologization and projection on constructed charismatic figures, values of authority and spiritual mediation. The collections of traditions certainly express the psycho-social-linguistic process through which collective memories shaped with heterogeneous elements, are preserved and enriched by selected values, ideals, attractive models of thinking, judging and behaving. Shīʿī Muslims never refer to Sunnī collections of *ḥadīth* presented as the most authentic teachings of the Prophet himself. The same taboo is observed by Sunnī believers in relation to Shīʿī and Khārijī collections. Each community sticks to the dogmatic enclosure built up by its traditional clerics obeyed as undisputable authorities, without caring or being disturbed by the fact that rival communities used the same patterns, followed the same procedures and refer to the same founding texts and initial authorities (Qur'ān, prophetic traditions, first transmitters) to eventually produce irreducibly opposing collective memories. A comparative literary and linguistic analysis of the biographies (*sīra*) of prophet Muḥammad and ʿAlī, his son-in-law, would show how competing collective memories have been constructed with the same existential needs, the same semiotic, literary and linguistic devices, the same historical pressures and anthropological patterns to perform the same psychological, social and political functions. These are more essential and relevant keys to understanding the nature and roles of religion and politics, rather than endless discussions about the authenticity of the narratives and the chains of transmission used in the written biographies, the collections of traditions and all historiographical literature.[1]

4.3. Collective Memories and Authority

The concept of collective memory was developed a long time ago by Maurice Halbwachs in three major books: *Les cadres sociaux de la mémoire*, Paris 1925; *La Topographie légendaire des Evangiles en Terre sainte. Etude de mémoire collective*, Paris 1941, and *La mémoire collective*, Paris 1950. Historians have used it to a lesser extent, especially those who explore societies related to Islamic influences. One important exception should be mentioned, that of Lucette Valensi who has devoted a very interesting monograph to the memory left in Morocco and Portugal by a very short battle in 1578 in which many people, including three princes, died; the book is: *Fables de la mémoire. La glorieuse bataille des trios rois*, Paris 1992. The most relevant study to my subject is *The Legendry Topography of Gospels in Holy Land*, because it explains how a collective religious experience expressed in what I have called prophetic discourse is memorized by the protagonists who took part in its first emergence, then transmitted through successive generations with semiotic manipulations to render the core of the initial experience and message more appropriate to the local needs and changing demands of an indefinite number of social groups. From a sociological point of view, all the 'sects', confessional communities and brotherhoods described in heresiographical literature as *firaq, milal, niḥal, ṭuruq*, have built their respective collective memories on the same founding texts, the same narrative devices, the same symbolic function for the integration of their own legendry topography, their own existential trials, their mythical Figures, saints and heroes, just as larger groups such as Sunnītes, Shī'ites, Ismā'ilites and Khārijites or Roman Catholics, Lutherans, Calvinists, Anglicans and Orthodox Christians have

1. For further developments on collective memories and historical consciousness, see my study 'Pour un remembrement de la conscience Islamique', in *Pour une critique de la raison islamique*, pp. 129–55.

done. In other words, a sphere of authority is needed as a supreme common reference by all social groups, regardless of their size and their real power and material resources; but the events, experiences, symbolic Figures and narratives in which authority is incarnated, are specific to each group or reworked according to the existing, already constraining collective memory.

In this perspective, the concept of collective memory becomes a *master key* to move from the factual formalist presentation of so-called religious history of sects to a more encompassing theoretical framework of analysis and interpretation concerning **social genesis and metamorphosis of meaning in human existence**. Religions had and still claim the privilege of 'revealing' to human beings the ultimate source of an eternal, intangible, indisputable meaning to enlighten and guide all levels of thinking, all fields of knowledge, all initiatives and actions required in changing circumstances. For centuries, religions invented and practised a kind of globalization in all human societies. Today, tele-techno-scientific reason is creating a different type of globalization with radically different philosophical postulates and more efficient procedures and technologies. Seeking a more elaborated framework of explanation and interpretation, in which both religious and the tele-techno-scientific projects of globalization are equally fully submitted to an encompassing critical reassessment, becomes an intellectual duty and an urgent scientific task.

I am writing this paragraph after a whole week of discussions, negotiations and debates over jurisprudence in the USA concerning the presidential elections. Beyond the arithmetic solution of the crisis, all observers are pondering or should be pondering over the problems of authority and power, legitimacy attached to authority, legality attached to power. If these problems are not addressed for their own significance and purport at the level of political philosophy, liberal democracy as a universalizable model in the present context of globalization, will suffer as a consequence. Not only the supporters of the fundamentalist religious alternative model will make a case of the American example, but political philosophy itself will loose the rest of its credibility and relevance.

I use this interesting event to ask the question: if we keep our search on the level of authority and power, legitimacy and legality, what will we have learned thus far from the debates within the Islamic tradition since the emergence of the Mecca-Medina Paradigm of God's caliph, the example of the charismatic *imām* and the struggle of clerics to control their sphere of influence? Which new questions are raised by the comparison between the model based on political theology and the secularized model based on political philosophy? To provide a fuller answer to this question, a historical survey is required and an examination of two subsequent stages in the handling of authority and power in Islamic contexts: from God's caliph/imām model to the routinization of the state power, especially since the emergence of democracies without any background of a democratic culture. I shall deal only with the first period here; for the second one concerning contemporary developments since the emergence of post-colonial states, I refer to Chapter 5 in this book.

4.4. From God's Caliph/Imām Model to the Routinization of the State Power

Classical theories on legal governance according to Sunnī tradition (*siyāsa shar'iyya*), or the just ruler according to the Imāmī tradition (*wilāyat al-faqih*), are the most frequently studied in the books already mentioned. There is no need to again stress that their presentations are merely descriptive. Today, these theories are of purely historical interest, because their institutional translation during the Caliphate, the Sultanate and the Imāmate were abolished in 1258 for the Caliphate and in 1924 for the Sultanate. The attempt of Khomeini to rejuvenate the Imāmī governance is very controversial; the nineteenth-century reactivation of the Ismā'ilī Imāmate with the family of the Aga Khan has achieved more promising results in the form of a modern connection between spiritual guidance and the necessities of bureaucratic administration. To shed more light on contemporary development since the emergence of the post-colonial regimes in all Muslim contexts, greater attention should be paid to the process of routinization of authority and power during the long period of Ottoman (1281–1924), Safavid and Qajars (1501–1732/1779–1924) and the Mughal (1526–1858) empires. Scholarship has devoted much less attention to this long and complex period, preferring to dwell on the more attractive classical time; intellectual and cultural development has been particularly neglected. The period in question is currently presented as a time of decay, scholastic repetition or summarized text-books (*taqlīd, mukhtaṣar*) of selected names and fragments from classical thought and culture. This is the typical vision imposed in Modern Europe by the nation-state. Only selected classical authors and works are studied, chosen for the school courses to develop a sense of admiration for, loyalty to and imitation of the glorious values and achievements of the nation in successive generations. This example has been followed by all the post-colonial nation-states; but it should be added that before the rise of the nations-states in Europe and elsewhere, the authorities of all religious-based regimes followed the same pattern of selection, retaining and teaching only 'orthodox' authors and works.

This general ideological control of education shapes the 'living' tradition in each line of transmission. It has an obvious impact on authority as a constructed corpus of references for each individualized community or nation. The critique of such an authority should then focus on the historical and social process which shaped different levels and types of authority during the said imperial periods. The point here is to get rid of the erroneous vision of an Islamic Ideal-Type of authority which is supposed to have existed and will remain unchanged from the time of the Prophet and God's caliph throughout all the great number of dynasties and regimes right up to the present day. This chapter would be too long if I were examine here all the aspects of authority and power in contexts as different as those of the Maghreb, Egypt, Syria, Iran, Turkey, Arabia, sub-Saharan Africa, India, Indonesia , and so on. For further research, I would rather refer the reader to five recent monographs which propose interesting lines of inquiry worthy of being pursued and expanded upon:

Touati, Houari, *Entre Dieu et les hommes: Lettrés, saints et sorciers au Maghreb (17e siècle)*, Paris, 1994.
Antoun, Richard T., *Low-key Politics: Local-level Leadership and Change in the Middle East*, SUNY, 1979.
Van Leeuwen, Richard, *Waqfs and Urban Structures: The case of Ottoman Damascus*, Brill, 1999.
Gerber, Haim, *Islamic Law and Culture*, 1600–1840, Brill, 1999.
Weismann, Itzchak, *Taste of Modernity: Sufism, Salafiyya and Arabism in Late Ottoman Damascus*, Brill, 2000.

H. Touati explores the cultural forms of the contact with God through the mediation of local saints, sorcerers and low-profile clerics sharing popular dialects and local cultures. *Sharīʿa* and *fiqh* are seen from below, in their daily popular expressions, customs and beliefs. There are concrete examples how authority and power are conquered, monopolized and translated, not in the theoretical classical frameworks, but in a more simplified vocabulary, accessible to the illiterate peasants, mountain-dwellers and nomads. Religious knowledge (*ʿilm*), virtuous endeavour (*ʿirḍ*) and enabling power conferred by the proximity to the saint or the prince (*jāh*) are the three pillars on which social, legal, ethical and political order rest. Houari Touati remains dependent upon the written documents and, although he reads them with an anthropological curiosity, he remains on the side of historiography rather than venturing in the direction of ethnology. The connection between historical writing and reasoning in an ethnological spirit, as well as exploration and interpretation, are not yet considered as a necessary epistemological step required by all the historical, social, cultural environment defined as 'Islamic', but still fragmented into two separated disciplines, namely, historiography on the one hand and ethnography and ethnology on the other. In fact, the whole field of research requires that a connection be made between these disciplines because oral cultures interact at all levels with written cultures and have done so from the first expansion of the scriptural tradition until modern times.

Focusing on *Kufr al-māʾ*, a small village in Jordan, R. Antoun tends to favour ethnographical-ethnological description and interpretation. Like many others, he draws attention to the facts, forces, practices, cultural visions and forms which are excluded from the historical analysis reserved for urban learned élites. The ideological line separating élites (*khāṣṣa*) from the masses (*'awāmm*) in all societies is thus maintained and reflected by the modern division into specialized disciplines. The point I want to make is adequately expressed in the following quotation:

'If every anthropologist were to become interested in a particular institutional pattern and did field work only where that pattern was most elaborated or developed, cross-cultural studies of those patterns would become impossible, for it is from variations in the magnitude of institutional factors that we test hypotheses concerning the functional relations of those factors with other variables. Studies of politics in stateless societies, of descent groups where there are no lineages, of lineages where there are no chiefs, prices where there is no money, of aggression among peaceful peoples, of history and science among the illiterate and technologically primitive, represent some of the most significant and subtle advances in anthropological understanding' (Antoun, pp. xii–xiii).

Anthropological understanding has never been a priority in the study of societies in which all the features listed in this quotation have always existed and still exist today. The Islamic Paradigm of knowledge, law, social and political order focuses on the eradication of stateless societies and human dignity, based on lineages with chiefs, aggression legitimized by patriarchal solidarity (*'aṣabiyya*), ignorance of divine revelation (*Jāhiliyya*) to replace it with 'true' knowledge (*'ilm*) preserved in the Heavenly Book and written down in the other books. With its ritual prescriptions, ethical and legal norms, educational practices, legal procedures and state strategies to exercise power in the name of divine authority, Islam as a religious promotion of the human being, succeeded in promoting its Paradigm as a deeply rooted aspiration to an ideal polity, but did not significantly change the anthropological structures and ethnological mechanisms of the societies converted to the Paradigm. In other words, Islam, as other living religions, has inspired a dynamic *politics of hope*, but believers as protagonists never succeeded in translating into positive law and institutions, critical knowledge extended to religious vision, this being the recurring protest against all those who stick to the '*jāhilī*' stage of human existence. To test the powerful recurrence of the Islamic Paradigm internalized as the politics of hope, it is sufficient to merely listen to or read the contemporary discourses of what is described as 'fundamentalist', 'radical', 'political' Islam.

Just as secular revolutions in Europe and the rise of the Nation-State model used the Christian Paradigm to transform it into the imaginary of progress based on scientific, technical and mathematical knowledge extended to the religious politics of hope, several nation-states emerged in Muslim contexts after colonial liberation and tried to secularize the Islamic Paradigm without going as far as Europe in the separation of the public space controlled only by the state and the private space to which religious authority should be confined. Yet, even in Europe, this dividing line has been unable to totally eradicate the more essential anthropological division between an oral and written culture, with its powerful expansions as a rationalist bureaucracy, an industrialized, capitalist economy, positive contingent law and a secular system of education. Social sciences have paid a great deal of attention to the first obvious, visible, pragmatic dividing line, but have not yet sustained a relevant approach to the second one; that is why sociologists, political scientists are obliged to admit a strong 'return of religion' after the enthusiast proclamation of the 'death of God' and even of 'man' or the human being, without providing the appropriate tools, methodologies and problematizations to go beyond all the obsolete paradigms. Again, in Islamic contexts, these issues are not only adequately addressed, they are declared **unthinkable** in the sense that anthropology, for example, is rejected in some countries as a 'colonial' science designed to destroy national unity and to dismiss the religious Paradigm.

The expression 'taste of Modernity', used by I. Weismann in his title, is particularly suggestive of the tactics, strategies and devices used by urban élites in an ancient city such as Damascus with its rich, active, conservative, conflicting collective memories, to create a '*resistance to the Emerging Modern State*' and to persist in 'remoulding Religion and Identity under the Populist Regimes (1883–1918): Returning to the Model of the Forefathers, Reviving the Arabic Heritage' (Chapters 6 and 7). The stakes in these struggles are the intellectual and cultural shifts required by the secularized nation-state model to abolish and replace the still powerful clerical culture and institution, with their belief-based manipulation of authority and power. This monograph and the two others – van Leeuwen and H. Gerber – are again on the side of learned culture and urban sociological forces. I. Weismann uses the expression 'populist regimes' without developing the difference between 'popular – relating to the general public as distinct from the learned élites – and 'populist', referring more specifically to the demagogic manipulation by leaders of the popular desires and claims, just as a springboard to rise to power. In the Communist regimes that prevailed until 1989, populism was represented by a single party and was the highway to power. It was the only way to monopolize ideological control of the whole of society; many post-colonial regimes in Third World countries, used and are still abusing of this populist discourse and culture. With the demographic growth in all these countries after the late 1960s, the sociological basis for state power became populist. The younger generations brought up in the nationalist, populist ideology, dominated the political scene, changed the urban fabric, and caused the traditional collective memories to deteriorate. So-called Islamic fundamentalism is the expression of this demographic, political, cultural shift. It refers more to the increasing pressures of these concurring factors than to Islam which became an illusory alleged cover. The sources of Islamic authority – *Qur'ān, ḥadīth, imām's and forefathers' teachings, sīra, sharīʿa, Nahj al-balāgha.* – are still quoted in populist discourse; but neither the spirit of their original content and contexts, nor the actual needs and goals of the actors, are adequately reflected in the discourses. Each quotation is a dual violation, destroying the mythical context of the emerging culture of authority and imposing an arbitrary dogmatic pressure on the contemporary historical contexts in order to negate its own dynamic creativity and force it to comply with the imagined, paradigmatic past.

To better explain this complex mechanism engaging language, thought, social psychology, political violence, individual alienation and shifts of paradigms, it should be remembered that the emergent and classical literature of authority simultaneously fulfilled three functions:

1. Mythologizing the new historical space ruled and controlled by the emerging new combination of authority and power under the leadership of God's caliph and the symbolic figures of the Prophet, the Companions, the Imāms. This creative stage of spiritual, divine authority produced a rich literature which would become the ultimate reference for future generations in restoring the true, effective incarnation of ideal authority and reinforcing those in power (*ūlū-l-amr*) who break the legitimate image of governance by illegitimate violence and illegal rule;

2. Preserving the symbolic Figures of authority as models to be contemplated, imitated and used as a refuge and a springboard in rebelling against the *unjust ruler*, while in the same time social necessity requires obedience to the existing order, as al-Ghazālī has put it.

3. *Mirrors of Prince* contributed, with the founding sources of authority, to spreading a culture of authority among the masses (*'awāmm*) through oral versions of the biographies, narratives going back to the biblical time of the prophets and the Inaugurating Time of Islam (see J. Dakhlia, *Le divan des rois: Le politique et le religieux dans l'Islam*, Paris, 1998).

These three functions are interrelated. They refer to the same stratified construction of the collective memories known as competing 'sects' or communities on the issue of the so-called Authentic Islamic Tradition. The three functions contributed to perpetuating the social structures and the cultural frameworks in which they flourished; in return, the continuity of the epistemic, socio-cultural context made possible the emergence of new symbolic figures of authority such as the Mahdīs in Sudan and Senegal in the late nineteenth century and, more generally, the local saints and spiritual guides of '*ṣūfī*' brotherhoods who founded autonomous political organizations whenever the central state became unable to impose its control. The irreversible historical and anthropological breakdown of this old, persistent system occurred after the World War II with the rise of the so-called modern states and the emergence of the populist ideology. The processes of this breakdown can be followed in a recently published monograph on *Myths, Historical Archetypes and Symbolic Figures in Arabic Literature. Towards a New Hermeneutic Approach*, Proceedings of the International Symposium in Beirut, June 25–30/1996, Beirut, 1999.

4.5. *'Aqīda, Authority and Struggle for Power: Taqlīd Supersedes Ijtihād*

'Aqīda means the system of beliefs and non-beliefs which are the basis for all levels of connection between authority and power. Power needs to be obeyed; but there is no loyal, free obedience to an arbitrary power that is not supported by authority. Jurists and legal authorities contribute by providing a rationalized foundation to the authority of those who have the responsibility of enforcing the law, law being the expression of the political power monopolized by the state. The intellectual discipline of *uṣūl al-fiqh* had to 'demonstrate' and teach that law is simultaneously the expression of the Will of God and the implementation of God's Commandments through a vertical hierarchy starting with the caliph/*imām* on top descending with the Great Judge (*qāḍī-l-quḍāt*), the judges (*quḍāt*) paralleled by the consultant-adviser (*muftī*) and the charismatic local mediator (saints, *walī, murābit, 'ālim, shaykh, marja' al-taqlīd).* I summarize this system by saying: **Islam is theologically Protestant and politically Catholic.**

The role of *marja' al-taqlīd* in Imāmī tradition deserves more explanation to differentiate it from the Sunnī practice. *Marja' al-taqlīd* is the instance occupied by scholars acting as a living supreme legal authority (*marja'*) accepted by all the members of the community. The civil structure of the Shī'ī community is, in theory, divided into those who lead – the scholars (*mujtahid*), and those who are led, the lay believers (*muqallid*); *taqlīd* is not only the acceptance by the lay believer in emulation of a living jurist's rulings (*fatwā*), in all fields of applied law; it is more significantly the recognition of the spiritual, moral and legal authority attached to the rulings mediated by the *marja'*. Thus, the authority of divine Law circulates without discontinuity from the Word of God and the twelve Imāms – its full charismatic mediators – to the *marja'* and the lay believers. To refuse to obey this spiritual chain of authority would mean that the acts performed might be declared invalid. The leadership of the *marja'* is conceived as a general deputyship (not designated as a leading expert in law, i.e. in spiritual and legal matters) on behalf of the hidden Imām (the last Imām's invisible existence is the core of the *Imāmī* Islam). Since the Safavid dynasty, the political rulers have manipulated this religious leadership for their political needs of legitimacy, reducing it to an officially appointed 'managers of the sacred'. This has been the case in Sunnī statecraft tradition since the Umayyād and with Ismā'ilī Imāmate under the Fatimids dynasty. In the three traditions, some *mujtahids* did not succumb to statecraft practice; they worked to keep the community autonomous in its religious life and loyal to 'spiritual' leaders able to validate their acts as believers. In Iran, a legal mechanism was introduced in the nineteenth century to declare allegiance to the *marja' mujtahid*. An explicit declaration of *taqlīd* became formally a part of the believers' obligation; otherwise their acts would be invalidated apart from any interference by the rulers. This enabled the growing 'authority/power' of the *marja'* who received voluntary religious taxes paid by the believers.

'The *marja'* was responsible for providing cohesion in maintaining the spiritual-moral identity and the related social-political identity of the Shī'ī community through his agents (*wukalā'*) recruited from his 'study-circles' who collected and distributed religious taxes. Before an Ayatollah died, the community leaders formed a consensus on his successor, to assure the continuity of the system. The supervisory and managerial roles of the *mujtahid* were legitimized under the jurisdiction of 'the guardianship of the jurist' (*wilāyat al faqīh*), strictly limited to the domain of Islamic Law. It did not include the political governance; this occurred for the first time in the history of Shī'ī Islam in the case of Khomeini. Al-Khū'ī became *marja'* in 1970; he had to face the rise of Khomeini and Bāqir al-Ṣadr who preached rebellion against the unjust rulers in Iraq and Iran. Al-Khū'ī chose the quietist attitude and pursued it until his death on 8 August, 1992.[1]

I shall not dwell on the tensions and confusions between authority and power, the degradation of authority under the pressures of all types and forms of the state (sultanate, emirate, monarchy, republic), of the corruption of the so-called religious 'élites' who served their material interests and power purposes. In my book *Penser l'Islam aujourd'hui*, I devoted a long chapter to these matters under the title 'Critique of legalistic reason in Islam'. It is appropriate now to summarize the main results of this historical, analytical, deconstructive survey of a topic which is central not only to the history of Islamic thought and political institutions, but to all systems of thought and political practices.

Conclusion

In all contemporary societies, developed and underdeveloped, the most recurrent debate is the competition, or radical opposition, between the religious and the secular model in building the best polity and assuring the safest and the most beneficial governance for its citizens. Authority as a concept, as an instance separate and distinct from power has lost its relevance, its functional importance, its theological and even philosophical topicality. This means that our societies and cultures have lost their capacity to generate, receive and support charismatic heroes or leaders,

1. For all this paragraph, See Abū-Qāsim al-Mūsawī al-Khū'ī, *The Prolegomena to the Qur'ān*, op. cit.

spiritual guides, thinkers or saints. We know the critical reactions generated by the saints recently canonised by the Pope John Paul II. The concept of power has invaded the whole sphere of theoretical debates and the bureaucratic administrative practice; authorities are those civil and military servants of the state; the highest ranked authorities – president of the republic, prime minister – who are removable through elections, or disposable under an authoritarian leader in non-democratic regimes. All languages have registered this degradation and disintegration of the concept of authority. In Arabic, *sulṭān* (power), has replaced *khalīfa* and *imām* since the fall of the Caliphate in Baghdad in 1258; the Ottoman regime could not restore the religious title 'caliph', only *sulṭān* prevailed; king (*malik*) or *amīr* (emīr) are used in contemporary Muslim monarchies. To gain some 'sacred' authority, the Saudi king promoted himself to the rank of the 'Guardian of the two sacred places' (*ḥāris al-ḥaramayn*), especially to counter the 'authority' claimed by the Ayatollah Khomeini.

Consequently, political theology lost its place and topicality since political philosophy dismissed it in Europe, for it to become the exclusive instance of theoretical debate not directly about authority, but on the legitimacy of political power monopolized by the state. Contemporary Islam has not developed a serious, reliable political theology, and even less a political philosophy which remains the unthinkable even for many intellectuals. Many debates take place in seminars, symposia and international conferences about civil society, democracy and Islam, religion and secularism. Based on my personal involvement in these debates since the late 1960s, I shall formulate the following provocative propositions both as concluding remarks and new points of departure.

Secularism is implicitly and explicitly included in the Qur'ānic discourse and the Medina historical experience.

The Umayyād-'Abbāsīd state is secularist in its sociological and anthropological basis, its military genesis and expansion, its administrative practice, its ideological discourse of legitimacy. The theological and jurisprudential endeavour developed by the *'ulamā'* contributed to concealing behind a religious vocabulary and sacralizing conceptualization, literary devices, the secularist, ideological basis of the so-called 'Islamic' polity and governance. Only Ṣūfī personalities developed a sense of religious experience of the divine in an autonomous spiritual sphere that was not only independent of the state management of religious affairs, but also from the demands of the lay believers. This experience is different from that which prevailed from the eleventh century onwards with local 'saints', founders of brotherhoods who reproduced on a smaller scale the strategies of central imperial states to instrumentalize religious authority for political leadership. All those scholars, Muslims and non-Muslims, who contend today that Islam confuses politics and religion, or Islam does not need to address the issue of secularism because – unlike Christianity – it never developed a clerical regime under the leadership of the Church, neglect the two major historical and sociological facts. These are the confiscation of spiritual autonomy by the top (the state) and by the bottom (lay believers mobilized by 'saints' in brotherhoods) that began in 661 and has lasted until today.

Very early in the history of the state, military power played a pre-eminent role in the caliphate, the imamate, the sultanate and all later forms of governing institutions in Islamic contexts (see P. Crone, *Slaves on Horses*).

Attempts to rationalize *de facto* secularism and to develop a shared secularized, intellectual attitude and political culture were made by philosophers (*falāsifa*) in the tenth century, under the Būyid regime, who succeeded in initiating a humanist attitude of mind shared by different social strata and supported by the merchant class. That is why I keep insisting on the necessity of writing a new history of Islamic thought that incorporates two key chapters on the sociology of the failure of philosophy, the impact of scholastic written culture whereby *taqlīd* attitude superseded *ijtihād* practice, and ethnographic culture under the leadership of brotherhoods.

Orthodox expressions of Islam – each community claiming the privilege to have preserved the original orthodox teachings, excluding the others as heretical sects – are the result of different ethno-cultural backgrounds, arbitrary selection of traditions referred to the Prophet, the Companions and the Imāms and ideological use and abuse of dogmatic exegesis and theological constructions.

The cognitive status of Islam as a religion needs to be reconsidered in the light of the comparative history and anthropology of religions. To achieve this task, epistemological options of modern reason, as instrumentalized in social sciences, should also be submitted to a more radical, critical evaluation.

The large majority of the political regimes which emerged in Muslim contexts after the liberation from colonial domination, are *de facto* secular in the sense that they have adopted legal codes, governmental procedures, administrative hierarchies and practices borrowed from liberal Western, or Socialist-Communist patterns of thought and institutional models. Eben in Saudi Arabia, secular forces are at work and creating tensions with the formal Islamic regime. This does not mean, of course, that these states have introduced a modern system of education, promoted a culture of democracy and human rights or accepted the emancipating principle of autonomy for the political and religious spheres. On the contrary, most of them have imposed the politics of traditionalization with strong support for the return to religious tradition.

From the anthropological and historical point of view adopted in this essay, secularism expresses the continuous effort of the human being to achieve the greatest adequacy between imagined, represented reality and objective, positive reality. In this perspective, the forms, trends, and content of secularism in its European/Western achievements is one possible historical expression of the search for more adequacy pursued in other cultural, historical performances. In this essay and in all my writings, I have tried to present, by using a comparative approach, the search for adequacy in what I prefer to call Islamic contexts.

FIVE

The Concept of Person in Islamic Tradition

In recent anthropological discussion, the moral (and aesthetic) aspects of a given culture, the evaluative elements, have commonly been summed up in the term 'ethos', while the cognitive, existential aspects have been designated by the term 'world view'. A people's ethos is the tone, character and quality of life, its moral and aesthetic style and mood; it is the underlying attitude towards themselves and their world that life reflects. Their world view contains their most comprehensive ideas of order.

Cl. Geertz

La personne est l'antinomie incarnée de l'individuel et du sacral, de la forme et de la matière, de l'infini et du fini, de la liberté et du destin.

Nicolas Berdiaev, *Cinq méditations sur l'existence,* Aubier, 1936, p. 180.

1. Theoretical Approaches and Cognitive Frameworks

It might be claimed that any social group, community or nation identified as such, constructs for itself a vision of what is called 'person' in our modern conceptualization. This vision may be expressed implicitly through beliefs, collective rituals and codes of behaviour or explicitly through precepts, proverbs, mythical narratives, religious corpora, law, systematic doctrines, arts and literature. For societies without writing, ethnologists have demonstrated the various conceptions of 'person' through exhaustive, ethnographical descriptions of all aspects and levels of cultural, social, political and ecological expressions of the groups. P. Bourdieu proposed an eloquent example in his book, *Le sens pratique* (Practical Sense) devoted to the study of the Kabylia people of Algeria. He emphasised the experiential character and the practical, empirical, unwritten scope of the 'values', norms and 'symbolic capital' which underlie and regulate the status of each member of the group, along with the mechanical solidarities that bind all the members together. 'Practical sense', so defined, forestalls the emergence of a person or autonomous individual who might conceivably be critical, or indeed dissident, vis-à-vis the group or religious community.

It is important to keep such data in mind if one is to correctly apply the difficult question of person within Islamic Tradition and various contexts. The historical, geopolitical and anthropological field under the impact of what I call the 'Islamic fact', is so vast and varied that analysts have thus far preferred to use the misleading global term 'Islam'. Even today, Islamic contexts encompass a number of peoples and groups that do not use writing and are thus more closely attached to the oral than to the written tradition, tied to behaviour, institutions and identities appropriate to the stage of 'practical sense' rather than that of the modern nation-state. So where and when, given all these facts, is one to identify the historical manifestations and the legal, political and cultural expressions of the person in Islamic contexts? What status has the human person been accorded, finally, after more than fifteen centuries of political experiment, the creation and practices of law and doctrinal teachings referring more or less correctly to 'Islam' and its Tradition?

Why, it may be asked, should we speak of Islamic 'Tradition', with a capital 'T'? And how is this Tradition to encompass, in practice, all the different historical, cultural and ethno-linguistic contexts in which it has been shaped and applied? Tradition is informed and conditioned by changing backgrounds, teaching, guiding and conditioning these backgrounds in return. This interaction is translated into the self-entitlement of each Muslim community to incarnate and monopolize the authentic expression of the 'orthodox' Tradition. The Sunnī majority calls itself 'the holders of the (authentic) Tradition and unified community' (*ahl al-sunna wa-l-jamā'a*); the Imāmī Shī'a opposes to this claim, and names itself 'the holders of the infallibility of the Imām and the Justice' (*ahl al-'iṣma wa-l-'adāla*). All the other groups are rejected as 'sects', 'heretics' and 'separate factions' according to the dogmatic definition of the 'orthodox' Tradition. Sociological and ethnological definition of the groups shows that there is no Tradition with capital 'T', but traditions that are more-or-less influenced by the scriptural tradition developed under the impact of four ideological forces: a central state, writing, learned written culture and thought – orthodoxy. The dialectic tension develops everywhere, in all contexts between the sacred Tradition and local, ethnographic traditions. In this sense, there are as many 'Islams' with their specific traditions as there are ethno-socio-cultural and linguistic environments sharing a long historical collective memory. One can speak of an Indonesian, Turkish, Uzbeki, Senegalese, Iranian or Indian Islam only in the sense that there is a centralized state that tries to achieve the unification of the nation and/or the community. The affirmation, promotion, protection or oppression and negation of the person will then depend on the social structures, the collective representations and the scale of values enforced by each central power or leading authority in limited communities such as brotherhoods, clans and tribes.

The Islamic Tradition that is shared by all Muslims, whatever their linguistic, cultural or historical background, entails three great and binding foundational sources (*uṣūl al-dīn* and *uṣūl al-fiqh*): the Qur'ān; the Prophetic traditions or *ḥadith* (to which are added the teachings of the twelve or seven Imāms in the case of the Twelver Shī'ites and Ismā'ilis respectively); and the religious law, or *sharī'a,* accepted as the legal codification of God's commandments by virtue of the technical work, known as *ijtihād,* undertaken by jurist-theologians. These three foundational sources were theoretically defined, in the hierarchical order set out above, during the period (c. 661–950) in which Islamic thought was formed; in other words, all the texts, teachings and doctrinal education laid down within this scripture-based Tradition, belong to a period of the general history of thought which is styled mediaeval. We shall return to the problems raised by the sequence of historical periods or stages (periodization) as it has been fixed by Western historians of civilizations from the sixteenth century onwards. For the moment, let us bear in mind that Tradition, so defined, can be written with a capital 'T' because it has always and everywhere sought to impose its supremacy, disregarding and, where possible, eradicating all previous local traditions, because these belong to the period that the Qur'ān calls *Jāhiliyya*, the state of ignorance of the true religion (*dīn al-ḥaqq*) as defined by God, for the last time, in the Revelation transmitted through the Prophet Muḥammad. This theological definition of Tradition, which is bound to supersede all others, naturally disregards the concepts of tradition and custom as these have been developed by ethnography and cultural anthropology since the nineteenth century. The old tensions between the scripture-based Tradition of the jurist-theologians and local traditions is today complicated by all the questioning which critical history, along with the various social sciences, has introduced into the study of every religious tradition, beginning with the traditions of Judaism and Christianity, which have been the direct focus of the ceaselessly renewed challenges of modernity. The capital 'T' also reflects the way in which present-day Muslim thought resists the most indisputable teachings of modernity, in the name of a 'true religion' which no longer allows itself to be questioned, even in terms of the educational tensions of its own past, when doctrinal pluralism was tolerated.

Neither 'noble' Tradition, having a universal value in the eyes of believers, nor local traditions reduced to residual functions by the combined action of learned 'orthodox' religion and the absence of a modern polity, have, as yet, benefited from the explanations and the historical alternatives provided by *critical intellectual modernity* (which I contrast with the politics of traditionalization imposed by the post-colonial states, upheld as these states are by untrained, conformist bureaucracies and the merchant classes who proved to be unable to enhance a sustainable economic development. The social and professional categories are isolated from each other, because the state itself is based on patrimonial mechanisms and cannot initiate a long-term political perspective, including a concrete, relevant plan aimed at the construction of a democratic arena of citizenship. European examples have shown how the legal and institutional emergence of the individual as a citizen fully protected by the rule of law, is a fundamental step in the complex process leading to the optimal formation of a person with humanistic attitudes. Immediately after the independence, gained in the late 1950s and 1960s, the emerging 'national' states could engage in the long, historical process of building a modern arena of citizenship similar to that of the Europeans who are engaged in building a larger entity of European citizenship beyond the limits of the nation-state. The so-called national élites were not acquainted, however, with the philosophy of the person underlying the modern democratic culture. They have never mastered the historical and intellectual conditions in which the learned, written Islamic Tradition has been developed and translated into mediaeval institutions. That is why the status of the human person including women, as defined in the Qur'ān, in the Prophetic traditions and in the legal codes received and applied as the 'Divine Law' (*sharī'a*), has barely begun to open itself to the necessary revisions and discussions inaugurated in Christian Europe, with the emergence, in the sixteenth century, of a humanist reason open to the pagan cultures of Graeco-Roman Antiquity and increasingly desirous of carving out its philosophical autonomy in the face of the dogmatic sovereignty of theological reason. This development continued with the reasoning of the Enlightenment, the philosophy of human rights and the establishment of a democratic rule of law, bound by renewable contract, within a civil society from which political sovereignty derives. This is how the citizen-individual, protected both in his relationships with other citizens and in the free legalistic construction of his private person, emerges as a human subject. The legal freedoms guaranteed by the rule of law do not, naturally, abolish the sociological, economic and linguistic constraints that strictly condition the construction and path of any human subject.

Contemporary Islamic discourse proceeds through a formal annexation of modern 'values' and principles, with the aid of an arbitrary selection of 'holy', sacralizing texts from the Qur'ān and *ḥadīth,* wrenched from their historical and cultural contexts so as to better serve their apologetic purpose. For this reason, I find myself unable to follow the lead of so many others in the operation of 'proving' that every modern development in the legal, political and philosophical status of the **individual-citizen-person** in Europe, is already clearly stated and prescribed in the three corpora of Islamic Tradition that have already been mentioned. The fact is that present-day social frameworks of perception, interpretation and knowledge within the societies called Muslim, better reflect the imaginary representations of the 'true religion' and of the overall Muslim community for which Salvation is promised, rather than support any scientific critique of all the alienating, apologetic and ideological instrumentalization of a so-called Islamic Model, as the historic alternative to the Western, secular, 'atheistic', 'materialist' model. In this connection, the place and role of the nationalist discourse of liberation was begun in the 1950s, but was replaced in the 1980s and expanded by fundamentalist discourse in terms of a phantasmagoric representation of the collective and individual self. It should be noted, nevertheless, that Muslims are not the only ones to practice this ideological patchwork in order to safeguard the validity of the living religious Tradition in the face of the competing model provided by modernity, which constructs the destiny of a human person without God. We are witnessing, rather, a situation in which each religious community strives to outbid the other in imposing its chronological precedence and its spiritual primacy, affirming and implementing such modern concepts as freedom of conscience, tolerance in matters of religious freedom, freedom of expression, freedom of association and the vocation of the human person to exercise full autonomy, more particularly in the fulfilment of individual spiritual destiny.

This is a very old debate between the three monotheistic religions, philosophical reasoning in its Greek version, and Roman law as it extended through the Mediterranean basin. Classical Islam underwent this intellectual experience during the period corresponding to the High Middle Ages in Europe. What marks the difference from Christianity and, to a lesser degree, Judaism, is that in Islamic contexts, philosophical reasoning was eliminated after the thirteenth century, while in Europe, it developed more and more influential interventions in support of the construction of a centralized, powerful state together with the rise of a civil society thanks to the economic, cultural and intellectual contributions made by the capitalist bourgeoisie.

The increasingly powerful role of the bourgeoisie in Europe led to new contradictions such as the exploitation of the labour force and the development of a formal, abstract discourse about so-called humanist values. The social revolutions of the nineteenth century generated this perversion of the philosophy of human rights in European societies, that even spread to the colonized countries. The historical effect of the social, economic and political developments in Europe on colonial societies needs to be clarified, because it continues to determine many essential consequences concerning the status of the person in so-called Muslim societies. How did Marxist-Communist ideology contribute its theories of alienation to economic and political practices during the crucial period of the first emergence of so-called nation-states in Islamic contexts? How did so-called leading 'élites' impose alien concepts, false cultural frameworks and a totalitarian bureaucracy on the peasantry and why were pastoral societies submitted to a brutal uprooting policy? This chapter of history should be written under the following title: *the perverting effects of modernity transferred during the Cold War through Marxist-Communist and liberal-bourgeois channels.*

A comparative, critical history of religions and modern secular ideologies is beginning to show how annexations in reverse – modern ideologies clothing traditional religious discourse on human person in secular atheist expressions – have also taken place in connection with the promotion of human rights and democratic values. The ideas of fraternity and equality, the moral and spiritual presentation of man as inspired, elevated by a free spirit or soul, who thus bears responsibility irrespective of ethnic divides, mechanical and social solidarities, illegitimate allegiances are all basic themes appealing to the promotion of the person and have already been presented in what I called prophetic discourse, to encompass the Jewish, Christian and Islamic traditions. The theoretical discussion of the chronological anteriority of the prophetic discourse to promote the spiritual and ethical status of the human person has, as usual, been more effectively studied, relatively speaking, on the Jewish and Christian side than under Islam, to which the questioning and new curiosity of the social sciences have always been tardily applied. Furthermore, Islam is suspected both by the two rival religions and modern secular thought, to be not only deprived of concerns about human person, but to have introduced into its system of beliefs and non-beliefs, negative teachings about the status of women in particular. We thus need to remedy the conceptual displacements and the various misunderstandings, nourished by two mental frameworks and cultural systems which perpetuate a mutual exclusion between two imaginary entities called 'Islam' and 'the West'.

Let us try and establish the critical course which will, today, lead to the crucial question of the person being adopted globally from the viewpoint of a humanism which should go beyond all those traditions of thought prior to the new cognitive practices which must accompany the historical process of globalization, without rejecting or seeking to invalidate them. It will obviously be necessary to examine the various contemporary Islamic contexts in order to determine how far they hold back or favour the emergence of an autonomous person, free in his choices and commitments to lead his own existence in solidarity with his society and change in the modern world. This will show that the person's course of life and contexts of socialization, the interactive relationship between the person and the group (patriarchal family, clan, village, district, community of orthodox believers) and the status finally accorded to the person in Islamic Tradition: all these basic elements of the traditional societies have been irreversibly upset since the end of World War II and the beginning of the struggles for national liberation. There is thus a *before* and an *after* in the political, institutional, semantic, sociological and anthropological development of the person in Islamic contexts. The study of the *before* places us within the perspective of the long period that begins with the appearance of the Qur'ānic fact and continues, with perceptible differences, but a profoundly marked structural and epistemic continuity, up to around 1940. The *after* constrains us to work within the short period in which brutal revolutions, violent upheavals and rapid disintegration of every traditional code whether customary, legal, semantic, semiotic or anthropological, have followed one another without preparation or transition, within a highly compressed time frame in which a number of heterogeneous temporalities are seen to clash. We shall refrain, therefore, from any static presentation of a 'paradigmatic Islam', unchanged and unchangeable since its foundation by a divine 'Revelation'. On the contrary, we are dealing with the concept of the person as one of the important issues to test the **unthought** and the **unthinkable** in contemporary Islamic thought.

2. The Qur'ānic Fact

Let us start from the Qur'ān, not with a view to seeking out any statements prefiguring our modern concept of person, but in order to distinguish the cognitive status of prophetic discourse from the normative devices subsequently introduced by theological-legalistic doctrines and by intellectual and cultural developments, especially in urban circles. The emergence and rapid expansion of a self-declared Islamic state (the Umayyād Caliphate, followed by the 'Abbasid Caliphate) favoured the construction of what I have called **Islamic**

fact in order to indicate its distinctive characteristics and functions when confronted with the **Qur'ānic fact**. This terminology aims to problematize the whole inherited conceptualization of classical and scholastic Islamic thought, transposed as it has been, without any critical deconstruction, either by Muslims themselves or by the classical Orientalist erudition. The question of the philosophical status of the person in the various doctrines developed in Islamic contexts, has not been raised and could not be addressed in the narrative transposition of the content of classical texts. The first task to this end is to rethink, or consider for the first time, all those questions relative to the person which have been thrust into the unthinkable and kept within the domain of the unthought by Islamic thought since the corpus of Islamic law was fixed by the founders of schools of law and their closest disciples. Paradoxically, it is in the course of the last fifty years, when the challenges of modernity, and now of globalization, are becoming more pressing, that the field of the unthinkable has become most broadened due to the ideological radicalization of the opposition between religious law and ethics on the one hand and secular law and ethics on the other hand.[1]

As has already been explained, the term 'Qur'ān' is too loaded with theological content to serve as an operational concept for a critical reassessment and prospective redefinition of Islamic Tradition as a whole. By speaking of Qur'ānic fact, in the same way as one would speak of biological fact or historical fact, I wish to set at a critical distance all the doctrinal constructions, theological-legalistic, literary, rhetorical and exegetical definitions and procedures that have been commonly regarded as indisputable since the open Qur'ānic discourse was turned into the Official Closed Corpus. Just when this shift occurred it is difficult to say exactly. One can only indicate some chronological points of reference, such as the two monumental works – *History* and *Tafsīr* – of al-Ṭabarī (d. 310/923), the *Risāla* of al-Shāfi'ī (d. 204/820) and the collections of *ḥadīth* completed by Bukhārī (d. 256/870), Muslim

1. I have already presented the main attitudes and teachings about the person in Islamic thought in *Rethinking Islam*.

(d. 261/875), Kulaynī (d. 329/940), Ibn Bābawayh (d. 381/991) and Abū Ja'far al-Ṭūsī (d. 460/1068).

The works left by all these authors are decisive landmarks in the slow historical process whereby concurrent Islamic orthodoxies were constructed with mythical narratives, theological and legal systems and political institutions. The collections of *ḥadīth* swiftly became, in their turn, closed official corpora, assuming the second rank in the hierarchy of foundational sources (*uṣūl*) defined as such by Shāfi'ī for an exegetically trustworthy development of the Law which would henceforth be styled divine (*shari'a*). As collective creations, the Prophetic and Imāmī traditions reflect the slow linguistic, cultural and psycho-sociological processes leading to the establishment of a Muslim *ethos* in the anthropological sense, as defined by Cl. Geertz (see the quotation at the beginning of this chapter). They are informative, too, about the interactions between the teachings of a Qur'ānic corpus that is in the process of closure and the ethno-cultural data proper to the various circles in which the Qur'ānic verses have been used as the ultimate authoritative propositions on all aspects and levels of existence – the physical world, human existence and all created beings. The Muslim *ethos* in process of formation, does not have an equal impact for every group within a vast historical area comprising, for instance, ancient Iran, the Berber regions, the Iberian Peninsula, the huge Turkish lands, Central and South-east Asia and Africa. Even after the establishment of closed official corpora and their circulation in written and oral form, the penetration of the Muslim *ethos* was never to be either generalized in extent and depth for all the groups, nor irreversible in time, nor totally in conformity with the ideal orthodox definition perpetuated in spiritual, ethical and narrative literature.

The ideal orthodox definition of the person in global Islam takes no account either of the historical and sociological dimensions, or of the anthropological problematization that I have set out above. Actually, the Qur'ān read by generations of the faithful as an Official Closed Corpus and a liturgical discourse, does not function linguistically, culturally or semiotically, either as it did at its stage of open oral delivery up to the death of the Prophet, or as it did at the second stage of a corpus in process of collection and written conveyance in a *Muṣḥaf* which was subsequently declared closed. Such were the numerous steps involved in the formation of the Muslim *ethos*. When we take into account all these concrete aspects of the Qur'ānic discourse, any attempt to create a Qur'ānic concept of person leads to two possibilities. Either one ends up with a more or less coherent lexicological construction based on the occurrences of *insān, nās, nafs, rūḥ, wajh, 'aql, fiqh, lubb* and other related notions elaborated in the corpus as a whole; or one follows the diachronic developments of the concept in various and changing contexts. Believers do not care about these academic distinctions and procedures; their reading obeys only the declarations and the statements validated by 'orthodox' faith and empirical collective memory. The construction of the person is pursued in daily empirical life with oral quotations from all verses to illustrate an immediate behaviour, reaction, discussion or event. The Muslim *ethos* is nurtured by this endless confrontation between the sacred and sacralizing, ideal, normative 'Word of God', expanded in the *sīra* of the Prophet as the incarnation of the noblest *ethos* (*makārim al-akhlāq*), and current personal and collective existence. This spontaneous, emotional integration of the sacred word into everyday life by believers should not lead to a disregard of the intellectual and socio-historical costs involved, to the extent that such a reading perpetuates both the alienation of the person and the conditions within which a scholastic culture, giving rise to **institutionalized ignorance**, can expand.

This is just what has occurred in a number of Islamic contexts from the fifteenth and sixteenth centuries onwards. I insist, in this connection, on the reversibility of the conditions whereby the person is promoted in Islamic contexts. The humanistic figure of the *adīb*, open to diverse cultural currents between the ninth and eleventh centuries (c. 800–1030), disappeared along with the social, political and cultural conditions which made him possible.[1]

1. See my description of the philosophical *adab* in the fourth/tenth century in my *L'humanisme arabe*.

A similar process can be seen with the figure of the mystic, who, at the same period, combined a rich personal experience of the divine with a considerable mastery of poetic and intellectual language, whereby this experience was recorded in major works. I am thinking, for example, of Muḥāsibī (d. 243/857), whose name refers to his critical self-examination (*muḥāsabat al-nafs*). This kind of mystical figure was transformed, from the thirteenth to the nineteenth centuries onwards, into a minor scholar who was to Islamize social groups in several societies that maintained an oral tradition and gather around himself disciples called brothers (*ikhwān*), finally establishing the Marabout dynasties governing quite powerful brotherhoods. We shall see later whether we ought to speak of regression or of a crisis of mutation with respect to the status of the person in the phase of national struggles for liberation and of Islamist opposition geared to seizing power.

Let us now briefly consider the means and mental tools provided by Qur'ānic discourse for the construction of a new person with a spiritual vocation, clearly opposed to the old anonymous member of a clan, or even a patriarchal family, whose religious horizons are limited to the local divinities in the *Jāhiliyya*. *Jāhiliyya.* This is worked out in the Qur'ān as a polemic concept pairing *Jāhiliyya/ 'ilm-islām*. It evokes the anthropological concept of 'savage, undomesticated thought' as opposed to 'domesticated thought'; but the opposition became a theological device for condemning a polytheistic culture and society and expanding the true religion revealed in the Qur'ān. I have shown in a long essay how Qur'ānic discourse associates with the terms *nafs, rūḥ, ins, insān, wajh* a rich vocabulary of perception and discursive activity[1] to construct, according to its appropriate spiritual perspectives, what it calls 'man' the son of Adam. It will be shown that the spiritual vocation and ethico-political definition of man at the Qur'ānic stage, masks the contents which are similar to, if not identical with, those found in the biblical and evangelical corpora. It is for this reason that I have introduced the concept of 'prophetic discourse' which, at

1. On the seminal importance of this vocabulary, see my study of the marvellous in the Qur'ān in *Lectures du Coran*, op. cit.

its initial oral stage, utilizes the same conceptual background and system of connotations running from the Biblical stage to our modern ethical definitions. This is particularly evidenced by the sign-symbol *wajh*, face. It is used seventy-two times in the Qur'ān to refer to the Face of God and man seeking this Face, desiring it and 'dedicating his own face to God' (*aslama wajhahu li-llāh*). 'Face' is the richest, still-living metonymy in all European and Semitic languages and all cultures related to Mediterranean area. There is the expression '*loosing face*'; in Arabic, benediction and curse, good and bad wishes are expressed by *red/black face.*[1] The following are some samples of verses often selected to assess an attitude, a behaviour or a judgment according to the ethico-spiritual scale of values concretely defined in the Qur'ān and expanded, as I have said, in the Muslim/Mediterranean *ethos*. Today, the quoted verses and many others are also currently used to annex modern values by placing them under the authority of the Word of God and Islamic tradition:

> *I [Abraham] have turned my face to Him who created the heavens and the earth, and I shall never be a polytheist* [6, 79].
>
> *On the day when some faces shall be white and some faces shall be black* [3, 106–7].
>
> *We offered Trust to the heavens, the earth and the mountains, but they refused to carry it and were afraid of it, but man carried it. He has indeed been unjust and ignorant* [33, 72].
>
> *When your Lord said to the angels: 'I am placing a representative on earth', they said: 'Will you place one who will make mischief in it and shed blood, while we sing Your praise and glorify Your sanctity?* [2, 29].
> *Had Allah not caused some people to repel others, the earth would have been corrupted* [2, 253].

---

1. For the symbolism of face in the Qur'ān, see A. Rippin, 'Desiring the Face of God: The Qur'ānic symbolism of Personal responsibility', in *Literary Structures of Religious Meaning in the Qur'ān*, edited by Issa J. Boullata, Curzon, 2000, pp. 117–24.

> *Say: We believe in Allah, in what has been revealed to us, what was revealed to Abraham, Ismā'īl, Isḥāq, Jacob and the Tribes, and in what was imparted to Moses, Jesus and the other prophets from their Lord, making no distinction between any of them, and to Him we submit* [2, 135].
>
> *Man is, indeed, a prey to perdition. Except for those who believe, perform righteous deeds, urge each other to seek the truth and urge each other to be steadfast* [103, 2–3].
>
> *Then, when the sacred months are over, kill the idolaters wherever you find them, take them [as captives], besiege them, and lie in wait for them at every point of observation. If they repent afterwards, perform the prayer and pay the alms, then release them. Allah is truly All-Forgiving, Merciful* [9, 5].

One could list an infinite number of statements in which the dialogue between God and man, man and God, develops within every register of discourse and within every sphere of knowledge and action. The Ten Commandments are represented in the most diverse contexts as the means to snatch man from the grip of blindness, violence, the 'uncultured' life (*Jāhiliyya*) and the constraints of the group, including parents who refuse to enter into the new Alliance (*mithāq*): 'That is part of what your Lord has revealed to you of wisdom' (17, 39). The verses quoted as a sample cannot, as has been said, reveal their true meanings, in the sense demanded by the historian, unless we duly consider the actual circumstances in which they were originally articulated in Mecca or Medina. This rule incumbent upon the historian is, of course, systematically disregarded by believers concerned only with norms immediately applicable to their empirical behaviour. According to the particular contingency faced, the development of a conversation or the necessities of a line of argument, they will invoke, with equal conviction, verse 9, 5 to legitimize *jihād* or other verses that are more peaceful and more geared towards the promotion of the positive aspects of the person. The Qur'ān as experienced has always had priority over the Qur'ān as analysed, expounded and known; yet the latter must retain primacy over the former if we are to limit the drift of the social and religious imaginary and reject manipulations performed with ideological ends in mind. This fight between priority and primacy lies at the heart of the history of all the founding texts, and, consequently, the meaning and the effects of sense (*effets de sens*) that always condition the construction and action of the person. Apart from the reading of the jurists, who are concerned to derive the laws and statutes they promulgate as part of an Islamic body of law *(sharī'a)* applicable to all, learned commentaries have had hardly any influence on common belief and individual acceptance of the Qur'ān, which is closely bound up with emotional ties, subjective expectations and group constraints on the expression of personal identity than with any learned exegesis. Memorized verses are at the disposal of all and are invoked spontaneously, without any concern for the original context, to utter a prayer, give thanks, meditate on the inner equivalence between a situation as experienced and its beautiful, concise, eternally true expression in the Word of the Most High. The person, as a human being faced with the vicissitudes of existence, constructs himself, blossoms out or else founders in alienation, according to his degree of nearness to Qur'ānic discourse in general (millions of Muslims do not speak Arabic and, even among Arabic-speakers, most do not have access to the archaic Qur'ānic language) and, according to the use he makes of scattered texts, knitted into the here and now of daily existence.

Note once more the relevance of the concept of 'prophetic discourse', which allows these analyses to be applied to all persons trained within the framework of identity associated with the long tradition of the teaching of the prophets from Abraham to Muḥammad, a tradition expressed linguistically in the same discourse of mythic structure, and using the same religious symbolism, the same metaphorical organization, to bring about '*the man of the Alliance*' with a Living, Speaking God, one who acts upon temporal history so as to enrich and broaden, in terms of a benevolent pedagogy, the reciprocity of the man-God and God-man perspectives. Thanks to the revelatory richness of 'prophetic discourse', man raises himself to the dignity of person through internalizing God as an inner protagonist, with the help of prayer, thanksgiving and a meditative deciphering of all the signs *(āyāt)* of creation and of that mark of Benevolent Care whereby man is singled out among all creatures to receive the heavy responsibility of directing a just order as '*God's representative on earth*'. All this leads to the emergence of a **consciousness of self** in relation to the Absolute of a God who is the ultimate Criterion and inevitable Referent for all the various activities of the '**person-creature**'. The change to be wrought by modernity to this mode of the awakening and realization of consciousness of self will lie in moving on from the 'person-creature' of God, bound to Him by a *debt of sense* and a loving acceptance of His commandments, to the '*person-individual-citizen*', bound to the state by a social and legal contract.

3. From the Qur'ānic Fact to the Islamic Fact and 'Modern Identity'

There is no chronological succession between these three historical and cultural facts, especially when it is borne in mind that modernity is less a matter of chronicling the history of thought than a problem of the *posture* of reason when faced with the question: **how can I gain adequate knowledge of the real and, if I arrive at this knowledge, how can I communicate it without alienating the consciousness of self in any recipient?** There is no room here to consider the analyses and historical restatements demanded by this definition of modernity (I have treated these at greater length in the second edition of my *Critique de la raison islamique*). The 'Qur'ānic fact', the 'Islamic fact' and the emergence of a modern 'posture' of reason co-exist at every stage of the history of thought, with interactions, educational tensions and direct confrontations that may be fruitful or negative, depending on the particular contexts or periods involved. To set out these complex and evolving connections would clearly require a comparative history of these three poles of meaning and action, which engage the destiny of the person differently within Islamic, Christian, Jewish, Buddhist, Hindu or secular modern contexts. We are a long way from this, however much the European viewpoint on modern thought imposes its periodization, categorizations, subject matter and segmentation of reality, which is thereby transformed into unassailable paradigms of knowledge.

In the case of 'Islam', the dialectic of the 'Qur'ānic fact' and the 'Islamic fact' remains to be defined. It presupposes the identification of the 'Qur'ānic fact' as a historical, linguistic, discursive stage different from the subsequent stage called Islamic fact with all the political, theological, juridical, mystical, literary and historiographical expansions, elaborations and doctrinal disputes. This distinction does not mean an endorsement of the theological status of the Qur'ān as the Revelation remaining above human history; both Qur'ānic fact and Islamic fact should be examined as components of concrete history; but they are different both in the intrinsic content of each fact and in the way they are received by their advocates, how they are interpreted and used to produce the concrete history. These differences need to be clearly identified in order to banish the current ideological confusions produced by believers and many interpreters of Qur'ān and Islam. Believers especially speak indiscriminately of the Word of God, Revelation, Qur'ān and Islam.

At the stage of the 'Qur'ānic fact', God presents Himself to man in a discourse articulated in the Arabic language. He sets Himself to perceive, receive and listen as the Person *par excellence,* possessing a fullness of fundamental attributes whose acquisition is only effectively possible for man through what mystics and philosophers have long called *ta'alluh,* 'the imitation of God'. Man must strive to attain the level of perfection embodied by God who reveals Himself in order to guide man in the fulfilment of this **essential Desire**, the celebrated *'ishq*,[1] that powerful motive for the moral, spiritual and intellectual search for the status of person (or, as it was known, Perfect Man, *al-insān al-kāmil*). Prophetic discourse was

1. See my article in the *Encyclopaedia of Islam*, s.v. *'Ishq*.

the inexhaustible spring wherein the saints, the friends of God, the servants of God and the great witnesses to spirituality found the living metaphors, fruitful symbols and myths of their experience of the divine. It runs through the history of many societies and cultures; and it is above political partisanship that is not based on the 'true religion' (the problems posed by this concept have been discussed in modern philosophy, but not definitively resolved). It relies, above all, on the trusting quest, dedicated to achieving the greatest closeness to the Altogether Other (expressed in the ritual phrase *al-lahu akbar*) and in the spiritual witness perpetuated for mankind by virtue of this search as unshakeable value.

The 'Islamic fact' retains and exploits this dimension of the 'Qur'ānic fact' as an area of sanctification, of spiritualization, transcendentalization, ontologization, mythologization, ideologization through all the doctrinal schemes, all the legalistic, ethical and cultural codes, all the systems of legitimation put in place by the *'ulamā'*. The 'Islamic fact', like the Christian, Jewish and Buddhist fact, or any other, cannot be dissociated from the exercise of political power in that the state, in all its historical forms, attempts to direct for its own benefit the spiritual *ethos* of the 'Qur'ānic fact', yet the Qur'ānic fact's connection with the 'Islamic fact' (notably ethical and legal codes) resists any total, irreversible annexation. It is the great moments and most pertinent areas of this ongoing psychological, existential tension that witness the affirmations, protests and resistance by those most conscious of the recurrent factors of a confrontation complicated by the claims of 'modern identity', as defined by Charles Taylor in his *Sources of the Self: The Making of Modern Identity*.

It is to the 'Islamic fact' that the development and historical action of what is called Muslim law should be linked, especially the aspect that is applied as positive law (*fiqh*). In practice, the role of 'Qur'ānic fact' boils down to operations of sacralization, indeed of divinization, of corpora of norms that have been transformed into religious law (*sharī'a*). We are now conscious of the fact that the formation of the schools of law (*madhāhib*) continued up to the fourth/tenth century; and it was from the ninth century that the work of sacralization came to be seen as a religious necessity, to restrict the infiltration of local customs and practices as well as strengthen the legitimacy of the central 'Islamic' state. The inroads that prophetic discourse attempted to make with regard to the emancipation of the person in law, have been only partially successful, either in time or space, since kinship solidarities continue to this day to interfere with the modern construction of the social bond and the emergence of a civil society, the rule of law and the *person-individual-citizen* as interactive dimensions of the human subject in the historical march towards intellectual, spiritual, ethical and political modernity, all linked indissolubly together. I have given a particularly enlightening example of the manipulations of Qur'ānic discourse itself, provided by jurists anxious to circumvent provisions considered too subversive for the customary order that preserved the force of patriarchal and clan solidarities in those key ethno-cultural areas in which the power of the new Islamic state, first Umayyād then 'Abbasid, was exercised.[1] After the triumph of what I have called the Official Closed Corpus, Islamic Tradition ratified all the *faits accomplis* of exegesis and of the *corpora juris* and accepted them as orthodox. For this reason, one cannot, today, either return to an open Qur'ānic corpus or easily liberate the person from the kinds of status defined in that part of private law called personal status, *al-aḥwāl al-shakṣiyya.* The *fait accompli* of the closed official corpus remains historically irreversible, unless *Muṣḥafs* can be discovered that are contemporary with the first official *Muṣḥaf* , and this is unlikely to happen. In the meantime, the *corpora juris* declared orthodox, continue to be perceived and experienced by the community of believers as legal categorizations (*aḥkām*) correctly derived from Qur'ānic verses.

In the light of these explanations, one may better appreciate the need to rediscover what I venture to call '**spiritual responsibility**', as a means of resistance, on the part of the human spirit, against the operations of reason itself as the latter works with the 'unthinkables' and 'unthoughts' of each socio-cultural environment and each

1. See my *Lectures du Coran*, Chapter 5: *De l'ijtihād à la critique de la raison islamique.*

historical period. I know how the concept of spirituality is dismissed within a scientific mindset which stresses the alienating functions of religion and a positivist, biological approach to the human person. I am introducing the concept of **spiritual responsibility**, not to reactivate the idealistic claims for religious spiritualism, but to problematize the current reference made to the '*dignity of human person*' in the declarations of many national committees for ethics that investigate the new threats posed by biotechnology and biology. This is recognized as a legitimate field of research with a view to rehabilitating and reactivating a concern lost as much in Islamic thought as in modem thought, that of the ethics of the person. I shall proceed with this heuristic definition in mind.

4. A Heuristic Definition

For the human spirit, assuming a spiritual responsibility means providing oneself with all the means, and at all times the necessary conditions, for resisting all activities (once they have been duly identified) that aim to alienate it (the spirit), enslave it, mutilate it or mislead one or several of its faculties in an attempt to achieve an end contrary to what makes it the seat, the agent and the irreducible sign of the eminent dignity of the human person.

An application of this definition to the concept of person, as sanctioned by the law of the *fuqahā'*, makes it possible to detect the limitations of the legal status that is typical of the mediaeval mindset, prior to the emergence of legal modernity; a legal modernity made possible by progress in scientific and philosophical thought as well as economic and technological development, that occurred first in Europe. In Muslim law, the full-blown status of person is reserved for the *orthodox Muslim who is male*, free (as opposed to being a slave) and entitled in law to respect the rights of God and human rights. Children, slaves and non-Muslims are potentially entitled to gain access to this status (the child when he reaches the age of responsibility (*mukallaf*), the slave when freed, the non-Muslims when converted). Woman, however, while raised to a spiritual dignity equal to that of man, is kept in an inferior ritual and legal status, since the Qur'ān itself did not succeed in removing all the taboos and restrictions weighing on the female condition in what it called the *Jāhiliyya*. It is a historical fact that all religions have perpetuated not only unthinkables and unthoughts with respect to the spiritual and legal status of the human person, but even in sacralized forms of religious status which continue, even now, to feed exclusions, schisms, inquisitions, persecutions, 'sacred' violence, claims and conquests in the name of a God whom living traditions have, in fact, linked arbitrarily to mechanical solidarities, strategies of power and all the constraints of the '*imaginary production*' of societies. Modernity may have abolished slavery, may have opened a space of citizenship in which distinctions between faiths are disregarded; but it has not yet finished the slow work of emancipation of the female condition and of the protection of the rights of the child.

It should be added that the theologies of 'true religion' – which is both a Qur'ānic and a biblical concept, adopted and developed by the three monotheistic religions, though Hegel attempted to give it a philosophical status – continue to disseminate their teachings and to erode the frontiers of the thinkable and unthinkable with regard to the status of the person. For its part, philosophical and scientific thought is less concerned to integrate the postures of theological thought and religious beliefs into its field of critical enquiry; in view of the extraordinary discoveries of biology and the neurosciences. Philosophers now prefer to shy away from any challenging posture about the changing status of human person. Even in the most secular societies, competition remains open between a 'humanism' centred on God, on whom man's salvation depends in this world and the next, and a 'humanism' centred exclusively on man. Note that the first borrows more from the second than the second from the first; but it should be added that the second increasingly distances itself from the classic concept of humanism, as the tele-techno-scientific reason behind the processes of globalization, is asserting its hegemony over the theological and philosophical stages of reason. The concept of humanism itself is so disputed, however, that it has almost fallen into disuse.[1] The status of the person thus finds itself fought over from several points of reference, ancient, traditional or new, while current debates and social scientific research fail to provide all the necessary enlightenment.

In contemporary Islamic contexts, the crisis of the status of the person is even more difficult to deal with. The rules of fraternity, solidarity and respect for the life and property of persons, already insisted upon in the Qur'ān and later in the whole living Tradition (*turāth*), are 'applied' with tragic rigour in the generalized context of national and international terrorism. I prefer to abstain from any comment on a phenomenon which throws into crisis every type of ethics and every system of legitimation, old and new: I refer to terrorism everywhere that is presented today as the only path left for a human group to attain or re-attain 'identities' wrested by other dominant nations, groups or powers. The various persecutions, imposed by the inquisitions at the time of theological certainty, have been taken up today, with the same sense of conscious justification, by the terrorist phenomenon. In both cases, it will be noted that the conflict of interpretations rests on the same, still surviving contradiction, namely that innocent persons are physically destroyed so that the self-proclaimed rights of other persons can be vindicated. We are not really concerned here with the political movements, ideological shifts, clans and factions, ideals and causes, which lead to such a radical negation of the human person; the main issue about terrorism is that the protection of human person should prevail in all circumstances, regardless of the ideological claims expounded in order to 'legitimize' a terrorist action. I know that this ethical principle cannot withstand the **structural violence** expanding in the world with the arbitrary forces operating in favour of a so-called international order. The **logic of war** is implicit in the economic and monetary 'order' imposed on the whole world. The human person is suffering a great deal from a semantic disorder that is affecting all cultures and all levels of existence under outdated international law.

1. I discuss this point in my book *Ma'ārik min ajl al-ansana fīl-siyāqāt al-islāmiyya*, Dār al-Sāqī, Beirut, 2001.

These trajectories and frameworks of realization of the human person on the world scale naturally impinge upon all Islamic contexts, in that the Islamic fact has practically imposed its priority as a platform of resistance against the 'cultural aggression' (*ghazw fikrī*) of the West or 'Westoxication'. The Qur'ān is quoted, but less involved as such in the battle. Not only is the distinction between Qur'ānic fact and Islamic fact, outlined above, unthinkable, but the terms 'Islam' and 'Islamic Law' have come to vaguely denote a populist brand of theological axiology, ritualization of collective behaviour, principles of political commitment and militant practices observed with the same ritual punctiliousness as religious obligations in the proper sense. We have, in this way, a complete system, sociologically and psychologically most efficient, for the education of a new human being who views himself as radically and authentically 'Muslim', the bearer of the one true message of salvation for all mankind, responsible for the historical action necessary to block the devilish forces of modernization and secularisation. Here are the lines of force of what I have just called populist brand of theological axiology. This terminology is dictated neither by a theological reasoning, that is more intellectually trustworthy, to which future reference would need to be made, nor by a philosophical or scientific reasoning laying claim to a role of absolute normative authority. It is merely a matter of broaching a typology of the social actors, of the kinds of discourse they produce, of regimes embodying truth, which they seek to impose through political, legal and economic institutions. I indicated earlier that populist culture, along with the theological axiology it conveys, has already led to political successes that make a mockery, in any substantial sociological or psychological sense, of what is called learned culture, the postures of philosophical and scientific reason. This inversion of 'values' spiritual, moral and intellectual on the one hand, political, economic and technological on the other, has been an incontrovertible fact of the history of thought, and therefore of the conditions within which the human subject is shaped and develops, ever since '*material civilization*' in the historical Braudelian sense of the term, first imposed its hegemony on the world.

5. Populist Theological Axiology

Consideration in more detail should be devoted to the concise content and cognitive status of this populist brand of theological axiology. In this way, it will be possible to measure more accurately the sociological extension of the concept of populist culture as I am trying to deal with it here.

I shall start with a remarkable series broadcast by the Qatari *al-Jazīra* television network under the general title *Religious Law and Life* (*al-Sharīʿa wa-l-ḥayāt*). The guest on the evening of 28 December, 1997, was Professor ʿAdnan Zarzur, the author of a number of learned works on Islamic thought. He gave a concise, perfectly orthodox definition, one accepted by all contemporary Muslims, of the theological status of the Qur'ān and of the procedures whereby all its verses are interpreted so as not only to base (*ta'ṣīl*) the thoughts and behaviour of believers in the divine Word, but to ensure the cognitive validity of all the divine statements *vis-à-vis* all forms of knowledge, present and future, up to the final Day of Judgement. As the ultimate manifestation of Revelation, the Qur'ān has divided the history of salvation, which embodies our chronological history on earth, into a before and an after of the year 632, to define the theological-legal status of every human act according to the limits (*ḥudūd*) fixed by God Himself in the legislative verses. The far more numerous verses speaking of the creation of worlds and beings are signs provided for the spiritual meditation and the reflection of believers so as to integrate, within their individual consciousness, the nature of the Being of God, the meanings of the actions He has undertaken and the everlasting scope of His teaching. Within this theological perspective, the term *turāth*, used to denote the classical cultural heritage bequeathed by what historians call the civilization of classical Islam, referring more specifically to the profane, mundane dimension of Arab classical culture including, of course, Islamic tradition.

The sum of the sacred texts collected in the Qur'ān and *ḥadīth*, authenticated by the authorized transmitters and correctly interpreted by competent, recognized exegetes, form the Divine

Body of Authority (*al-marji'iyya*) to which every subsequent product of human activity on earth must be referred, so as to determine its theological and legal status according to the five legal categorizations (obligatory, forbidden, recommendable, reprehensible, permitted). This referral of the whole of human history on earth to a tribunal decreed to be divine, although its members are mere mortals, elevated *post factum* to the rank of infallible Imāms (for the Shī'ites) or authoritative duly qualified doctors (*a'imma mujtahidūn*) (for the Sunnīs), is to be continuously applicable through History of Salvation.

There is, in this formulation, an undeniable inner coherence which satisfies religious reasoning, a kind of reasoning indivisible from what anthropologists call 'the social imaginary'. Reason invoked in the course of theological enquiry is indifferent to all the reasonings of the human and social sciences. On the other hand, it is highly attentive and stringent regarding all the discursive operations made necessary by the collection and authentification of the official corpora it will pronounce closed. Once the process of dogmatic closure has been achieved, this same reasoning will, for the protection and everlasting preservation of the 'faith', use the ready-prepared arsenal of axiological postures, methodological practices, argumentative proceedings, rhetorical forms and strategies of selection, insertion, rejection and total destruction of facts prior to and following on from the time of closure. Thenceforth, what the human and social sciences call 'representations', images that each individual or collective subject possesses of itself, will dwell within the sphere of the unthinkable. It can be seen here how the unthinkable and the unthought trace a psychological dividing line between two mental configurations structured by two cognitive practices which, once systematized, permit the reproduction of two differentiated frameworks of the formation and development of the person.

I do not know how far Professor Zarzur would share these analyses, which, it will be seen, endeavour to problematize the two concurrent cognitive practices, and try never to affirm, even implicitly, the handling of concepts and the primacy of one or the other. I am speaking, alternately, the language of the social sciences and that of dogmatic theological reason, so as to transfer both alike to a cognitive practice whose legitimacy and productivity will emerge as this confrontation develops. The dogmatic posture makes no corresponding concession to concurrent kinds of discourse. Thus, in his presentation of theological axiology through a powerful media outlet, even someone like Professor Zarzur consigned to silence all the discussions set up between the multiple schools before the closure of the official corpora and the construction of an orthodox *turāth*, on the strength of which he gives a warning that is both theological and 'scientific' to the regime of religious truth as such; a regime that functions for millions of Muslims throughout the world (a good many listeners to the series take part in the discussion from Europe). This is a measure of the sociological dimension, political weight and historical scope of what I have called the populist brand of theological axiology.

What turn might the programme – or rather the very numerous programmes in the same style – have taken if Professor Zarzur, or any other teacher and scholar of his calibre, had been confronted with an advocate of the (still largely utopian) project of a *critique of Islamic reason* such as I have been working on in all my writings since the 1970s? The problem of *communicability* between the two mental configurations and the cognitive systems they generate and reproduce would then arise; and, if communication proved possible to the fullest extent, then, the unthinkables and the unthoughts accumulated on both sides would be incorporated and examined within a **necessarily new space of the thinkable**; reason, imagination, the imaginary and memory would receive different statuses, entering another psychological dimension, thus generating new regimes embodying what continues, globally, to be called truth. I stress, with sadness, that neither the western media, nor those of Muslim countries, nor even the universities and research institutions, have considered organizing, encouraging and multiplying activities which would hasten the emergence of a new thinking to give more opportunity for the rise of a new human person.

While awaiting a time when this utopia is accorded an initial concrete realization, there is a need to explain why the dominant Islamic discourse has taken on such broad proportions and mobilizes so many fervent militants. I shall merely list the most decisive factors. The internal factors include the demographic growth which, in a short period of time, has considerably expanded the sociological bases of a social imaginary fed both by the nationalistic discourse of the anti-colonial struggle and the Islamist discourse regarding the 'refounding' of an 'identity' betrayed by secular 'élites'; the use of the media and public education for the purposes of ideological conditioning by one-party states that are voluntarist, militarist and devoid of democratic culture; recourse to a policy of 'traditionalization' aggravating the split between the modern and the 'religious' construct of the human being; the uprooting of peasant or nomadic populations, who flock to the cities where traditional customary and cultural codes disintegrate, being replaced by a *populist* social imaginary that is simultaneously isolated from the urban élites and from those witnesses (increasingly rare and marginalized) to an Islamic tradition concerned with obedience to the sole authority *(ḥukm)* of God and, as such, being independent *vis-à-vis* every type of power. I make a distinction here between, on the one hand, *'ulamā'* who are adept at handling the media, who lend their assistance to the policy of traditionalization and add their substantial weight to the 'populist' imaginary, and, on the other, intellectuals, teachers, scholars, essayists, writers and artists who strive, in their respective spheres, to introduce a modern culture of perception, interpretation and creative interaction between a reconsidered Islamic tradition and a self-critical modernity. Unfortunately, this latter current of thought and action exists only precariously, since its proponents are dispersed throughout the world, far from the sociological terrain that is now virtually abandoned to the mechanical forces of the factors enumerated above.

The external factors comprise, basically, the continuous pressures of economic and technological modernity on all those societies which have never taken part, at any stage, in the production and direction of this modernity. All the political 'élites' who have assumed control in these societies since the 1950s have taken immediate steps to ensure the acquisition of *power* in the practical sense of the term (through military disciplines, police networks for the control of the whole national territory, heavy industry and technological tools) over the development of the means for searching for *sense.* The imbalance created by this policy has been aggravated all the more rapidly in that modernity, has accelerated the rhythms of change in all fields of the historical production of societies. Thus it is that historical research into the past of each society is the most urgent kind of research for restraining and correcting the excesses of ideological manipulation, but it is also the most neglected. The perverse effects of material modernity continue to feed global rejections of modernity as a project of liberation for the human condition, while the legitimate needs of a vast population everywhere demand recourse to modern means of production and trade. The internal and external factors do not act separately; rather, the historical dialectic of the forces of modernity has a multipling effect on the increasingly ungovernable interaction of all the factors.

I have, I hope, sufficiently shown how the 'Qur'ānic fact', the 'Islamic fact' and 'modern identity' face one another, challenge one another and exclude one another; how they condition one another in their expressions and in their struggles for survival and hegemony. I have, I hope, sufficiently pointed out the gaping chasm that separates the respective protagonists advocating open competition between the model called *Islamic* and the other called *Western* in producing the history of mankind for the third millennium. There remains the problem of listing the resources and present orientations whereby a 'modern identity' seeks to open the way to the historical solidarity of mankind, to put an end to the cultural and intellectual systems of reciprocal exclusion which continue to legitimize civil wars, structural violence, systems of inequality and hegemonic conquests, under the pretext of the historical necessities of globalization.

'Modern identity' is a historical given as massive, and as broadly encompassing in its definitions and applications, as 'religious identity' in its various forms. This is why they compete for the privilege of leading man towards his 'true' salvation. It should be clear by now that my position in the face of this age-old rivalry, disfigured by wars and costly revolutions, can be summed up in three verbs: **infringe, displace, transcend**. I have described at length the methodological and epistemological scope of these three cognitive operations as applied to the writing of the history of societies fashioned by the 'Islamic fact'; I refer the reader to the relevant study in *Arabica*, 1, 1996, republished in *Penser l'Islam aujourd'hui*, 2002. I note that Christian theology is witnessing significant moves towards the displacement and transcendence of questions and solutions bequeathed by a two-thousand-year-old practice of living Tradition whose frontiers are now infringed. I am thinking especially of the recent work by Father J. Dupuy entitled *Vers une théologie chrétienne du pluralisme religieux* (Towards a Christian Theology of Religious Pluralism). The interest of this orientation of religious thought in the face of the productive or arrogant challenges posed by 'modern identity', lies in its demonstration of the possibility and promise of a systematic problematization of the two identities by one another. It should not be forgotten that the reason of the Enlightenment liberated mankind from what Voltaire called a "wild beast' (meaning the dogmatic theological reasoning employed by the institution of the Church as a way of wielding its power over souls and bodies). By the same token, this reasoning ratified recourse to the violence of war in order to impose a new political legitimacy – a historical fact which is not without bearing on the barbarous instances of violence in the nineteenth and twentieth centuries and on what has been stated here about 'modern' terrorism. The establishment of the revolutionary violence of the modern political symbolism, in place of the religious symbolism now declared obsolete, has driven back into the so-called *darkness of the Middle Ages*, i.e., into ignorance, the unthought, and indeed the unthinkable, about numerous questions of an anthropological and philosophical nature. The so-called *return of God*, following the vaunted declaration of His death, must not mean a return to mythologized 'values' and illusory visions of the 'perfect man', but the opening of new spaces of intelligibility and more reliable possibilities for the emancipation of the human condition.

Conclusion

I shall conclude this critical investigation by drawing the reader's attention to one of those new paths that neither religious thought nor modern thought has explored in any exhaustive or even relevant manner. I refer to what I have called the anthropological triangle of Violence, Sacred, Truth. I am well aware that countless meditations, sermons, exhortations, analyses and inquiries have been devoted to these three themes in every tradition of thought. Nor am I ignorant of the contributions made by contemporary anthropology and psychoanalysis; and René Girard has, I know, reflected on the link between violence and sacred, the only relevant response, according to him, being that proposed by Christianity. The point made is very debatable, especially since truth has been considered separately from the Violence, Sacred duality. But there still remains much to be done in this direction. In an earlier study,[1] I broached the problem of what St Augustine called the '*just war*' and the Qur'ān has called *jihād* – a concept taken up once more by the Western countries allied against Iraq during the Gulf War. Throughout the history of humanity, people have invoked 'the just war', the sacred struggle to protect the superior interests of a 'Truth' assailed by 'enemies' external to it. Examples are the defence or expansion of Christian territory, of the *Dār al-Islām,* of the modern capitalist nation states, of colonized regions and of the geopolitical spheres of the Great Powers. I have analysed at length a text by Muḥammad 'Abd al-Salam Faraj entitled '*The Absent Canonical Obligation*' *(al-Farīḍa 'l-ghā'iba),* showing how the author's efforts to reactivate the obligation of *jihād* within a majority Muslim society – Sādāt's

1. See my *Rethinking Islam*, pp. 86–106.

Egypt – and more generally within the *umma* as a whole, so as to vindicate exclusively the warring and terrorist face of *jihād,* runs counter to all the teachings of the Islamic Tradition on the dignity of the human person This study, like so many others that have been translated into Arabic, has nevertheless found no significant echo either among intellectuals or within enlightened Muslim opinion. As for the western public, it naturally prefers to reinforce its own imagery of an Islam championing Holy War against the Infidels. So long as it is a question of confrontation, about a truth of self which each protagonist opposes to that of the other, without either side being prepared to reflect in depth on what such a truth of self actually implies, then the question of the human person is not on the agenda. The logic of war is rooted in the founding logic of truth itself. The culture which fosters this two so-called 'logics' – logics which refer, in each case, to the same processes for the construction of the human subject – is not yet available even in those places most permeated by 'modern identity'.

I realize the need to delve further and more deeply into the exploration of an Islamic consciousness as yet unreconstructed by the positive contributions of modernity. For this reason I have, for some years now, been working on expanding the space of thinking in Islamic thought. We cannot continue to invoke formal kinds of humanism taught by the great religious and philosophical texts, while treating violence as a manifestation which is exceptional, which simply happens to occur within archaic societies, or imperfectly integrated sections of civilized societies, or committed by wayward individuals who are immediately condemned or brushed aside in the name of a dominant morality and an effective law. Violence is a driving force inherent in the human being and in social life; there are always, within each person, quite strong and recurrent tensions between impulses to violence and aspirations for Good, Beauty and Truth. *Sura 2, 253,* quoted earlier, provides a very simple reminder of this dual aspect of man. In his attempts to check the ravages of violence, man has long had recourse to what is still called the 'sacred', referring things to a substantial reality endowed with effective powers, when it is really rather a matter of rituals and procedures of sacralization aimed at shielding individuals, places and periods of time from profanation and sacrilege through violence. Sacrifices are instituted to turn the effects of violence toward a category of human being, toward a part of the human body, toward animals or natural elements. These functional and notional bonds are woven between **Violence, Sacred and Truth**, just as clearly stated in *sura* 9:5. This objectification of interactions between realities still being posed and experienced as powers external to man, simultaneously shows the person moving on to a new stage of knowledge and self-realization.

Struggles for respect for the rights of man, woman and child are joined in every country and every regime in which Islam, Islamic Tradition and *sharīʿa* remain points of reference that are impossible to bypass. The spiritual, moral and cultural wholeness of the person can be ensured only by way of a democratic regime, a rule of law, monarchical or republican, according to the history of each country, and a civil society recognized as a partner from which the sovereignty of the state derives. It has been conclusively shown, since the 1950s, that movement towards these institutions is more strongly conditioned by the acquisition and diffusion of a *culture of democracy* than by material prosperity, which nevertheless remains a trump card when managed with the democratic participation of all the participants. I have shown the decisive role played by the philosophical postulates which, implicitly or explicitly, govern all religious, legal, moral and political thought. For this reason, I would maintain that there is no viable democracy without open, free, fruitful, critical debate, initiated in each society; and these debates cannot attain the humanistic aims of democracy unless they incorporate philosophical interrogation on the prevailing systems of thought used by competing protagonists. We know the extent to which a dogmatic religious attitude or modern ideological mindsets exclude philosophical education and interest; and we are familiar, too, with the weakness, or often the total absence, of the teaching of philosophy not only in the educational systems introduced by post-colonial regimes, but also in the secondary schools of several Western societies. If we add to this the total absence, everywhere, of a teaching of theology founded on a critique of theological reason, it can clearly be appreciated what the kind of educational programme should be introduced as a matter of urgency, in order to create the modern intellectual and cultural conditions for the emergence and optimum development of the person in Islamic contexts and elsewhere.

SIX

Aspects of Religious Imaginary

The Examples of the Crusades and the Battle of Lepanto

Great importance is attributed to the concept of the 'imaginary', not only in the social and political sciences but also in psychoanalysis, literary and artistic criticism. Theoretical debates in France, when Marxist epistemology was defended by many influential scholars and thinkers, provided such rich dimensions of the *imaginaire social* that in the late 1960s and 1970s it became the subject of subversive works such as *L'institution imaginaire de la société* (1975) by Constantin Castoriadis and *Les structures anthropologiques de l'imaginaire* (1961) by Gilbert Durand. Historians such as J. Le Goff and G. Duby made valuable contributions to a new area of history known as the '*anthropology of the past*' and '*the archaeology of the daily life*', to use the expressions of G. Duby. Few significant contributions in that field of knowledge have been added in Islamic contexts. The works of Henry Corbin focused on what he called 'the *imaginal*' and 'the *creative imagination*' as demonstrated by thinkers such as Soharawardi, Avicenna and Ibn 'Arabī; but he ignored the wider scope of the functions fulfilled by the imaginary. In two essays published in *Arabica*, 1988, vol. 35: *Imaginaire social et leaders dans le monde musulman contemporain*, and in *Lectures du Coran*, 1991: *Peut-on parler de merveilleux dans le Coran?*, I have shown how the concept can be fruitfully applied to the study of ancient texts as well as to contemporary society.

Obviously, religions ought to have been the richest field in which the functions of the *imaginaire* could be identified, described and differentiated from the interventions of reason and rationalization. The contrary has happened; theology has been and remains a constant effort to translate into coherent, rational, systematized doctrines, beliefs that were originally expressed and transmitted in mythical narratives more closely related to the creative imagination and the social expansion of the collective *imaginaire* than to the adventurous consistencies created and sustained over the centuries by theological thinking. Until now, this sociological and historical fact is not even currently recognized as an important subject for research and teaching. When political scientists presented fundamentalist discourses, as they have done in many societies in the name of several religions, they limit their interpretations to the postulated framework of 'rationality', but neglect to point out to the irrational, emotional, imaginary dimensions of the representations spread by such discourses. They do not introduce any rational coherence between the manipulations of the mythologized, ideologized past and the concrete realities, expectations and needs of the present. The main trend of contemporary Islamic thought is dominated by the will to 'rationalize' and 'modernize' the whole Qur'ānic discourse that is used as a screen on which to back-project all of the scientific and technological discoveries of modern science; in the same way, any metaphoric organization or mythical structure of the discourse would be vehemently denied. This collective practice is encouraged and even nurtured by famous physicists, medical doctors, engineers and mathematicians. Such a rich psycho-socio-cultural field of reality remains unexplored, because the concept of the *imaginaire* is marginalized, minimized, if not negated by neo-scholastic reason as P. Bourdieu has deconstructed it.

The above remarks are designed to introduce the two examples I have chosen to illustrate the concept of the religious *imaginaire* and its functions in all social contexts, from the most archaic to the most 'modern'. The Crusades have been and are still used in European and Muslim discourses, even in schools, as a theme of **mutual exclusion** and **contempt**. It took a long time for the European side to shift the historical presentation from its one-sided self-legitimating narration to the modern, critical, open exploration of both sides, using archives and new interpretive approaches. I remember the efforts of my own teacher, Claude Cahen, in the late 1950s and 1960s, to balance the biased, Western historiography with the Arab Islamic vision of the events. On the Arab side, the Crusades remain a recurrent theme of the imaginary perception of Christianity and the colonial, imperialist 'West'. Many important works published on the subject in European languages during the last 30 years are ignored in contemporary Arab and Islamic discourse. All these facts lead to the necessity to think what remains unthinkable on both sides about the Crusades.

The example of the Battle of Lepanto is particularly enlightening for historians, teachers, theologians and preachers who continue to disregard the role of the collective *imaginaire* in the biased, nationalistic construction of the values, criteria and regime of truth underlying the concept of *Jihād* in Islam, Just War or Holy War in Christianity and secular Europe. My contention is that the concept of *Jihād*, a Just War or Holy War should be reinterpreted in the conceptual framework of the anthropological triangle: **Violence, Sacred, Truth**. The following texts will, I hope, reinforce my claim.

I. Rethinking the idea of the Crusades

> *History is the most dangerous product ever concocted by the chemistry of the intellect. Its properties are well-known. It makes peoples dream, intoxicates them, gives them false memories, exaggerates their reflexes, keeps their old wounds open, disturbs their rest and drives them to heights of greatness or depths of persecution, rendering nations bitter, unbearable and vain* [Paul Valéry].

> *The Crusade comes to life (rather than making sense), in the book you are about to read, both through the epic power of the popular*

> *masses and through the panicky life of an eschatology. Accentuating the popular spirit of the Crusade, more than the rest of us have done for fear of hardening into a theory what ought to be a leaning; and reducing the preoccupation with eschatology more than we have done for fear of accusing psychic states of collective participation, that is what, in my opinion, with the greatest possible certainty of being right, places Paul Alphandéry's discovery in the depths of the Crusade* [Alphonse Dupront].

> *Thus the link between jihād and al-Quds (Jerusalem), the Holy City) was relaxed, but a hundred years of holy war (1144–1250) had irrevocably changed the status of Jerusalem in the Islamic consciousness. After that period, its status underwent essential change both in doctrine and in the popular consciousness. The sacred character of the city was no longer open to question. The era of the Crusades had banished the remaining doubts, and a very powerful association of ideas grew up between the city, occupied by the infidels, and the treasures of psychic and physical energy invested in liberating it both by sovereigns and their subjects. Jerusalem became one of those mechanisms necessary to the faithful, one of those intermediaries between humans and God that help attenuate the believer's feeling of powerlessness in the face of the immeasurable majesty of the divine* [Emmanuel Sivan, *Mythes politiques arabes*, p. 98].

The three quotations that introduce this essay clearly define the ambitions and the limitations of what is intended as a critical evaluation that looks to the future rather than clinging to disputes about the past. Paul Valéry's disillusioned remarks on the dangerous delusions encouraged by national and community historiographies are still relevant, especially where the Crusade/*jihād* duality is concerned. In their book, *La chrétieneté et l'idée de croisade*, Paul Alphandéry and Alphonse Dupront helped restore confidence in a history that aims specifically at **de-alienating** our relationship with the most sacralized past. They inaugurated in France the application of the new methodology and research objectives of *historical psychology* to the idea of the Crusade. The narrative and descriptive material is enriched with explanatory analyses covering the mental agenda, imaginary representations, psychological mechanisms and cognitive systems. To tell the truth, the authors do not always go as far as one might wish in all these new areas of historical knowledge, especially since the subject is very rich in cultural, religious, political, social and economic problems. What is more, they limit themselves to the Christian context; the Muslim protagonist of the Crusades being left, as usual, to the 'orientalist'. That is why I am hoping to draw attention to the need to **think**, in this day and age, about the idea of the Crusade from a comparative perspective in both contexts, Christian-Jewish and Muslim, by extending the enquiries of historical psychology to a theoretical take on the functions and cognitive status of the religious phenomenon in the Mediterranean area based on the examples of Christianity, Judaism and Islam. E. Sivan helps us on our way by showing how the sacralization of Jerusalem in the Muslim psyche is the product of military and symbolic resistance to the earlier (but also contingent) sacralization initiated by the crusaders.

This ambition to bring the same critical scrutiny to bear on the psycho-cultural processes that generated (and still maintain) the idea of Crusade/*jihād* has not to my knowledge, been clearly asserted, let alone attempted. Amin Maalouf wrote a successful book called *The Crusades through Arab Eyes* (Saqi Books, 1984), with the praiseworthy intention of redressing the balance from the one-sided accounts established by Western historiography. In the event, apart from weaknesses in the project from the viewpoint of a modern professional historian, the author was content merely to reverse the point of view by placing it on the side of the 'Arabs' (itself a somewhat dubious designation since the protagonists on the Muslim side in the battles included Turks, Kurds, Armenians and Copts). So we have still to state the methodological conditions, cognitive strategies and practical objectives of a comparative approach to an historical subject that should, if the enquiry is conducted properly, open the way to a retrospective and prospective re-reading of the Mediterranean geo-historical arena.

In order to understand the historical and psychological genesis of the concept of Crusade in Christendom and the corresponding idea of *jihād* in Islam, a few mutual conditions for the construct of the human subject in the monotheist context should be expounded. The definitions and roles assigned to Crusade and *jihād* by the theologies legitimizing armed action, should then be examined, and finally an explanation is required as to explain why Crusade and *jihād* have been resorted to constantly down the centuries and why, since 1990, they have tended to come back into favour in a number of religious as well as secular contexts, impressively so at a time when most people were looking forward to a more enlightened progress towards new horizons of hope and meaning.

1. The Construction of Religious Imaginary

The three monotheistic religions have developed traditions so all-enveloping, so rich and yet so specific that it seems impossible, pointless even, and somehow unacceptable, to go back to the shared *symbolic capital* they have continuously exploited over time through the procedures of *mimetic rivalry* described by René Girard. Theological systematization for community purposes, the legal structures required by state bodies, individual and collective rituals for reinforcing faith as an experience of the divine, strategies for incorporating 'orthodox' traditions into the innovations imposed by historical developments, the obligatory references in each community to the founding narratives, are all cultural expressions and historical actualizations which become the known (or knowable) manifestation of each religion, while the common *symbolic capital* is disguised and repressed into the experienced implicit. Studies of religion by the social sciences are too often limited to a more or less exhaustive exploration of what I call 'the **knowable explicit**', the sociological, cultural and jurisprudential manifestations of each religion. This leads to a fragmentation of the undivided structure of the overall religious phenomenon, but fails to provide the means for using systematic

deconstruction to reveal hidden mechanisms, strategies for the production of meaning or simple **effects of meaning** (*effets de sens*) by constant interplay between the original symbolic capital and its so-called religious extensions in the different religions. In the case of monotheism, with which we are concerned here, the common symbolic capital underwent an initial fragmentation, or historic diversification, in the constitution of what I call the three **Official Closed Corpuses**, the Hebrew Bible (known as the Old Testament in the Christian tradition), the Gospels and the Qur'ān. These corpuses are historical constructs in which the initial symbolic capital has undergone a more or less detailed cultural and institutional development, but not to such an extent that the strong relationship with the common symbolic capital, which is productive of meaning, has been severed. This is why, in the case of communities which set them up as founding narratives, the three corpuses become the beginnings of new codes (*nouveaux départs de codes*) that, in each case, go beyond their predecessors. The Qur'ān insists quite clearly on both the break and the relationship with the preceding corpuses by introducing the concept of the Seal of the Prophets into the development of the History of Salvation in the monotheist context.

Theological development of Judaism and Christianity never incorporated the continuity asserted and exploited in its own way by the Qur'ān, of a History of Salvation inseparable from the common symbolic capital. For its part, Islamic theology insisted, in the polemical context of reciprocal exclusion during the Middle Ages, on the rupture and abrogation of the earlier corpuses. We are therefore still living on the assertions of preeminence of each version of 'Revelation', as understood by each community and embodied in its concrete history, while the relationship between symbolic capital and the theological constructions dictated by the **will to power** and expansion in the Muslim, Byzantine and Western Christian empires after the emergence of Islam as a rival historic model in the Mediterranean region, was relegated to the unthought and gradually become the unthinkable. Crusade and *jihād* both derive their legitimacy from theologies of armed action to make one or other version of 'Revelation' prevail on the political and economic front, justifying over the centuries, through all the struggles between the Ottoman Empire and Christian Europe, the colonialist expansions of the latter as it transformed itself into a secularized, capitalist Europe; and culminating, in our own time, in the wars of colonial liberation, giving way to fundamentalist so-called Islamist violence in response to the structural violence of the globalization processes managed by the hegemonic West.[1]

The common symbolic capital has been obscured or reduced to rigid paradigms by theologies based on systems of beliefs and non-beliefs, although to differing degrees, depending also on the individuals concerned, historical events and changing cultural and intellectual contexts. I should specify at the outset that when discussing symbolic capital, I am in no way prejudging the symbolic, real and substantial character of the concepts involved; I leave open the question of the cognitive status of all of the prophetic discourse articulated in Semitic languages (Hebrew, Aramaic and Arabic, before the involvement of 'profane' languages not used by the first enunciators and mediators of the divine Message). The symbolic capital considered here is a body of concepts, representations, images, metaphors and virtual meanings already worked over in the **prophetic discourse**, but not yet fenced in by dogmatic doctrinal statements of theological systems. At the stage of **prophetic discourse**, symbolic capital still had its function and the power of promoting creative thought.

In the perspective thus defined, four main themes that organize and traverse the three great Official Closed Corpuses will be focused upon, namely:

1. This short historical survey should be read as a psycho-socio-historical analysis, not at all as a theological statement opposing a 'true' theology to 'wrong', 'altered' theological systems. I know through contacts with a great number of Western audiences, that when a person named Muḥammad speaks or writes, he can only express theological claims on the superiority of Islam. In spite of all my efforts to extend a deconstructive criticism to Islam, I have not been successful in gaining even Western Islamicists to that new cognitive posture of mind.

- the eternal Pact of Alliance (*'ahd* or *mīthāq* in the Qur'ān, a repeat of Jahweh's alliance with the Chosen People, which even implies commitment on behalf of fellow believers at war) between a living, speaking, omnipresent, omnipotent God, a stern but compassionate and benevolent Judge; and His weak, straying, fallible, lovingly obedient creatures.
- the prophetic discourse mediating the Word of God, given to be understood and lived by the faithful as a transcendent, intangible Revelation, an ultimate Referent, illuminating and compelling, for any thought or action concerned with Salvation.
- eschatological hope implying the quest for Salvation through a constant search for meaning in the scrutiny of the Word of God to nourish spiritual life and illuminate the earthly path towards eternal Life.
- the Law regarded less as a legal-moral code extracted from the Word of God through the exegetic effort of jurist-theologians, than as the authentic manifestation of God's teaching and Order in creation. At the level of symbolic capital, the Law with a capital L is that which puts the thoughts and behaviour of men in ideal conformity with God's intentions or Plan for the whole of creation; it is an absolute space for the emergence, circulation and actualization of meaning in the dual sense of direction of progress (the primary meaning of the word *sharī'a* in the Qur'ān) and significant content. A Muslim author describes this assembly of values as follows:

> *Being good or being bad are not attributes of those who are good or bad, nor the modes in which they act; good and bad have no other meaning than the very promulgation of Commandment and Prohibition by God* [Abū-l-Qāsim al-Anṣārī (d. 1118)].

These themes of true significance – that which guarantees eternal Salvation – control all levels of the religious discourse in a monotheist context: all the way from the most elaborate speculative theology to the simplest sermon addressed by rabbi, priest or imām to believers remote from scholarly thought. In this way, the believing subject's 'faith' is structured through the matrix of perception, interpretation, expression, rejection or adhesion that comes into play in all existential situations. In all societies marked by the phenomenon of the Holy Book (the theological name for what I call Official Closed Corpus, in reference to the linguistic, historical, political and cultural conditions under which it emerged and became established as such), the continued faith of the believer is ensured by guardians of the 'orthodoxy' of the system of beliefs and non-beliefs, itself inscribed within the space delineated by the themes of the symbolic capital.

This powerful construct, which combines the symbolic function with discursive activities, is further reinforced by ritual behaviour whose regular repetition in sacred and sacralizing places, situations and times, ensures the absorption and assimilation by the physical body of the meanings, representations and beliefs conveyed by the mythical narratives and the didactic religious discourse. A. Dupront and many others have shown the role of pilgrimages in the physical and psychological preparation for the idea of Crusade. It is the same for *jihād*. In the time of the Qur'ān, Bedouins who were not yet converted to the new axiology and Muslim ritual, refused to take part in the struggle for God's Cause.

This short summary of the discursive and ritual apparatus for constructing the believing subject in a monotheist context, would not be complete without the examination of the psychological configuration of cognitive faculties postulated by the progressive assimilation of the system of beliefs and non-beliefs described above. What importance and what roles have been attributed, respectively, to reason, imagination and memory? Can one speak of rational (or even merely rationalizable) assent, or should one assume an emotional sense of belonging, reinforced by ritual observances and by the aesthetic/ethical impact of the marvellous, the miraculous supernatural beings and events and the reassuring and poetic (or threatening and terrifying) evocations of heaven and hell, inherent in mythical narratives? This is a whole continent of historical knowledge that researchers in European societies have just started to explore through works such as Jean Delumeau's on *La peur en Occident*, or the ways in which paradise is represented. The Islamic domain has not yet had the benefit of equivalent researches, which should help to confirm the existence of a continuum of the psychological configuration of the mediaeval mindset – including, of course, the Islamic domain – influenced by the phenomenon of the revealed Book or holy Scriptures along with their imaginary, ritual, semantic, cultural and cognitive amplifications. It would thus be better understood that Crusade and *jihād* are two words which refer to the same notional processes in psychological configurations which are similar if not identical. It would also be easier to understand why the idea of Crusade and *jihād* persist, and reappear forcefully not only in socio-cultural contexts hardly touched by modern scientific rationality, but also in the most secularized areas of political thought, as we shall see from some of the many examples thereof.

2. Crusade and Jihād: Theology and Anthropology of the Just War

Urban II's appeal to the Council of Clermont in 1095 was based on a theology of armed action. During a commemoration of the appeal, at Clermont-Ferrand in November 1995, Monsignor Sabbah, Latin Patriarch of Jerusalem, made the following declaration:

> *What gives birth to religious extremisms and religious wars is not dogma, but men who transform dogmas into specific cultures and national identities. For if all the faithful limited themselves to the effort to seek God and to adore Him, the search for God and his adoration could not be the causes of wars, hatreds or discrimination.*

Muslim, Jewish, Hindu and other dignitaries would spontaneously concur with this position which is clearly fideist and apologetic. What this means is that after the passage of several centuries, official religious thought continues to conceal the real content and workings of the founding texts, which can therefore be reactivated every time a threatened or threatening community desires to mobilize its members for a struggle that is invariably described as defensive. It is certainly the case that the Qur'ān contains more explicit passages inciting to *jihād* than can be found in the Gospels directly preaching the idea of Crusade as later theology was to construct it; but the God of Israel in the Old Testament is equally warlike, playing a preponderant role in the imposition and expansion of the sole Truth approved by Him, absolute respect for which is a precondition of eternal Salvation. On this subject today, however, it is necessary to go beyond theological disputes as to the interpretation of the founding texts and the dogmas generated by them, and to incorporate the problem of righteous or holy war into an anthropological issue.

Still using the three Official Closed Corpuses as the starting point, it is easy to assemble convergent texts supporting a theory of violence as a bio-physiological, socio-cultural, political and anthropological factor present in all human societies, in combination with two other universal forces, Sacred and Truth. Violence, Sacred and Truth comprise a triangle of forces that has always and everywhere ruled the historical output of societies, from the smallest and most archaic groups to the most progressive and secular contemporary nations. René Girard has analysed the combination of violence and sacred but left aside the status of truth, especially religious truth, since he concludes that only Christianity offers the possibility of emerging from violence through a radical transformation of sacrifice and the expiatory victim through the mysteries of the Incarnation and Redemption. The triangle of the three forces cannot be broken, however, by a theoretical construct without engendering an unthinkable and an unthought in relation to the force set aside or attached to another area of reality with the aid of a reductive operation. This is a characteristic of the very strategy common to classical theological and metaphysical thought. In order to offer mankind ontological security, they linked Truth with a capital 'T' exclusively to what Michel Foucault described and criticized as '*the mytho-historico-transcendental thematic*'. Truth, sacralized and transcendentalized by the intervention of religions, then of classical theologies, extended by the 'rational' procedures for disguising and reducing reality as used by modern political philosophies, legitimizes recourse to violence in the higher interests of God and the chosen community (nowadays the country, the nation, the right of peoples to self-determination, human rights, the duty to intervene for 'humanitarian' reasons, etc.); so that violence is incorporated, as a functional necessity, into a system of values universally held to ensure the safety and survival – but also very often the expansion – of the group, community or nation. The founding religious texts have contributed extensively to the establishment of a **structural violence** that erupts frequently in all societies in which, along with a single God, the idea has spread of an equally single Truth, one that excludes all competing versions and is held up as the obligatory source of all laws, all political and jurisprudential order, all ethical, semantic and cultural values, and all the legitimization procedures that differ therefrom, however slightly. We know, of course, how this ultimate form of control, that becomes totalitarian and oppressive in many historical contexts, has led in several of today's European societies to serious, so-called revolutionary confrontations. The anthropological theory of violence makes it possible to go beyond the tenacious idea that so-called wars of religion use a specific form of violence from which modern, secular revolutions are supposed to have delivered us. The difference between the two types of violence resides in the importance and function provided or denied to the sacred. Religions locate it concretely in the space and time between the transgression called *sacrilege* and the form of worship called *sacrifice*; secular revolutions relegate it to conceptualist abstraction, enclose it in the archaic and the magical and conceal it behind 'rationalized' official civic celebrations and commemorations.

In the light of these recurrent devastating conflicts, in which the will to power hides its violence behind meaning-related objectives as attractive as they are ill-defined (cf. the French Revolution with its substitution of the Supreme Being to the God of Abraham and Jacob; or the eschatological promises of the Khomeinist revolution), the pertinent – and urgent – question is how can there be progress beyond, on one hand, the potentially totalitarian structure of religious Truth with its functions of sacralization, transcendentalization, ontologization, mythologization and mystification and on the other, the generalized corrosive, demobilizing relativism that is just as liable to generate violence, which has resulted from a certain practice of modernity. We are entering the twenty-first century with the idea that the clash of civilizations – the spirit of crusade/*jihād* – could assume catastrophic proportions with the resurgence of a religiosity that has not been mastered scientifically, philosophically, theologically or politically. The fact is that '*The Revenge of God*',[1] whose death was announced in the nineteenth century, is arousing the anxieties of some and the vengeful jubilation of others, without our understanding of the religious phenomenon having progressed much beyond either the traditional representations or the reductive scientific explanation that confirms the death of God, followed by that of man.

In his book entitled *Jihād versus McWorld*, Benjamin Barber, an advisor to President Clinton, promotes the term *jihād* to the level of a wider political concept embracing all the disagreements, rejections and fundamentalist rebellions springing up all over the world against the irresistible expansion of economic, monetary, technological and data-handling globalization, symbolized by worldwide corporations such as Macintosh and McDonald's. This intuition is a penetrating one, as can be seen from the way in which so-called Islamist movements have, in practice, secularized the concept of *jihād*, initially bound (such as that of Crusade) to the impetus for conquering and preserving a terrestrial site for the reign of God on earth. The permanence of the Crusade/*jihād* idea can also be measured from the need people feel to rebel collectively

1. A totally irrelevant title to one of Gilles Kepel's most successful books, translated in many European languages. The success of the book is related to the same psychological-ideological reception by Western imaginary of the theory of the *clash of civilizations*.

against anything that opposes, genuinely or allegedly, their concept of their earthly and/or spiritual salvation. In addition to its recurrence, the idea of Crusade/*jihād* thus receives psychological, ideological and historical support that give it anthropological significance. No longer can this idea be relegated to the religious fanaticism of an obscurantist period, still less to an Islam that propagates its faith with the scimitar while Christianity has made love prevail. It is certainly the relationship between violence, sacred and truth that has mobilized men for millennia and continues to arouse them against false divinities in the name of the one true God (the convenient name for what, in different historic settings, might be local saints, agnatic solidarity, the charismatic leader, dictator, fatherland, nation, identity, profit, money, power, etc.). To isolate the physical or structural violence (the state's monopoly of legal violence, the violence of the economic 'order', that of 'orthodox' customs, traditions and beliefs) from the truth whose victory it has achieved, and which legitimizes it in return, from the sacred which transforms it into meritorious action in the service of God, the community or the nation, is to contribute to the collective function of sublimating 'values' and of disguising the real foundations of the political, religious, ethical or jurisprudential order. But by the same token, therefore, it is also to deprive oneself of the search for new instruments of thought and more effective strategies of action to eliminate false knowledge, detect the alienating tendencies of the ideologies and of what P. Bourdieu has called *practical sense.*

3. Religion and Politics as Interacting Instances

We can see by now that an historical and anthropological approach to the idea of Crusade/*jihād* makes it necessary to reconsider the difficult and inflammatory question of the relationship between the religious and the political. The present state of this relationship varies from one society to another, even within a relatively homogeneous historical and cultural space such as western Europe. Separation of Church and State, along the lines of the secular French model, has not been established in any other country with the same doctrinal and legal rigidity. In this example, the State alone has the power to trace and supervise the frontier between public and private spaces. The Minister of the Interior is also the Minister of Religious Affairs, although religion, in the first instance, is really a matter of culture and education. In all known cases, there is a single constant that prevails everywhere, namely, the establishment of legal and institutional compromises that has led to imbalances and inconsistencies in the management of the public and private spaces. In France, a debate is starting to emerge regarding the need for intellectual training adequate for a proper comprehension of the religious dimension of the cultural heritage; but there are still strong reservations and resistance to proposals for teaching the comparative history of religions which would, of course, make no concessions to the transmission in state schools of the faith in the orthodox forms proper to each community. Under these conditions, the history of the Crusades, or of any other event in which religious forces played a preponderant role, continues to follow the duly established narrative and descriptive procedures for political, social and economic facts, using authenticated documents; explaining what was really at stake, the effects of meaning as postulated by religions, the techniques for revealing and disguising reality employed by the protagonists and the weight of the collective psyche in the emergence and instrumentalization of facts, representations and beliefs. In short, anything to do with the historical psychology and anthropological problematization of any manifestation seen as religious, is whisked out of sight, passed over in silence, repressed into the unthought and established as unthinkable for all the generations subject to this cognitive system, coupled with cheerfully (but scandalously) reductive teaching practices.

In the Islamic contexts, the situation is more alarming. Not only are secular compromises unknown, but the teaching of social sciences, too often under official control, has not yet reached the stage of becoming critical, deconstructive of inherited systems of thought; in other words at least able to attenuate the destructive effects of false knowledge (which I prefer to call **institutionalized ignorance**, as it is disseminated in the schools and from all public platforms). Once again, the period of the Crusades provides an illustration, as striking as it is sad, of the intellectual and scientific bankruptcy of the educational discourse, and of the ever more restrictive domination of ideological and apologetic opportunism. The political struggle is waged against the West and the superiority of Islam established by portraying it as a victim, without ever bringing the ideas of Crusade and *jihād* together, as we have just done, in a psychological and anthropological analysis. It is appropriate, however, to delve deeper into the archaeology of the psychic forces that continue to set a post-Enlightenment West fundamentally against a murky Orient mingling esoteric dreams, superstitious beliefs, uncontrollable fanaticisms and recurrent violence. The schism between Western Latin Christianity and Eastern Orthodox Christianity is as instructive, in this respect, as the more radical, explicit and continuous exclusions between the three major historic forms of Christianity and what is known globally, if confusingly, as Islam with a capital I, emphasizing an ideological perception rather than a valorising definition. People at present would rather shelter behind the stereotyped courtesies projected in official discourse by the religious authorities and heads of state, exchanging snatches of superficial Islamo-Judaeo-Christian dialogue, than pursue archaeological exploration of the powerful imageries that still haunt the social psyche on all sides.

A good example is the immense media operation that reactivated the idea of Crusade/*jihād* during the Gulf war. François Mitterrand, president of a fiercely secular French Republic, used the expression '*just war*', a concept first postulated by St Augustine. In fact, Western public opinion on all levels of class and culture, had a deeply rooted feeling, as in the time of Pope Urban II's appeal, that a new Jerusalem was being delivered from barbarians who were outside international law (which, it was also admitted, urgently needed redefinition). Is it necessary to retrace Bonaparte's conquest of Egypt, as did the historian René Grousset in his 1930s classic *Histoire des Croisades* in which he developed the idea of continuity between the crusaders' plan and the French conquest of Algeria, the procession of children in crusader costumes at the Carthage Eucharistic conference in 1930, the tripartite expedition against the Naṣṣer regime in 1956, the justifications for the Algerian war (1954–62)? Clearly these are not isolated or fortuitous examples; they express a very ancient and irrepressible hope, a tenacious concept of a revealed Truth later confirmed, although carefully disguised with the 'scientific' procedures of reasoning of the Enlightenment, a will to power justified by the 'humanist' discourse of that same Enlightenment, a discourse today based on the themes of democracy, human rights and humanitarian aid. Behind them looms the whole majestic, sovereign march of a West whose hegemony first showed itself, still timidly of course, with the First Crusade, but still being pursued before our eyes in every corner of the planet. There is a strong case for a rigorous history that would not ignore this negative aspect, deliberately minimized or omitted in national historiographies, one that would show that the reactivation of *jihād* on the Islamic side in the form of fundamentalist outbursts does not correspond to a new eruption of some spiritual force, but expresses the reaction of an imagination fed, since the nineteenth century and perhaps earlier, on representations of an inexorable march by the spirit of the Spanish *reconquista* and the successive Crusades raised and pursued all over the planet after the postulate of *the right of peoples to self-determination* had conferred a 'modern' spin on Crusade/*jihād* formerly conducted in the sacred cause of God.

It would be interesting to make a detailed study of the themes and conceptual usage in the many texts produced in 1995 when the Clermont appeal was being commemorated on all sides. They certainly express a growing wish to broaden the area of enquiry and rework the points that have not been adequately explained on the Western side. The Muslim adversary is still always mentioned as an external protagonist, an obstacle to the advance and peaceful settlement of the newcomers; the job of studying his cultural and religious universe is still left to the 'orientalists' who, with a few exceptions, are not yet converted to the modes of enquiry and problematization made available by anthropology and historical psychology. Arab researchers themselves are excluded from the profession of historian, rightly so in many cases, so much more ignorant are they (even more so than classical orientalists) of the elementary rules, especially when a theme such as the Crusades with its strong, ideological baggage is involved. So this subject that more than ever, on the Arab-Muslim side, is dominated by collective imaginaries solidly constructed centuries ago, is still awaiting historians capable of exposing the various manipulations of a symbolic capital common to all the protagonists; of bringing an anthropological scrutiny to bear on the monotheistic religious phenomenon and its cultural and ideological functions throughout the Mediterranean area. Only if this is done, will we at last accede to a new area of intelligibility, not only of the religious phenomenon, but also of the sacralizing ceremonies and rituals of the political, even after the great political thinkers and all the scientific and intellectual revolutions. Political undertakings will no longer hide behind the sacralizing cloak of religion; and religion will no longer make arrogant or indirect use of the secular arm in order to exercise arbitrary control over intellectual freedoms. There will no longer be talk of separation of the Church and State, with both institutions still competing to manipulate the same symbolic values of legitimacy (justice, equality, fraternity, liberty, formal humanism, human rights, spiritual, moral and civic authority, etc.); but a concrete, cooperative, critical quest for principles, foundations, instruments of thought and procedures, that would no longer be used to impose conquering wills or hastily constructed identities, but will bring to life a universalizable body (not another resurrected one! people will say) for elucidating and regulating all enterprises of emancipation of the human condition.

Postscript

This text is the expanded version of a lecture given in Belgium in 1995. The war launched by NATO against Milosevic's Republika

Srbska provides a number of concrete illustrations of the analyses and interpretations suggested in this text. The Patriarch of the Russian Orthodox Church was seen arriving in Belgrade to support Milosevic's cause and condemn the NATO allies' unjust aggression before an audience of thousands of Serb believers; Pope John Paul II on the other hand, while calling for a just peace, tended to support the NATO initiative. The high-profile Paris intellectual Julia Kristeva suddenly became aware that there is an Orthodox Christianity that is very different from the Western, Roman, Latin Christianity. She seemed to be aware, for the first time, that the religious factor can still play a determining role in a late twentieth-century European society, even going so far as to recognize the urgency of rising above the schisms by re-evaluating the treasures and detecting the bottlenecks on both sides (the Serbian Orthodox side and the secularized Western European side) in her article entitled '*Le poids mystérieux de l'orthodoxie*', *Le Monde*, 18/19 April 1999. In times of peace, leading intellectuals are utterly indifferent to the religious question and disdainful of anyone who tries to draw attention to the damage caused by the religious illiteracy officially cultivated by an education system that leaves to private religious schools and the spiritual 'authorities' of each community, the task of managing the inheritance and doctrines of salvation! If the ignorance and reciprocal exclusion that persist between Orthodox, Catholic and Protestant Christianity are only discovered with consternation at moments of crisis, what is can be said about the divides that have been deepening for fifteen centuries between the unanimously rejected Islam and the other competing religions in the Mediterranean area? Tomorrow, when peace has returned, the same influential intellectuals who now call for schisms to be set aside and institutionalized ignorance to cease will take up the cudgels again in France, especially against any suggestion of introducing a comparative anthropology of religion into the public education system. Religion, along with the political discourse of electoral campaigns, must be maintained as sources of renewal and driving forces of the **imaginary production of society**. Without these instruments, it would be difficult, perhaps impossible, to accede to power or remain in power for any length of time, to mobilize believers and patriots for just wars or to construct legitimacies that deny and destroy the human individual. It is not merely important to keep these two sources safe from **subversive** critical analysis, sheltered behind all the religious and secular orthodoxies; but since the abolition of religious wars through genuine enlightenment, it has become crucial to prevent the same abolition from being extended to the substitute quasi-religions invented by the high priests of modernity, absorbed, obeyed and served by the armies of managers who administer knowledge, technology, economics and political systems that have become disposable. This is not to say that a comparative anthropology of cultures and religions will necessarily be sufficient in itself to put an end to disposable thought and break the **Violence, Sacred, Truth** triangle; but along with reflective philosophy it should help to open new paths towards the re-evaluation of all intellectual, spiritual and cultural heritages, and hence to a better understanding of the optimal conditions for the deployment of the human condition.

II. The Lepanto Example

> *From the depths of time, the cortege of saints, heroes and ordinary men who have steadfastly upheld human dignity rises up from the cemeteries of the world and asks: 'What have you decided to sacrifice, and to what?'* [Charles De Gaulle].

The battle of Lepanto – 7 October 1571 – was one of the major episodes in the competition between Islam and Christianity for Mediterranean supremacy. As in many other confrontations between the two rival powers, each side invoked 'the laws of God' and the revealed Truth, ignored or rejected by the 'infidels' opposite.

Religion was fully mobilized to legitimize cynical strategies of political and economic dominance. A commonplace situation, one might say. Wars always take place between what my friend Paul M.

G. Levy calls '*possessors of the true*'. Even today, however, it is to be noted that religious thought has still not drawn all the conclusions from these commonplace situations in which religions played and still play leading roles. Instead of reflecting on the true functions of religion to advance our knowledge of the religious phenomenon, the guardians of orthodoxy in each community have tended to interpret victory over the enemy as a sign of God's approval, and to erase the compromises present in official religion while continuing to exalt the 'transcendence' of eternal belief.

What does the Battle of Lepanto tell us about this aspect? If we take the trouble to examine impartially the language, conduct and ideologies of the two sides, we find that Islam and Christianity performed the same functions of masking reality, twisting the meaning of events and transcendantalizing profane behaviour, with the same later results of individual and collective alienation. This last, it will be claimed, is the price paid for the survival and temporal growth (*spiritual* growth, believers will insist) of each community. If that is an unbreakable boundary in the human condition, it is well worth a thorough investigation of its causes and consequences with the aid of historical examples such as the Battle of Lepanto.

This exercise will be attempted 1) by describing the protagonists; 2) by defining what was at stake in the battle; and 3) by bringing out the common mode of thought underlying the Christian and Islamic discourses.

1. Description of the Protagonists

On the Christian side, the Republic of Venice had a firm ally in Pius V who headed the thirteenth crusade against the Muslim infidel. The Pope had no difficulty in recruiting Philip II, King of Spain (1527–1598), by making him a beneficiary of the papal bull that launched the crusade, ensuring him an annual income of 400,000 ducats extracted from Church property. Philip had abandoned his father Charles V's dream of a universal monarchy and was seeking to rebuild the power of Spain, having lost Preveza in Greece in 1538, Djerba in 1559–60, Malta in 1564 and Tunis in 1570; Granada, in Spain itself, was under threat from the Moors. The king hoped, with the help of Venice, to eliminate the Calabrian 'renegade' Uludj Ali who held Algiers and Tunis in the name of the Ottoman sulṭān. This power strategy had aroused Venetian suspicions, the more so when Pius V helped manoeuvre Don John of Austria (1545–1578), fresh from his harsh repression of the Mooorish revolt (1568–1570), into supreme command of the allied fleets. Within this command, Marc Antonio Colonna, Constable of the Kingdom of Naples, favoured Venice; the Genoese admiral Andrea Doria supported Philip II.

On the Muslim side, the Ottoman Empire, in 1570, covered the Balkan peninsula and the Eastern and Southern Mediterranean; pirates of various origins, operating out of Tripoli, Tunis and Algiers, maintained (with the help of their Christian competitors) a climate of insecurity, making it possible for example for the Turks to take the Venetian colony of Cyprus in 1570. But, although Turkish power looked threatening from the outside, internally the regime had a number of weaknesses. Sulṭān Selim II, who had succeeded his father, Suleiman the Magnificent, in September 1566, was seen by Western contemporaries as '*a sovereign both unworthy and incompetent, odious, squat and obese . . . the first of the indolent sulṭāns*'.[1] Continuity of imperial power was in the hands of the Grand Vizier Mehmed Sokoullou (or Sokolovitch), one of those astonishing individuals characteristic of the whole age. Sokollou

1. See Michel Lesure, *Lepante: La crise de l'empire ottoman*, Paris, 1972. Since our objective is to reflect on religion as a factor in peace and a factor in war, but not to enrich the subject from the documentary angle, we refer several times to this exemplary monograph, which is new from the very point of view we are concerned with. Michel Lesure has the merit of confronting Turkish archives and Christian accounts in an equally rigorous manner, while pointing out that the battle of Lepanto has continuously fed a myth that 'can still be found in the work of some twentieth-century authors' (p. 12). I cannot recommend too highly this alert and intelligent book to the Muslim and Christian believers.

was actually a Bosnian, born in Ragusa (now known as Dubrovnik) and taken from his family as a child under the *devshirme*[1] of press-ganging Christian boys to fight for the Ottoman Empire. Raised and educated in the seraglio, he had learned how to assert his authority without losing his footing among court intrigues, merciless struggles between foreign clans, demanding Janissaries and over-ambitious Pashas. While accepting sumptuous presents and fabulous sums of money from vassals of the empire (but also from Venice and the Greek Patriarch of Constantinople), he maintained an attitude of obedience and devotion to the Sulṭān.

In their battles in Cyprus, Lepanto and elsewhere, both sides depended on galley-slaves (oarsmen) and mercenaries of every origin and provenance. Thus, when the peasants of Crete showed extreme reluctance to assist, Venice was obliged to call upon the Bohemians. But it is also true that when the Sacred and Perpetual Union against the Turk was proclaimed in May 1571, Italy and Spain were once again swept up by crusading fervour and every town and city wanted to raise a contingent. The Turks, by combining calls for holy war (*jihād*) with the practice of *devshirme*, managed to assemble a force of 25,000 men and 2,500 Janissaries.[2] Sickness, desertion and treachery spread confusion and uncertainty on both sides in the run-up to the battle, exacerbated by internecine violence, incompetence and squabbling among the leaders.

It would be interesting to dwell on the extraordinary characters who figure in the preparations and negotiations before the battle, the battle itself and its aftermath. Popes, kings, ministers, viziers, cardinals, ambassadors and military officers of all ranks, all deserve detailed biographies to map the status of the human individual in Muslim and Christian settings. How can the importance for each of them of genuinely religious motivation be measured, given the general predominance of ambition, appetites for power and revenge, obsessions and private fantasies? Thus, Don Juan '*recognized as a*

1. The Turks periodically took children from Christian families to supplement the corps of Janissaries and to fulfil certain functions in the seraglio.
2. Lepante, op. cit., p. 92.

royal prince from the age of 16 (but) known to all as "the bastard" . . . eaten up with the lust for action, he at last found, with his nomination, the opportunity for revenge on his destiny . . .' Marc-Antonio Colonna '*descended from an illustrious Roman family . . . quarrelled with Pope Paul IV, stripped of estates, excommunicated . . . remains indebted to the King of Spain . . .*' Veniero '*whose difficult character was already known . . . not pleased at having to obey an inexperienced young man . . . also scornful of his worldly character, and jealously protective of Venetian prestige . . .*'[1]

Uludj Ali (known as Kilidj Ali or 'Ali the scimitar') had even more of the characteristic features of the age than those described above.

> *He was both choleric and melancholy, ostentatiously devoted to the Empire and suspected of treason. Like many other of the Ottoman dignitaries, he was a Christian renegade. Born into a very poor family in Calabria, he had always been a child of the sea, as fisherman, galley-slave and finally pirate. Captured by the Turks at the age of 16 and mocked by his fellow galley-slaves when afflicted by scurvy, he killed one of them in a brawl and abjured Christianity to avoid the death penalty. He later amassed a colossal fortune as Beylerbey of Algiers.*[2]

Many other such portraits could be quoted but it is already apparent that religion counted for very little in the behaviour of the most visible protagonists, and even less among the mercenaries greedy for loot or the press-ganged rowers who cowered under the lash of their guards. There remain the many peasants and humble townspeople who had responded with fervour to appeals from a Pope and a Sulṭan venerated as 'spiritual' leaders. It will be seen that the language of the official discourses employed all the stereotypes most likely to arouse eschatological visions and millenarian aspirations in the popular consciousness.

Nothwithstanding all this, can it be claimed that the stakes

1. Ibid., pp. 106–7.
2. Ibid., p. 225.

over which the battle of Lepanto was fought were as varied as the interests of those individuals, parties, communities and ethno-cultural groups? Or is it possible to discern amid this tangle of violent appetites, explosive hatreds and deep-seated rivalries certain more universal and permanent aims?

2. What the Battle was About

Lepanto is an episode in the secular struggle between all the Mediterranean peoples. The geo-historical facts of this competition were admirably described by F. Braudel in his major book on *the Mediterranean world in the time of Philip II.* The emergence of Islam in the seventh century and its impact first on Byzantium and, from the eleventh century onwards, on the expanding Christian West, came increasingly to be presented as an intolerable challenge to the temporal and spiritual power of the Church. In the minds of both sides, a religious motive was thus substituted for the real reasons which were (and remain to this day) strategic and economic. The wealth of polemical Islamic and Christian literature[1] makes it possible to monitor the construction of what I have called a cultural system of reciprocal exclusion, on which the perceptions that Islam and Christianity have of each other are still based today. For the Muslims, the 'arguments' and framework of the polemic were fixed for all time by the Qur'ān, which reflects the climate of opposition to the Prophet maintained by the Jews and Christians first in Mecca, then in Medina. For the Christians, a haunting collection of imagery has been built up in the course of many Crusades against the infidel in the East, in Spain and in the Maghreb. Modern research has so far failed to establish the correct historical, cultural and theological

1. For an exhaustive bibliography, see R. Gaspar and his collaborators, *Bibliographie du dialogue islamo-chrétien: lea auteurs et les œuvres du 7e au 10e siècle*, 1975–76, vols 1 and 2. See also Y. Moubarac, *Recherches sur la pensée chrétienne et l'Islam dans les temps modernes et à l'époque contemporaine*, Beirut, 1977 (comprehensive bibliography). For an updated bibliography, see *Isalmochristina*, from 1977 to 2001.

perspectives for the study of the Mediterranean area.[1] Historiography, based on Western sources, has seen the region principally as the theatre in which Western power was deployed. Even today, the history of the eastern and southern shores of the Mediterranean is not an integral part of degree courses in most Western universities; it is only covered marginally by a (deplorably small) number of specialist Islamicists. Symptomatic of this state of mind, which may be too deeply ingrained to be reformed, is the fact that the international congress of orientalists held in Paris in 1973 thought fit to treat North Africa as part of the oriental, or even Asiatic, domain. Not until 1972 did Michel Lesure publish a book in which the Ottoman archives concerning Lepanto were at last opened.[2]

By considering historical turning points such as Las Navas de Tolosa, Granada, Oran, Algiers, Tunis, Tripoli, Alexandria, Lepanto, Constantinople and the Palestinian tragedy today, I am trying to establish the nature of the major concern at stake in our own time. Since religious imagery has been attached to struggles for political and economic hegemony in order to give them 'divine' legitimacy,[3] and since such imagery has for centuries fixed *a priori* the forms of sensitivity and intelligibility in the Jewish, Christian and Muslim communities, it is reasonable to suggest that the history and anthropology of the Mediterranean area needs to be given a cognitive basis that is radically different from the one established by mediaeval theologies and continued by positivist, colonial, Eurocentric historiography until at least the 1950s.[4] Academic research hardly bothers with this purifying

1. See my essay 'Penser l'espace méditerranéen', in *Penser l'Islam aujourd'hui.*
2. I should also refer to several new publications on the Ottoman period; see *Encyclopaedia of Islam*, s.v. *'Othmanli.*
3. An unexpected manifestation of this phenomenon is to be found today in *Islamochristina*: the archeological research being encouraged by Israel and Syria in former Palestine is being used to confirm or undermine the alleged rights of the 'chosen people'. It is to be hoped that historical knowledge will progress rapidly enough to prove the inanity of the ideological conflict, held by one of current of Jewish thought to be an essential theological theme.
4. I would advise anyone who doubts this to examine the French political

function although it is of great importance currently, especially in the Mediterranean world, where serious conflicts have built up, not only over territorial issues but more essentially in what I will call the metaphysical structure of the three great religious universes. Thus, for example, although Michel Lesure reveals to the reader many valuable texts redolent of the mentality of the age, he takes no interest in the common structure of thought that produced these utterances; so he does not help the unprepared reader to understand that, although couched in obsolete sixteenth-century linguistic forms, their underlying thought still prevails to this day in the three communities. The whole literature of the Israel-Arab conflict broadly confirms the current status of the legitimization discourses used during all the Crusades and, notably, at Lepanto. Although the Christian discourse appears to be more 'modern' since Vatican II, it should be recognized that the hard core of traditional theological thought successfully resists all attempts at reform.[1]

To better outline the cognitive background to the debates launched in the Mediterranean world by the successive emergence of the three monotheist religions, it is worth analysing some significant texts quoted by Michel Lesure.

3. Observations on Historical Psychology

The defeat of the Turks at Lepanto was greeted by all the Christian peoples as 'Christ's victory'. A durable imagery was crystallized in

literature from the time of the Algerian war (1954–62) until the confrontation between 'Islam' and the 'West', that about the Rushdie affair, or the so-called Islamic scarf at public schools in France. Also worth a glance is H. Serouya's *La pensée arabe*, Que Sais-je?, no. 915, of which I was asked to supervise an entirely new edition by PUF, as late as 1975.

1. Until today, the Islamo-Christian dialogue could not seriously approach the main theological issues raised in the Qur'ān itself in the perspective of compared history of Jewish, Catholic, Protestant, Sunnī, Shī'ī doctrinal systems. The anthropological problematization remains the unthought in the great majority of seminars, conferences, organized frequently since Vatican II.

the popular consciousness during the widespread celebrations that followed, encapsulated in songs such as this one:

> *Did you think, booby, you could confront*
> *Italy and Spain with your rabble*
> *And did you believe Mahomet would vanquish Christ?*
> *O my Selim, what's become of you? And Mahomet,*
> *What a lot of help he gave you!*
> *Your pashas have all gone up in smoke* [pp. 10–11].[1]

The text of the Holy League signed in Rome on 19 May 1571 includes the following:

> *After first invoking the name of the Father, the Son and the Holy Ghost . . . in the presence of our Holy Father and the Most Reverend Cardinals . . . has been published this Sacred League . . . They (the Confederal members) wish and agree, through the grace and favour of God, that to destroy and ruin the Turk, this league be perpetual, and not only to defend the kingdoms and principalities of the Confederal members against the Turk, but also to go and cause him damage and invade his territories, both by land and by sea, and in these enterprises are included Algiers, Tunis and Tripoli in Barbary . . .* [p. 42].

Christian convicts serving life sentences were 'permanently set free and encouraged to fight for Jesus Christ through whose grace they had been delivered from servitude . . .' [p. 118].

Pius V, who had 'received from heaven on 7 October the revelation of victory', wrote to the king of Spain:

> *My very dear son in Jesus Christ . . . since receiving the happy news of the most glorious victory won by the army of the Sacred League over the army of the arrogant tyrant and enemy of the Christian name, we have not ceased giving thanks to the Lord God who, in*

1. This and the following quotations are from Michel Lesure, *Lepante*, op. cit.

> *his mercy and infinite bounty, did not fail to fulfil the hopes He had given to that effect* . . . [p. 157].

The Turkish texts are just as thickly sprinkled with propitiatory formulae, invocations to God and the Prophet to ensure victory. The enemy is referred to as '*the fleet of the vile Infidels*', the '*boats of the miserable Christians*'. '*War is uncertain in its results*,' wrote Selim to Pertev Pasha. '*Judgement belongs to God, the High, the Great, the Master and the Benefactor. We hope that Almighty God will soon make possible all sorts of humiliations and the crushing of the enemies of the Religion and the Empire* . . . [p. 182].

After the defeat, Sokoullou called on Selim. It is said that he took up the Qur'ān, read two chapters and closed it; but he opened it again at random and fell on a verse that said: '*I am suffering because of the victory of the Christians over the inhabitants of the earth; but they will not have occasion to rejoice in their victory in future*' [p. 214].

In his instructions to the Kapudan Pasha, Seyit-Ali, Sokoullou wrote:

> . . . *with the help of Almighty God and placing your absolute trust and resignation in the ultimate assistance of the All-Highest, relying on the abundant blessings of the Prince of Prophets, and seeking the aid of the Prophet's four Companions – God's grace be upon them – and all the holy spirits, you will come down from the direction of Corfu* . . . [pp. 237–8].

These texts support three observations:

1. In the Christian discourse, there is a function of equivalence, if not of status, of Jesus and Mahomet but the Muslims do not refer to Christ as the protagonist to be defeated, in conformity with Qur'ānic teaching on the subject of the Son of Mary. This difference of perception of the religious figures on both sides, around whom the concept of the True Religion was constructed, was the main axis of opposition between Islam and Christianity from the Middle Ages to the present.

On both sides, the theme of the *True Religion* is evoked in the same fashion by direct and constant references to God, rather than to the collection of signs, symbols, myths, rituals and narratives that, over time and with effort, gradually form the specific consciousness of a community. We call this 'religious' to the extent that historical events are integrated (as in the case of Lepanto) into the setting and with the aid of religious symbolism; we call it 'national' when the system of legitimation is secular (territory circumscribed by a political frontier, mother country, historic individual, etc.). The passage from one system of legitimation to another takes place with very different frequency in different socio-cultural environments. Apart from that, these recurrences are becoming ever more important in the present phase of history, as the political monoliths of 'modern' regimes restore to the traditional religions their function of ultimate refuge for marginalized or silenced social groups. I refer, of course, to the rapid proliferation of 'sects' of different kinds in the Western societies and the role of Islam in the expression of political opposition. That is why those of ostensibly modern and secular consciousness should not be too quick to dismiss the texts quoted above as clichés and ritual formulae from another age.

2. The operation of sacralizing and transcendentalizing material objectives and profane behaviour can be seen clearly by a modern analyst of the discourses of religious legitimation, but it escapes those who continue to move exclusively within the confines of what is currently known as 'faith'. While Christian theology is starting to embark upon a serious investigation into the changing content and functions of faith, beliefs and spirituality under various determining factors, the same cannot be said of Muslim or Jewish thought which continue to fulfil dialectical, polemical and self-establishing functions in the context of the Israel-Arab conflict and more generally the structural violence exerted in international economic and cultural relations.

Legitimating discourses that refer directly to other

communities or hegemonic powers are especially revealing of the way in which certain individuals or secular historical events are transcendentalized in the collective memory of each group. These moves should be discerned in the first instance in the founding texts or discourses that become Holy Writ for each community. When villagers all over Europe celebrate 'Christ's victory', when Catholic kings confer with the Holy Father to found the Sacred League, when Sokoullou discovers 'at random' a Qur'ānic verse predicting the later restoration of the true order and values, we see living examples of the exercise of a single mode of semiotic organization. In victory as in defeat, the Scriptures are given confirmation of their transcendent nature; in exchange, they bestow upon the event the value of a deliberate sign from God aimed at informing the faithful of His approval in one case, and of their need to return to the 'true path' in the other.

Guardians of 'orthodoxy' and the transcendent will certainly object to the reductive side of this analysis. This objection has two meanings. It confirms that contemporary consciousness, despite all the positive achievements of modern rationality, continues to acquiesce in spontaneous operations of transcendentalization; but it also signals the philosophical quest that ought to accompany '*the new scientific spirit,*', illustrated by the explorations of human and social sciences. This is what I am pursuing personally by attempting a re-reading of the Scriptures, not through the axioms of traditional theologies, but by using all the instruments of a greatly expanded historical sciences.

3. The third observation is an extension of the second. The processes involved in the transcendentalization, its extent and scale, vary according to the socio-cultural group and the individuals involved. It is difficult, for example, to describe with any certainty the religious beliefs or stance of a 'renegade' such as Uludj Ali. There were many like him. And what about

the mercenaries and galley-slaves 'in the service of God'? The fact is that these protagonists were major contributors to God's victory or defeat, the real but unacknowledged agents of a transcendantalizing process which is really the work of managers of religious 'values' whose permanence is ensured by the strict reproduction of ritual formulae, beliefs and behaviour.

It goes without saying that these notes are provisional, intended to contribute to the questioning process required by our time. I cannot conclude this consideration without mentioning the Lebanese tragedy,[1] in which I discern a terrifying concentration of all the disputes, imageries, fantasies and 'modern' ideological distortions so piously accumulated over long centuries of competition between the three monotheistic religions. However great the civilizations, however rich the cultures produced by these three religions – civilizations and cultures that have yet to be re-considered and re-interpreted by a problem-centred history (*histoire-problèmes*) – the fact remains that all three have claimed the same monopoly of revealed Truth. Dogma – that of the Chosen People, of the Church as the only way to Salvation and of Islam as the last religion to be given God's personal endorsement – has never ceased functioning, both as the common horizon of a single metaphysical universe and as the web of fault lines between three cultural systems of reciprocal exclusion.

1. The original version of this chapter goes back to 1979. Since the Lebanese civil war, we had (and still do) many tragedies, politically programmed, both by the national regimes, emerged in the 'third world' countries, and by the rivalry between the two big powers until the end of the Cold War (1989), followed by the triumph of the free market and so-called liberal philosophy. The functions of religion, especially in the case of Islam and Judaism, have been perverted; this phenomenon is reactivating a Manichean dualist opposition between 'Good' and 'Evil', to a point that we cannot discern any horizon of spiritual hope and philosophical meaning.

SEVEN

The Rule of Law and Civil Society in Muslim Contexts

Beyond Dualist Thinking[1]

Fetishism of each one for his merchandise: jurists walk on the head because they think that law is the reality.

K. Marx, *German Ideology*

I want to know how long we can go on doing this stuff in defence of western society without ceasing to be the sort of society that is wealth defending. That's all. And what stuff maddening with thin pots Third world countries, bullying them, smashing their economies, rigging their elections, assassinating their leaders, buying their politicians like pop corn, ignoring they are starving, they are uneducated, kicking their peasants from the land, arming their oppressors to the teeth, turning their children into tomorrow's terrorists, manipulating the media, lying constantly.

John Le Carré, Lecture at John Hopkins University, 1986

1. This chapter is the result of several contributions I have made to seminars, conferences and courses on recurrent issues such as religion and secularism; religious and secular law; religion and peace; the rule of law, civil society and governance; religion, ethics and governance. I have lectured on these burning, but yet unthought problems in several places including Jakarta, Casablanca, Amsterdam, Washington, London, Bonn, etc.

Islamism is a fecund fuel.

Hassan II, *Le Monde* 9/8/1988

The rule of law and civil society are a modern historical construct; they are still in the process of construction on the basis of the new needs and demands of various societies and the political culture available in each tradition of thought. Apart from the advanced European and North American democratic regimes, large-scale, ongoing experiments are taking place in every contemporary society, such as China, India, Brazil, Mexico. Yet, there is no one recognized 'model' or archetype of a Civil Society with its correlated rule of law. One can even speak of the crisis of political reason in the most advanced experiments in the construction of a civil society such as those that are ongoing in United Kingdom, France, Holland and Scandinavia. On the other hand, there are societies in which political thought is paralyzed, dangerously diverted by a perverted and perverting instrumentalization of the religious tradition. This is the case in several of the so-called Islamic regimes or rather regimes which claim Islam to be the official religion of the state. To encompass all societies in which Islam is represented by a large majority or a minority of citizens, I prefer to use the expression 'Muslim contexts'. This enables Muslim minorities living in European and American societies to be included in the general exploration of the attitudes and approaches to civil societies that are more or less inspired by references to 'Islamic' principles, values and political vision.

Surely, in all Muslim contexts, the issue is continuously and passionately debated in the ongoing political struggles between the established regimes and opposing movements in which opposition is tolerated. There are also many international conferences, seminars and political and religious meetings which provide opportunities for dialogue. These activities have an important educational role and should be systematically developed everywhere to fill the gaps where there is a deprivation and emptying of modern critical conceptualization of vital issues concerning the creation of a worldwide civic citizenship starting, of course, from various national experiences. I have personally insisted on the pedagogic necessity of liberating all nationalist collective imaginaries from the alienating ideological representation of so-called national or religious 'identities'. I have indicated the negative functions of the mythological identities built and taught in all national historiographies, including those of the already well-established modern democratic regimes. All the epistemological, intellectual, linguistic, political and legal obstacles that have been analyzed in the previous chapters continue to prevent and delay significant progress towards radical reassessments of the religious, legalistic and political legacy related to the 'great Islamic Tradition'. The concepts of secularized law and democratic culture are not only misunderstood and even totally ignored, and certainly strongly rejected by a large majority of Muslims, on the basis of what I called **'institutionalized ignorance'**. The ideological competition between the two blocs constructed under the names of 'Islam' and the 'West' is increasingly distorting, disrupting and breaking down any positive experience that may be emerging in certain countries ruled by precarious political regimes.

One of the most negative results of the mutual exclusion that has developed since 1945 by the negative polarization of 'Islam' and the 'West', is that both ideological poles instrumentalize a dualist, Manichaean thinking whenever they have to express their perception of each other. How is it possible to break free from these historical, cultural, intellectual impediments? There can be no political cooperation and positive communication as long as the basic political vocabulary is not available for both protagonists. I mention such simple and current words as democracy, rule of law, human rights, citizenship, justice, liberal philosophy, free market . . . Through translation – at least when it is accurate – ideas and representations can be transferred from one culture to another; but the concepts will remain abstract, cut off from their initial existential, historical content as long as the process of conceptualization has not become rooted, initiated by the historical experience that shapes the living collective memory of each social group, community or nation.

This collective memory also needs to be expressed and transmitted in the original language used through all the historical experience of the group. This is not the case for the majority of marginalized groups and societies, since the modern secularized languages, developed in European societies from the seventeenth century onwards, were spread all over the world during colonial expansion, followed by the increasing pressures of the ideology of development/underdevelopment and now by globalization with its constraining economic, monetary and technological rules and mechanisms.

In each society of what has been known for some time as 'the Third World', increasing gaps have been created between a rich, powerful economic and political so-called elite and the marginalized masses who are submitted to a continuous process of social exclusion. Such a sociological structure generates strong authoritarian, repressive, non-accountable States, in which the emergence of a civil society is nigh impossible. It is difficult, under such conditions, to identify a middle class with the roles, the status and restrictions currently experienced in advanced democratic regimes. The middle classes and a dynamic, creative bourgeoisie have a precarious existence in undemocratic countries; they remain too weak, unable to reach the critical mass required for recognition by the State as a necessary partner for the enhancement of the historical building process of a civil society, backed by the state and supporting, in return, the construction of a rule of law. This process took place in Europe in the seventeenth and eighteenth centuries; it has obviously failed to develop in contemporary Muslim contexts, although the States that emerged in the late 1950s and 1960s had access to two dominant competing models, the Communist regime claiming the construction of a so-called democratic popular republic and the Western, liberal model applied in Western Europe and North America. The result of the Cold War competition that broke down in 1989 is well known. New ideological obstacles have been added everywhere to those inherited from colonial regimes between 1800 and 1945, and from a long, disintegrating historical process that dates back at least to the thirteenth and fourteenth centuries in all Muslim contexts.

All these historical, cultural and ideological facts still have a determining impact on the deep political, economic, social and semantic crisis that has been exacerbated by the new pressures of globalization in all of the former Third World societies. The end of the Cold War has opened an horizon of a short-lived new hope of more shared and controlled emancipation for all these societies. This ended as quickly as 1990-91, with the Gulf War and the new geopolitical strategies for mapping the frontiers between the Big Seven and the rest of the world, inaugurating a new phase in the 'just war' between the 'West' and 'Islam'. My colleague, S. Humphreys, used a very evocative title for he last book: *Between Memory and Desire: The Middle East in a Troubled Age*. Any inquiry as to the political attitudes and the theoretical approaches to the rule of law and civil society in Muslim contexts since 1945 should start with the following questions:

Which memory of Islam was alive in Muslim societies before and immediately after the independence of each country? How was this idealized collective memory interacting with the still strong, living, collective, local, ethno-cultural memories of each society? How did the new states consider and take decisions about the 'Islamic' memory used as an ideological tool to legitimize their power and initiate a unifying process between the imagined Nation on one side, the local ethno-cultural and linguistic memories marginalized, ignored and doomed to dilution on the other? And which *desires* inspired and motivated the political decision-makers, compared to the *desires* and expectations of various social groups that were still subject to the mechanical solidarities of the tribal, patrimonial and patriarchal archaic systems, that originated long before the birth of Islam? Not one of these questions has been adequately considered so far in the current literature about political Islam as well as in the so-called Muslim societies prior to their clashes with modernity, industrial civilization and the forces of globalization. That is why all scholars continue to use the political vocabulary developed in European contexts under the epistemological guidance of the reasoning of enlightenment as the reliable criteria for locating intellectually, ethically, philosophically and through jurisprudence, all the discourses and the decisions made elsewhere concerning the rule of law and civil society. Very few Muslim intellectuals and scholars share the critical analysis performed in Europe in rethinking the whole nation-state experiment embarked upon since the eighteenth and nineteenth centuries which has been replaced by the new political entity of the European Union. The importance of the transition which Europeans have been experiencing since 1945 is crucial for all contemporary nation-states. |It must be said that this experience has been rejected, minimized and ignored by many intellectuals and decision-makers, who prefer to insist on the priority and primacy of the imagined, desired Islamic Model, constructed with anachronistic arrangements of mythological fragments of what I called the Inaugurating Age of that Islamic Model.

These are the prevailing conditions in which the debates about a civil society are engaged in Muslim contexts. It is undeniable that these basically romantic, emotional, frustrating, even phantasmagorical conditions generate clashes between two conflicting imaginaries. The geopolitical strategies of the West have clearly accelerated the dialectic 'answers' of radical political Islam; the geopolitical sphere called 'the Middle East' in American terminology is particularly affected by several ongoing conflicts over vital stakes: oil, the strategic positions for Western forces, the place of Israel in the whole area, the conflicting religious memories since the emergence of Islam as a new rival in the semiotic manipulation of the monotheist legacy. This is really too much; it is an explosive mixture of material interests, the desire for authoritarian rule and a dispute over jointly held symbolic symbolic capital all of which are disputed, fragmented and dismantled by the modern ideologies that are designed to support self-promoted national interests.

To shed more light on this complex situation, there is a need to consider key substantive themes concerning the historical dialectic which has ordered world history after '*the end of history*'. The analysis will concentrate on the following major themes:

1. Does culture matter?
2. The ethics of intellectual and political responsibility;
3. *Siyāsa shar'iyya*, rule of law, civil society.

1. Does Culture Matter?

Does Culture matter? Politics and Governance in the Mediterranean Region. This was the title of a two-day seminar held in Bonn, Germany on 19–20 June 2001. The theme is inspired by a book published by Lawrence E. Harrison and S. P. Huntington entitled *Culture Matters: How Values Shape Human Progress* (Basic Books, 2000). The aim of the authors is to consolidate, expand upon and illustrate the famous theory of the clash of civilizations. Thoughtful contributions are made on the most basic debatable fields of knowledge and reality: culture and economic development; culture and political development; The anthropological debate; culture and gender; culture and American minorities; the Asian crisis; and promoting change.

From the perspective of my own research published in *The Unthought in Contemporary Islamic Thought*, I would make two remarks. Firstly, there is not one contribution on the example of Islam as a commanding, cognitive framework imposed on a great number of cultures and languages in the world; nevertheless, S. Huntington has built his famous theory of representations of 'Islam' borrowed from a very limited and biased Islamicist literature. Secondly, the approach used by all of the contributors confirms the scientific relevance of my concept of **Applied Islamology** which I defended for the first time in 1973 (see my *Critique of Islamic Reason*). There is no question that **culture matters**, and it does so on two important levels. For the individual, the group, the community and the nation, it mirrors the existential experiences, values and performances which enhance the civic consciousness, the sense of ethical and spiritual growth of the human subject and the aesthetic emotional participation in humanistic creativity. Culture is also responsible for the building process of the cognitive frame of perception, interpretation and expression of the human, historical, cosmic reality within which reason, intelligence, imagination and memory can either expand, create and innovate, or regress, degenerate and deviate from their optimal activities. There are cultures that emancipate the human condition, cultures addressed to and instrumentalized by social imaginaries. It is the task of the social, political and economic science as well as of philosophy to detect and expound upon the alienating elements and functions of each culture. This approach to culture, taking into consideration all living cultures in the world, is absolutely new; it is made possible by anthropology as cultural criticism and archaeology as a deconstructive analysis of the systems of thought as exemplified in the works of Jacques Derrida and M. Foucault.

The two editors of *Culture matters* allocated only three chapters to culture and political development. This question is vital in all Muslim contexts, however. Which culture has been supported, chosen and imposed by all the post-colonial states since the 1950s? Is it the emancipating, liberating, liberal, pluralist modern culture, or, its antithesis, the ideological, restrictive, alienating, oppressive culture aiming first and foremost at political manipulation of the collective memories and the social imaginaries? A few ethnologists have addressed these questions in limited monographs. Political scientists have essentially been busy with the narrative and descriptive transcription of the fundamentalist discourses into European languages in order to build up a strong negative imaginary of Islam, Muslims and Muslim societies; a few have paid scant attention to the interaction between different forms and levels of the official 'culture' and political development in order to evaluate, for example, the chance given or refused to the rise of a civil society. The monolithic, closed image of fundamentalist Islam has led to the marginalization, and eventually the elimination, of other cultures which have been rejected and ignored both by the state policy of education and the powerful political movements for the *Islamisation* of the surviving remnants of idolatry and 'savage' (*Jāhiliyya*) cultures. Christian minorities, the languages and cultures of groups converted to Islam, such as the Berbers of the Maghreb and the Kurds of the Middle East are living examples of what I have described elsewhere as the historical dialectic of the powers and residues in all societies and at all periods of history (see *Penser l'Islam aujourd'hui*). Here we have a case study of the role of the Jacobin centralizing states using religious orthodoxy, whether or not it is linked to the ideology of the unified nation in order to transform the emancipating function of a humanist culture into a psychological alienation of the individual and the collective consciousness. There are enabling liberating cultures and disabling, regressive, schizophrenic cultures.

The ideological manipulation of the social imaginary by political and/or religious leaders, parties and brotherhoods is exemplified not only in Fascistic, totalitarian experiences, but even in theocentric regimes, such as those of the Middle Ages, or in some contemporary democratic regimes. The level and the styles of manipulation differ, of course, from one context to another. The style of the Third Republic in France is different from the Italian process of national unity, and the Spanish democratic transition from the Franco regime to the present, decentralized state. In Muslim contexts, the role of culture changed radically during the struggle for liberation (1945–67) followed by the so-called socialist and Islamic fundamentalist revolutions (from 1970 onwards). The changes and their consequences have not yet been studied; it would be enlightening, for example, to compare the progressive, critical attitude of the reformist Muḥammad ʿAbdu to the regressive, dogmatic positions of his so-called disciple Rashid Ridha, or the later conservative sage Muḥammad ʿAmāra. Even more significant would be the comparison between the well-known liberal writer and thinker Taha Ḥussein and the fundamentalists who rejected his contributions as too favourable to Western culture and close to a 'bourgeois' anti-socialist ideology. The shift from a socialist collectivist revolution to the Islamic revolution mainly concerns the substitution of Islamic vocabulary and references for a socialist secularized ideology. In both cases, liberal philosophy and political institutions are rejected and maintained in the domain of the unthinkable, order to avoid the dissolution of Islamic belief. The Nobel prizewinner, Naguib Mahfuz, was able to encompass both revolutions without ever making concessions to any regime of political control; for this reason, at an advanced age, he was the victim of terrorist aggression. This regressive evolution demonstrates that what matters in cultural life is to carefully monitor the fault line between ideological alienation and positive, innovative, liberating subversion of inherited 'false' values and ideals. This has been shown in the case of *The Satanic Verses.* What I am saying about culture in Islamic contexts can be extended to all the cultures that are employed to defend 'national identities' and collective 'identity', as a springboard for seizing political power. If we agree on the principle that a civil society and the rule of law should both be founded on the defence of and strong support for a humanist, liberal culture, the expression *'Culture matters'* will be seen to mean that culture, like knowledge, is a subject and a domain of continuous inevitable conflict. The best result achievable in this domain is to restrict the conflict to peaceful, constructive debate and enlightened rivalry.

2. The Ethics of Intellectual and Political Responsibility

Max Weber insisted on the distinction between the *Ethics of responsibility* and the *Ethics of conviction.* Yet there is still a need to clarify the interaction between these two levels of practical moral conduct, especially in the light of the new ethical challenges produced by discoveries in biology, the problems of genocide, crimes against humanity, humanitarian help in many places in the world, international terrorism and the movement of people across rigid political frontiers. I would be very cautious with the ethics of conviction in the sense that a suicide attack by terrorists, as has been repeated in the second Palestinian *Intifada*, has for each individual perpetrator and his whole community a highly valid legitimacy based on deeply-held, sacred 'convictions'. We know how each attack of this kind generates a more 'civilized', less 'barbarian', more legitimate 'reprisal'. It is an historical fact that since the creation of the State of Israel, there has been no single national or international instance of authority which has been able to put a stop to this circle of violence by means of a just solution to the conflict. It would be wrong to speak only of political and ethical failure; the concept of **intellectual responsibility** needs to be introduced here. My contention is that intellectual responsibility cannot be separated, put aside, or even more so, deliberately ignored in any reflexive process leading to political and ethical decision-making. If it is accepted that the building process of a rule of law, with its related civil society, cannot do concrete, full, continuous justice to human dignity in all contexts, at all times, in all cultures and all regimes of truth, one can no longer ignore 'convictions' founded on religious belief, philosophical options and social solidarity. That is the meaning of my chapter on believing and the human subject.

The ethics of responsibility means that any political, scientific, religious, ecological or economic decision engaging the future of all living generations, as well as those yet unborn, should evaluate all the consequences of each decision for the immediate present and the foreseeable future. President Bush recently refused to subscribe to the international ecological agreement to reduce air pollution in the next few years; similarly, the Clinton administration refused to endorse the creation of the Penal International Tribunal, to say nothing of the US refusal to pay its annual dues to UNESCO and United Nations. All these decisions raise problems of the ethics of intellectual and political responsibility concerning the state as applying rule of law and the civil society which supports or rejects this rule of law as applied by the state. The immediate pressures of *Realpolitik* have made obsolete any reference to the ethics of responsibility not only in matters that depend on the decision-makers at the highest level of government, as well as in the domain of scholarship, scientific research and the teaching or scholarly transmission of the knowledge produced by the most reliable scholarship. Certain scholars have chosen to focus their research on what Pierre Bourdieu in France has illustrated with the concept of *reproduction*. The idea is that scholars are not always innovative in their methodology, approaches to aspects of reality, vocabulary and systems of thought and interpretation; they tend to reproduce the substance and cognitive framework of what is already available, supported and imposed by the academic establishment. This attitude has clear repercussions on the shape of government, the style of governance and the type of civil society that is necessarily dependant on the scientific culture and the space of the **thinkable** created and transmitted from behind the scenes on the highest level. In other words, the rule of law is more the product of a political philosophy (or theology in the case of states tied to an official religion) than it is the direct initiator and manager of the dominant mainstream of what I call the shared space of the **thinkable**. The intellectual, ethical and scientific scope, the thematic dimensions of the thinkable tolerated in each **regime of truth**,[1] is itself the product of interactive sociological forces, collective memories and social imaginaries on the one hand and the type of political regime imposed by the central state on the other. In other words, the dialectic evolution of the two main factors called the rule of law and civil society is so complex and specific to each society that its investigation cannot be restricted to an extensive logosphere such as the native speakers of Arabic, Persian or Hindi, the Muslim community that is often confused with 'Islam', modern, secular societies or 'Islam' and the 'West'.

Consultants, administrators, engineers, bankers, the uncultured, illiterate and ideologically motivated politicians are the modern protagonists who cross every social, economic and political divide in order to shape the 'spirit' of the nation, i.e. its arbitrarily defined identity, regardless of the historical, cultural, religious

1. The **regime of truth** is the term I use for epistemic organization of knowledge, the common cultural framework, the active axiology and postulates commanding the articulation of all manifest discourses within the confines of a logosphere, a collective memory, a religious community, a nation or a society with clear-cut political frontiers. In large pluralistic, democratic societies like the United States, the United Kingdom, Canada or France . . . many regimes of truth co-exist, interact, exchange and open new possibilities for a dynamic intercreativity. In large multi-ethnic, multi-lingual, multi-religious societies that are hindered by fragile democratic institutions and strict political control on the freedom of association, expression and cultural manifestations, the regimes of truth are also numerous, but more conservative, rigid and reduced to the necessity for each group or community to secure the reproduction of its identity on the basis of officially acceptable 'values'.

and scientific differences between societies in which modernity emerged and shaped new mentalities with critical regimes of truth, and those societies in which the same modernity has been imposed from outside, and is manipulated and instrumentalized as a disintegrating, alienating, delinquent force. The intellectual gap is not only widening between developed and underdeveloped societies. Sociologists have produced a more complex picture; the attention paid to intellectual responsibility, together with the ethics of responsibility and conviction, is certainly more effective in democratic societies than it is in vassal states and disadvantaged societies, but it remains generally restricted to social categories such as critical intellectuals. In other words, the developed world has active supporters in each satellite country striving for its emancipation through inadequate systems of thought, forms of rationality and institutions. The defenders of national interests and identities during wars of liberation, have managed to live in social, cultural, economic **enclaves** in their own societies while simultaneously procuring advancement for themselves to the more enabling level of the professional categories in the ex-colonial, developed societies in which they are choosing more and more to live. This worldwide re-composition of social links, ideological alliances and visions of the future is not the result of the 'brain drain' phenomenon, lack of political security for innovators and entrepreneurs, or the economic necessity of finding employment, when it is mostly to be had in the wealthy countries. It is also a manifestation of the historical failure of those nationalist regimes that emerged after so-called liberation from the colonial domination. Through their individual political options, people who were unable to enjoy modern, completely reliable citizenship in their own countries are proving that civil society and its correlated rule of law are the basic attributes of a worldwide modern polity. Emigration to foreign countries or to social and economic enclaves within oppressive regimes has two consequences. It delays the emergence of a civil society in disabling societies and it enhances the construction for the future of pluralist spaces for a wider citizenship in advanced democratic regimes. These critical observations need to be expanded upon by introducing some key substantive themes, often considered by those who aim to bring about the rule of law to a civil society, and moving from utopian aspirations to the concrete historical empirical ground of states, societies, nations and international institutions.

The key substantive themes are those related to the distance, if not the brutal split between the total triumph of the **tele-techno-scientific** civilization that leave all the pre-modern societies with their traditional cultures totally marginalized, excluded from the new imaginary of progress and intellectual emancipation. This divide and its political, economic, cultural consequences cannot be compared to what prevailed during the late 1960s and the 1970s, when the ideology of development-underdevelopment was taken care of by the two competing solutions of the socialist-collectivist secular revolution, as opposed to the liberal bourgeoisie contention that economic progress could not be achieved without a democratic rule of law as the protector of human rights and those of the citizen. The post-colonial states could thus sustain the political illusion that poor societies would able to achieve their industrialization in a shorter time than Europe had done in the nineteenth century, since this was considered as the required first step for attaining a rule of law and a civil society more concretely committed to social justice and political freedom. This ideological representation of the future of a common world civilization was the determining factor in the Cold War. When the Communist supporters of Socialist Revolution disappeared from the political international scene, the Third World regimes demonstrated their failure to offer a workable alternative vision of the future of those many peoples and cultures exposed to stronger dismantling forces than those of the industrialization and urbanization that had been experienced in the previous century by the First World, but in this case without the massive, radical uprooting, disintegrating process of the peasantry. The majority of the Third World regimes had to replace their so-called Socialist liberation plans by a reversion to a traditional faith-driven 'national identity'. This ideological leap prevailed in Muslim contexts in which the demographic explosion provided a large sociological basis for the so-called 'Islamic revolution'.

Many 'organic' intellectuals supported the new historical alternative to the previous secular, revolutionary model. In both cases, they supported recurring demands for the restoration of 'national identities,' officially related to an illusory, imaginary, defective representations of 'Socialism', and to an even greater extent of 'Islam' because illiterate peoples could relate more easily to Islamic justice than to 'Socialist, secular' justice. The role given to this imaginary 'Islam' expanded so quickly and widely throughout the world that it has itself become the most unwieldy unthought in contemporary Islamic thought. It involves systematic references to an Islam that is isolated from the most elementary historical reasoning, linguistic analysis or anthropological decoding, operating as a psychological, cultural and intellectual obstacle to a serious approach to the major twin themes of rule of law and civil society. The constant amalgam between the modern cognitive framework and the West depicted as a hostile, destructive force imposed on Muslim societies and culture is systematically used as a decisive argument in order to preserve 'Islam' from all the intellectual and scientific challenges.

A stronghold has been thus created in which a large number of social protagonists, including the *'ulamā'*, intellectuals, scholars, jurists, physicists, journalists, politicians and wealthy influential citizens, can present themselves as the defenders of an 'orthodox', 'authentic' dogmatic Islam while simultaneously enjoying a comfortable, privileged lifestyle in social, economic enclaves that are closer to the civil society in Western democratic regimes than they are to the overwhelming sector of their own society (workers, peasants, low-grade civil servants, the unemployed, women as a marginalized category). This socio-economic segregation is the result of the political will imposed since the several societies gained their independence. Of course, it has had many adverse consequences on the new expressions and distorted functions of religion, the lack of a civil culture common to the global society, the strategies used by the state in order to balance the conservative 'religious' opposition with the secular modernizing trends, or the reverse, according to King Hassan II's metaphoric definition of fundamentalism as a 'fecund fuel'. Where can change come from if there is no leading group, no authoritative creative voice capable of initiating a reliable plan of action for a modern polity in a dynamic, challenging historical environment? Any intervention from outside would generate violent indignation in the name of the state sovereignty; diplomatic relations are limited to negotiations about trade, transfer of technology, economic assistance and immigration problems; there is no place for cultural, scientific or educational issues for improving the communication of common values and preventing the clashes of the so-called 'conquering civilizations'. To shed more light on these matters, we need to consider the tensions between the conceptualisation and the values proposed in the traditional construction of the *siyāsa shar'iyya* or *wilāyat al-faqīh* expounded in militant Islamic discourse in order to challenge and dismiss the Western concept and practice of the rule of law and civil society.

3. Siyāsa Shar'iyya, Rule of Law, Civil Society

How can the rule of law and civil society be located within political and religious culture using the thought processes claimed by contemporary Muslims as the ultimate legal instance of authority on which an 'authentic' Islamic governance should be exclusively based? Those who defend this position minimize, ignore or even reject a fruitful dialogue, and refuse to identify any reliable, universal model leading to garnering legitimacy for the planned civil society. They constantly point out to failures, deviations, perverted ideologies and unfulfilled promises of all the existing models experienced in several democratic regimes. The historical experiences of Europe and North America societies offer the possibility of detecting the solid, sustainable elements of a dynamic civil society. One example is the very successful French law of freedom of association promulgated in 1901. This also makes it possible to *falsify* – according to Karl Popper's definition of falsification – theoretical visions based on purely ideological options in Muslim contexts. This is the only way out of the recurrent conflicts about religious and secularized models, Oriental and Western 'values', the universal and the local outreach of human rights, etc. For this search, the 'light' of both Euro-American and Muslim post-colonial experiences might be helpful on condition that both are approached through a radical criticism. The failures of post-colonial states to foster a democratic civil society should be clearly identified with their actual internal genesis and external contexts. Describing the opposition of fundamentalist defenders of a so-called 'Islamic model of state' to the existing regimes accused of introducing Western secularized norms and institutions is insufficient. In fact, all states in all countries have more or less used and imposed Islamic references and a will to protect the *Sharī'a*; there is a mimic rivalry between the state and the opposition, to outdo each other in closeness to the 'authentic', 'pure' and 'original' teachings of the Qur'ān and the Prophet. This debate on old theological, exegetic and legal issues unknown historically to both protagonists, has overwhelmingly occupied the political space and eliminated the intellectual and scientific endeavours to trace a clear-cut line between the ideological, instrumentalized so-called Islam, and two other problems neglected and maintained in the unthinkable and the unthought: the historical, doctrinal Islam, according to the critical studies published since the last nineties (see the bibliography) on the one side; and the crucial new debates enlarged and enriched by the current experiences of the European Community, in particular, on the other.

In my upcoming book *Penser l'Islam aujourd'hui*, I have devoted a long chapter to the critique of juridical reason in contemporary Islam, to show the extent to which existing political regimes and their Islamist conservative opponents disregard books dealing directly with major issues of the *Sharī'a*, like those of B. Johansen, G. Makdisi, N. Calder, W. M. Ballantyne, D. J. Stewart, B. Weiss, W. B. Hallaq and many others. Even among those who can read English, French or German, there is a reluctance to trust 'Western' scholars on Islamic matters of 'faith'. This means that faith is not a matter of critical knowledge, but only of orthodox reproduction of what the 'Tradition' B itself preserved from any criticism B has transmitted since the age of the 'pious ancestors' (*al-salaf al-ṣāliḥ*). The result of this policy and mental attitude is that the modern conceptualization of the rule of law and civil society is continuously postponed until a future is to be found in the past, not to be invented, imagined, planned and made present with relevant decisions. The more public opinion is receptive to the idea that *Sharī'a* should replace all secularized laws and institutions, the more likely that freedom of expression and publication is restricted to what the state, the dominant opinion or both, allows. Examples of this can be observed in several countries and contexts inside and outside the Muslim world. Another contradiction should be mentioned here: many intellectuals, writers, artists who stand on the side of democratic values prefer to stress the responsibility of the West in supporting conservative regimes than to insist on the role of national so-called 'elites' who have monopolized political power since the independence of each country. We shall come back to the role of intellectuals and their status in society later.

Such aspects and critical analysis are not always properly integrated into the current research programs of political and social sciences, which prefer either to maintain the descriptive, narrative erudite presentation of the 'facts', or to endlessly point to the abstract, biased theory of the 'clash of civilizations' built, on what I call the 'intellectual irresponsibility coupled with an obvious ideological vision of the present map of geopolitical and geocultural spheres in the world'. This is a matter of top priority in negotiations between democratic states and all post-colonial states, where the democratic culture and modern legal and philosophical frames of thought are dramatically absent. Therefore, a strictly shared modern, legal, historical and philosophical culture should take precedence in all negotiations between states and peoples around the world; this would fill the intellectual and institutional gaps created by the colonial period, and deepened by nationalist, alienating and authoritarian policies imposed by the post-colonial states of an imagined, arbitrary so-called identity opposed to the 'cultural aggression' (*al-ghazw al-fikrī*) of the 'West'. It is true that the Western discourse on democracy and human rights, presupposes the existence of a reliable, already set model of rule of law and civil society in all 'backward', traditional and patriarchal societies. At the same time as those official voices urge the spread of democratic responses to the current history, they continue to support conservative regimes strongly opposed to the rapid and successful emergence of a strong, efficient civil society. In the case of some states, like Morocco and Turkey, candidates to the European Union and later the Community itself, but as long as Islamic institutions, laws, customs and culture officially prevail in these regimes, it will be impossible to harmonize the legislative process, the *sine qua non* condition, to the admission of new members. This is a very significant and concrete case study testing the possibility for contemporary societies claiming an Islamic identity, to radically rethink this identity in the framework of a criticized, enlarged, eventually revised intellectual, scientific and secular modernity.

From this perspective, there is also a difficulty on the side of the European approach to political debates in the modern polity. We mentioned the issue of intellectual and ethical responsibility. It is currently debated by several NGOs, that priority should be given to the capacity-building of an ethical reasoning and judgement process. Certainly, ethical reasoning is not only weakened, if not totally absent, but made obsolete by the triumphant experimental, empirical, pragmatic and managerial reasoning spread by the social, political and managerial sciences. Long ago, R. Musil described the substitution in industrial societies of the *Man without Qualities* (*L'homme sans qualités*) to the traditional man, trained to aspire to ideals codified in rigorous ethical and civic programs of education. At the same time, Guy Debord showed the other shift, from societies of personalized relationships to the 'society of spectacles' (*La société du spectacle*, 1967). Even philosophy tends to comply with the rules of the 'society of entertainment' when authors supported by the media, focus their reflexive activities on the problems and ideas raised within the limitations of the national language, cultural identity, religious or positivist tradition of thought. We have witnessed this phenomenon in France with the wave of 'new philosophers' after 1968. The culture of disbelief and the criteria of economic and political reasoning have marginalized, disqualified all forms of ethical discourse, except in the idealist apologetic sermons of religious leaders and official calls for a civic secularized conscience. Both discourses hide, or exclude, the urgent need to reactivate ethical concerns with the task of building civil societies as new historical platforms for the genesis of a worldwide space of solidarity and citizenship, foreseen and claimed by a still reduced number of influential voices. The concept of **worldwide space of solidarity and citizenship** is not considered in the diplomatic discourse and geopolitical strategies of any contemporary state, especially the Western democratic states who are rather developing theories of clashes, threats of fanaticism, violence, terrorism, Islamist/Islamic movements against 'Western values and civilization'. This Manichean dualist frame of the present geopolitical struggle is becoming the main obstacle for a serious consideration of the building process of a **worldwide space of solidarity and citizenship**.

Mindful of all these observations, we shall explore three issues which, in my view, have prior relevance to the necessity of moving from a diplomacy of national interests and hegemony to a new vision of history based on two harmonized principles: the protection of specific national cultural rights, and the commitment to a common effort to reach a worldwide space of solidarity and citizenship:

1. Beyond the dichotomy of religion *vs* secularism.
2. Rethinking the trilogy religion, ethics, rule of law.
3. The status and the role of 'intellectuals' in Islamic contexts.

3.1. Beyond the Dichotomy of Religion vs Secularism

This dichotomy is the product of history; developed by religions claiming the monopoly on Truth[1] as a whole: the truth of beliefs and non-beliefs, the truth of the Just Law, the truth of the answers to all questions in the universe, physical phenomena, terrestrial history and the history of salvation, life and death, human nature and activities, etc. Reason, imagination and memory are associated in the articulation, the transmission and the protection of the Truth, from deviations, destruction and negation. All these definitions and strategies that deliver, explain, teach, apply and protect the Truth can be called the 'religious regime of Truth'. Pre-modern states have adopted, supported and utilized this 'regime of Truth' as the ultimate instance of their legitimacy; the 'managers of the sacred' (priests, rabbis, *imams*, wise men) and the secular rulers agreeing to respectively share their responsibilities B religion being the instance of authority, the state, the instance of power B to implement, serve and protect the Truth to which the head of state himself submits as a human being. The alliance between religion and politics has generated a dogmatic control on all levels of the 'subjects'' life and expression, submitted to the religious law itself as mediated by the ruler and his delegates.

Modern revolutions have substituted their own 'regimes of Truth' to the religious ones, which are still claiming full validity against the most constraining scientific evidence established by linguistics, critical history, cultural anthropology, psychology, historical epistemology, etc. Scientific arguments cannot remove religious Truth once rooted in the human subject; it can be transformed, focused on different 'values', activities, but the 'ethics of conviction' continue to determine the perception, interpretation and motivation of each person. This construction of the subject needs to be better studied along with the scientific knowledge, used as a mere expertise and technical reproduction, which superficially affects the deep psychological, emotional structure of the individual's life. For this purpose the French Revolution is a rich case study: it was particularly violent and radical in its will to overthrow the 'old Regime' and

1. I write Truth with a capital T because it is represented and used as the absolute divine Truth, while modern truth will be more and more revitalized.

a king invested with the divine Right as sacralized by the Church at Reims. When Louis XVI had been judged and executed by the courts in the name of the sovereignty of the people, the sacralizing power of the divine Right was finally abolished. When Khomeini came to power in February 1979, he did just the opposite of what the French revolutionaries imposed: he decided to arrest the Shah, presenting him as *Firʿawn*, the Qurʾānic symbol of the unjust ruler who usurped the right of the charismatic guide to enforce God's law on earth. That way the Shah could be arrested, judged and executed in the name of God as represented by the Imam.

In human affairs, all things start with mystical, high hopes, transcendentalizing visions to end up with politics, and the constraining power imposed by a 'legal' violence. The chronological order of the chapters of the Qurʾān (*sūras*) as presented by the Muslim tradition, suggests this process: the last *sūra* (*al-tawba*) contains the verse 5 called by jurists the *sword verse* and several polemical verses addressed to the Peoples of the Book and those Arabs who refused to participate in the Just war (*jihād*) against the idolaters. This historical, anthropological and psychological fact should be integrated in our reflection on the conditions of the emergence, construction and positive use of civil society. If we still need to search for Just governance as the *sine qua non* condition for building the capability of becoming a civil society, we should also pay more attention to violence as a structural force at work in each society. We are accustomed to speaking of violence just as the religious sermons and the civic training of the citizen in secular, democratic regimes have taught us. Violence is linked exclusively to the *others*, perceived, described and condemned as barbarians, uncivilized and uneducated, who are ignorant of the true teachings provided only by the True Religion, or the true philosophy, the objective history taught in the public schools of the modern *laïc*[1]

1. This concept has no equivalent in any European language; it refers to the specific French historical experience since the Revolution, considered by the French Republican state as the Inaugurating Moment of a new era of Truth, just as the emergence of Christianity or Islam are the Inauguration of other competing eras of Truth.

state. If we consider French or American newspapers produced at the time of the Vietnamese and Algerian colonial wars, or Israeli literature about Arabs, Muslims and Palestinians, to say nothing of Communist and Nazi literature, we come to the conclusion that the building process of any type of society involves at some level, in given circumstances, the Manichean split between a civilized, cultivated, peaceful, humanist *we* radically opposed to a terrorist, fanatic, rebellious, unenlightened *he/them*. This sociological psycho-cultural rule also applies to the foreign immigrants in modern civil societies, in the spite of the legal attempts to correct the situation introduced by the rule of law. Structural violence is also manifested in the field of education. The intellectual competition between different schools of thought is translated into political rivalries leading to the monopoly of legal violence exercised by all types of states, including those built on democratic majorities.

These short historical, anthropological remarks show clearly that religion and secularism are mostly handled as polemical concepts referring to *contingent* ideological regimes of Truth. This contingency is already displayed in the founding texts of the three monotheist religions. God himself is involved in the polemical disputes and violent conflicts between the true, loyal believers and all the groups who, for various reasons, refuse to receive and hold on to the true Revelation. This polemical framework is accepted, enforced and perpetuated in the religious Law developed by theologians-jurists recognized as orthodox authorities of the three religions (Jewish Law, Christian canon Law, *Sharīʿa*). European revolutions endorsed the same polemical affirmative action leading to the triumph of a lay/secular regime of truth. The most important problem here, that has not yet been fully and convincingly addressed by modern historians, can be explained in the following terms.

While in Islamic contexts, the stakes of the battle as shaped in the paradigmatic, Prophetic Discourse, ended with the political and cultural defeat of the philosophical, scientific regime of truth, in Europe – mainly Catholic and Protestant Europe – the contrary happened , after the contributions of Descartes, Spinoza, Leibniz, Locke, Hobbes, Rousseau, Diderot, Voltaire and many others.

Critical reasoning was directed at the task of building modernity as an alternative framework of thought and action, while religious reasoning in Islamic contexts has not only survived until today, but has consented to regress from the intellectual, scientific levels it reached in its classical period (700–1400). Muslim supporters of the reformation movement (*iṣlāḥ*) that began in the nineteenth century and lasted until 1940, had an apologetic, naïve answer to this question. They claimed that regression back to the 'authentic' Islam taught by God and his Messenger started with the opulent, materialistic, secular civilization that prevailed under several dynasties and contemporary regimes. Muslims went astray and deviated from the ideal Righteous, God-given Rule which can be recovered and restored by learned, pious, reliable authorities . . . this genuine mythologization of the mythical structured message of the Prophetic Discourse was defended as an answer that challenged modernity and would be replaced after 1945, by the nationalist, secular ideology of liberation. The transition from *iṣlāḥ* to the so-called socialist revolution lasted until the late 1970s, when the political failure of the post-colonial regimes with a single-party system opened the way to a fundamentalist Islamic solution, or radical Islam.

In the present crises of all regimes of truth and inherited systems of legitimation, the new waves of 'believers' are happy with 'the return of religion' as a platform of resistance to the 'materialist', secular, corrupted, corrupting regimes; but they are unable to rethink the new status and functions of this religion manipulated, in fact, by politically oriented and obscurantist 'leaders'. In European contexts, the social sciences provide more reliable approaches to the religious phenomenon and its traditional and contemporary expressions. At the same time, the secular regime of truth is revisited and reinterpreted in the wider perspectives and the new cognitive frameworks offered by the combined revolutionary discoveries of social, information and hard sciences. The intellectual and philosophical follow-ups of the technological leaps with their impact on contemporary societies as well as on the formation of the new human subject, is obviously not in the line and on the level of the hopes, demands and repressed needs of various populations and social classes. We see, rather, a growing fear and anger in the face of so many forms of violence generated by the powerful and obscure forces of globalization. As far as Islam and societies referring to it are concerned, acts of terrorism and physical violence in the name of a so-called Islamic Revolution, have replaced the reformist discourse (*iṣlāḥ)* in reactivating the so-called 'authentic Islam' bequeathed by the pious pure sanctified Ancestors, *al-salaf al-ṣāliḥ*. Examples of this structural move are provided in several contemporary Islamic contexts. The social, political, cultural and economic conditions to generate or negate the emergence of a modern peaceful civil society, are changing as a result of tragic murders and ideological pressures. The search for a more concrete, effective, liberating interaction between thought, knowledge and action is again delayed and distorted, if not deleted by uncontrolled, invisible forces. Obviously, these forces are not only opposed to the orientation I am proposing, but the majority of social actors are prevented by political, social, economic, cultural impediments from even thinking of the possibility to take the initiatives precisely required to get out of their present impasse. Demographic pressure, unemployment, social marginalization, material, psychological and sexual frustrations, precarious conditions of daily life, authoritarian distant state, inefficient bureaucracy, irrelevant system of education, disintegration of cultural, ethical and semantic codes, uncertain future and populist religious expressions. These are themes for sociological analysis to show how problematic and, indeed, almost impossible is the emergence of a civil society with all its attributes, institutions and functions.

More will be said about the status and the role of 'intellectuals', the place and levels of cultural life; but we can already make the following statement as regards the disputed issue of the separation between Mosque and State as institutional entities. A brutal separation along the lines of that used by Kemal Atatürk to eradicate Ottoman institutions, cannot be on the political agenda of any party in power as long as the state ultimately remains patrimonial and the social mentalities are deeply shaped and commanded by patriarchal kinship mechanisms. I have observed these common features in all the Muslim countries in which I have lectured from Indonesia to Morocco, from the Caucasus to South Africa. Systematic ethno-linguistic surveys of all contemporary Islamic contexts would show how gender segregation is reflected in the separation of private and public space, in the division of daily work, in the vertical power of the father or the elder bother, in the culture transmitted by the mother to her daughters, the father to the males. When rural or nomadic populations are uprooted and move to the slums surrounding the overpopulated cities, the patriarchal order breaks down, to be replaced by a specific **populist** system of inner solidarity and outer hostility which deserves the special attention of sociologists. A rampant secularization permeates these emerging micro- societies through the media, but the intellectual and cultural dimensions of what we call secularism in Western contexts – more specifically in Western Europe – are as absent and unthinkable as they are in the upper, wealthier classes in whom material modernisation is too often combined with cultural traditionalization. Under such socio-cultural and anthropological conditions, asking for a separation of Mosque and state is just imposing a foreign formal ideological model on societies in which the problem of increasing *structural violence*, reflected in the architecture and urban fabric, is not addressed either by the patrimonial states, nor by the 'élites' obliged to negotiate their conditional freedom with the powerful bureaucracy or levels of power at the service of the established regime.

The issue of religion, ethics and rule of law deserves further clarification.

3.2. Rethinking the Trilogy of Religion, Ethics and Rule of Law

I singled out this issue just to determine under which conditions and in which sense references to religion and ethics can be relevant to set a rule of law and locate civil society in Islamic contexts. In other words, when we consider the case of Islamic contexts, we need to re-examine from the outset the principle accepted by the majority of Muslims, according to which Islam is simultaneously religion, state and society, the three inseparable 'D's – *Dīn, Dawla, Dunyā* – often discussed in classical Islamic thought.[1] The rule of law and civil society are the result of modern conceptualization, based on the legal and institutional principle of the separation or autonomy of the *religious sphere* with its specific, theological speculation on spiritual and ethical values, and the *political sphere* with its secular, philosophical approach to governance, legitimacy, popular sovereignty, positive law and the separation of the three instances known as the legislative power, the executive power and the judicial power. In the modern concept of political legitimacy, God and Revelation, prophetic authority are no longer the source of the True Knowledge, the Just Law, the ultimate spiritual and ethical values; all types and levels of which are called *values*. They are doomed to be re-discussed and reassessed in the perspective of the interface between political theology and reflexive philosophy, unless theology and philosophy are totally separated, pursuing different lines of thinking to create two competing frameworks of thought, interpretation and action.

This is exactly what happened historically in the development of Islamic thought. After the death of Ibn Rushd (1198), the creative interface between theology, religious law and philosophy was disrupted; theology as a rationalizing attempt at faith building or even criticism, disappeared after the thrirteenth–fourteenth centuries; schools of law stopped their disputations (*munāẓara*) and became isolated from each other; ethics elevated by Miskawayh (1020) to the rank of a key discipline in the curriculum of a learned humanist human subject,[2] was disregarded as well as a critical, rationalizing endeavour to consciously discern the positive, operative, emancipating virtues from the traditional, uncriticized, unthought collective habits ritually reproduced in patriarchal societies.

1. See my *L'humanisme arabe au IVe/Xe siècle*, Paris, 1982.
2. See my recent book, *Ma'ārik min ajli-l-ansana fī-l-siyāqāt al-islāmiyya*, Dār al-Sāqī, 2001; French version: *Combats pour l'humanisme en contextes islamiques*, forthcoming, 2002.

We cannot ignore this historical transformation of the intellectual scene in all Islamic contexts from around 1300 to 1850. The second radical transformation of intellectual activity concerning all the issues related to the three 'D's, began after 1945 and is still in progress. All so-called Muslim societies have been challenged by the modern intellectual, institutional shift that occurred in Europe during the seventeenth and eighteenth centuries, but they had to be cautious and finally reject a historical experience introduced from the outside under colonial domination. There is an urgent need to re-write the whole history of the colonial phenomenon, bearing in mind the important distinction between the local traditional cultures of the colonized countries and the colonial, ideological translation, in the nineteenth century, of *intellectual modernity* by Europeans themselves for their own peasant population and industrial workers. The colonized societies were actually based on the patriarchal system more than on Islamic Law and ethics. That is why I prefer to speak of Islamic contexts, or the so-called Muslim society in order to escape from the ideological confusions spread throughout the contemporary world by Muslim discourses 'objectively' (I mean by that, without any deconstructive criticism) transcribed, reported by the media and even a great number of well known scholars.

Highly respected and influential Muslim personalities and leaders refer with pride and conviction to the intangible superseding Islamic spirituality and Ethics, without taking into consideration all that I have just mentioned about the historical, sociological and ideological transformations inside Islamic thought itself on one hand and the undisputable challenge of modernity as a mental, historical shift, on the other. Such positions based on personal belief, or constraining responsibilities for those in charge of religious, political and educational leadership, contribute to maintaining the ideological, apologetic confusions and, as a result, delay the inevitable radical criticism of values – whether spiritual or ethical – introduced by Nietzsche in his *Genealogy of Values*. Because this criticism is ignored and unthinkable, of course, in its philosophical inspiration and consequences, wherever the neo-patriarchal regime of authority, values and truth is prevalent, ethical thinking cannot articulate today for pluralist civil society a single normative code of ethical 'values'. This is the experience of many national ethics committees for the life sciences. I was a member of the French committee from 1990 to 1998 and I know how each member was very careful to not refer to his personal scale of ethical values to share the consensus of the committee on the basic universal principle that the dignity of human person should take precedence in all the positions publicly declared in the name of the committee. This is the typical French laic approach to the issue of ethics in a pluralist society.

The debate remains open as to the philosophical postulates of different approaches to the ethical issue. There is a place, of course, for a specific approach in each of the religious traditions; but there are also a number of common founding principles recognized by cultural anthropology in traditional and modern systems of thought. My contention is that philosophical ethics and Islamic ethics developed as two competing, differentiated systems until the eleventh and twelfth centuries. The competition ended with the elimination of the philosophical trend of thought; this historical fact generated an intellectual handicap and a cultural gap which prevent contemporary Islamic thought from joining in the debate on ethics on its constraining level: namely biological, anthropological, sociological, psychological and ultimately philosophical. Insofar as ethics and law generate knotty problems that need to be unravelled, the Islamic rule of law, with its relevant civil society, cannot be proclaimed if we do not even recognize that we have inherited from classical Islamic thought many such complex problems that were left untackled in the reject pile of unthinkable issues. Religion and secularism are just frameworks of thinking and interpreting which generate different knots, with the important difference that in the religious framework, values and legal norms are sacralized, deified and declared intangible, while in the secular framework, all values and norms are doomed to change, to be changed under the pressure of historicity.

Mindful of all these considerations, we can trace a programme of research and action to enhance the emergence of a rule of law, with its civil society, in Islamic historical contexts. An outline of the programme of research is proposed in every chapter of this book. The problem is that such a programme cannot be considered either by the popular and populist sector of societies, nor by the upper class of managers, entrepreneurs and decision-makers. It cannot be supported either by the existing political regimes whose legitimacy is radically subverted in terms of the critique of religious, legal, historical and anthropological reason and cognition. States in general do not mind of this kind of subversion, as long as it cannot affect the social 'order'. 'Successful' politicians are those who detect and monitor the main structuring representations, expectations of the social psyche to manipulate it with an appropriate ideological, mobilizing discourse.

The most impressive illustration of this strategy is provided by Khomeini's conquest of power. His discourse mixes religious symbolism of righteously guided Islamic governance with prospects of eschatological salvation, judgements rooted on the Shīʿī high instance of spiritual authority (*marjaʿ al-taqlīd*) and last, but not least, an exceptional sense of political action. Another example of this attention given to the social psyche as a springboard, a social platform for legitimizing the monarchy and its head, is provided by the late king Ḥassan II. He supported a policy of traditionalization while fully supporting the modernisation of sectors of social development, apart from so-called personal status, especially concerning the legal status of women, the religious institutions of learning and places of worship, the ceremonial of allegiance to the king and the royal family and the ceremonial of religious teaching during Ramaḍān lead by the king himself, with his sons seated on the ground to listen humbly to the teachings of God, delivered from a magnificent seat symbolising the throne of God, by learned men officially invited for that purpose. A third, different example is provided by the Algerian president, Houari Boumediène, who imposed a socialist collectivist government inspired by the Soviet regime, but supported a paralleled policy of Islamization through the annual Seminar of Islamic Thought, the

University of Islamic studies on the model of Zaytūna in Tunis, Qarawiyyīn in Morocco, al-Azhar in Egypt, and the great number of mosques built throughout the country. Boumediène thought that with this dual strategy he could introduce a 'modern' Islam, compatible with the socialist collectivist ideology brutally imposed upon the Algerian peasantry and pastoral nomads of the Saharan Desert. This tragically mistaken vision translates clearly into the emergence of the FIS party and the civil war that broke out in 1990, illustrating the devastating political and cultural consequences of the unthought in contemporary Islamic thought.

After such conclusive experiences (I could give more examples), the question arises: as to what kind of contribution can be made in the ongoing battle as to the type of state and civil society are claimed by two radically opposed visions. The stakes in the battle become ever more similar to those engaged in French Revolution versus Roman Catholicism, that began in 1789. But there are decisive differences. Islam with its so-called ethics and law were radically changed after the use and abuse made of it for mere political, ideological purposes by all the regimes that merged in post-colonial societies. Even the five canonical obligations deviate, in many aspects, from their essential meaning as spiritual expressions of the human person, and are transformed into an ostentatious display of social and political loyalty, or even into opportunities for small and big business, during Ramaḍān and the Ḥajj. Mosques are used, either by the state or by religious parties, as places for political militancy. Scarf, veil, keffiyeh, moustache, dress and other rituals are also transferred to the semiological expression of political options under the cover of religious faith. The re-conceptualisation of Islam as a religion becomes impossible when the frontier between religious expression and political struggle is blurred in almost all daily activities and discourses. I personally experience this obstacle in every lecture I deliver, even in Europe and America , at which Muslim attendance is always high.

Intellectually and scientifically, there is no way of subscribing to the apologetic anhistorical confusion which projects back on an 'imagined' Islamic tradition, separated from the historical facts or about selected fragments from the Qur'ān and *ḥadīth*, a so-called Islamic democratic model, with an Islamic constitutional Law.[1] It is possible that some formal aspects of the modern rule of law are recognized and incorporated into 'Islamic' regimes such as the Iranian one initiated by Khomeini. But the question arises: either the empirical, pragmatic experience of Iran since 1979, eventually leads to the process of an original articulation of the religious sphere of authority within the political sphere, similar to the one accepted long ago in United Kingdom, or it ultimately fails to integrate intellectually, spiritually, politically, legally and institutionally the whole modern *re-conceptualisation* of the three 'D's in Islamic thought. In the first hypothesis, we can speak of the first radical revolutionary mental shift through the whole Islamic tradition with major historical consequences for all the societies linked to the Islamic traditional model; in the second case, there are again two possibilities:

A rule of law with its civil society founded on specific Islamic principles, attributes and style, is historically viable not exclusively for Muslim believers, but in the sense that it would be an intellectual, spiritual, ethical, legal and institutional challenge to the so-called secular model achieved and presented in Europe as universal, or at least universalizable. Without such a challenge, the viability of an Islamic polity would be at most *functional* in terms of psychology, cultural expressions and chronological duration, since it would be limited by the contingency and subjectivity of what I described as the *dogmatic theological enclosure*. Teaching Islam as a system of beliefs and non-beliefs is compulsory at all elementary and secondary levels; children and students are taught that there is no point in teaching the history of religions, even less a compared anthropology of religions, since the Qur'ān has clearly and for

1. It is impossible to exhaust the critical discussion of this immense issue in the present chapter; I refer to all the chapters of this book, and the expanding literature in the line of the *Siyāsa shar'iyya* of Ibn Taymiyya and the *Wilāyat al-faqīh* of Khomeini. See also the literature presented by A. Sachadina on the *Just Ruler in Shī 'ite Islam: The Comprehensive Authority of the Jurist in Imamite Jurisprudence*, OUP, 1988.

ever 'demonstrated' with irrefutable 'arguments' that the cycle of revelation is closed and all previous religions are abolished. The psychological result of this teaching desired and paid for by the state to support the official religion, is that historical, anthropological reasoning is utterly inconceivable. I have given many lectures on social sciences as applied to the study of Islam to various Muslim audiences; regularly, I should say ritually, the first question I generate is: 'do you believe that the Qur'ān is the word of God or not'? As it is phrased, the question aims to deny whatever is proposed and explained in order to retreat into the dogmatic enclosure. The most remarkable and also disappointing phenomenon is when women struggling for their emancipation, ask the same question after a whole lecture on the history of so-called Islamic law. There is no way to out of the enclosure, the paradise inside the enclosure. Those Muslims who have received a good training in the methodology of the social sciences or on philosophical reasoning would never dare to approach the problem of the cognitive status of revelation. In other words, the search for a rule of law should either include the *sharī'a* as defined in the classical orthodox collections, or provide the opportunity of offering an unpredictable solution, unless the Algerian, Iranian, Sudanese and Afghan civil wars are deliberately chosen as a third possibility for entering or exiting the dogmatic enclosure. The continuous brain drain is another answer to the lack of communication imposed, as I explained, by the political strategies of the state-party to gain the support of the public opinion shaped with the culture of traditionalization and nationalist identity.

If, on the contrary, we consider the hypothesis of the challenging Islamic model on the level we have indicated, the European model would be intellectually and scientifically constrained to stop looking down on all ancient and contemporary experiences of an Islamic polity. We know how political scientists, historians and philosophers have theorized about what they called 'Oriental despotism', 'Islamic Law' and so-called Islamic regimes. It is interesting to observe that neither the Japan experience, nor the potential Indian and Chinese experiences are likely to be admitted in contemporary political and legal philosophy as an actual or potential challenge in the sense that we are envisaging for the Islamic historical line of polity construction. It is an indisputable fact that the discourses produced outside the Western/European geopolitical, cultural and intellectual sphere of influence, are purely *reactive*, at most narrative and descriptive, not *active* and *creative* on the subjects and the themes under discussion in this section. In my own terminology, I would say that the existing Western/European model of governance, rule of law and civil society is generating themes, issues, institutions, evolutions and experiences that are intellectually challenging for all other systems and traditions of thought that are still alive in our world; this intellectual dimension remain largely the unthought critically, or a priority programme for critical thinking, especially in Islamic contexts.

The second possibility concerning the Iranian example is that it ultimately fails to produce a challenging Islamic model, just as the Saudī regime, established in 1932, or the much older Moroccan monarchy that dates to the rise of the first Islamic dynasty with Idris I at 789, have failed to do. The so-called Republican regimes, with formal modern constitutions, have been no more successful in handling the Islamic references in initiating a challenging sustainable model and filling the gap between the new leaps forward that we are witnessing in the construction of a new European space of governance and citizenship. It is very likely that political and jurisprudential discourses in Islamic contexts will remain *reactive*, dependent on the conceptualizations and the implementations carried on within dynamic, self-challenging European thought. There are urgent pressures on the younger generations who are more and more heavily influenced through the worldwide diffusion of a standard culture, to rid themselves of the patrimonial state and the patriarchal social order and affiliate to the more attractive regime of the rule of law with its democratic civil society. How long will the present transition be maintained under the 'republican', 'parliamentary' veil, hiding the totalitarian nature of several states obviously isolated from their people and rejected by large segments of their societies already committed to building a free, civil society? In the meantime, the rule of law remains a strong claim, civil society an obsessive dream of the populace, a theme of empty official discourse trying without success to offer a prospect of hope to sceptical populations still deprived of the full status of citizenship. It is also a device used by officials to refute the NGO criticism and prevent the objections of international organizations to totalitarian regimes.

We have several illustrations of this struggle for human rights, freedom of thought and belief and expression in societies in which the official religion is stated in the constitution. In Egypt, Tunisia, Malaysia and Turkey, well- known intellectuals and scholars such as Sa'd al-Dīn Ibrāhīm, Naṣr Abu Zayd are put on trial and convicted just because they introduced discussions on religious issues that had been declared unthinkable, or civic problems casting doubt on the legitimacy of states when they exercise arbitrary 'legal' violence. The idea that a rule of law should protect all citizens, even when they debate issues of religious law and ethics is negated, although it might be formally recognized in the constitution. It is true, nevertheless, that in the Egyptian constitution, it is explicitly written that Divine Law supersedes any law developed on the basis of human opinion; this principle provides judges with every possibility of overruling prior judgements in the name of the *sharī'a*.[1] How can a civil society ever be developed when such a confusing constitutional law exists, that adopts the mediaeval mindset, dating from a time when the theocracies commanded and governed all legal systems in Christianity, Judaism and Islam? Under the secular rule of law, religious and ethical issues can be debated and studied on a scientific basis in the public sphere; they can also be kept in their orthodox expressions in private institutions of learning and practice.

Regarding the legal distinction between the public and the private space, several options are debated in Europe; in Islamic contexts, the frontier remains rigid between the private space to which a large majority of women are still confined in many

1. See the important essay by Baudouin Dupret, *Au nom de quel droit*, CEDEJ, 2000.

societies, the public space being monopolized by male activities and decision-making at all levels. Changes are certainly taking place, but this segregation has very negative consequences on all attempts to generate a civil society in which the role of women is and will be more and more crucial for the first time in the history of all forms, all places and at all times of Islamic polity. The Turkish example, in which a secular state was proclaimed in 1924, should be examined to determine how far the frontier between public/private spheres has moved in the 77 years of political struggle. I am not speaking only of the socio-legal, visible frontier, but of the psychological, invisible motivations, needs, hopes and criteria also traced in the present conflicting contexts, the deep fault lines between men and women.

All religions and systems of ethics are a matter for scientific research, philosophical debate, sociological and anthropological reassessment. This cannot be done without the protection of a rule of law and the support of a pluralist civil society in which many traditions of thought, many postures of mind and many religious experiences can be tackled. For this precise reason, I repeat that the building capacity of any level of ethical reasoning and judgement is a totally different task and will lead to different consequences in the fields of education, governance and construction of the human subject depending on where it is performed, whether in the arena of lay citizenship or under the control of an official religion imposed by the state. There is a cognitive, philosophical, legal and psychological barrier between the modern and the religious regime of truth. Because such a barrier has existed in Europe since the seventeenth and eighteenth centuries, it became one of the decisive criteria to assess a typology of political regimes, civil societies, the philosophy of law and the status of human subjects which are favourable or hostile to the expansion of an enabling, emancipating, sustainable civil society with the rule of law as its necessary partner. Like all criteria, that which I mention is fiercely debated among 'religious' believers and '*laïc*/secular' believers. In both spheres, I speak of **believers** in order to avoid the unjust prejudice that religious believers are not open to scientific criticism, while secular minds are necessarily supporters of enlightening scientific knowledge. Secularism – *laïcism* in French – had and still has its believers, unconscious of the philosophical, social, psychological and political challenges of their belief, that exist just as they do in the case of a religious society. The Manichean division between the so-called traditional, conservative believers and the modern, enlightened, progressive citizens of a progressive, advanced *laic/* secular democracy, still governs the discourses of both militant parties, less and less in western societies, but more and more in Islamic contexts. In both positions, as in all doctrinal options, belief is always present. That is why the two opposing parties should start by discussing the place and the role of **belief** in their philosophical, theological, ethical, juridical, historical reasoning and judgement and their ability to make constructive contributions. This is not yet the case either among the defenders of either one option, nor among scholars who specialise in these matters.[1] The fact is that the *laic/*secular state has generated a culture of systematic *disbelief*, rejecting religious reasoning and motivations in the obsolete past of the so-called Dark Ages, while the theocratic states have and are still imposing a stultified culture, rigid rituals and contingent 'sacred' law on their hapless subjects (it is not appropriate to call them 'citizens' in this case). Christian readers of this last statement will protest at its arbitrary generalization. I should add for their benefit that Roman Catholic Christianity resisted and is still resisting in many places the struggle of reasoning for autonomy and independence from any imposed statement about matters of knowledge, human beliefs and interpretations. We know how John-Paul II is exercising his theological *Magisterium* after Vatican II. Protestant Christianity, born as one of the first claims for modern intellectual freedom, is often linked with the emergence and growth of secular regimes and culture together with European capitalism. As for orthodox Christianity and Judaism they are in some aspects closer to the case of Islam than to the two first expressions of religion versus secularism. This is the historical and

1. There are exceptions, such as the Protestant theologian Pierre Gisel and the philosopher Paul Ricœur.

doctrinal platform from which we must start – at least as far as what I have described elsewhere as the 'societies of the Book-book' – to open a new historical space for rethinking the inherited systems of beliefs, values and norms, or thinking for the first time about the problems of the present and future.[1]

What are the implications for the civil society of this necessity to go beyond the dichotomist and the binary thinking of religion *versus* secularism?

A modern civil society should, of necessity, be pluralist. It provides all the individual citizens belonging to different ethnic, cultural and religious groups with all the required democratic freedoms. Debates are multi-faceted, cross-cultural, cross-disciplinary and are not subject to the restrictions imposed by monolithic religious, ideological communities or nation- states. Dichotomous thinking accepts the Aristotelian principles of contradiction and identity: a proposition is true or false, teaches good or evil. But pluralist logic is more flexible, offering a variety of ways and possibilities for expressing religious values and spiritual experiences through secular, political institutions or philosophical postures. In such a civil society, different cultures and world visions are not juxtaposed without significant appropriate interactions in the same space of citizenship, as has been the case so far in many democratic societies in which communities are situated in specific urban locations; *inter-creative* activities are made possible, even postulated, by the new style of thinking, the new political and legal concept of citizenship and the human subject.

3.3. The Status and Roles of 'Intellectuals'

The contributions of 'intellectuals'[2] to the conceptualization of civil society in Islamic contexts cannot be assessed if no

---

1. For more detailed analysis of the issues raised and concepts used in this paragraph, I refer to my book in Arabic, *Al-fikr al-uṣūlī wa-stiḥālat al-ta'ṣīl*, Dār al-Sāqī, 1999; see also Chapter 2 in the present book.

2. I refer to a long chapter on the status and functions of intellectuals in Islamic contexts, to be published in my *Penser l'Islam aujourd'hui*, op. cit.

definition is provided of their social and political status, strategies of intervention in the political and intellectual fields and the reception of their work compared to the large audiences of the *'ulamā'* who control religious orthodoxy. For our purpose here, it is more enlightening to evaluate the reception or rejection of their interventions than to insist, as is often done, on the eventual relevance and the substance of their work.

I have written 'intellectuals' in quotation marks to remind the reader of the yet unanswered question: what is an intellectual? In the French philosophical tradition of thought, this debate has been raging since the eighteenth century. Scholars and writers are not necessary intellectuals; physicians, lawyers, journalists, politicians and executives can be intellectuals. To reach the widest consensus about the status and role of the intellectual in any cultural tradition, I propose to consider the following attributes:

1. The *sine qua non* condition for a person to be considered as an intellectual is the constant commitment to the *critical function* regarding not only all the discussions about cognitive and scientific activity – debates shared in principle by all reputable scholars – but also all the important social, political, religious, ethical and legal issues raised in the current daily life in the limits of the nation-state as well as on the world level. For intellectuals, the critical quest for meaning and the right should in all circumstances prevail on any ideological option even if this option is shared by the greatest majority of the members of one's nation or community. The crucial point is that the critical function applied to concrete existential, social, political, ethical and legal debates should first focus on the suspicion of reason itself, just as the scientist remains suspicious of the results of his experiments in the laboratory. The intellectual is keen to generate, enrich and enlighten the debates with the purpose of enhancing the public awareness of the ultimate stakes of the discussed issues; thus, he brings precious contributions to the process of building a duly informed civil society with a shared civic responsibility and an emancipating sense of citizenship.

Every listener or reader should feel more enabled to share the critical thinking on the basis of more reliable information and ways to approach the problems under discussion.

2. The second attribute is the *intellectual, scientific, moral authority* to elucidate complex issues disputed among professionals, political parties, religious authorities, judges, philosophers, historians, etc. To gain this reputation, the intellectual needs to declare explicitly the epistemological postulates which command his own discourse and eventually his personal options as a citizen, believer or a defender of a particular case. This means that he has to listen to all the objections, and take any expressed disagreement seriously in order to rethink, adjust and absorb all relevant facts.

3. As a corollary of the attributes mentioned, the intellectual should always regain total *independence* from any political option, religious or philosophical commitment that would affect the authority of the critical function.

4. The discourse and writing of the intellectual should reflect at all times, all levels, the loyalty and fairness to the authors, the social actors and categories, the rulers, the communities, the doctrines, the peoples, the nations, the states, the cultures under debate.

I am aware that I am presenting an ideal archetype; intellectuals themselves need touchstones to pinpoint their positions and initiatives in a full scale of values and responsibilities. The reputation gained by the French writer Emile Zola with his letter '*J'accuse*', concerning the Dreyfus affair, or Voltaire with the Calas affair, shows how powerful intellectual writers such as the aforementioned or J. P. Sartre, M. Foucault and P. Bourdieu can be, though they also might lose respect, because they have not scrupulously respected the frontier between the critical function and political militancy on behalf of one party, social category, or particular interpretation.

In my *L'humanisme arabe au 4e/10e siècle*, I have shown to what extent the critical function has been claimed and discussed among intellectuals belonging to what I called the generation of Miskawayh (d. 1029) and Tawḥīdī (d. 1023). The mindset, cognitive options and the activities of these intellectuals in the Islamic polity (*al-madīna*) can be compared to those displayed on a larger scale, with more appropriate scientific tools and social support, by the European philosophers and writers of the seventeenth and eighteenth centuries. That is why scholars agree now to speak of 'Arab humanism' in that exceptional period favourable to the first ephemeral emergence of a type of civil society aware of the necessity and the conditions in which it could attain a 'virtuous city' – the *madīna fāḍila* described by al-Fārābī – based on a strong philosophical trend. In other words, the role of intellectuals in constructing a civil society is crucial either in fostering the process or in allowing it to slow down and fail. It is worth saying more about this dialectic because historically, attempts have been made in Islamic contexts to institute a civil society; but they soon failed, while, as has been said, the process in Europe has been sustained and has been gaining greater momentum since 1950–60.

I would like to focus on a responsibility that is specifically that of intellectuals, mindful of the social, economic and political contexts in which this responsibility can be fully implemented. To develop the concept of *intellectual responsibility* and its relationship to the process of constructing a civil society, I shall use two examples. One concerns the highest level of authority, namely the interpretation of the Qur'ānic verse 5, 44; the other refers to the lowest social status imposed on marginalized groups almost excluded from many rights theoretically guaranteed to all citizens.

The verse says:

> *We, indeed, did reveal the Thora wherein is guidance and light; by its norms, the prophets who bowed [to God's Will] judge the Jews; so do the rabbis (rabbāniyyūn) and the doctors of law (aḥbār), for having been entrusted to safeguard the revealed part of God's Book and they were its witnesses thereto. So fear not mankind, fear Me;*

> *do not sell My signs for a little gain. Whoso judges not by that God has revealed, such are disbelievers.*

The Shīʿī scholar Muḥammad Bāqir al-Ṣadr used this verse to contribute to the constitution of an Islamic state as Khomeini did in his book *The Rule of the Supreme Jurist* (*Walāyat al-faqīh*). The whole verse is interpreted as a commandment for the believer to intervene in political affairs. According to Bāqir al-Ṣadr, *rabbāniyyūn* refer to the twelve Shīʿī Imāms (known as the Twelver) and *aḥbār* are those authorities enabled to fulfil the function of *marjaʿ*, the supreme jurist who is, in the new constitution, the mouthpiece and the ultimate reference for the implementation of divine Law on earth. Since the political triumph of Khomeini's theory, this interpretation has been officially translated in terms of the constitutional law of the new Iranian Republic, under the leadership of learned authorities who monopolize control of Qur'ānic interpretation.

Faced with this concrete, historical situation, what would be the place, the role and the initiatives of intellectuals aware of the historical, doctrinal and legal objections to the normative interpretations of leading religious 'authorities' who enjoy the status of Bāqir al-Ṣadr, Khomeini and so many '*ulamā*'?

During the revolutionary struggle to defeat a political regime, there is no place whatsoever for intellectuals aspiring to the profile I have described. Some totally subscribe to the principles and goals of the revolution and become the leading ideologues during and after it; others keep silent or emigrate. This has been, and is still, the case in several contemporary societies. Of course, many intellectuals engaged in the battle become organic supporters of the triumphant single party-state; they could and do even argue against their fellow intellectuals who have chosen to fulfil the critical function beyond all ideological options. I personally have many colleagues and friends in the Maghreb and elsewhere who have suffered from this situation. Intellectual life and scientific research are considerably distorted, postponed and impoverished in such ideological conditions, since decision-making is monopolized by ideologues who continue to impose themselves as intellectuals dedicated to the construction of a modern polity. Critical debates on cultural and educational issues are very rare, unless influential members of the party initiate them. When the FLN party in Algeria had full control over the party, Mostefa Lacheraf, the Minister of Education who was respected as a critical intellectual and a loyal supporter of national independence, had to resign from office because he criticized the demagogic politics of arabisation. This is not an isolated example in the political practices of all post-colonial states.

Many reasons obliged many intellectuals to emigrate to Western democratic countries. This option translates clearly the difficulties and pressures imposed on intellectuals in their own countries. In the 1960s and 1970s, organic intellectuals condemned this attitude as a betrayal of sacred national obligations. Renouncing one's own nationality in order to accept the nationality of the colonizing nation-state was judged to be an insult to the heroes and martyrs who died for the liberation of the nation. This kind of moral pressure on many intellectuals generated a guilty conscience, which prevented each person from thinking and acting as a genuinely free citizen of both the original and the new country of citizenship. This psychological and moral aspect of intellectualism which spread all over the world, especially to Europe and North America, should not be minimized or ignored when one is asked evaluate the contribution of intellectuals to the positive development of their respective countries. They have solved their own problems in different ways. There are those who preferred to forget about their origins and who, with their families, became totally integrated into their chosen society. Others maintained a nostalgic link to their original, imagined identity '*waiting in the dreamed of future for the past to come*' to borrow the phrase used in a Tunisian novel by Ṣabīḥa Khemīr. Then there are those who decided to cross all the cultural, religious and nationalist boundaries to share with the new visionary thinkers, the humanist option for a world space of citizenship, using the historical platform of the emerging European Union. All ethnic, linguistic, religious, cultural and national groups and communities are represented in European and North American democratic societies. This is a unique opportunity offered to so many frustrated people, dramatically uprooted from their own culture, land, region and nation, to re-conquer new horizons of meaning and hope for their existence. Those intellectuals who are fully convinced of this privileged historical position – especially if they compare their position to that imposed on the previous generation immediately after the first liberation from colonial domination in the time of Cold War – will make a more efficient contribution to the new liberation of the people ignored, oppressed, exploited and submitted to tragic civil wars by their so-called national elites.

Whether inside or outside them, there are few intellectuals so far who have faced this responsibility regarding their native societies. The *'ulamā'*, on the other hand, have not emigrated; they are much closer to the lay people and have managed to perpetuate the old alliance with a patrimonial state exploiting society as its private, inherited property. This is the opposite of the modern status of a civil society. In the patrimonial regime, the head of state occupies second place in a vertical line descending from God to the ancestor of the clan and the father of the patriarchal family. While the state monopolizes power with its patrimonial logic, societies in Islamic contexts develop an underground system of exchange and regulation, parallel to the official 'legal' codes and bureaucracies. The word 'corruption' covers complex social and economic local practices called *bakhshīsh* and *trabendo*; practices that are tolerated as a functional dimension of the patrimonial state; they even reach an international level with what is described as *petro-Islam* and *business Islam,* with the support of the wealthy Arabian dynasties with their most deeply rooted patrimonial states. There are also patrimonial states disguised as democratic republics, including Indonesia, Algeria, Libya, Iraq, Syria and the Sudan. Algeria, still officially named the Algerian Democratic Popular Republic, is the country in which *trabendo* and what so-called *political financial mafias* have reached the structural importance described recently by Luis Martinez in *La guerre civile en Algérie*. Gilles Kepel in his *Expansion et déclin de l'islamisme*, gives other examples in the so-called Muslim world. The anthropological basis for the patrimonial, patriarchal system in Islamic contexts is clearly deconstructed by 'Abdallah Ḥammoudi in his *Masters and Disciples*, and Hishām Sharābī in *Neopatriarchy: A Theory of Distorted Change in Arab Society*.

The second example will produce enlightening conclusions about two conflicting models of the civil society in Islamic contexts. Soumaya N. Guessous, a Moroccan sociologist, published in the June, 2001 issue of the magazine *Femmes du Maroc*, an impressive report on the brokers who provide rich urban families with teenage girl servants. The whole text should be translated because it describes a large segment of rural society in which girls are used by their own parents as chattels displayed in the market for sale. 'Citizens' of high social and economic profile, from the learned, cultivated, wealthy class, accept to enslave teenaged girls wrenched from their families, thrown into a hostile urban environment and forced to toil day and night as servants. Furthermore, they are exposed to the sexual harassment of the young boys and even the father or other males close to the family. This is not peculiar to Moroccan society; it is a worldwide phenomenon that has been studied by NGOs and other international institutions. The problem remains: neither the state, nor the society as it is, nor the moneyed classes, nor even the religious authorities and intellectuals who have been so far unable to eradicate such an intolerable contradiction in societies such as Morocco in which significant steps are being made towards a promising civil society.

Another important aspect should be underlined here. The populist, political movements, generally described as the fundamentalist 'Muslims', display an ambivalent approach to the construction of a civil society. On the one hand, they provide the most relevant and significant social help and protection to those rural and urban population disabled, marginalized, excluded and often exploited both by the official middle class bureaucracy and the privileged socio-economic categories already mentioned. They cover health expenses for the poor; they provide transportation, material support and schooling for isolated families; contribute to maintaining a sense of morality among the younger generations cut off from their families and all traditional kinship protection. At the same time, they are developing their concept of an 'Islam' transformed into a *refuge*, or an ideological *springboard* from which to oust and replace the 'corrupted-corrupting materialist, secular' regimes. This positive and negative intervention in the building process of a civil society is a structural element of current developments in all Islamic contexts.

How is one to identify a civil society under such conditions? The wrong approach currently followed points to the constitutive attributes and practices of a consistent, coherent civil society as it is conceptualized and more or less achieved in advanced, democratic regimes. With this model in mind, one looks to detect signs, aspects, promises and institutions of a similar society in contemporary societies presented *a priori* as 'Islamic'. Other authors, mainly apologetic or militant Muslims, select formal, idealized attributes displayed in concrete democratic examples, to project them back on the imagined Islamic Model achieved in Medina under the guidance of Prophet Muḥammad; by this device, the contemporary Islamic (the so-called fundamentalist) discourse restores for the popular psyche the original, 'authentic' archetype (according to the well known sociological concept) achieved in a mythical time and space (Medina during 610–632), while, in concrete contemporary historical development, one can see the evidence of patrimonial states delaying and obstructing by the politics of *traditionalization* the emergence of a rule of law with its expressly civil society. Methodologically, the same critical analysis needs to be applied to the ongoing social dialectic between the forces of the common Islamic *imaginaire*, the persistence of the patrimonial political order sacralized and 'legitimized' by 'divine' Islamic Law and modern democratic culture imposed from the outside through international organizations and the worldwide expansion of scientific knowledge, the new economy, the new monetary order, and new technology. How do these three trends interact in each particular society? The effectiveness of intellectual modernity and secular institutions in societies like Tunisia, Morocco, Egypt, Syria and Turkey, needs to be more accurately differentiated by comparison with other countries which have different historical memories and sociological constraints such as the Sudan, Indonesia, Malaysia, Mali, Uzbekistan, etc. As long as political and social sciences stick to their linear, descriptive, fragmented surveys of turning points, isolated movements or ideologies, we shall remain ignorant of the underlying operating mechanisms and protagonists.

To summarize the central arguments concerning the rule of law and civil society in Islamic contexts, past and present, I can propose the following brief statements in the hope to enlarge, deepen and enhance scientific research and enrich the debate with more concrete facts, more examples of experiences developed here and there in contemporary societies. I wish that my propositions had been received and used as *heuristic hypothesis*, because there is still a long way to go in Islamic contexts to achieve the rule of law claimed everywhere in the dreamed of civil society. Even the level of democratic practices and institutions already achieved and in process of improvement in the Western and Scandinavian European societies, goes a long way to achieving this goal.

1. The biological and social sciences have established the constraining evidence that the activities of the human mind are all based on and conditioned by bio-socio-historical mechanisms. Philosophers draw conclusions from this evidence; but theologians and managers of the sacred resist this 'materialist', reductionist theory. The collapse of the Marxist-Communist ideology has liberated an area of scientific research and critical reassessment of the dichotomist, binary framework of analysis and interpretation concerning the two conflicting spheres of spiritual authority *versus* political power (*ḥukm/sulṭa; auctoritas/potestas*), intangible ethical principles and virtues *versus* relational truths and values, sacred law and contingent law. But such scientific leaps are not integrated into the populist culture and ways of reasoning used in daily life, educational practices and social and official discourses. This discrepancy is, of course, far wider and more influential in Islamic contexts.

2. The content, functions and authority of religion are changing profoundly under the impact of the new forces and options offered by globalization. The problem for Islam and Muslims is to know whether they should resist against these forces as they did modernity, or whether globalization will be more effective in changing the status of the state and political institutions, the collective mentalities concerning traditional beliefs, rituals and values, educational practices, channels of communication and the relationship to scientific knowledge, especially in the domain of human, social, political and legal sciences. The changes that might take place are unpredictable, because all the societies considered in this essay are under-analysed, or as it used to be put, they are economically and culturally underdeveloped. Not only is scholarship a very slow process, but institutions for scientific research and learning, well-trained scholars and professors, educational and cultural activities are either rare, or poorly-funded and ill-prepared for heavy and difficult tasks. So how can the problems, demands and expectations be tackled of so many peoples who are forced to make use of obsolete knowledge, archaic bureaucracy, disintegrated urban spaces and architecture, decontextualized beliefs, values and references?

3. According to these historical statements, it becomes irrelevant to keep asking whether or not Islam is compatible with secularism, democracy and human rights. Islam is controlled by the state; there is strong opposition to establishing a secular, liberal regime, and a desire to substitute it for a more 'authentic orthodox' Islamic regime following the example of Iranian Islamic revolution. In terms of theology, if any political regime monopolizes the control of Islam, it loses its legitimacy *ipso facto*. That is why, the caliphate, the imamate, the sultanate, the emirates and the so-called republican regimes of today pay a college of official *'ulamā'* to maintain a fiction of religious legitimacy.[1] I use the following expression to

1. See Malika Zeghal, *Gardiens de l'Islam: Les oulémas d'al-Azhar dans l'Egypte contemporaine*, Paris, 1996.

describe this historical and doctrinal situation of Islam: **Islam is theologically Protestant and politically Catholic.**

4. Contemporary societies use many devices for resisting and overcoming the oppressive policies of their regimes; but they have greater difficulties when the vast majority of the female population is confined to the home and private domestic activities and there is an increasing number of jobless, illiterate, homeless orphans cut from any collective memory, deprived of a promising vision of the future, unconscious of the rights attached to modern citizenship and consequently unable to discover and respect the necessity and the functions of the connection between society and social responsibility. Sociologists do not address this crucial issue often enough, because the silent majority of the population can be heard only when it resorts to demonstrations, rioting and violence. So where are the chances and opportunities that promote the emergence of a modern enabling civil society? With slight modifications, these structural impediments are to be found today in all Islamic contexts.

5. Can the paradigms of contemporary international relations accelerate the shift of post-colonial or Third World states from their patrimonial, patriarchal order to the democratic features and functions of the rule of law? Confronted with modern pluralist states, all the authoritarian states present themselves as full supporters of democratic values and institutions; but their domestic policy remains contrary to this image which is merely for show. To achieve empowerment through the 'governed' population, the state should pay more attention to developing a relevant culture of citizenship that provides greater social cohesion, less division and tension between the heterogenous collective psyche, a high level of universal education, adequate distribution and maintenance of skills and a humanist vision through the building process of national purposes. It is a historical fact that these conditions were very seldom fulfilled or even thought of in that perspective in any known Third World

state. It is true that the leap from a bipolar to multi-polar world has resulted in more instability, violence, wars and a single major power dictating the international agenda. '*We (USA) will retain the pre-eminent responsibility for addressing selectively those who are wrong, who threaten not only our interests, but those of our allies or friends, who could seriously unsettle international relations*' (Arab Studies Quarterly, 1993, vol. 15/4, p. 15).

6. The whole of the present chapter can be re-written under the general title '*Umma* and Civil Society'. *Umma* as a spiritual Utopia was inaugurated with the prophetic discourse, developed and enriched through a great diversity of religious, political, ethical and social experiences, articulated intellectually in a large number of major works. This *umma* is still alive as a terrestrial and eschatological hope, project and aspiration in the collective minds of millions of believers. The main problem to be addressed today that is facing the modern secular unachieved – unachievable? – plan of civil society is the following: does the traditional Utopia of the *umma* with its specific culture and mindsets, constitute an intellectual, spiritual, ethical and legal obstacle to the acceptance and contribution of the historically advanced building process of a modern, secular, civil society? Conversely, does such a civil society which is still an idealized imaginary one, pursued and partially achieved in the democratic regimes of Western Europe and North America, present ontological, spiritual, ethical and humanistic perspectives for the overall emancipation of the human condition, which definitely supersede those taught and still held valid by the traditional religions and their adherents? Expressed in these terms, the problem requires much critical, modern investigation using comparative history and the anthropology of all religious and secular systems of thought and action.

7. There is a last vital problem concerning not only the 'rest of the world', but the powerful hegemonic Western states where the intellectual and scientific agenda is defined, fixed, prescribed, although continuously debated, and imposed on the future of

human existence and the status of human dignity. It is clear from the themes, questions and points, that I have raised throughout this book that tele-techno-scientific reasoning coupled with the Management of the so-called Human Resources (MHR), are mobilizing all human attention and energy in the service of the free market. Anthropology as cultural criticism, ethical definition of the limits in which any historical action by an individual or a community should take place, philosophical resistance to any form of violence justified by the promise of liberation from oppression and the negation of human dignity, are minimized, narrowed, neglected, disqualified, if not declared useless whenever the 'rights', 'interests', and 'comfort' of those in a hegemonic position are threatened. What is left then to those on the side of the victims, the oppressed, those 'without history' to be fully admitted among those who hold the monopoly on being the dignified? We know the answer of the revolutionary movements for liberation since the British, American and French Revolutions to Lenin, Stalin, Trotsky, Milosevic and all twentieth century leaders of wars against colonial domination who led criminally devastating operations to end up with even more violence, collective tragedies, semantic disorder and intellectual perversions still expanding at the dawn of the twenty-first century. If we are to consider the significance of the tragic failure of 'Western' reason on the horizon of meaning and hope for all living peoples on our small planet, we should also rethink the case, still unthought, of Hitler and his 'final solution'. To enlighten this crucial point, I add this ethical principle:

For the third millennium, the struggle against semantic disorder and perversions of the intellect should supersede, precede and be sustained in all cultures, religions, systems of thought and political regimes whenever there is a historical necessity to initiate a war of liberation from oppression, domination and exclusion. Violence is a fact to be contained, refused, eradicated by all means; it is not a thesis to be discussed, be it the structural violence codified, legalized everywhere in all cultures and religions, or the physical, military violence. There is no way to legitimize any level, any form of violence between human beings or against animals and the environment, as long as human beings are unable to find the irreversible way out from what I called the anthropological triangle of **violence, sacred and Truth**'.

Select Bibliography

The guiding principles to establish this bibliography are those required by *historical epistemology*: in all times, all scientific and cultural contexts, articulating meaning in a given language is always commanded by implicit and/or explicit postulates that are more or less shared by the author, whoever the author may be, with a trend, a school of thought of his time, an official ideology, a belief or non-belief system. Each trend or school is itself related to the common *épistémè* which traces the limits of reasoning in a given period of the history of each logosphere. There are English, German, French, Arabic, Chinese, Latin and Greek logospheres. The selection is determined by the introductory remarks on the present situation characterized by an emerging reasoning from the still existing, competing, conflicting inherited frameworks of thought in contemporary logospheres, including the conflicting logospheres of 'Islam' and the 'West'. I could not include German, Italian and Spanish bodies of literature because I do not have a sufficient command of these languages. As for Arabic scholarly production, I consider it to be the primary source that a researcher-thinker should master and know perfectly; so from that viewpoint, I cannot make a relevant distinction between ancient classical sources and contemporary sources. The most erudite scholarly literature provides scientific and psychological information; but I am more interested in the way in which it could illustrate the central issue studied in the present book. Other scholars and thinkers who have mastered the main languages used in Islamic contexts will, I hope, contribute to the kind of research and thought that I have been trying to introduce for three decades. From my perspective, a comprehensive critical bibliography in Arabic, Persian and Turkish languages is terribly missing; I am still working on a bibliography of Arabic production.

'Abed, Shukri B. (ed.) *Aristotelian Logic and the Arabic Language in al-Fārābī*, New York: SUNY, 1991.

'Ajina, Muhammad: *Mawsū'at asāṭīr al-'arab 'ani-l-jāhiliyya wa dalālātuhā*, vols I-II, Beirut, 1994.

Akbar, A. and Hastings, D. (eds.) *Islam, Globalisation and Postmodernity*, London: Routledge, 1994.

Aktouf, 'Omar *Traditional Management and Beyond. A Matter for Renewal*, Paris: Morin, 1996.

Alter, Robert: *L'art du récit biblique*, Antwerp: Lessius, 2000.

Amir-Moezzi, M. A.(ed.) *Le voyage initiatique en terre d'islam. Ascensions célestes et itinéraires spirituels*, Leuven; Peeters, 1996.

Annales, Economies, Societés, Civilisations, Paris: Editions Armand Colin.

Archives de Sciences Sociales des Religions: Croire et modernité, Paris: CNRS, 1993/81.

Astington, Janet Wilde *Comment les enfants découvrent la pensée*, Paris: Editions Retz, 1999.

Audouard, Xavier *Sortir de la croyance : L'ici-au-delà*, Paris: L'Harmattan, 1997.

al-'Azmeh, 'Aziz *Muslim Kinship. Power and the Sacred in Muslim, Christian and Pagan Polities*, London and New York: I.B. Tauris, 1997.

Badiou, Alain *Saint Paul: La fondation de l'universalisme*, Paris: PUF, 1997.

Ballantyne, W. M. *Essays and Addresses on Arab Laws*, London: Curzon, 2000.

Bar-Asher, Meir M. *Scripture and Exegesis in Early Shiism*, Leiden: Brill, 1999.

Bashear, S. *Arabs and Others in Early Islam*, Princeton: Darwin Press, 1997.

Bedarida, F. *L'histoire et le métier d'historien en France (1945–1995)*, Paris: Maison des Sciences de l'Homme, 1995.

Bensaid, Daniel *Marx l'intempestif: Grandeurs et misères d'une aventure critique*, Paris: Fayard, 1995.

Benmakhlouf, Ali *La raison et la question des limites*, Casablanca: Editions Le Fennec, 1997.

Bleuchot, Hervé *Les cultures contre l'homme? Essai d'anthropologie historique du droit pénal soudanais*, Aix-en-Provence: Presses Universitaires d'Aix-Marseille, 1994.

Bloch, Maurice *La violence du religieux*, Paris: Editions Odile Jacob, 1997.

Bois, Guy *La grande dépression médiévale: XIV-XVes siècles; le précédent d'une crise systémique*, Paris: PUF, 2000.

—— *La Mutation de l'an mil: Lournand, village mâconnais de l'Antiquité au féodalisme*, Paris: Fayard, 1989.

Boon, James *Other Tribes, Other Scribes: Symbolic Anthropology in the Comparative Study of Cultures, Histories, Religions and Texts*, Cambridge: CUP, 1982.

Botiveau, Bernard *Loi islamique et droit dans les sociétés arabes*, Paris: Karthala-IREMAM, 1993.

Brockopp, Jonathan E. *Early Mālikī Law. Ibn 'Abd al-Ḥakam and his Major Compendium of Jurisprudence*, Leiden: Brill, 2000.

Boutier J. and Julia D. *Passés recomposés: Champs et chantiers de l'histoire*, Paris: Autrement, no. 150–151, 1995.

Brunner, R. and Ende, W. *The twelver Shī'a in Modern Times*, Leiden: Brill, 2001.

Bulliet, Richard W. *Islam. The View from the Edge*, New York: Columbia University Press, 1994.

Burton, John *The Sources of Islamic Law: Islamic Theories of Abrogation*, Edinburgh: EUP, 1990.

Calder, Norman *Studies in Early Muslim Jurisprudence*, Oxford: Clarendon Press, 1993.

Canto-Sperber, Monique *Dictionnaire d'Ethique et de philosophie morale*, Paris: PUF, 1997.

Caroll, D. (ed.) *The States of 'Theory': History, Art and Critical Discourse*, New York: Columbia University Press, 1990.

Carter, Stephen *Culture of Disbelief: How American Law and Politics Trivialize Religious Devotion*, New York: Anchor Books, 1993.

Chabbi, Jacqueline *Le Seigneur des tribus: L'Islam de Mahomet*, Paris: Noêsis, 1996.

Chabry, Laurent and Annie *Identités et stratégies politiques dans le monde arabo-musulman*, Paris: L'Harmattan, 2001.

Chaumont, Eric *Le livre des rais illuminant les fondements de la compréhension de la loi. Traité de théorie légale musulmane, traduction du Kitāb al-luma' fī uṣūl al-fiqh d'Abū Isḥāq Ibrāhīm al-Shīrāzī (m. 476/1083)*, Berkeley: Robbins collection, 1999.

Colonna, Fanny *Les versets de l'invincibilité*, Paris: Presses de la fondation nationale des sciences politiques, 1995.

Comte-Sponville, André and Ferry, Luc *La sagesse des modernes. Dix questions pour notre temps*, Paris: Editions Robert Laffont, 1998.

Cook, Michael *Commanding Right and Forbidding Wrong in Islamic Thought*, Cambridge: CUP, 2000.

Crone, Patricia *Roman, Provincial and Islamic Law*, Cambridge: CUP, 1987.

Crone, P. and Zimmermann, F. W. *The Epistle of Sālim ibn Dhakwān*, Oxford: OUP, 2001.

Dakhliya, Jocelyne *Le divan des rois. Le politique et le religieux dans l'Islam*, Paris: Aubier, 1998.

Dartiguenave, Jean-Yves *Rites et ritualité. Essai sur l'altération sémantique de la ritualité*, Paris: L'Harmattan, 2001.

Debashi, Ḥamīd *Truth and Narrative. The Untimely Thoughts of 'Ayn al-Quḍāt al-Hamadhānī*, London: Curzon, 1999.

Donner, Fred M. *Narratives of Islamic Origins. The Beginnings of Islamic Historical Writing*, Princeton: Darwin Press, 1998.
Duchet, Michèle *Anthropologie et histoire au siècle des Lumières*, Paris: Editions Albin Michel, 1995.
Duprat, Annie *Le roi décapité: Essai sur les imaginaires politiques*, Paris: Editions du Cerf, 1993.
Dupret, Baudouin *Au nom de quel droit?*, Paris: CEDEJ, 2000.
Dutton, Yāsīn *The Origins of Islamic Law*, London: Curzon, 1999.

Ellis, John M. *Against Deconstruction*, Princeton: PUP, 1989.
ESS, Josef van: *Theologie und Gesellschaft im 2 und 3 Jahr hundert Hidschra. Eine Geschichte des religiösen Denkens im frühen Islam*, 6 vols, Berlin: De Gruyter, 1991–1997.
Fernhout, Rein *Canonical Texts. Bearers of Absolute Authority. Bible, Koran, Veda, Tipitaka*, Amsterdam: Editions Rodopi Bv, 1994.
Firestone, Reuvin *Jihad: The Origin of Holy war in Islam*, Oxford: OUP, 1999.
Flori, Jean *Pierre L'Hermite et la première croisade*, Paris: Fayard, 1999.
—— *Croisade et chevalerie*, Paris and Bruxelles: De Boek Université, 1999.
Fontana Dictionary of Modern Thought, 2nd ed., London: Harper Collins, 1999.
Fontenay, E. de *Le silence des bêtes: La philosophie à l'épreuve de l'animalité*, Paris: Fayard, 1998.
Fukuyama, Francis *The End of History and the Last Man*, London: Macmillan, 1992.
Fraade, Steven D. *From Tradition to Commentary: Torah and its Interpretation in the Midrash Sifre to Deuteronomy*, New York: SUNY, 1991.
Gauchet, Marcel *Révolution des pouvoirs*, Paris: Gallimard, 1995.
—— *La religion dans la démocratie: Parcours de la laïcité*, Paris: Gallimard, 1998.
Geertz, Clifford *After the Fact: Two Countries, Four Decades, One Anthropologist*, Cambridge: HUP, 1994.
Gellner, E. *Post-modernism, Reason and Religion*, London: Routledge, 1992.
Gerber, Haim *Islamic Law and Culture, 1600–1840*, Leiden: Brill, 1999.
Gilliot, Claude *Exégèse, langue et théologie en islam: L'exégèse coranique de Ṭabarī*, Paris: Vrin, 1990.
Girard, René *Je vois Satan tomber comme l'éclair*, Paris: Editions Grasset, 1999.
Gisel, Pierre *La théologie face aux sciences religieuses*, Geneva: Labor et Fides, 1999.
Gisel, Pierre and Evrard, Patrick (eds) *La théologie en postmodernité*, Geneva: Labor et Fides, 1996.

Gleave, Robert *Inevitable Doubt: Two Theories of Shīʿī Jurisprudence*, Leiden: Brill, 2000.
Gleave, R. and Kermely, E. *Islamic Law. Theory and Practice*, London and New York: I.B. Tauris, 2001.
Goldingay, John *Models for Interpretation of Scripture*, Carlisle: Paternoster Press, 1995.
Goody, Jack *The Domestication of the Savage Mind*, Cambridge: CUP, 1977.
Gosselin, Gabriel and Lavaud, Jean-Pierre *Ethnicité et mobilisations sociales*, Paris: L'Harmattan, 2001.
Graham, William *Divine Word and Prophetic Word in Early Islam: A Reconsideration of the Sources, with Special Reference to the Divine Saying, or Ḥadīth Qudsī*, The Hague: Mouton, 1977.
—— *Beyond the Written Word. Oral Aspects of Scripture in the History of Religion*, Cambridge: CUP, 1987.
Greimas, A. J. and Courtes, J. *Sémiotique. Dictionnaire raisonné de la théorie du langage*, Paris vol. 1, 1979; vol. 2, 1986.
Gutas, Dimitri *Greek Thought, Arabic Culture*, London: Routledge, 1998.
Habermas, J. *Critique de la raison fonctionaliste*, Paris: Fayard, 1987.
Habermas, J.: *Der philosophische diskurs der Moderne*, Frankfurt/Main: Suhrkamp, 1985.
Halbwachs, Maurice *La topographie légendaire des évangiles en terre sainte: Etude de mémoire collective*, Paris: PUF, 1941.
Hall, John A. (ed.) *Civil Society: Theory, History, Comparison*, Cambridge: Polity Press, 1995.
Ḥallāq, Wā'el B. *Law and Legal Theory in Classical and Medieval Islam*, London: Variorum Reprints, 1992.
—— *A History of Islamic Legal Theories: An introduction to Sunnī Uṣūl al-Fiqh*, Cambridge: CUP, 1997.
—— *Ibn Taymiyya against the Greek Logicians*, Oxford: Clarendon Press, 1993.
Ḥammoudi, Abdallah *Masters and Disciples*, Oxford: Clarendon Press, 1993.
Henderson, John B. *Scripture, Canon and Commentary: A Comparison of Confucian and Western Exegesis*, Princeton: PUP, 1991.
Hervieu-Leger, D. *La religion pour mémoire*, Paris: Editions du Cerf, 1993.
El-Hibri, Ṭayyeb *Reinterpreting Islamic Historiography: Hārūn al-Rashīd and the Narrative of the ʿAbbāsīd Caliphate*, Cambridge: CUP, 1999.
Hick, John *An Interpretation of Religion: Human Responses to Transcendent*, London: Macmillan, 1989.
History and Theory (journal).
Hooker, Morna D. *The Signs of a Prophet. The Prophetic Actions of Jesus*, London: SCM Press, 1997.

Hoyland, R. G. *Seeing Islam as Others Saw it: A Survey and Evaluation of Christian, Jewish and Zoroastrian Writings on Early Islam*, Princeton: PUP, 1997.

Humphreys, R. S. *Islamic History Revised*, Princeton: PUP, 1991.

Humphreys, R. S. *Between Memory and Desire. The Middle East in a Troubled Age*, Berkeley: University of California Press, 1999.

Iogna-Prat, Dominique *Ordonner et exclure: Cluny et la société chrétienne face à l'hérésie, au Judaïsme et à l'Islam*, Paris: Aubier, 1998.

Jackson, Sherman *Islamic Law and the State: The Constitutional Jurisprudence of Shihāb al-dīn al-Qarāfī*, Leiden: Brill, 1996.

Jammard, J-L., Terray, E. and Xanthakou, M. (eds) *En substances, textes pour François Héritier*, Paris: Fayard, 2000.

Journal of Islamic Law and Society, Leiden: Brill, 1994.

Johansen, Baber: *Contingency in a Sacred Law: Legal and Ethical Norms in the Muslim Fiqh*, Leiden: Brill, 1999.

Kelsen, H. *Théorie générale du droit et de l'état, suivi de la doctrine du droit naturel et le positivisme juridique*, Brussels: Librairie générale de droit et de jurisprudence, 1997.

Khālidi, Ṭarif *Arab Historical Thought in the Classical Period*, Cambridge: CUP, 1995.

Kozakaï, Toshiaki *L'étranger, l'identité. Essai sur l'intégration culturelle*, Lausanne: Payot, 2001.

Kugel, James L. *The Bible as it Was*, Cambridge: Belknap Press, 1997.

Kohlberg, Etan *Belief and Law in Imāmī Shī'ism*, London: Variorum Reprints, 1991.

Lacoste, J. Yves *Dictionnaire de théologie*, Paris: PUF, 1998.

Lagardère, Vincent *La vie sociale et économique de l'Espagne musulmane aux 11e et 12e siècles à travers les fatwas du Mi'yār d'al-Wansharīsī*, Madrid: Mélanges de la Casa Velasquez and Paris: Editions de Boccard, 1990.

Lambert, Jean *Le Dieu distribué: Une anthropologie comparée des monothéismes*, Editions du Cerf, 1995.

Laot, Laurento *La laïcité, un défi mondial*, Paris: Editions de l'Atelier, 1998.

Layish, Aharon *Bedouin of the Judean Desert: Islamization of a Tribal Society: A Study Based on Legal Documents of Arbitrators and Sharī'a Court.*

Lecker, Michael *Muslims, Jews and Pagans: Studies on Early Islamic Medina*, Leiden: Brill, 1995.

Leeuwen, Richard van *Waqfs and Urban Structures: The Case of Ottoman Damascus*, Leiden: Brill, 1999.

Lepetit, Bernard *Les formes de l'expérience: Une autre histoire sociale*, Paris: Editions Albin Michel, 1995.

Levering, Miriam (ed.) *Rethinking Scripture: Essays from a Comparative Perspective*, New York: SUNY, 1989.
Lloyd, Geoffrey E. R. *Demystifying Mentalities*, Cambridge: CUP, 1990.
Lüdemann, Gerd *The Unholy in the Holy Scripture: The Dark Side of the Bible*, London: Westminster John Knox Press, 1997.
Lurol, Gérard *E. Mounier: Le lieu de personne*, Paris: L'Harmattan, 2000.
McChesney, R. D. *Waqf in Central Asia: Four Hundred Years in the History of a Muslim Shrine, 1480–1889*, Princeton: PUP, 1991.
Madelung, Wilferd *The Succession to Muḥammad: A Study of the Early Caliphate*, Cambridge: CUP, 1996.
Madigan, D. A. *The Qur'ān's Self-image. Writing and Authority in Islam's Scripture*, Princeton: PUP, 2001.
Magonet, Jonathan *The Subversive Bible*, London: SCM Press, 1997.
Makdisi, Georges *Ibn 'Aqīl: Religion and Culture in Classical Islam*, Edinburg: EUP, 1997.
Mallāṭ, Shibli *The Renewal of Islamic Law*, Cambridge: CUP, 1993.
Malrieu, Philippe *La construction des imaginaires*, Paris: L'Harmattan, 2000.
Mardin, Serif *The Genesis of Young Ottoman Thought: A Study in the Modernisation of Turkish Political Ideas*, Syracuse: Syracuse University Press, 2000.
Martinez, Luis *La guerre civile en Algérie*, Paris: Karthala, 1998.
Martinez-Gros, Gabriel *L'idéologie omeyyade: La construction de la légitimité du Califat de Cordoue*, Madrid: Bibliothèque de la Casa de Velázquez, 1992.
Mas'ūd, Muḥammad Kh., Messick, Brinkley and Powers, David (eds): *Islamic Legal Interpretation. Muftis and their Fatwas*, Cambridge: HUP, 1996.
Mas'ūd, Muḥammad Kh. *Iqbāl's Reconstruction of Ijtihād*, Lahore: Iqbal Academy, 1995.
Melchert, Christopher *The Formation of the Sunnī Schools of Law, 9th–10th Centuries*, Leiden: Brill, 1997.
Merlin, Donald *Origins of the Modern Mind: Three Stages in the Evolution of Culture and Cognition*, Cambridge: HUP, 1991.
Meslin, M. *L'expérience humaine du divin*, Paris: Editions du Cerf, 1988.
Minois, Georges *Histoire de l'athéisme*, Paris: Fayard, 1998.
Moaddel, Mansoor *Class, Politics and Ideology in the Iranian Revolution*, New York: Columbia University Press, 1993.
Mojaddidi, Jawīd A. *The Biographical Tradition in Sufism*, London: Curzon, 2001.
Momigliano, Arnaldo *Problèmes d'historiographie ancienne et moderne*, Paris: Gallimard, 1983.

Namer, Gérard *Halbwachs et la mémoire sociale*, Paris: L'Harmattan, 2000.

Nāṣir, Jamāl *The Islamic Law of Personal Status*, London: Graham and Trotman Ltd, 1990.

Nerhot, Patrick *Law, Writing, Meaning. An Essay in Legal Hermeneutics*, Edinburgh: EUP, 1992.

Newman, Andrew J. *The Formative Period of Twelver Shī'ism: Ḥadīth as Discourse between Qum and Baghdād*, London: Curzon, 2000.

Nock, Arthur Darby *Conversion: The Old and the new in Religion from Alexander the Great to Augustine of Hippo*, Baltimore: Johns Hopkins University Press, 1998.

Noth, Albrecht *The Early Arabic Historical Tradition: A Source Critical Study*, 2nd edn with L. I. Conrad, Princeton: Darwin Press, 1994.

Nyiri, J. C.: *Tradition and Individuality*, Dordrecht: Kluwer Academic Publishers, 1992.

Patton, Laurie L., ed. *Authority, Anxiety and Canon: Essays in the Vedic Interpretation*. New York: SUNY 1994.

Pearl, David *A Text Book on Muslim Law*, London: Croom Helm, 1979.

Pellat, Charles (ed.) *The Life and Works of al-Jāḥiẓ*, London: Routledge, 1969.

Peters, F. E. *Muhammad and the Origins of Islam*, New York: SUNY, 1994.

Porter, Roy *The Creation of the Modern World*, New York: W.W. Norton & Company, 2000.

Posner, R. *Sex and Reason*, Princeton: HUP, 1992.

Powers, David *Studies in the Qur'ān and the Ḥadīth: The Formation of the Islamic Law of Inheritance*, Berkeley: University of California Press, 1986.

Price, Daniel E. *Islamic Political Culture: Democracy and Human Rights: A Comparative Study*, Westport: Praeger Pub Text, 1999.

Rawls, John *Political liberalism*, Cambridge: CUP, 1993.

Raynaud, Ph. and Rials, Stéphane *Dictionnaire de philosophie politique*, Paris: PUF, 1997.

Rémond, René *Religion et société en Europe*, Paris: Editions du Seuil, 1998.

Resweber, Jean-Paul *Le pari de la transdisciplinarité: Vers l'intégration des savoirs*, Paris: L'Harmattan, 2000.

Reynolds, D.F. (ed.) *Interpreting the Self: Autobiography in the Arabic Literary Tradition*, Berkeley: University of Cal ifornia Press, 2001.

Riche, Pierre *Les grandeurs de l'an mille*, Paris: Bartillat Editions, 1999.

Ricœur, Paul *La critique et la conviction*, Paris: Editions Calmann-Lévy, 1995.

—— *La mémoire, l'histoire, l'oubli*, Paris: Editions du Seuil, 2000.

Ricœur, Paul et LaCoque, André *Penser la Bible*, Paris: Editions du Seuil, 1998.

Rippin, A. (ed.) *Approaches to the History of the Interpretation of the Qur'ān*, Oxford: Clarendon Press, 1988.

Rosen, Lawrence *The Anthropology of Justice. Law as Culture in Islamic Society*, Cambridge: CUP, 1989.

Rosenfeld, Michel *Just Interpretations: The Law between Ethics and Politics*, Berkeley: University of California Press, 1998.

Rossi, Paolo *La naissance de la science moderne en Europe*, Paris: Editions du Seuil, 1999.

Rouland, Norbert *Introduction historique au droit*, Paris: PUF, 1998.

Rubin, Uri *The Eye of the Beholder: The life of Muḥammad as Viewed by the Early Muslims*, Princeton: Darwin Press, 1995.

Sacks, Jonathan *Politics of Hope*, London: Jonathan Cape, 1997.

Saint-Sernin, Bertrand *La raison au XXe siècle*, Paris: Editions du Seuil, 1995.

Sanguin, André-Louis (s.d.) *Mare Nostrum: Dynamiques et mutations géopolitiques de la Méditerranée*, Paris: L'Harmattan, 2000.

Savage, Elizabeth *A Gateway to Hell, a Gateway to Paradise: The North African Response to the Arab Conquest*, Princeton: PUP, 1997.

Schmitt, J. Cl. et LE GOFF, J. *Dictionnaire raisonné du Moyen-Age*,Paris: Editions Fayard, 1999.

Serjeant, R. B *Customary and Sharī'a Law in Arabian Society*, London: Variorum Reprints, 1991.

al-Shāfi'ī *La Risāla: Les fondements du droit musulman*, traduit et annoté par Lakhdar Souami, Paris: Sindbad, 1997.

Sharābī, Hishām *Neopatriarchy: A Theory of Distorted Change in Arab Society*, Oxford: OUP, 1988.

Shaykh al-Mufīd *Kitāb al-irshād, (The Book of Guidance)*, tr. by I. K. A. Howard, London: Balāgha Books/The MuhammadiTrust of Great Britain and Northern Ireland, 1981.

Shinn, Tery 'structures épistémologiques des relations Nord-Sud', in *Les sciences hors d'Occident au XXe siècle*, Colloque UNESCO, 19–23/9/1994.

Stetkevych, Jaroslav *Muḥammad and the Golden Bough: Reconstructing Arabian Myth*, Cambridge: CUP, 1996.

Stewart, D. J., Johansen, B. and Singer A. *Law and Society in Islam*, Princeton: Markus Wiener Publishers, 1996.

Stewart, Devin *Islamic Legal Orthodoxy: Twelver Shī'ite Responses to the Sunnī Legal System*, Salt Lake City: University of Utah Press, 1998.

Stroumsa, Sarah *Free Thinkers of Medieval Islam: Ibn al-Rāwandī, Abū Bakr al-Rāzī and their impact on Islamic Thought*, Leiden: Brill, 1999.

al-Ṭabarī *The History of al-Ṭabarī*, vol. 1, tr. by F. Rosenthal, New York: SUNY, 1989; and vol. 28, tr. by J. D. McAuliffe, New York: SUNY, 1995.

Tardieu, Michel *La formation des Canons scripturaires*, Paris: Editions du Cerf, 1993.

Todorov, Tzvetan *Le jardin imparfait*, Paris: Grasset, 1998.

Touati, Houari *Islam et voyage au Moyen-Age*, Paris: Editions du Seuil, 2000.

Valdès, Mario (ed.) *A Ricœur Reader: Reflection and Imagination*, Toronto: University of Toronto Press, 1991.

Vansina, Jan *Oral Tradition as History*, Madison: University of Wisconsin Press, 1985.

Versteegh, C. H. M. *Arabic Grammar and Qur'ānic Exegesis in Early Islam*, Leiden: Brill, 1993.

Veyne, Paul *Comment on écrit l'histoire: essai d'épistémologie*, Paris: Editions du Seuil, 1970.

Wansbrough, John *The Sectarian Milieu*, Oxford: OUP, 1978.

Warnke, Georgia *Justice and Interpretation*, Boston: MIT, 1993.

Weinstein, Fred *History and Theory after the Fall: An Essay on Interpretation*, Chicago: University of Chicago Press, 1990.

Weiss, Bernard G. *The Search for God's Law: Islamic Jurisprudence in the Writings of Sayf al-dīn al-'Amidī*, Salt Lake City: University of Utah Press, 1992.

—— *The Spirit of Islamic Law*, Athens: University of Georgia Press, 1998.

Wheeler, Brannon M. *Applying the Canon in Islam: The Authorization and Maintenance of Interpretive Reasoning in Ḥanafī Scholarship*,, New York: SUNY, 1996.

White, James Boyd *Heracles' Bow: Essays on the Rhetoric and Poetics of the Law*, Madison: University of Wisconsin Press, 1985.

—— *Justice as Translation: An Essay in Cultural and Legal Criticism*, Chicago: Chicago University Press, 1990.

Wild, Stefan (ed.) *The Qur'ān as Text*, Leiden: Brill, 1996.

Wilson, Robert *Genealogy and History in the Biblical World*, New Haven and London: Yale University Press, 1977.

Woodman, A. J. *Rhetoric in Classical Historiography*, London: Croom Helm, 1988.

Woodword, Martin *Defenders of Reason in Islam*, Oxford: OUP, 1997.

Yūnis, 'Ali and Moḥamed, M. *Medieval Islamic Pragmatics: Sunnī Legal Theorists' Models of Textual Communication*, London: Curzon, 2000.

Zeghal, Malika *Gardiens de l'Islam: Les oulémas d'al-Azhar dans l'Egypte contemporaine*, Paris: Presses de Science Po, 1996.

Zumthor, P. *La lettre et la voix: De la 'littérature' médiévale*, Paris: Editions du Seuil, 1987.

Index